Contents

*The Michelin Maps
you will need
with this Guide are:*

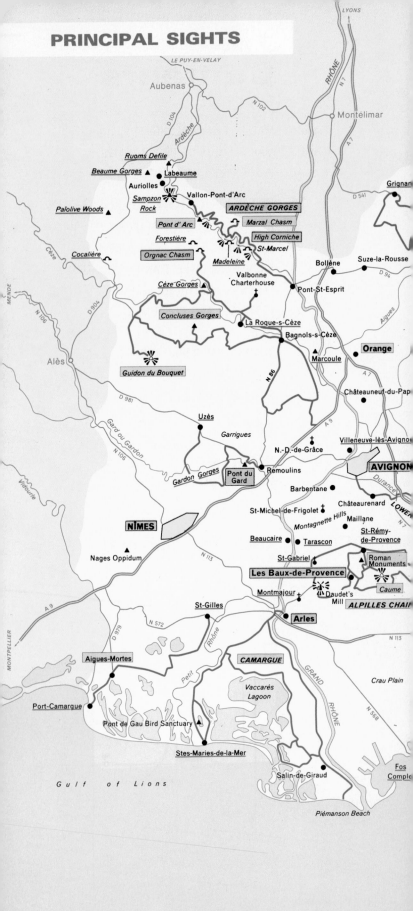

LYONS

LE PUY-EN-VELAY

Aubenas

Montélimar

RHÔNE

Ruoms Defile

Beaume Gorges Labeaume

Auriolles

Sampzon Rock Vallon-Pont-d'Arc

Païolive Woods

ARDÈCHE GORGES

Grignan

Pont d'Arc *Marzal Chasm*

Forestière High Corniche

Cocalière *Orgnac Chasm* *Madeleine* St-Marcel

Bollène Suze-la-Rousse

Valbonne Charterhouse

MENDE

Cèze Gorges Pont-St-Esprit

Concluses Gorges La Roque-s-Cèze

Bagnols-s-Cèze

Orange

Aigues

Alès Marcoule

Guidon du Bouquet

Châteauneuf-du-Pap

Uzès

Garrigues

N.-D.-de-Grâce Villeneuve-lès-Avigno

Gardon Gorges Pont du Gard Remoulins AVIGNON

Durance

Barbentane

St-Michel-de-Frigolet Châteaurenard

LOWER

Montagnette Hills Maillane

NÎMES Beaucaire Tarascon St-Rémy-de-Provence

Nages Oppidum St-Gabriel

Roman Monuments

Les Baux-de-Provence Caume

Montmajour Daudet's Mill ALPILLES CHAIN

St-Gilles Arles

Aigues-Mortes N 113

CAMARGUE

Crau Plain

Port-Camargue

Vaccarés Lagoon

Pont de Gau Bird Sanctuary

Stes-Maries-de-la-Mer Salin-de-Giraud

Fos Comple

Gulf of Lions

Piémanson Beach

0 20 km

MEDITERRANEAN

4

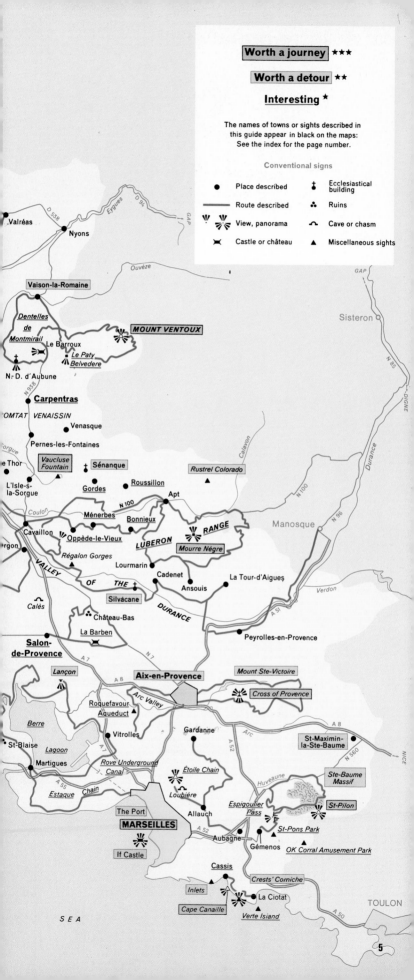

TOURING PROGRAMMES

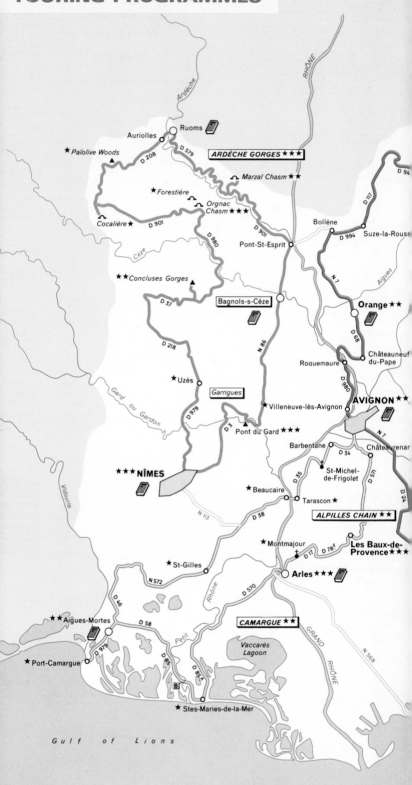

Ardèche

Ruoms
Auriolles
★ Païolive Woods

ARDÈCHE GORGES ★★★

◠ Marzal Chasm ★★

★ Forestière

D 579
D 208

◠ Orgnac
Chasm ★★★

Cocalière ★

D 901

D 980

Bollène

D 94

D 117

Suze-la-Rouss

Pont-St-Esprit

D 994

Cèze

★★ Concluses Gorges ▲

D 37

Bagnols-s-Cèze

Orange ★★

D 68

N 7

Aigues

D 218

N 86

Roquemaure

Châteauneuf-
du-Pape

D 980

★ Uzès

Garrigues

Villeneuve-lès-Avignon ★

AVIGNON ★★

Gard ou Gardon

D 979

D 5

Pont du Gard ★★★

Barbentane

D 34

Châteaurenar

N 7

D 571

St-Michel-
de-Frigolet

D 24

★★★ NÎMES

D 35

★ Beaucaire

Tarascon ★

ALPILLES CHAIN ★★

N 113

D 38

Vidourle

★ Montmajour

D 17

D 78ᴱ

**Les Baux-de-
Provence ★★★**

★ St-Gilles

N 572

Arles ★★★

D 570

D 46

Rhône

CAMARGUE ★★

★★ Aigues-Mortes

D 58

Vaccarès
Lagoon

GRAND

RHÔNE

N 568

D 979

Petit

D 85

D 85ᴬ

★ Port-Camargue

B

★ Stes-Maries-de-la-Mer

Gulf   of   Lions

0   20 km

MEDITERRANEAN

6

Alpilles Chain-Camargue:200 km-124 miles
(4 days including 1 day for Avignon)

Marseilles Region: 300 km-186 miles
(5 days including 1 day for Marseilles)

Lower Vivarais and Garrigues: 300 km-
186 miles (3 days)

Mount Ventoux-Luberon: 400 km-248 miles
(6 days including 1 day for Avignon)

Overnight Stop

CAMARGUE ★★   Name under which a route is described
see the index for page number

Valréas

Nyons

Eygues

D 538

D 938

★★ Vaison-la-Romaine

Ouvèze

Dentelles de Montmirail ★

MOUNT VENTOUX ★★★

C O M T A T

Carpentras ★

V E N A I S S I N

Pernes-les-Fontaines

D 938

Calavon

Durance

★★★ Vaucluse
Fountain

Sénanque ★★

D 22

▲ Rustrel Colorado ★★

Sorgue

D 25

D 2

L'Isle-s-
la-Sorgue

Gordes ★

Roussillon ★

D 209

Coulon

LUBERON RANGE ★

D 109

★ Oppède-le-Vieux

★ Bonnieux

D 943

Durance

Cadenet

Verdon

★ Calès

D 25

D 17D

★★ Silvacane

N 7

Salon de Provence ★

D 67A

D 572

N 7

D 16

★★ Aix-en-Provence

D 10

✳ Cross of Provence ★★★

Mount Ste-Victoire ★★

Berre Lagoon ★

Arc

St-Maximin-
la-Ste-Baume ★★

N 7

Ste-Baume Massif ★★

D 5

Estaque Chain ★

D 49

MARSEILLES ★★★

Huveaune

N 560

D 5

D 80   ✳ St-Pilon ★★★

Aubagne

D 2

★★ If Castle

Cassis ★

D 559

Crests' Corniche ★★

Callelongue

★★ Inlets

La Ciotat

S E A

PLACES TO STAY

The mention Facilities under the individual headings or after place names in the body of the guide refers to the information given on this page.
The map below indicates towns selected for the accommodation and leisure facilities, which they offer to the holidaymaker. To help you plan your route and choose your hotel, restaurant or camping site, consult the following Michelin publications.

Accommodation

The **Michelin Red Guide France** of hotels and restaurants and the **Michelin Guide Camping Caravaning France** are annual publications, which present a selection of hotels, restaurants and camping sites. The final choice is based on regular on the spot enquiries and visits. Both the hotels and camping sites are classified according to the standard of comfort of their amenities. Establishments which are notable for their fortunate setting, their decor, their quiet and secluded location and their warm welcome are distinguished by special symbols. The Michelin Guide France also gives the address and telephone number of local tourist offices and tourist information centres.

Planning your route, sports and recreation

The **Michelin Maps** at a scale of 1:200 000 cover the whole of France. For those concerning the region see the layout diagram on page 3. In addition to a wealth of road information these maps indicate beaches, bathing spots, swimming pools, golf courses, racecourses, air fields, panoramas and scenic routes.

THE SEASONS

Climate. – Poets and writers have acclaimed Provence's temperate climate, lack of rain and exceptional light. And yet climatic conditions are, nevertheless, irregular from year to year (examples of freezing winters – the most recent one being winter 1985-6 – do occur), while the rhythm of the seasons somewhat fluctuates, especially in the spring; even in winter the temperature can rise or fall in one day.

Provence's land relief and the sea play an important role. Maritime Provence enjoys a more agreeable climate (less rain and hotter) than Provence's hinterland, where the question of altitude modifies the temperature considerably. But the dominant factor remains the extraordinary presence of the sun (more than 2 500 hours per year) in the region.

Summer. – This is "the" season. During those three or four months which give Provence both its laughter and charm, the heat and lack of percipitation attract the sun-loving tourist. It rains no more than 70mm-2 1/2in and the temperature rarely goes below 30 °C – 86°F. This dry heat is neither depressing nor overpowering; its constancy is explained by the presence of a hot air mass from the Sahara, protected from the west's humid depressions by the Massif Central.

Autumn. – The reflux of high pressure of tropical origin opens the way to Atlantic depressions. From mid-September to late November rain appears; sometimes violent rainstorms provoke flashfloods. There can fall more than 100mm – 3 3/4in of water in 1 hour (for a total of 600mm – 23 1/2in annually).

Winter. – The cold season is relatively mild and dry. Often sunny, it is above all because of the *mistral* blowing that the temperature can drop 10 °C – 50°F in several hours. The Mediterranean's liquid mass attenuates the cold and prevents snow falls except on the peaks.

Spring. – The disappearance of high pressure of Siberian origin, beginning in February, allows the Atlantic rains to fall on the region. Nevertheless, these rains are less violent than those in the fall and fine bright and clear days are frequent. The *mistral* especially in March, can provoke a suprising chill for those who are not used to the whims of a Provençal spring.

Winds. – The wind is an essential part of the Provençal climate. The most famous is the **mistral** (*mistrau* means master in Provençal), thus masterwind; this strong, dry, cold north-northwest draught sweeps down when the pressure is high over the mountains from the Massif Central to the Mediterranean, funnelling through the narrow Rhône Valley. This violent blast of air clears the sky of clouds and purifies the soil: the farmers call it *mange fange* (mud eater) as the *mistral* dries up the mud pools.

When the *mistral* rages a storm-like atmosphere reigns: the Rhône makes waves, the lagoons and ponds foam and just moving about becomes difficult. The master-wind disappears as suddenly as it arrives; in a couple of hours nature goes back to normal. Alphonse Daudet *(qv)* had counted some 30 different winds. In fact besides the *mistral,* two other winds are to be mentioned: *marin,* a southeast wind which brings rain and fog and *labech,* a southwest wind which brings rainstorms. All the other winds are local.

OUTDOOR ACTIVITIES

For addresses and other details see the chapter Practical Information at the end of the guide.

Rambling. – Discovering Provence on foot is truly enchanting for the observer as the luminosity which pervades enhances the beauty of the countryside, wild and unruly or orderly villages bearing the mark of man. To leave your car behind is the way to capture the past and to understand a multi-faceted region.
Many long-distance footpaths (Sentiers de Grande Randonnée) enable ramblers to discover the region covered in this guide; they are the signposted white and red horizontal lines. The GR 4 crosses Lower Vivarais to Mount Ventoux; GR 42 follows the Rhône Valley; GR 6 follows the Gard River to Beaucaire and then plunges into the Alpilles Chain and the Luberon; GR 9 follows the north face of Mount Ventoux and then crosses Vaucluse Plateau, the Luberon, Ste-Victoire and Ste-Baume; GR 63, 92, 97 and 98 are variants.
Local short-distance footpaths (Sentiers de Petite Randonnée) of a couple of hours to 48 hours have also been set up; they are the signposted yellow horizontal lines.

Riding holidays. – Several possibilities are offered to lovers of horse-riding: a number of riding centres and ranches organise day tours and treks. In Camargue – horse country – a number of different ways to ride through the area are offered.

Boating. – Regular boat lines sail to If Castle. The inlets *(calanques)* are visited from Marseilles and Cassis. In addition excursions are organised on the Rhône and Petit Rhône Rivers and some of Camargue's canals.

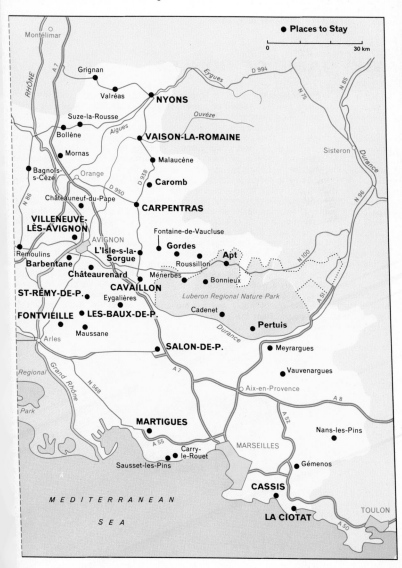

Water sports. – Sailing, windsurfing and water skiing can be done along the coast, on reservoirs and some lagoons. The canoe and kayak allow the tourist to reach the most inaccessible sites of the Rivers Ardèche, Cèze, Sorgue (from its origin at Fontaine-de-Vaucluse), Durance and Rhône. Scuba-diving is a fascinating sport especially in the Marseilles inlets.

Deep-sea fishing. – The Mediterranean Sea has less fish than other seas bordering the French coast and yet there are masses of rock fish: scorpion fish, the queen of bouillabaisse *(qv)*, red mullet, congers, morays, octopuses, spider crabs, varied shellfish and a few spiny lobsters. In the sandy zones skate, sole and lemon sole can be found. Out in the open sea shoals of sardines, anchovies and tunnyfish as well as sea bream, sea bass and grey mullet can be caught.

Freshwater fishing. – The water network of Provence is not very dense and is subject to numerous variations. There are a number of streams which run after a rainfall; nevertheless, the Rivers Ardèche, Gard, Durance (and of course the Rhône), canals and reservoirs (Cadarache, Brinon) are good for catching trout, chub, carp, tench, pike...

Hunting. – Most of the game known of in France can be found in Provence where hunting is a very popular sport.

Mountaineering. – Climbing is possible all year round on the limestone ridges of the Provençal heights (Dentelles de Montmirail) and the cliffs of the Marseilles inlets.

Speleology. – The importance of this region's karstic network *(p 19)* offers a wealth of caves and chasms for speleologists and avid, untrained amateurs alike.

Archaeological excavations. – Provence is rich in archaeological sites; in summer, especially, volunteer excavators are welcome.

Walkers, campers, smokers
please take care
fire is the scourge of forests everywhere

THE GAME OF BOULES

This is the favourite popular game. It is played with balls strengthened with iron. Contests are played between teams of three *(triplettes)* or of four *(quadrettes)*, amid attentive and enthusiastic spectators. The *pointeurs* have to throw their balls as near as possible to a smaller ball *(cochonnet)*, which has been set at the end of the bowling ground; the *tireurs* have then to dislodge the balls of the opposing team by striking them with their own, and the most skilful succeed in doing this and in taking the exact place of their adversary *(faire le carreau)*. Over short distances play is *à la pétanque*, which means with the feet together placed in a circle. Over longer distances, above 10m – 30ft, the game is called *la longue;* the *tireurs* take a running start and throw their balls after having made three hopping steps from the throwing-point.
Amid all these shirt-sleeved players the two Provençal types form a piquant contrast. The one, a native of the mountains, somewhat reserved and frigid, shows his pleasure or his disappointment by a smile or a frown; the other, a descendant of the traditional Marius, enacts quite a little drama, which has been happily described: "Here, then, is the last ball; it rolls out before the player and you can watch its progress in his face; he broods over it, protects it with his gaze; gives it advice, strives to make it obedient to his voice, hurries or slows its course, encourages it with a gesture or urges it on with a heave of his shoulder, slackens it with his hand; perched on tip-toe, his arm flung out, his face animated by a wealth of varying emotions, he wriggles his body in bizarre undulations; one could almost say that his soul had passed into the ball."
Play is frequently held up by noisy and excited disputes about the distances which separate the various balls from the *cochonnet;* play resumes once the measurements have been taken.

Introduction
to the tour

The region described in this guide does not exactly correspond with the historical and administrative Provence.

Using the Rhône River as its centre, the region overflows largely to the west annexing part of the Vivarais to the north and the Languedoc to the south. To the east Sault Country and the coastline beginning at Les Lecques are described respectively in the Michelin Green Guides Alpes du Sud – Haute-Provence *(in French only)* and French Riviera.

Beneath its exterior appearence of geographic and social unity, Provence is a country of varied facets: "It is a complete whole, a microcosm of contrast and harmony" wrote Marie Mauron *(qv)*.

Gordes

In order to give our readers the most up to date information the times and charges for admission to sights described in the guide are listed at the end of the guide.

The sights are listed alphabetically in this section either under the place – town, village or area – in which they are situated or under their proper name.

Every sight for which there are times and charges is indicated by the symbol ⓥ in the margin in the main part of the guide.

APPEARANCE OF THE COUNTRY

LOCAL GEOGRAPHY

Formation of the land. – During the Primary Era (c600-220 million years ago) what is now Provence was covered by a sea which surrounded the continent of Tyrrhenia, contemporary with the Massif Central. It was formed by crystalline rocks and vestiges of this land mass included the Maures, Corsica, Sardinia and Balearic Islands.

During the Secondary Era (220-60 million years ago), Tyrrhenia was gradually levelled by erosion; before the Cretacaeous Sea covered practically the whole region. Variations in sea level were caused by the materials from the Primary strata carried down by rivers and deposited at the bottom of the sea forming sedimentary deposits composed either of limestone (e.g. from Orgon) or of marl and transformed into regular and parallel layers of rock (strata) in a strip of land lying east to west; this was the Durancen Isthmus surrounded by the sea.

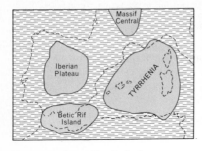

Primary Era: Tyrrhenia

Quaternary Era: Mediterranean Sea

The Tertiary Era (60-2 million years ago) was marked by important tectonic upheavals creating the young folded mountains of the Alps and Pyrenees by uplifting the sedimentary cover. The strata were uplifted and folded in an east-west direction creating the Provençal secondary mountains; to the north of Marseilles (Ste-Baume, Ste-Victoire, Mount Ventoux, Baronnies, Alpilles Chain, Luberon), Toulon and Draguignan. The sea level rose to the presentday Rhône Valley and while the Alpilles Chain was thrust upwards, the Crau Plain sank.

During the Quaternary Era (beginning about 2 million years ago) evolution continued: Tyrrhenia was submerged beneath the presentday Mediterranean Sea leaving such outliers as the Maures, Esterel and Canaille Mountains. The relief adopted the form it now has, the Rhône corridor emerged, widened and became an important routeway. The Durance River was modified by the subsiding of the course of Crau Plain and deviated to join the Rhône. Erosion during glaciation and interglacial periods put the final touches to the landscapes (inlets).

The plains. – The plains were formed by reclaiming territory from the sea with the constant deposits of alluvial sediments i.e. Rhône Delta. They first spread over the Rhone's east bank, **Comtat Venaissin** *(qv)*, then they spread over both banks. On the west side of the river the plains extended to the Lower Languedoc dominated by the *garrigues (qv)* near Nîmes, to the east they became the fertile **Petite Crau** and Grande Crau.

Romans, medieval monks and small property holders throughout the centuries have improved the land with drainage and irrigation schemes. Two regions, especially, have profited from such schemes: Comtat Venaissin and Petite Crau. Market gardens now cover the land creating a fine pattern of tiny plots separated by windbreaks of tall cypress and lower screens of reeds.

The **Grande Crau** *(qv)* is separated from Camargue by the Grande Rhône. An immense desert of pebbles and boulders between which grow tufts of grass known locally as *coussous*. It was used traditionally for the winter pasturing of large flocks of sheep. The expansion of Fos's industrial zone and the clearing the land of stones and irrigation schemes have transformed the area; it has lost its pastoral image and with it much of its charm.

Olive groves, almond trees, vineyards and undulating grass-land make up the new wealth of these areas.

The **Camargue** *(qv)* is a delta of recent alluvium or silt formed by the Rhône. This delta regained from the sea is salt-impregnated, and is one of France's most picturesque regions. The *sansouires*, vast salt-marshes, bring to the area an immense wild appearence.

Plateaux, hills and massifs. – The Provençal plains are flanked or penetrated by folded mountain chains lying east to west which rise quite abruptly blocking the horizon. The relief often appears confused presenting an undisciplined alternance of limestone heights and partitioned off fertile basins: Apt Country, Aigues Country (south of Luberon), Aix Country (irrigated by the Provence canal) where very varied crops (grain, vineyards, fruit, market gardening) are cultivated. East of the Rhône from north to south different landscapes follow one after another.

The western fringe of the **Baronnies** form a complicated structure of hills and slopes of real beauty where olive groves and the hybrid lavandin *(qv)* reign. The rocky summits of the **Dentelles de Montmirail** *(qv)* display a finely carved out relief (*dentelle* means lace) which is unique in Provence: oak and pine forests with vineyards carpeting the slopes. Backed up against the Baronnies is **Mount Ventoux** *(qv)*, an imposing limestone massif, dominates the Comtadin Plain at a height of 1 909m – 6 263ft.

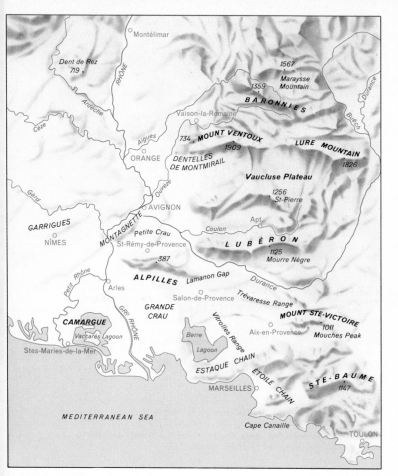

The **Vaucluse Plateau** – also known as Vaucluse Hills – a vast arid area devoted to sheep raising and the cultivation of lavender *(photograph p 15)* is a land of karstic relief. This limestone countryside is potted with chasms *(p 19)* and carved out by gorges. A mysterious underground hydrographic network penetrates through the limestone and opens out at Vaucluse Fountain *(qv)*.

The **Luberon Range** *(qv)* stretches over some 60 odd kilometers – 37 odd miles; cut in half north to south by the Lourmarin Coomb and culminates in the Grand Luberon at Mourre Nègre (alt 1 125m – 3 691ft). This region is an enchantment with the beauty of its rugged sites to which cling precariously perched villages; it offers a striking contrast between its forest ridden, wild north face and its more cultivated south face.

In the middle of the Rhône Plain stand two picturesque ranges: **Montagnette Hills** *(qv)* and **Alpilles Chain** *(qv)*.

East of Aix, **Mount Ste-Victoire** *(qv)* a limestone mass, pock-marked with caves and chasms, dominates the Aix Basin while to the southeast the Ranges Trévaresse and Vitrolles bar it from Berre Lagoon. The lagoon is closed to the south by **Estaque Chain** *(qv)* separated from the St-Mitre Hills by the Caronte Depression.

The Chains **Étoile** *(qv)* and St-Cyr and Marseilleveyre Massif *(qv)* surround Marseilles while on the horizon looms the long rocky barrier of the **Ste-Baume Massif** *(qv)* which reaches an altitude of 1 447m – 3 763ft at the Ste-Baume Signal Station.

West of the Rhône River, the Cévennes foothills lie north to south receding in the river's direction and the vine carpeted plain via the *garrigues (qv)* of Nîmes.

A series of desolate limestone plateaux cut by canyons and gouged out by sometimes huge chasms succeed in tiers; it is arid, rocky terrain good only for sheep grazing. In the past picking (aromatic plants, olives, almonds...) and goat cheese *(migou)* constituted a way of making income. The countryside is criss-crossed by a multitude of dry-stone enclosures in the middle of which stood a modest hut *(mazet)* or *capitelle* (similar to the *bories*). There are, however, a couple of isolated fertile areas: Uzès Basin, Vistre Plain and Vaunage (southwest of Nîmes) which are devoted to crop growing (orchards, vineyards, etc).

Waterways. – On its Provençal flow, the Rhône receives from the west the Rivers Ardèche and Gard, which come down from the Cévennes and from the east the Rivers Aigues, Ouvèze and Durance, which come down from the Alps. They all have the same torrential appearance: a trickle of water in a stony bed too wide during periods of draught which transforms itself into an avalanche of foaming water during rain storms. The Cévennes receives rainfalls of unusual violence – a single downpour exceeds the annual rainfall of Paris. The rivers expand dramatically, the Ardèche has been seen to rise 21m – 69ft in one day and its flow from 2.5m³ per second to 7.500m³ – 88.3ft³ to 264 855ft³; often enough the water rises 10m – 33ft and more. Frequently the flow of the Ardèche cuts through the Rhône like a rocket striking the dikes of the left bank, across the way; these flash-floods 5m – 16 1/2ft high are known as the blows of the Ardèche *(les coups de l'Ardèche)*.

For the tributaries of the east bank which come down from the Alps, it is the melting snows which multiply considerably the volume of water. For the Durance, for example, it expands proportionally from 1 to 180. Fortunately these spates occur in the spring, when the Rivers Ardèche and Gard are low. Contrarily speaking the Durance is almost dry in winter and autumn while the rains from the Cévennes expand the tributaries of the west bank.

Coastline. – From the Languedoc coast to the Marseilles inlets the coastline often changes form.

As far as Fos Bay, the shoreline is marked by vast **lagoons** separated from the sea by narrow sand bars: the mass of alluvial deposits dropped by the Rhône and shaped by the coastal currents has formed offshore bars closing off the lagoons. The encroachment of sand had pushed inland old ports like Aigues-Mortes.

With the Estaque Chain reappear the limestone relief which cuts the coastline. From Marseilles to La Ciotat the littoral is cut into a great number of inlets of which the deepest and most uneven are called **inlets** – *calanques* – they are in fact the submerged extremities of the valleys, when the sea level rose after the Quaternary Era's glacial period. Steep cliffs, brown and reddish rocks plunge vertically into the deep blue sea from which emerge a number of islands not far out. Small well sheltered ports, lovely wild creeks, the inlets are the kingdom of deep-sea divers and climbers alike.

The sea. – This is the bluest of European seas. This deep tint – cobalt, the painters call it – arises from the great limpidity of the water.

The temperature of the water surface varies from 20°-25 °C – 68°-77 °F in summer falling to only 12°-13 °C – 53°-55 °F in winter (in depth 200 to 4 000m – 656 to 13 123ft, the temperature is at a constant 13 °C – 55 °F). This is an important factor in the climate; this great liquid mass cools in summer, warms in winter. As a result of very rapid evaporation the water is noticeably more salty than that of the Atlantic.

The tide is very slight: 0.25m – 9 1/2in average and yet variation in height caused by strong winds can be as much as 1m-3ft. This relative stability has singled out the Mediterranean as base level for all the French coast's altitude.

A calm sea, with small short choppy waves, the Mediterranean can suddenly become violent: in the lapse of a couple of hours a *mistral,* which rises can provoke dangerous storms which have often surprised the careless yachtsmen.

Gourmets...
The country's gastronomic specialities and fine wines
are described on page 41.
Each year the **Michelin Red Guide France** *proposes a revised selection*
of establishments renowned for their cuisine.

LOCAL ECONOMY

The Provençal economy is, perhaps in France, the region which has encountered the most impressive mutations in the past fifty years: agricultural revolution, increased industrialisation especially along the coast, adaptation to large scale tourism, runaway urbanisation.

The Different Facets Of Agriculture

Rural life of the past depended on three crops – wheat, vineyards, olives – which, with sheep raising and a variety of other products gathered locally (herbs, olives, almonds...) assured the existence of a mass of small farmers very attached to their native soil. This traditional polyculture has almost disappeared, replaced by a modern speculative agriculture, making the most out of the Provence's natural resources, thus enabling it to become the garden of France.

Early produce. – The alluvial soil of the Rhône Plain, the high mean temperature, and irrigation schemes have favoured the development of early market gardening and fruit producing several crops a year in the Comtat Venaissin and Petite Crau. The whole region is now divided up into little parcels of land protected from the *mistral* by screens of cypress and reeds.

Strawberries, tomatoes and melons from Carpentras, asparagus, new potatoes and melons from Cavaillon, cabbage from Rognonas, asparagus from Lauris, cherries from Remoulins, peaches, pears and apricots from the Rhône Valley are all sold in the markets of Paris, north and eastern France as well as foreign countries.

Early produce, picked in the morning, is either sold to a private packer or sent to a cooperative where it is sorted, graded, packed and conditioned (cooperatives have been established at St-Remy, Châteaurenard, Barbentane, Cabannes and St-Andiol, west of Cavaillon etc).

From the main railway heads – Châteaurenard, Cavaillon, Carpentras, Barbentane, Avignon – leave the rapid early produce trains which go up the Rhône Valley to Paris and other large cities.

Cereals and vineyards. – The area between Arles and Tarascon, hitherto the main centre for growing wheat in Provence, is now producing maze, rape and rice as well, and the windmills so dear to Alphonse Daudet have been replaced by modern milling machinery in the towns.

Vineyards occupy some 110 000ha – 424sq miles and in the plains produce large quantities of common wine *(vin ordinaire)*. Whereas on the hillside where the vineyards are cultivated with more care a more delicate wine is produced carrying the general name Côtes du Rhône. The Côtes du Rhône's most celebrated vintage is Châteauneuf-du-Pape *(qv)*. It has an estimated 15 000ha – 37 050 acres of vineyards which produce table wine.

Lavender and lavandin. – Who does not know the scent of lavender so unique to the Provence? It has adapted beautifully to the climate and calcareous soils of Provence and Haute-Provence *(see Michelin Green Guide Alpes du Sud, in French only).* Lavandin, a more productive but less fragrant hybrid is cultivated on the lower slopes (400-700m – 1 312-2 297ft) and in the valleys. Today, about 8 400ha – 20 748 acres of lavender are cultivated and 2 350ha – 5 805 acres of lavandin. The harvest takes place from July to September according to the region; most of the picking is now done by machinery but the inaccessible or closely planted older fields are still picked by hand. After drying 2-3 days, the picked lavender is sent to a distillery equipped with the classic still.

Lavender on the Vaucluse Plateau

Lavender essence is reserved for the perfume and cosmetic industries whereas the hybrid lavandin perfumes laundry soap and cleaning products. The lavender flower can also be dried and placed in scent bags.

Superb lavender fields can be spotted on Vaucluse Plateau and in the Drôme and Gard *départements,* north of Nîmes.

Almonds and olives. – Almond trees which grow all round the shores of the Mediterranean were first imported into France from Asia in 1548; the development of later blossoming varieties have led to increased cultivation. The most famous of the local almond confectionary are *calissons* from Aix and Salon.

The silver green of the olive groves is a common sight in the country round Salon, Nyons and the mountains' southern slopes.

Sometimes, in the olive plantations, old trees have been cut low to the ground and four suckers can be seen growing in a crown-like shape; these are kept as they create handsome new trees. The black olives of Nyons, preserved in brine, are a delicacy.

Truffles. – The truffle is an edible, subterranean fungus which develops from the mycelium, a network of filaments invisible to the naked eye. They live symbiotically in close association with the root of the downy oak *(qv),* known in Provence as the white oak. The truffle harvest is in the winter when they are ripe and odorous.

These small stunted oaks are planted in rows in fields called *truffières.*

They are found mainly in south Tricastin, Comtat Venaissin, Claparèdes Plateau and in the Luberon. A superficial breaking-up of soil and a specified pruning favours the truffle crop which is harvested November to April and marketed mostly in Apt, Carpentras, Richerenches, Uzès and Valréas, where several tons of this black diamond pass through annually.

Lime trees and herbs. – Although found in most parts of France, the lime tree is cultivated mainly in Provence between Buis-les-Baronnies and Carpentras. At the end of the 19C, the lime tree bordered most of the French roads whereas today they are planted in orchards and pruned. The flower is picked in June, depending on the blooming, dried in a shaded, airy dry room then sold in bags or by the ounce for tea. Aromatic plants also called Herbes de Provence (Herbs of Provence) have doubled in popularity in recent years. Certain varieties are cultivated traditionally: basil and marjoram are cultivated around St-Rémy-de-Provence, tarragon on the Vaucluse Plateau while other varieties such as thyme, rosemary and savory are still gathered from the hillsides where they grow wild, and supply a large proportion of the herbs gathered.

Stock raising. – Provence is centred on sheep raising, an essentiel resource of all Mediterranean rural economics. Wool, no longer profitable was discarded and butcher's meat adopted. The Merino variety from Arles is predominant in the Bouches-du-Rhône *département,* however, the area allocated to it diminishes daily. It grazes on the meagre *coussous (qv)* from Crau Plain *(qv)* from 15 October to 15 June and then transhumes to the Alps; the transhumance, once a picturesque procession, is now done in trucks. In the *garrigues (qv)* there again the flocks of sheep graze on the meagre vegetation that they find when roaming these vast territories; they spend the summer in Larzac or in the Lozère Mountains.

Camargue *(qv)* is the land of large plantations and concentrates on the rearing of black bulls and white horses living in liberty and grouped in herds called *manades.*

Fishing

Fishing is a traditional activity which takes place in the ports of Languedoc (Le Grau-du-Roi) and Provence (Port-St-Louis, Martigues, Carry-le-Rouet, Marseilles, Cassis) and yet, it occupies a minimal position and frequently suffers from water pollution. Nevertheless, several thousand tons of sardines, anchovies, mackerel and eel are caught annually.

The coming and going of these sailor-fishermen unloading their catch, drying their nets still remains one of the ports most attractive scenes.

At Marseilles, the recent port of Saumaty, located at the foot of the Estaque can shelter as many as 180 trawlers (1 400m – 4 593ft of quays) and offers all the necessary equipment for the preservation of fish.

Small fishing boats still supply the fishmongers of Marseilles's Old Port whose cries echo in an atmosphere so vividly rendered in several of Pagnol's *(qv)* novels.

Industrialisation

Provence taking advantage of its geographical location propitious to commercial exchange encountered a spectacular industrial development in the 1930s.

Around Berre Lagoon a vast industrial complex was built – oil refineries, chemical, aeronautic and iron and steel (today threatened) works – with Fos Complex, inaugurated in 1968 as its centre. From Marseilles to Aix industrial zones have multiplied and offer a vast range of activities from soapmaking plants to the most modern electronics factories including the Gardanne thermal power station.

The hydro-electric installations of the lower valleys of the Rhône and Durance have also contributed to the profound economic upheavals. Hydro-electric production combined with nuclear (Marcoule) production has allowed France to strengthen its energy potential. However, the domestication of the two undisciplined rivers has resulted in the possibility of irrigating an immense agricultural area, until then, hindered by draught. All these transformations have made Provence one of France's great industrial areas juggling between two types of industry:

– traditional: minerals (ochre, bauxite, lignite), shipbuilding, foodstuffs, soapmaking (Marseilles area), building materials, construction and saltworks;

– modern: petroleum and its derivatives, aeronautics, electronics, nuclear (Cadarache Centre on Nuclear Studies), chemicals.

Light industries have also developed: packaging in Valréas and Tarascon, confectionary in Aix, Apt and Nyons, fruit preserving, garment and shoe making in Nîmes.

Ochre and bauxite. – The Apt-Roussillon *(photograph p 159)* area is one of the main mining and treatment regions of ochre (an earthy red or yellow and often impure iron ore essentially used as a pigment for paints or as a wash applied for its protective value) in France. The mineral beds can at times be 15m – 49ft thick. Ochre in its natural state is a mixture of argillacaeous sand and iron oxyde. To obtain a commercially pure ochre product, the mineral is first washed, the impurities which tend to be heavier, settle to the bottom, while the lighter weight "flower", which is made of iron oxide and clay is passed through the filter and into settling tanks where after drying it assumes the look of ochre, which is then cut into blocks. After drying, the ochre is crushed, sifted and at times baked in ovens to darken the pigmentation and obtain a reddish orange colour. This process is called ochre calcining; it then becomes an unctuous, impalpable powder used commercially. The quality of the ochre from Vaucluse has made France one of its most important producers – annual production is about 3 000 metric tons. The production of bauxite (a mixture of hydrous aluminium oxides), the name of which comes from the village of Les Baux de Provence *(qv)* where it was discovered in 1821, has somewhat declined in Lower Provence for the benefit of Var and Hérault *départements*. With a production capacity of 1 700 000 metric tons, France still assumes 2/3 of its needs (the depletion of its resources estimated at 14 000 000 metric tons should occur within a short period of time). Bauxite is the essential raw material used in the production of aluminium and has taken on an increased importance as a structural material in transportation, construction, electrical industry, packing and housecleaning articles.

Olive oil. – Typically Provençal oil has always been olive oil. Olives are treated when they are ripe and are picked while still green if used for food preservation. The quality of the oil depends on the quality of the fruit and treatment (number of pressings). Once picked, the olives are crushed whole with the pit either by a millstone, hammer mill or roller. The paste obtained is then distributed on a trolley's nylon disks. The trolley now loaded is placed on the sliding piston of a hydraulic press, pressure is exerted and the resulting mixture of oil and water is collected in tanks and then pumped into centrifugal machines where the oil and water will be separated. The oil which comes out of the machine is a virgin oil obtained by a first cold water pressing. The residual pulp *(grignon)* can be pressed again.

In the past the olive paste was spread by hand onto coconut mats *(scourtins)* which were stacked under the press. For a long time the presses were worked by hand and the horse turned the millstone. The residual pulp was remashed with lukewarm water: a mixture of refined and virgin oil was obtained classed as second quality called second pressing. With the arrival of electricity and the improvement of techniques, the quality and production have increased. Today, as in the past the residual pulp treated with chemical solvents in large factories in Italy obtain oil used for cutting or soap-making. Before this last pressing the pit can be separated from the pulp: the pit is ground down into powder and is used by the baker and pastry cook; the pulp is used for compost.

Salt marshes. – Two large salt marshes are worked in Camargue: one south of Aigues-Mortes spreads over 10 000ha – 24 700 acres; the other south of Salin-de-Giraud *(qv)* spreads over 11 000ha – 27 170 acres. Already improved by the monks in the 13C, the salt marshes increased production in the mid-19C, progressed and then decreased. The present day global annual production is evaluated at 850 000 metric tons.

VEGETATION

In addition to its beautiful countryside, underlined by an always (or almost) luminous sky, Provence possesses one of the most original natural habitats.

Trees and plants. – All vegetation combined is closely dependent on climatic conditions. In Provence blossoming occurs as elsewhere during the spring, and a second blossoming in the autumn which goes on well into winter; the dormant period is during the summer when the heat of the climate only permits plants which are especially adapted to resist drought to grow: long tap roots, glazed leaves which reduce transpiration, bulbs which act as reservoirs of moisture and a protective perfumed vapour. The olive tree and holm oak mark out the Mediterranean area as such, spotted with *garrigues*. In Upper Provence the *garrigues* disappears replaced by the forest cover (downy oak, Scots pine, beech) and the moors (broom, lavender, boxwood). In Vivarais the presence of chestnut adds a unique touch to the landscape.

Olive trees. – The Greeks brought olive trees to Provence 2 500 years ago because they grow equally well in limestone or sandy soils. The olive has been called the immortal tree for, grafted or wild, it will continually renew itself. Those grown from cuttings die relatively young at 300 years of age. Along the coast the trees reach gigantic dimensions attaining 20m – 65 1/2ft in height, their domes of silver foliage 20m – 65 1/2ft in circumference and trunks 4m – 13ft round the base. The olive tree of which there are more than 60 varieties will grow up to 600m – 1 968ft and marks the

Olive Tree

limit of the Mediterranean climate. It grows mainly on valley floors and hillsides often mingling with almond and fig trees. The olive tree begins to bear fruit between 6-12 years and is in full yield at 20-25 years; it is harvested every two years *(p 16)*. Under the light, evergreen foliage of the olive tree early vegetables are cultivated.

Oak trees. – There exist several varieties of oaks.
The **holm oak** *(quercus ilex)* has a short thick-set trunk with a wide-spreading thick dome. It grow on arid calcareous soil at less than 1 000m – 3 281ft. It is an evergreen oak, the leaves of which remain a fine dark green. In stunted form it is a characteristic element of the *garrigues (qv)* in association with all sorts of shrubs and aromatic plants.
The **kermes** or **scrub oak** is a bushy evergreen shrub rarely exceeding 1m – 3ft in height. It has a trunk of grey bark with a thick dome of shiny, tough, ragged, prickly leaves. Its name kermes comes from the scale insect which lives on its branches and from which is obtained a bright red dye. The tree grows on stone free dry soil but prefers a fertile, cool soil.
The **downy or white oak** *(quercus pubescens)* is a deciduous tree (the underside of the leaves are covered with dense short white hairs) which requires more water than the preceeding evergreens. It will be found in the valleys and on the more humid mountain slopes. It is at times associated with the maple, service tree and rowan. In its undergrowth a variety of shrubs and flowers, notably the orchid, grow. It is also on the root of this tree that the truffle lives *(p 15)*.

Pine trees. – The three types of pine to be found in the Mediterranean may be easily distinguished by their outline.
The **maritime pine** *(pinus pinaster)* grows on limestone soil; its foliage is dark blue-green and the bark a purply red.
The **umbrella or stone pine** *(pinus pinea)* is one of the Mediterranean's most characteristic sights; it owes its name to its easily recogniseable shape. It is often found singly, growing alone.
The **Aleppo pine** *(pinus halepensis)* is a Mediterranean species which grows well in the chalky soil along the coast. Its foliage is light and graceful with a trunk covered with a grey bark and twists as it grows.

Umbrella Pine

Other Provençal trees. – In towns and villages the streets and squares are shaded by the smooth-barked **plane trees** or the dark green canopy of the branching **lotus tree** *(micocoulier)* which yields a fruit mentioned by Homer in the *Odyssey* as inducing a state of dreamy forgetfulness and loss of desire to return home – hence lotus-eaters. It has also been identified by some as the jujube tree. The outline of the dark **cypress** a coniferous evergreen marks the Mediterranean landscape with its tapered form pointed towards the sky. Planted in serried ranks the pyramidal-shaped cypress forms a windbreak.
The variety with scattered branches is used for reforestation programs. From the rosaceous species the common **almond tree** prevalent in Provence delights the eye with its lovely early spring pink blossoms. The noble elm has practically disappeared.

Almond Tree

Cypress

17

Forest cover. – There are not many forests in the Provence and those that exist grow especially in the mountain ranges below 1 600m – 5 249ft.

Fine forests of holm or downy oak grow in Grand Luberon on Mount Ste-Victoire, and Vaucluse Plateau. Petit Luberon is covered with a fine cedar forest; on the north face of Ste-Baume Massif grow forests of beech trees. Spread along the limestone peaks is a moor of broom.

The designation of the word forest beyond these areas indicates copses carpeting vast areas north of the Durance.

| Globe-Thistle | Grey-Leaved Cistus |

Garrigues. – In Provence this word is used to describe vast expanses of rocky, limestone moors. It is generally made up of a stretch of low limestone hills with minute parcels of land between the outcrops of white calcareous rock; sometimes the rain has washed the soil down into the valleys leaving vast rocky table-lands.

Vegetation is sparse consisting mostly of holm oaks, stunted downy oaks, thistles, gorse and cistus as well as lavender, thyme and rosemary interspersed with short dry grass which provides pasture for flocks of sheep.

Small *garrigues* can be found in most parts of Provence, however, the *garrigues*, as such, is found especially north of Nîmes where it was carved deeply by the River Gardon.

In addition to the wild aromatic plants which grow in the *garrigues,* such herbs as basil, majoram, savory, sage, melissa, mint, laurel and absinth, which are cultivated commercially and are sold for herbal and medicinal use *(p 15),* also appear.

French Lavender

Environmental battle. – The influx of tourists, industrial and urban development are the cause of constant attacks against the Mediterranean and Provence's natural habitat.

Forest fires. – The Provençal forest is particularly exposed to fires (those of 1979, 1985 and 1986 were catastrophic), the majority of which are due to carelessness or pyromaniacs. The fire has two natural allies draught and wind.

During the summer the dried-up plants of the underbrush, pine needles, resins exuded by leaves and twigs are highly combustible and sometimes catch fire spontaneously. Once a fire has started, it spreads to the pines and if the wind is strong disaster may follow.

Enormous walls of flame, sometimes more than 10km – 6 miles in length and 30m – 98ft high, spread at speeds of 5-6kmh – 2-3mph. When the fire has passed, nothing remains standing except the blackened skeletons of the trees while a thick layer of white ash covers the ground.

Often the fire wins, stopping only at the coast, unless the wind drops or alters direction. The fires alter little by little the ecological balance; thus, for example, the oak forests are receeding and the soil is barren for a long time. The many different means of fighting forest fires will not solve the problem, fire prevention (systematic watch, periodically cleaning the underbrush, creation of fire-breaks etc) public awareness, especially that of tourists, should help combat this enemy of nature.

Dial 18 to obtain the fire department.

Pollution. – The fast-developing urbanisation and industrialisation programs which occurred in Provence have dropped a heavy blow on the beauty of several natural sites. The Fos-sur-Mer industrial complex is devouring Crau Plain, the area around Berre Lagoon, especially its eastern side has become the active, bustling suburb (airport, refineries etc) of Marseilles. Already in 1957 due to the high level of polluted water, fishing was strictly forbidden in the lagoon. The discharge of used water from the surrounding towns, St-Martin-de-Crau garbage dump and the Marseilles main sewer dumping into Cortiou Inlet etc are all very harmful. The flow of traffic (constantly on the increase) has resulted in the construction of more and more road networks which are cutting up the countryside and leaving but a smaller and smaller area to nature.

CAVES AND CHASMS

In contrast to the deeply dissected green valleys with their many settlements, the Lower Vivarais limestone plateaux roll away to the far horizon, stony, grey and deserted. The dryness of the soil is due to the calcareous nature of the rock which absorbs rain like a sponge.

At the end of the last century, the methodical and scientific exploration of the underground world, with which the name of **E.A. Martel** is associated, led to the discovery of a certain number of caves and their organisation as a tourist attraction. In 1935 **Robert de Joly** *(qv)* explored Orgnac Chasm and discovered its wealth of cave formations; later on the discovery of a gaping hole in the chasm led to the discovery in 1965 of a vast network of upper galleries. Our knowledge of the underground system is at present very incomplete and a great many chasms remain unknown to speleologists.

Water infiltration. – Rainwater, charged with carbonic acid, dissolves the carbonate of lime to be found in the limestone. Depressions, which are usually circular in shape and small in size and are known as **cloups** or **sotchs,** are then formed. The dissolution of the limestone rocks, containing especially salt or gypsum, produces a rich soil particularly suitable for growing crops; when the *cloups* increase in size they form large, closed depressions known as **dolines.** Where rainwater infiltrates deeply through the countless fissures in the plateau, the hollowing out and dissolution of the calcareous layer produces wells or natural chasms which are called **avens** or **igues.** Little by little the chasms grow, lengthen and branch off communicating with each other and enlargening into caves.

Underground rivers. – The infiltrating waters finally produce underground galleries and collect to form a more or less swift flowing river. The river widens its course and often changes level, to fall in cascades. Where the rivers run slowly they form lakes, above natural dams, known as **gours,** which are raised layer by layer by deposits of carbonate of lime. The dissolution of the limestone also continues above the water-level in these subter-

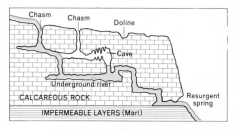

Development of a resurgent spring

ranean galleries: blocks of stone fall from the roof and domes form, the upper parts pointing towards the surface of the earth. Such is the case with the Upper Chamber at Orgnac *(qv)* which lies only a few feet beneath the surface of the plateau. When the roof of the dome wears thin it may cave in, disclosing the cavity from above and opening the chasm.

Cave formation. – As it circulates below ground, the water deposits the lime with which it has become charged, thus building up concretions of fantastic shapes which defy the laws of gravity and equilibrium.

In some caverns, the seeping waters produce calcite (carbonate of lime) deposits which form pendants, pyramids and draperies. The best known formations are stalactites, stalagmites and eccentrics.

Stalactites form from the cave roof. Every droplet of water seeping through to the ceiling deposits upon it, before falling, some of the calcite with which it is charged. Gradually layer by layer the concretion builds up as the drops are attracted and run down its length, depositing particles before falling.

Stalagmites are formed in the same way but rise from the floor towards the roof. Drops of water, falling always in the same place deposit their calcite particles which build up to a candle-like shape. This rises towards a stalactite with which it ultimately joins to form a pillar linking the cave floor with the ceiling. Concretions form very slowly indeed; the rate of growth in a temperate climate is about 1cm-3/8in every 100 years.

The **eccentrics** are very fine protuberances which seldom exceed 20cm – 8in in length. They emerge at any angle either as slender spikes or in the shape of small, translucent fans. They are formed by crystallisation and seem to disregard the laws of gravity. Orgnac and Marzal Chasms and Madeleine Cave contain remarkable examples.

Marzal Chasm

HISTORICAL TABLE AND NOTES

Events in italics indicate milestones for the local history

From prehistory to the Roman conquest

BC	
c6000	Neolithic impressed pottery: the first potters begin turning to agriculture and settle on the sites of Châteauneuf-les-Martigues and Courthézon.
c3500	Chassey culture: the appearance of true stock raising farmers living in villages.
1800-800	Bronze Age. Ligurian occupation.
8-4C	Progressive installation of the Celts.
c600	*Founding of Massalia (Marseilles) by the Phocaeans (p 128).*
4C	Massalia is at its apex; travels of the Massaliote, Pythéas, into the northern seas.
218	Hannibal passes through Provence and crosses the Alps.
125-122	Conquest of southern Gaul by the Romans. Destruction of Entremont *(qv)* and founding of Aix *(qv)*.
102	Marius defeats the Teutons at Aquae Sextiae (Aix) – *(p 46).*
58-51	Conquest of long-haired Gaul by Julius Caesar.
55	Caesar lands in Britain.
27	Augustus establishes the Narbonensis: Roman civilisation spreads.
AD	
2C	Nîmes at its apex.
284	Narbonensis is divided into two provinces: Narbonensis on the Rhône River's west bank, and Viennoise on the east bank.
4C	Arles at its apex; establishment of the dioceses.
416	Jean Cassien, from the Far East, founded the Abbey of St-Victor in Marseilles.

Head of Venus from Messius's House in Vaison-la-Romaine

Establishment of the County of Provence

471	Arles taken over by the Visigoths.
476	Fall of the Roman Empire.
536	Provence ceded to the Franks.
843	By the *Treaty of Verdun* Provence, Burgundy and Lorraine are restored to Lothaire (one of Charlemagne's grandsons).
855	Provence is made a kingdom by Lothaire for his 3rd son, Charles.
879	Boson, Charles the Bald's brother-in-law, is King of Burgundy and Provence.
2nd half of 9 and 10C	Saracens, Vikings and Magyars terrorise the land.
1032	Provence is annexed by the Holy Roman Empire; the Counts of Provence, however, retain their independence; the towns expand and assert their autonomy.
1066	*William the Conqueror lands in England.*
1125	Counts of Barcelona and Toulouse divide Provence up between themselves.
c1135	First mention of a consulate in Arles.
1215	*Magna Carta*
1229	By the *Treaty of Paris* Lower-Languedoc returns to France; founding of the royal seneschalship in Beaucaire.
1246	Charles of Anjou, brother of St Louis, marries Beatrice of Provence, the Count of Barcelona's daughter, and becomes Count of Provence.
1248	St Louis embarks from Aigues-Mortes on the 7th Crusade.
1274	Cession of the Comtat Venaissin to the papacy.
1316-1403	The popes and anti-popes at Avignon. Great Schism of the West (1378-1417).
1337-1453	*Hundred Years War.*
1348	Clement VI bought Avignon from Queen Joan I. Great Plague epidemic.
1409	University of Aix founded.
1434-80	Reign of Good King René, Louis XI's uncle.
1450	Jacques Cœur set up his trading posts in Marseilles.
1481	Charles of Maine, nephew of René of Anjou, bequeaths Provence to Louis XI.

The Estates of Provence

1486	The Estates of Provence meet at Aix to ratify the union of Provence to the crown.
1492	*Christopher Columbus discovers America.*
1501	Inauguration of the Parliament of Aix as supreme court of justice with limited political authority.
1509-47	*Henry VIII's reign.*
1524-36	Provence is invaded by the Imperialists (soldiers of the Holy Roman Empire).
1535	*Jacques Cartier sails up the St Lawrence River.*
1539	*Edict of Villers-Cotterêts* decrees French as the language for all administrative laws in Provence.
1545	Suppression of Vaudois heretics from Luberon *(p 23).*
1555	Nostradamus *(qv)* publishes his astrological predictions, *Centuries.*
1558-1603	*Elizabeth's reign.*
1558	The engineer Adam de Craponne *(qv)* builds a canal.
1567	Michelade tragedy occurs in Nîmes *(p 143).*
1588	*Defeat of the Spanish Armada.*
1609	*Hudson sails up the Hudson River.*
1620	*Pilgrim fathers land at Plymouth, Ma.*
1622	Louis XIII visits Arles, Aix and Marseilles.
1660	Solemn entry of Louis XIV into Marseilles.
1664	*British capture New Amsterdam, which they rename New York.*
1685	Revocation of the *Edict of Nantes.* Huguenots flee France.
1713	Under the *Treaty of Utrecht* the Principality of Orange is transferred from the House of Orange-Nassau to France.
1714-27	*George I's reign*
1720	The great plague which originated in Marseilles decimates Provence.
1763	*Peace of Paris ends French and Indian War (1754-63); it marks the end of France's colonial empire in North America.*
1771	Suppression of Aix's Parliament.

From the Revolution to the present

1790	The constitutional Assembly divides southeast France into 3 *départements:* Basses-Alpes (capital: Digne), Bouches-du-Rhône (capital: Aix-en-Provence), Var (capital: Toulon).
1791	Avignon and Comtat Venaissin are annexed to France.
1792	500 Marseilles volunteers parade in Paris to the song of the Rhine Army, henceforth called the *Marseillaise (p 129).*
1805	*Battle of Trafalgar.*
1815	*Battle of Waterloo; Napoleon's fall.*
1837-1901	*Victoria's reign.*
1854	Founding of the Provençal literary school: Félibrige *(qv).*
1859	Frédéric Mistral publishes the Provençal poem *Mirèio (p 126).*
1861-65	*American Civil War.*
1886	*Statue of Liberty erected.*
1899	*Second Boer War.*
1933	Founding of the National Rhône Company for the harnessing of the river.
1942	German forces invade Provence.
1944	15 August: Allied troops land on the Côte d'Azur. 22-28 August: General de Montsabert and his troops aided by the Resistance movement liberate Marseilles from German occupation.
1962	First hydro-electric power stations of the Durance begin operating.
1965	Construction of Fos Complex *(qv)* begins.
1970	A6-A7 motorways link Paris and Marseilles.
1977	Marseilles's underground begins service.
1981	The high-speed train, TGV, links Paris and Marseilles.

A RICH PAST

Southern Gaul before the Roman conquest

Origins: a melting pot. – During the Bronze Age (1800-800BC) the region was inhabited by Ligurians, probably descendants of the native neolithic population. Beginning in the 7C the Celts began infiltrating while the first Greeks were settling. Massalia (Marseilles) was founded in 600 (or 620) by the Phocaeans in agreement with a Celtic tribe. And yet the arrival of Celts in hoards did not come about until the 5-4C. This resulted in a mixture of populations which provided ancient Provence with roots in the Celtic-Ligurian civilisation. These diverse populations settled progressively on *oppida,* fortified hill sites. Nages, near Nîmes, St-Blaise overlooking Fos Bay, Entremont near Aix were important settlements, in reality fortified townships.

Greek presence. – The Greeks were an essential part of the history of Provence's civilisation. The Rhodians most likely gave their name to the great Provençal river (Rhodanos), however, the Phocaeans, from Asia Minor (Ionia) were the first to establish a permanent colony: **Massalia.** Massalia rapidly became a powerful commercial city which founded in turn a number of trading posts: Glanum, Avignon, Cavaillon and had commercial exchanges with the people of the north (wine and pottery for pewter from Armorica and agricultural products and livestock from Brittany). And yet Greek culture spread slowly; not before 2C, a period when the relations between the natives and the Phocaeans from Massalia were deteriorating. The Salian Confederation (which had grouped together the Provençal population) rose against Massaliote imperialism.

Rome and Massalia. – During the Second Punic War (218-201), Massalia supported Rome whereas the Salian Franks helped Hannibal cross the region in 218. In 154 Massalia, worried about the threat of attack by the Gauls, obtained the protection of Rome. In *c*130 the powerful Arverni empire posed a problem of security to southern Gaul, the key trading centre between Italy and Spain.

In 125 Rome came to Massalia's aid, the Roman legions conquered with ease the Vocontii and Salian Franks, of which Entremont, their capital, fell. In 122, date of the founding of Aquae Sextiae (Aix-en-Provence), the Arverni and Allobroges suffered a bloody defeat. The consul Domitius Ahenobarbus delimited the boundaries of a new province, **Transalpine** which became **Narbonensis** (from the name of the first Roman colony of Narbonna) in 118. Massalia remained independent, it was recognised as a territory. The Roman domination, which at one time was threatened by the Cimbrian and Teuton invasions in 105 (disaster at Orange) and halted by Marius near Aix in 102 spread irreversibly over the region, not without abuse and pillaging.

Roman colonisation

Pax Romana. – Gaul Transalpine rapidly became integrated in the Roman world and actively supported the Preconsul Caesar during the Gallic Wars (58-51BC). Marseilles, as a result of having supported Pompey against Caesar, was beseiged in 49BC, fell and lost its independence. The important towns were Narbonne, Nîmes, Arles and Fréjus. Romanisation accelerated under Augustus, the Narbonensis *(see above)* was reorganised in 27BC. Antoninus Pius's *(p 143)* reign (2C) marked the apogee of Gallo-Roman civilisation. Agriculture remained Provence's principal activity and trade enriched the towns, mainly Arles which profited from Marseilles's disgrace. Urban affluence was reflected in the way of life which was entirely focused on comfort, luxury and leisure. Excavations have given us a glimpse of that life.

Arles, the favoured city. – After the troubled times of the 3C, the 4 and 5C brought considerable religious and political transformations. Christianity, which did not seem to appear before the end of the 2C, triumphed over the other religions after Constantine's conversion; he who made Arles his favourite town in the west *(p 64)*.

Marseilles remained a commercial centre, Aix became an administrative capital while Nîmes declined and Glanum was abandoned. The rural areas suffered due to the general impoverishment of the Gallo-Roman world; the large landowners placed heavy demands, the feeling of insecurity brought about the resettlement of fortified hill sites such as St-Blaise *(qv)*.

From the fall of the Roman Empire
to the Popes at Avignon

Invasion after invasion. – Until 471, the date of conquest of Arles by the Visigoths, Provence had been relatively spared of invasions. After the Burgundian and Visigoth domination, which lasted from 476-508, followed the Ostrogoth restoration, a period of some 30 years whereupon the Ostrogoths, considered themselves the mandatories of the Far Eastern emperor and revived Roman institutions: Arles, thus, recovered its praetorian prefects. Religious life continued progressing; several synods were held in Provence towns (Vaison-la-Romaine). The bishop of Arles, Caesarius, had a vast following in Gaul. In 536, Provence was ceded to the Franks and followed the same uncertain destiny as other provinces, tossed from hand to hand according to the Merovingian dynastic divisions. Decline was rapid.

The first half of the 8C was confusion and tragedy: Arabs and Franks transformed the region into a battleground. Charles Martel from 736-40 went through it with an incredible brutality. The Saracens were a constant threat. In 855 Provence was made a kingdom, the limits of which corresponded more or less with the Rhône Basin. It was weakened by the Saracens and Vikings terrorising the land. It, thus, soon fell into the hands of the kingdom of Burgundy, whose possessions spread from the Jura to the Mediterranean and were placed under the protection of the Holy Roman Emperors who inherited it in 1032; this was a major date in the history of Provence as it made Provence a part of the Holy Roman Empire with the area west of the Rhône under the yoke of the Counts of Toulouse.

Occitanian Provence. – The 10 and 11C marked a break in the evolution of Provence's civilisation, until then dependent on its Greco-Roman past. A new society developed out of the feudal anarchy. Rural life, henceforth, was concentrated in the perched villages – Luberon, Ste-Baume, Vaucluse Mountains – which depended upon the seigneuries. The towns attempted to recapture their expansion and began administrating themselves. The Oïl language spread... Close links were established between Provence and Languedoc. The failure of Occitania facilitated Capetian intervention. The Albigensian heresy resulted in the delayed union of the Catalan and Toulousain peoples who until then had been fighting over Provence, against the invaders from the north; but the defeat at Muret in 1213 dashed all hope for a united Occitania.

Louis VIII's expedition (seige of Avignon in 1226) and the *Treaty of Paris* in 1229 brought about the founding of the royal seneschalship in Beaucaire: the west bank of the Rhône was part of France. In the east the Catalan Count Raimond-Bérenger V maintained his authority and endowed Provence with an administrative organisation. The towns became powerful locally: as early as the 12C they elected their own consuls, whose power increased to the detriment of the traditional lords (bishops, counts, and vicounts); in the 13C they were seeking to gain independence.

House of Anjou's Provence. – The marriage of **Charles of Anjou**, St Louis's brother, to Beatrice of Provence, Raimond-Bérenger V's heir, in 1246 links the Provence to the House of Anjou. Charles had large political ambitions: he interfered in Italy and conquered the kingdom of Naples in 1266 before turning towards the Far East.

In Provence Charles of Anjou's government was very much appreciated: security was reestablished, and honest administration managed public affairs and prosperity returned. Concerning the territories, Comtat Venaissin was ceded to the papacy in 1274, by the king of France, and evolved seperately.

Charles I's successors, Charles II and Robert I, continued their father and grandfather's political ideas and a political order and peace reigned during the first half of the 14C. Aix was raised to administrative capital with a seneshal and a court where the officers who presided were in charge of the finances of the county.

The key city was, henceforth, Avignon where the Bishop Jacques Duèse, elected pope in 1316 under the name John XXII established himself. Clement V was already residing in Comtat Venaissin and benefited from the protection of the king of France; thus John XXII's decision was of no surprise to anyone and was confirmed by his successor Benedict XII, who began the construction of a new papal palace.

The popes' stay in Avignon, which lasted almost a century brought expansion and extraordinary brilliance to the city (bought in 1348 from Queen Joan): banking capital, large market centre, a perpetual construction site, an artistic centre; it surpassed all its rivals from afar.

From its annexation to the French crown to the 20C

The end of Provence's independence. – After the second half of the 14C, Provence entered a difficult period. Famine and the plague (which appeared in 1348), the pillaging road bandits and the political instability brought about by Queen Joan's (grand-daughter to King Robert, she was assasinated in 1382) slackness did great damage to Provence's stability. The population was decimated and the country was in ruins. After a violent problem of succession, Louis II of Anjou (nephew to the King of France, Charles V) aided by his mother, Marie de Blois, and the pope, reestablished the situation (1387).

Pacification was temporarily slowed by the activities of a turbulent lord, Vicount Raymond de Turenne *(p 86)* who terrorised the country (1389-99) pillaging and kidnapping. His lairs were the fortresses of Les Baux and Roquemartine. Peace was not achieved until the early 15C.

Louis II of Anjou's (d1417) youngest son, **King René,** inherited the county at the death of his brother in 1434. He was primarily concerned with the reconquest of the kingdom of Naples but every attempt of his failed, thereupon he turned all his attention to Provence (1447) and came to love it. His reign left happy memories; it coincided with a political and economic restoration which was felt through all of France *(p 46)*. He was a poet and had a cultivated mind due to his love of art; he attracted a quantity of artists to Aix which came to take up where the popes' Avignon had left off.

His nephew Charles of Maine briefly succeeded him and in 1481 ceded Provence to Louis XI.

The history of Provence and France were henceforth intwined inspite of the Rhône boatsmen who, for a long time, continued to distinguish between the Holy Roman Empire and the Kingdom of France.

Vaudois and Huguenots. – As early as 1530, the Reformation spread in the south of France, due for the most part to merchants and colporteurs; through the Rhône and Durance Valleys and Vivarais, Protestantism was stimulated by the brilliance of the Vaudois church located in the Luberon village communities.

The Vaud heresy went back to the 12C: **Pierre Valdo,** a merchant from Lyons had founded in 1170 a sect preaching poverty, Evangelism and refusal of the sacraments and ecclesiastical hierarchy. Excommunicated in 1184, the Vaudois had since then been pursued as heretics. In 1540 the Aix Parliament ordained the destruction of a Vaud village, Mérindol. François I temporised and prescribed a deferment. Instead of calming things down, the religious controversy was brought to a head: Sénanque Abbey was pillaged by the heretics in 1544; as a ripost the Parliament's president obtained from the king the authorisation to apply the Mérindol decree and organised a punitive expedition. From 15-20 April 1545 blood ran through the Luberon village streets: 3 000 people were massacred, 600 were sent to the galleys and many villages were razed.

Nevertheless, Protestantism continued to spread especially west of the Rhône in Vivarais, Cévennes, Nîmes and Uzès; east of the Rhône it was Orange (a Nassau Family principality since 1559) which became a Reformation stronghold. In 1560 the inevitable happened. Numerous churches and abbeys (St-Gilles, Valbonne Charterhouse) were pillaged by the Huguenots; violence brought on violence and with it the fall of Orange (1563) by the Catholic partisans which was answered by the fall of Mornas *(qv)*.

During these tumultuous times Provence and Languedoc-Cévennes split taking different paths. Provence opted for Catholicism and the League recruited fervent partisans in such cities as Aix or Marseilles (both of which would have liked to become an independent republic. On the Rhône's opposite shore the situation was different. The people, influenced by the merchants and textile craftsmen who kept the Reformation alive, generally tended to believe in the Protestant movement with Nîmes as its capital.

The violence of the Wars of Religion in southern France ended up bringing face to face two opposing mentalities who were to meet again during the Camisard Insurrection (1702-04) and who were never able to forget this crucial period of their history.

The 17 to 20C. – Provence licked its wounds and revived, particularly in the 18C, which was the golden age for agriculture and commerce.

However, the 19C was a less successful period: industrialisation progressed but rural life suffered from the failure of the silkworm farms and phylloxera which spread through the vineyards.

Facing these changes Mistral sought to defend the Provençal identity and its traditions. When he died in 1914, Provence was, nevertheless, wholeheartedly engaged in modernisation, today highly successful with its heavy industry, speculative agriculture and tourism.

PROVENÇAL DIALECT AND LITERATURE

The Provence is an ancient civilised land, Greco-Latin then Occitanian, which has never stopped influencing poets and writers alike, who expressed themselves in Provençal (a group of South Occitan dialects).

Language of the troubadours. – From vulgar Latin spoken at the end of the Roman Empire evolved the Roman languages : Italian, Rumanian, Catalan, Spanish, Portuguese and in France Oïl language *(langue d'oïl)* in the north and Oc language *(langue d'oc)* in the south. *Oïl* and *Oc* were the words used for yes in the north and south, respectively. This distinction which was formed as early as the Merovingian period was advanced enough in the 10 and 11C that the two languages seperately entered into literature. Provençal, which appeared in Latin texts for the first time in the 11C, owed its place and influence to the success of 12C

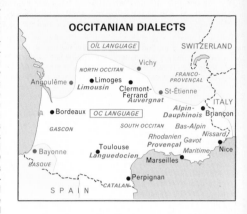

courtly literature. In fact the art of the troubadours, which developed in the feudal courts of Périgord, Limousin and Gascony was not confined purely to Provence but encompassed all of Occitania, from Bordeaux to Nice.

These troubadours (*trobar* = to find) inventors of musical airs both melodies and words in the Oc language, created a linguistic community independent of political divisions: Jaufré Rudel from Blaye, Bernard de Ventadour, Peire Vidal from Toulouse and from the Provence Raimbaut of Orange, Countess of Die, Raimbaut of Vaqueiras and Folquet of Marseilles.

Under the Provençal name, Occitanian was appreciated by noble foreigners and most of the European courts. The essential inspirational motive of the troubadours was love, not a passionate love but a courtly love where the patience and discretion of the poet-lover finally weakened the lady who accepted the hommage of her vassal. Using sound, word pattern and stanza-structure these poems verbalised the troubadours anxieties and hopes. This literary form declined in the 13C: the themes of courtly love had been exhausted and the wealthy seigneurial castles, which served as a backdrop, had lost their influence (due to the penetration of French influence in the south, favoured by the Crusades' embarkation points, the Inquisition and the expanding Capetian monarchy). Provençal, nevertheless, retained its importance: Dante (1265-1321) almost used it to write his *Divine Comedy* and it was the language spoken at the pontifical court of Avignon. With Latin, Oc language was, in the Middle Ages, the only written administrative language. And yet beginning in the 14C regional differences began appearing and the Oc language began to lose ground.

Provençal literature moved to Italy where it was revived thanks to Dante and returned in force into the Rhône Valley in the form of a sonnet with **Petrarch** (1304-74). Exiled in Avignon, Petrarch fell passionately in love with the lovely Laura de Noves in 1327; his love was personified at her death (d 1348). His *Canzonière* were a group of sonnets where he expressed his unrequited love for Laura. The poet, who had retired to Fontaine-de-Vaucluse *(qv)*, also wrote in his letters descriptions of Provençal life; he spoke of shepherds, the Sorgue fishermen and his climb to Mount Ventoux.

The Provençal language's fatal blow was in 1539 with the adoption of the *Edict of Villers-Cotterêts* which decreed that for all administrative use the French language – the dialect spoken in Ile de France, thus Paris – be employed. Inspite of that, Provençal literature survived until the 19C in the theatre, poetry, short stories and legends, chronicles, didactic and erudite works (dictionaries and anthologies).

To be cited at this time are the writers Bellaud de la Bellaudière and Nicolas Saboly.

Folquet de Marseille (13C manuscript)

Bellaud de la Bellaudière. – Born in Grasse in 1534, Bellaud de la Bellaudière lived a very active life as a soldier; he was opposed to the Huguenots. When he was in prison, he wrote 160 sonnets his *Œuvres et Rimes*. His poetry, inspired by Marot, Rabelais and Petrarch, was essentially personal due to its familar realism. It brought to the Provençal language a renewal. He was joined by Claude Bruey, Raynier from Briançon and François de Bègue.

Nicolas Saboly. – In the 17C, while the moralist Vauvenargues was born in Aix and Madame de Sévigné resided at Grignan *(qv)*, Nicolas Saboly was composing Provençal **Noëls**, charming, simple works of popular poetry. These happy yet pious canticles depicted beside the angels the touching characters of an entire small world running in the night towards the newly born baby Jesus.

As a vulgar language, however, Provençal continued degrading, breaking up into different provincial dialects.

In the 17C services were still said in Provençal in rural villages as well as in the cities. When Racine *(qv)* resided in Uzès in 1661, he had a great deal of difficulty making himself understood. Until the Revolution, Provençal was the language spoken day-to-day; it was but a small elite which spoke French, and even then they were bilingual.

The Félibrige. – In the late 18C, Provençal, weakened by the centralised state, was reborn through literature. In 1795, Abbot Favre made history with his *Siège de Caderousse* (Caderousse's Seat), a satirical poem written in dialect amusing because of its Rabelais like truculence. In the 1840s there was an explosion: Joseph **Roumanille** (1818-91), teacher in Avignon and the author of a work *Li Margarideto* (1847) awakened in the young Mistral *(qv)* a passion for the Provence, its culture, history and Oc language. As early 1851, Mistral began writing *Mirèio* and in 1852 the first congress of future *Félibres* was held in Arles. The decisive date was 21 May 1854 at the castle of Fort-Ségugne, seven young poets, writing in Provençal (Roumanille, Mistral, Aubanel, Mathieu, Tavan, Giéra and Brunet) founded the Félibrige (*félibre* was a word taken from an old song meaning doctor), an association, the goal of which was, to restore the Provençal language and to codify its spelling; it published a periodical *Armana Provençau* which was to spread its ideas making them widely known.

In 1859 **Mistral** published *Mirèio* an epic poem of twelve cantos which brought him immense success – Lamartine praised his work and Charles Gounod made it into an opera in 1864. His literary works included: *Calendau* (1867), *Lis Isclo d'Or* (1875), *Nerto* (1884), *La Reino Jano* (1890), *The Song of the Rhône* (1896), *Lis Oulivado* (1912). In 1904 he was awarded the Noble Prize of Literature. Mistral was also a fine philologist who patiently collected the scattered elements of the Oc language and restituted its spelling in a monumental dictionary *Lou Trésor dóu Félibrige* published 1878-86, which still serves as a reference book. The Félibrige grouped Occitanian poets and novelists as different as: Alphonse Daudet, Paul Arène, Félix Gras, Baptiste Bonnet, Joseph d'Arbaud, Charles Rieu, Dom Xavier de Fourvière, Jean-Henri Fabre, Folco de Baroncelli-Javon *(qv)*, Charles Maurras (political theorist), Jean Alcard (a member of the Academy, he wrote *Maurin of the Moors);* and on a totally different level, Émile Zola (went to secondary school in Aix) who with his Rougon-Macquart series evoked the evolution of a family from the south and Edmond Rostand (born in Marseilles) who wrote the unforgettable *Aiglon.*

Mistral

In the present. – Although Provence is always present in their works, the contemporary writers have gone beyond the regional level and attained the ranks of top French writers: Jean Giono from Manosque, Marcel Pagnol *(Marius)* from Aubagne, René Barjavel from Nyons, René Char (one of France's greatest poets) from Isle-sur-la Sorgue and Marie Mauron to name but a few.

Among the English and American writers who have settled in Provence are: Lawrence Durrell, Graham Greene, F. Scott Fitzgerald, H.G. Wells.

Paradoxically speaking Provençal as a spoken language regressed whereas as a language of culture (successor to the troubadours and *Félibres*) it progressed. Admittedly the local dialects remain but they are most often ignored by the young and are more prevalent in the rural than urban areas. While the centralising and unifying role of the state has, instead of weakening, enhanced the language: Oc language is, henceforth, recognised in the official teaching programmes. A harmonious language, Provençal, counts a wealthy vocabulary, which allows for an infinite variety of nuance. The goal of the Institute of Occitanian Studies is to seek beyond the different dialects issued from the Oc language, the unity of a common language similar to what Occitania's influence was in the Middle Ages when it extended over the political limits from the Atlantic to the Mediterranean.

LEGENDS AND TALES

The legends and tales of Provence are a colourful account of history and geography; in these stories are depicted the men, customs, institutions, lifestyles, beliefs, monuments and sites. Perhaps the Greco-Roman heritage must be recognised in the Provençal tradition where the wonderful accompanies daily life in its humblest activities, as in the ancient Roman and Greek myths where the gods were everywhere and when they intervened miracles occurred.

Ancient myths. – For the ancient Greeks the western Mediterranean was awe inspiring, at the same time frightning and wonderful where each evening, the sun set with Apollo's chariot. **Hercules,** son of Jupiter, had been to this land and had married Galathea from Gaul; accorded an incredible strength he had opened the passages through the Alps; to protect his son's crossing through Provence, Jupiter had showered his enemies with stones and boulders which became a desert, the Crau. The attraction of this western Mediterranean land inspired the Phocaeans to later found a colony here. The legend of **Protis and Gyptis** illustrate this episode *(p 128)*. The Marseilles navigator, **Pytheas** in 4C BC, is said to have sailed between the columns of Hercules (Straits of Gibralter), sailed the waters to Cornwall and onto Iceland.

Legends of the Saints. – Christianity, too, brought its collection of stories. A thousand year old tradition ascribes the conversion of Provence in the 1C to the miraculous landing of a boat from Judea bearing Lazarus, Mary Magdalene and Martha and their saintly companions, disciples of Christ *(p 172)*. With St Victor and Cassien they formed a sort of mystic Provençal state and are credited with many wondrous acts including the overcoming by Martha of the Tarasque *(p 179)*. Local saints were not lacking. **Eleazarius of Sabran** *(p 57)* was no less precocious and every Friday refused milk from his milk nurse for mortification. Whereas **St Mitre**, the beheaded martyr, as the legend recounts it, picked up his head, kissed it and bore it to the cathedral where he placed it on the altar. Then there is **St Caesarius**, who captured in his glove a puff of sea air to carry it back to Nyons country, locked in an amphitheatre of impenetrable mountains, from then on a light wind blew over the region; the local people took heart and began to cultivate the land. The prosperity of Nyons country dates from this period and its privileged climate has allowed it to cultivate olives.

Troubadour tradition. – Then there are the legends of Provence which have been inspired by epic poetry *(chansons de geste)* and courtly prose.
Pierre of Provence a valiant knight and talented troubadour lived at his father's court in Cavaillon Castle. On simply seeing her portrait, the knight fell in love with Princess Maguelone, daughter of the King of Naples, and set out to fetch her. Received at the Neapolitan court, he came out winner of a number of tournaments where he wore Maguelone's colours. But one day Pierre was kidnapped by Barbary pirates and taken to Tunis where he was imprisoned for seven years. Having served his term he was finally able to set sail for Provence but his boat sunk not far from Aigues-Mortes. Mortally wounded, he was brought to the Aigues-Mortes hospital, headed by Princess Maguelone, herself, who had sought through charity a way to cure herself of her love. The lovers met and recognised each other, Pierre was cured...
Not all endings were so happy... One day **Guillem de Cabestaing,** a son of a noble and well-known troubadour came to sing at the court of the lord of Castel-Roussillon, an ugly, vulgar old man who had a lovely young wife named Sérémonde. Love kindled quickly between these two young people. The lord having discovered this killed the handsome Guillem in an ambush, ripped out his heart and served it to his wife as dinner; Sérémonde responded with: "My lord you have served me such delicious fare that nothing could ever equal it and so I swear before Christ, in order to keep the taste fresh for all time, I will never eat again." She then threw herself from the top of a cliff in Roussillon; her blood as it spread coloured the soil; that is the origin of ochre!

Sorcery. – Rare were the villages that had not encountered a *masc* or a *masco*. These people had the power to bewitch people and animals. If a baby stopped suckling, if horses stopped for no apparent reason, if hunting dogs lost their scent, they had been *emmasqués*. Méthamis in Vaucluse is still, even today, a sanctuary of Provençal sorcery. To fight against evil spells a *démascaire* was called in, this person was often a shepherd, because the shepherd was a holder of supernatural powers but a sworn enemy of the sorcerers, it was said, and held the secrets of nature. The *démascaire* was good and broke the evil spell; he was also a bonesetter and cured ills with plants. Other ways of distancing the evil spell were possible such as wearing a piece of clothing inside out or in back instead of front, throwing salt into the hearth or saying different entreaties while crossing yourself at the same time. To protect houses from the evil eye the custom was to cement into the wall a vitrified pebble; on the sheep pen door was nailed a magic thistle. Some places are totally magical, mysterious... Such as Garagaï at Vauvenargues an unending chasm where strange things happen. Between Arles and Montmajour is the fairys' hole peopled with supernatural beings.

Child heroes. – A great number of Provençal legends recount the memorable exploits of children and adolescents gifted with a force and extraordinary ingenuity; they generally appeal to all mighty God, the intervention of the saints or magic. This is the case of little **Bénézet** from Avignon, who built the bridge at Avignon *(p 80)*. **Jean de l'Ours**, so-called because he had been brought up with a bear, was another: at the age of 12, he conceived the idea of journeying round France. He forged himself a stout iron staff and thus armed killed the horrible dragons which kept a young princess in an enchanted castle. He married the princess and lived happily ever after... **Guihen l'orphelin** thanks to his mysterious white hen, which he would stroke while murmuring a special incantation, could become invisible. He was able to free a king and his daughter imprisoned by a wicked baron. To thank him the king promised his daughter to Guihen and they lived happily ever after...

FESTIVALS AND COSTUMES

Festivals. – The people of Provence have always had a taste for celebration. In the past it was the men who were in charge of the festivities. The fairs, either secular or religious, (remnants of solemn Christian celebrations mixed with pagan tendencies) were numerous; there are the classic feast days which happen throughout the year and the larger festivals, more or less traditional, attracting thousands of people in a typically colourful Provençal atmosphere.

From April to September, Nîmes and Arles rival each other in the organisation of their famous *férias* attracting *aficionados* whether it be the *corrida* with picadors and the kill or simply the bull run through the streets (the bulls wear a *cocarde,* a rosette between their horns: it must be removed by the *razeteurs,* handrake holders.

In Camargue the roundup (*ferrade – p 97*) is always an exciting time: the young calves are thrown to the ground and branded with the mark of their owner; there are also the horse races between *gardians*.

There is also the quite different Venetian Water Festival held at Martigues where a nocturnal procession of decorated boats occurs.

And of course there are the theatre, opera and dance festivals which take place in Provence; whether it be Avignon, Aix-en-Provence, Orange, Vaison-la-Romaine, Carpentras, Salon-de-Provence or Arles each of these cities is the venue for an annual artistic festival of top quality.

See the table of principal festivals pp 199-200.

Costumes and farandoles. – Most of the festivals are a wonderful time to admire the traditional costumes while listening to the fife and *tambourin*. The Provençal costume is best summarised with the **traditional dress from Arles** (Museon Arlaten in Arles has an excellent collection). The women wear long colourful skirts and a black blouse *(eso)* with long tight sleeves; on top a pleated shirt is covered with a shawl either made of white lace or matching the skirt. There are different varieties of head-dress; they are all, however, worn on top of a high bun: *à la cravate* consists of a white percale handkerchief knotted like rabbits' ears; *à ruban:* the bun is fitted with a wide velvet ribbon hemmed with lace on the front and running down the back, at the crown of the head, there is a flat ribboned surface (held with cardboard); *en ailes de papillon*, a lovely old lace ribbon knotted around the head in the form of butterfly *(papillon)* wings *(ailes)*. The fan accompanies the Arles traditional costume.

Arles woman in costume

The mens costume is less colourful, more sober. They wear a white shirt knotted at the collar by a thin tie or ribbon, sometimes covered by a dark coloured vest upon which hangs a watch chain, canvas trousers are held at the waist by a wide red or black woolen belt. They wear black felt hats with a wide slightly raised rim. The peasants dress consists of a lovely brightly coloured shawl and small white hat on top of which is a wide flat straw hat for the women while a black velvet vest and straw hat for the men.

The **farandole** is a Mediterranean dance which goes back to the Middle Ages if not to Antiquity, and was danced throughout Arles country. Young men and women, either holding each others hands or a handkerchief dance, to a six-beat rhythm. The typically Provençal instruments played by the *tambourinaires* are the **galoubet,** a small 3-holed flute which produces a piercing sound and the **tambourin** a type of drum 75cm – 29 1/2in high and 35cm – 13 1/2in wide beat by a *massette* held in the right hand while the other hand holds the *galoubet;* on the drum itself, the head of which is made from calf-skin is stretched the *chanterelle*, a thin strand of hemp or a violin chord which produces a rasping sound poetically called the song of the cicada.

ABC OF ARCHITECTURE

To assist readers unfamiliar with the terminology employed in architecture, we describe below the most commonly used terms, which we hope will make their visits to ecclesiastical, military and civil buildings more interesting.

Ecclesiastical architecture

illustration I

Ground plan. – The more usual Catholic form is based on the outline of a cross with the two arms of the cross forming the transept: ① Porch – ② Narthex – ③ Side aisles (sometimes double) – ④ Bay (transverse section of the nave between 2 pillars) – ⑤ Side chapel (often predates the church) – ⑥ Transept crossing – ⑦ Arms of the transept, sometimes with a side doorway – ⑧ Chancel, nearly always facing east towards Jerusalem; the chancel often vast in size was reserved for the monks in abbatial churches – ⑨ High altar – ⑩ Ambulatory: in pilgrimage churches the aisles were extended round the chancel, forming the ambulatory, to allow the faithful to file past the relics – ⑪ Radiating or apsidal chapel – ⑫ Axial chapel. In churches which are not dedicated to the Virgin this chapel, in the main axis of the building is often consecrated to the Virgin (Lady Chapel) – ⑬ Transept chapel.

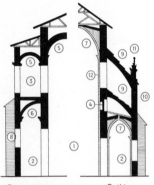

Romanesque   Gothic

◀ illustration II

Cross-section: ① Nave – ② Aisle – ③ Tribune or Gallery – ④ Triforium – ⑤ Barrel vault – ⑥ Half-barrel vault – ⑦ Pointed vault – ⑧ Buttress – ⑨ Flying buttress – ⑩ Pier of a flying buttress – ⑪ Pinnacle – ⑫ Clerestory window.

illustration III ▶

Gothic cathedral: ① Porch – ② Gallery – ③ Rose window – ④ Belfry (sometimes with a spire) – ⑤ Gargoyle acting as a waterspout for the roof gutter – ⑥ Buttress – ⑦ Pier of a flying buttress (abutment) – ⑧ Flight or span of flying buttress – ⑨ Double-course flying buttress – ⑩ Pinnacle – ⑪ Side chapel – ⑫ Radiating or apsidal chapel – ⑬ Clerestory windows – ⑭ Side doorway – ⑮ Gable – ⑯ Pinnacle – ⑰ Spire over the transept crossing.

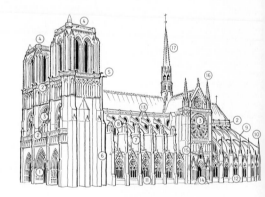

illustration IV

Groined vaulting:
① Main arch – ② Groin
③ Transverse arch

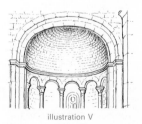

illustration V

Oven vault:
termination of a barrel
vaulted nave

illustration VI

illustration VII

Lierne and tierceron vaulting:
① Diagonal – ② Lierne
③ Tierceron – ④ Pendant
⑤ Corbel

Quadripartite vaulting:
① Diagonal – ② Transverse
③ Stringer – ④ Flying buttress
⑤ Keystone

▼ illustration VIII

Doorway: ① Archivolt. Depending on the architectural style of the building this can be rounded, pointed, basket-handled, ogee or even adorned by a gable – ② Arching, covings (with string courses, mouldings, carvings or adorned with statues). Recessed arches or orders form the archivolt – ③ Tympanum – ④ Lintel – ⑤ Archshafts – ⑥ Embrasures. Arch shafts, splaying sometimes adorned with statues or columns – ⑦ Pier (often adorned by a statue) – ⑧ Hinges and other ironwork.

illustration IX ▶

Arches and pillars: ① Ribs or ribbed vaulting – ② Abacus – ③ Capital – ④ Shaft – ⑤ Base – ⑥ Engaged column – ⑦ Pier of arch wall – ⑧ Lintel – ⑨ Discharging or relieving arch – ⑩ Frieze.

Military architecture

illustration X

Fortified enclosure: ① Hoarding (projecting timber gallery) – ② Machicolations (corbelled crenellations) – ③ Barbican – ④ Keep or donjon – ⑤ Covered watchpath – ⑥ Curtain wall – ⑦ Outer curtain wall – ⑧ Postern.

illustration XI

Towers and curtain walls: ① Hoarding – ② Crenellations – ③ Merlon – ④ Loophole or arrow slit – ⑤ Curtain wall – ⑥ Bridge or drawbridge.

◀ illustration XII

Fortified gatehouse: ① Machicolations – ② Watch turrets or bartizan – ③ Slots for the arms of the drawbridge – ④ Postern.

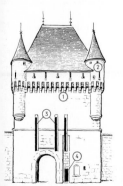

illustration XIII ▶

Star fortress: ① Entrance – ② Drawbridge – ③ Glacis – ④ Ravelin or half-moon – ⑤ Moat – ⑥ Bastion – ⑦ Watch turret – ⑧ Town – ⑨ Assembly area.

ART AND ARCHITECTURAL TERMS USED IN THE GUIDE

Acroterion: ornaments placed at the apex and ends of a pediment of a temple.

Aedicule: a small house or room; a niche.

Aisle: illustration I.

Altarpiece or retable: illustration XX.

Ambulatory: illustration I.

Apsidal or radiating chapel: illustration I.

Archivolt: illustration VIII.

Axial or Lady Chapel: illustration I.

Barrel vaulting: illustration II.

Basket arch: depressed arch common to late medieval and Renaissance architecture.

Bay: illustration I.

Bishop's throne: Gothic chair with a high back.

Buttress: illustrations II and III.

Capital: illustration IX.

Cardo: main street of Roman town running north-south.

Caryatid: female figure used as a column (atlantes are male caryatids).

Chevet: French term for the east end of a church; illustration I.

Cippus (i): small pillar used to mark a burial place or serve as a sepulchral monument.

Coffered ceiling: vault or ceiling decorated with sunken panels.

Corbel: illustration VI.

Crypt: underground chamber or chapel.

Curtain wall: illustration XI.

Decumanus: main street of Roman town running east-west.

Depressed arch: three centred arch sometimes called a basket arch.

Diagonal arch: illustrations VI and VII.

Dome: illustrations XIV and XV.

Exedra: seated section in the back of Roman basilicas; curved marble bench (covered), rounded niche.

Flamboyant: latest phase (15C) of French Gothic architecture; name taken from the undulating (flame-like) lines of the window tracery.

Flame ornament: ornamentation used in classical art representing a vase spewing flames.

Foliated scrolls: sculptural or painted ornamentation depicting foliage, often in the form of a frieze.

Fresco: mural paintings executed on wet plaster.

Gable: triangular part of an end wall carrying a sloping roof; the term is also applied to the steeply pitched ornamental pediments of Gothic architecture; illustration III.

Gallery: illustrations II and XVII.

Gargoyle: illustration III.

Génoise: decorative frieze under the eaves, composed of a double or triple row of tiles embedded end-on in the wall.

Groined vaulting: illustration IV.

High relief: haut-relief.

Hypocaust: an underground furnace designed to heat the water for the baths or the rooms of a house.

Keep or donjon: illustration X.

Keystone: illustration VII.

Lintel: illustrations VII and IX.

Lombard arcades: decorative blind arcading composed of small arches and intervening pilaster strips; typical of Romanesque architecture in Lombardy.

Low relief: bas-relief.

Machicolations: illustration X.

Modillion: small console supporting a cornice.

Mullion: a vertical post dividing a window.

Oppidum (a): Latin word for a fortified agglomeration, usually set on a hill or height.

Organ: illustration XVII.

Oven vaulting: illustration V.

Overhang or jetty: overhanging upper storey.

Ovolo moulding: egg-shaped decoration.

Peribolus (os): sacred enclosure or court around a temple.

Peristyle: a range of columns surrounding or on the façade of a building.

Pier: illustration VIII.

Pietà: Italian term designating the Virgin Mary with the dead Christ on her knees.

Pilaster: engaged rectangular column.

Pinnacle: illustrations II and III.

Piscina: basin for washing the sacred vessels.

Porch: covered approach to the entrance to a building.

Portico: a colonnaded space in front of a façade or in an interior courtyard.

Postern: illustrations X and XII.

Quadripartite vaulting: illustration VII.

Recessed arches: see voussoir.

Recessed tomb: funerary niche.

Roodscreen: illustration XVI.

Rose or wheel window: illustration III.

Rustication: large blocks of masonry often separated by deep joints and given bold textures (rock-faced, diamond-pointed...); commonly employed during the Renaissance.

Santon: fired and brightly painted clay figurines; traditionally used in the Christmas cribs in Provence.

Segment: part of a ribbed vault; compartment between the ribs.

Semi-circular arch: roundheaded arch.

Spire: illustration III.

Splay: a slope; applied usually to the sides of a door or a window; illustration VIII.

Stalls: illustration XIX.

Stucco: mixture of powdered marble, plaster and strong glue; used for decoration.

Tracery: intersecting stone ribwork in the upper part of a window.

Transept: illustration I.

Triforium: illustration II.

Triptych: three panels hinged together, chiefly used as an altarpiece.

Twinned or paired: columns, pilasters, windows... grouped in twos.

Voussoir: illustration VIII.

Watchpath or wall walk: illustration X.

◀ Illustration XIV
Dome on squinches:
① Octagonal dome –
② Squinch – ③ Arches of transept crossing

Illustration XV ▶
Dome on pendentives:
① Circular dome – ② Pendentive –
③ Arches of transept crossing

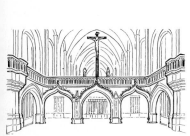

Illustration XVI

Rood screen. – This replaces the rood beam in larger churches, and may be used for preaching and reading of the Epistles and Gospel. From the 17C onwards many disappeared as they tended to hide the altar.

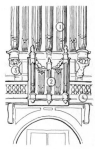

Illustration XVII
Organ:
① Great organ case
② Little organ case
③ Caryatids – ④ Loft

Illustration XVIII
Renaissance ornament
① shell – ② vase – ③ foliage
④ dragon – ⑤ nude child
⑥ cherub – ⑦ cornucopia
⑧ satyr

Illustration XIX
Stalls:
① High back
② Elbow rest
③ Cheek-piece
④ Misericord

Illustration XX
Altar with retable or altarpiece
① Retable or altarpiece – ② Predella –
③ Crowning piece – ④ Altar table –
⑤ Altar front
Certain baroque retables consisted of several altars; contemporary liturgy tends to eliminate them.

Provençal bell cages. – Built to resist the *mistral* which would blow through the wrought iron instead of blowing and knocking down the stones, the Provençal bell cage *(photograph p 43)* crowned buildings: religious, civil or military. Either simply (bell-shaped or spherical) or elaborately shaped (bulbous, cylindrical or pyramidial), these wrought iron cages grace the Provençal sky with their delicate silhouettes.

ANCIENT ART

Before the Roman conquest

Ligurians and Celts settled in fortified hill sites *(oppida)* such as Nages *(qv)* and Entremont *(qv)* and created true towns organised on a regular plan. Within the fortified walls stood a group of uniform dwellings, a type of hut in unfired stone and brick. Celtic-Ligurian sculpture honoured, before anything else, the cult of the dead warrior, the town's hero, which was presented in the form of warriors' statues seated cross-legged with people either free-standing or in relief. An important ritual consisted of putting in the stone lintels the beheaded victims of the conquered peoples either alive or in the carved version. The sculpture exhibited at Roquepertuse demonstrates perfectly the Celtic form of expression. Hellenistic influence was capital for the region; it directly influenced the native peoples accelerating the development of their economy and society. Greek construction techniques infiltrated into the building of St-Blaise *(qv)* and Glanum *(qv)*. Numerous pottery fragments and Greek black figure vases were excavated at Arles, and the stelae found Rue Négrel in Marseilles, are the oldest examples (second half of the 6C BC) of Greek sculpture in France.

Roman towns

Provence covered itself with towns which adopted the Roman urban plan. They were all constructed with remarkable public and private buildings, some of which are still well preserved, giving them a charm all their own.

Towns. – The great Provençal towns, without totally dropping all Hellenistic influence, took Rome as their model.

Urban plan. – Most of the towns were built either on native Hellenistic or Gallic sites. And yet, very often the desire to settle in a particular spot was instilled by a colony of veteran legionaires as was done in Nîmes and Orange who were soon after joined by the civilian population. The foundation was set according to precise rules: after having determined the future town centre two major streets were traced – the *cardo maximus* (north-south orientation) and the *decumanus maximus* (east-west orientation) which created a regular grid pattern where the grids were squared with sides some hundred square yards wide. In fact this

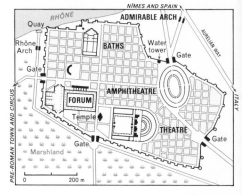

Roman Arles

geometric exactitude could only appear on sites, where the local topography was suitable such as with Orange or Arles as opposed to Nîmes and Vaison-la-Romaine. When previous edifices had existed, they were razed such as at Glanum, to make room for the new buildings. These towns were not surrounded with walls except at Nîmes, Arles and Orange, which were granted the honour of surrounding themselves with ramparts (permission obtained from Rome). Defensive walls did not appear until the end of the 3C, they were then built with towers and gates corresponding to the main streets.

Streets. – The main streets were lined with sidewalks, at times 50cm – 19 1/2in high and bordered by porticoes which protected the people from sun and rain. The roadway paved with large flagstones laid diagonally, was crossed at intervals by stepping-stones laid at the same level as the pavements but between which horses and chariot-wheels could pass and pedestrians could cross over above the dust and mud. Gutters also ran beside the road and were slightly rounded.

Forum. – The forum, a large paved open space surrounded by an arcade, was the centre of public and commercial life in a Roman town. Government offices were located round the forum; these included a temple devoted to the imperial cult, a civil basilica (a type of town hall where judicial and commercial affairs were treated); the *curia* or headquarters of local government, and at times a prison.

At Arles the forum had the particularity of being lined with a vast underground gallery, *cryptoporticus (p 67)*, the origin of which remans a mystery.

The art of building. – The art of building was very advanced with the Romans. The rapidity in which their buildings went up was not due to the number pf people working on a site but more due to the special training of the workers, their organised working methods and the use of lifting devices such as levers, hoisting winches, tackles, to move heavy material into place.

Building materials. – For building material the Romans used the local limestone, which was not hard to dress; the stone was easily extracted and shaped into blocks. They originally had adopted the method of using large blocks of stone without mortar, that is to say by the weight of the stones themselves, and with dowels or cramps. They, thereupon, revolutionised wall construction by the use of concrete, a manufactured material not unique to any one country; it could, therefore, be used in the construction of buildings throughout the Empire giving a uniformity and similarity to their buildings. It could be used to fill in the cracks or joints, or give to a public building a uniformed surface such as at the Maison Carrée and Amphitheatre in Nîmes *(p 144)*, or to wedge the stones between themselves allowing the expansion of the vault.

Orders. – The Roman architectural orders derived from the Greek orders but with some variation. Roman Doric, still called the Tuscan Order, the simplest and most solid was found on the monuments' lower storeys; too severe it was rarely used by the Romans. The Ionic Order was very elegant but not pompous enough for the Roman architects. Whereas, the Corinthian Order was used frequently for the richness of its ornamentation. The Composite Order was a combination of the Ionic and Corinthian Orders.

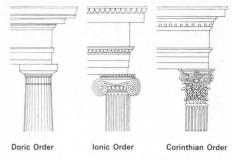

Doric Order   Ionic Order   Corinthian Order

Roofs. – The public buildings sometimes had rectangular shaped roofs held by colonnades inside the rooms. But more often the Romans used rounded vaulting in the corridors and galleries where the walls were parallel, groined vaulting in square rooms and the dome in the circular rooms.

Public Buildings. – The inhabitants of Roman towns enjoyed bloody combats as much as the more peaceful theatrical representations *(p 144)*.
The gladiator fights were forbidden in 404 under the influence of Christianisation; the games were abandoned at the same time.

Amphitheatre. – The amphitheatre, also known as **arena,** had on the outside two tiers of arcades surmounted by a low storey called the attic. On the attic were fixed posts to carry a huge adjustable awning, the *velum,* to shelter the spectators from the sun and rain. The arcades were divided by rectangular pillars decorated with engaged half-columns on the first storey. Inside, enclosing the arena, a wall protected the spectators in the front rows from the wild animals released in the ring. The *cavea* – terraces for the spectators – was divided into *maenia* – tiers of seats generally in groups of four individually separated by a passage. The seats were strictly reserved; nearest the arena being for the men with the superior social station: the first *maenia* were reserved for consuls, senators, magistrates and members of local guilds (such as the boatmen of Arles) who arrived in litters. In another section sat priests, knights and Roman citizens while freedmen and slaves sat in the attic. The arcades and three circular gallery-promenades, the hundreds of staircases and passages enabled spectators to reach or leave their stepped seats directly – at Nîmes it took less than five minutes for the audience of 20 000 to leave.

Theatre. – The Roman theatre, in the form of a half-circle lengthened by a deep stage, was divided into three sections: the *cavea* (auditorium) built in the hollow of a hillside, as in Orange *(p 150)* and crowned by a colonnade; the *orchestra,* the semi-circular section in front of the stage with moveable seats reserved for dignitaries; the stage flanked by side rooms, rectangular in shape which were higher in level than the orchestra. At the back of the stage was a wall (which was as high as the *cavea*) with three doors through which the actors entered.

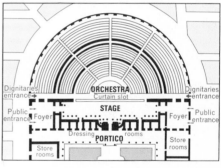

Roman Theatre in Arles

The stage wall was the finest part of the building; its decoration included several tiers of columns, niches containing statues (the central niche contained the emperor's statue), marble facing and mosaics. Behind this were the actors' dressing-rooms and store rooms. Beyond these again was a portico open to the garden, through which the actors entered the theatre. In it the spectators would stroll during the intermissions or take shelter from rain. As in the arenas, a huge adjustable awning (the *velum*) could be opened to shelter the spectators from the sun and rain.
Scenery and machinery were ingenious. Some scenes were fixed; some were superimposed and uncovered by sliding others sideways.
The curtain was only 3m – 10ft high. It dropped into a slit at the beginning of the play and rose at the end. The basement contained the machinery and communicated with the stage through trap-doors on which the actors could rise from or sink into the ground. Other machines, mounted in the flies, lowered gods or heroes from the heavens or raised them into the clouds. The effects men knew how to create were smoke, lightning, thunder, ghosts and the accompaniment of apotheoses.
All sorts of means were used to obtain perfect acoustics. The mouths of the actors' masks were little megaphones; the large sloping roof over the stage threw the sound downwards, the upward curve of the seats received it smoothly, the colonnades broke up the echo and carefully graduated sounding-boards under the seats acted as loud-speakers. One detail will show how far these refinements were carried: the doors on the stage were hollow and made like violins inside. When an actor wished to amplify his voice he would stand against one of these sound-boxes.

Circus. – These were huge rectangular arenas, one end of which was oval, where chariot and horse races were held. All that remains of the circus at Arles is the obelisk which stands before St-Trophime.

Temple. – The temple stood on a podium surrounded by columns and consisted of two rooms: the *pronaos* (a vestibule) and the *cella* (a place for the statue of the divinity). The prime example of a temple is the Maison Carrée at Nîmes *(p 145)*. In the countryside existed small local temples, *fana* (singular *fanum*).

Triumphal arch. – The arches in Orange, Glanum, Carpentras and Cavaillon resemble the triumphal arches of Rome, raised in honour of victorious generals, but were built to commemorate the founding of the cities in which they stand and the exploits of the veterans who settled there. They had either one or three openings; the columns decorating the four sides and flanking the central arch were all engaged; later on they became detached. The upper storey was decorated with statues, horse-drawn chariots, and their feats of arms usually in gilt bronze.

The Baths. – The Roman baths, which were public and free, were not only baths but centres of physical culture, casinos, clubs, recreation centres, libraries, lecture halls and meeting-places, which explains the amount of time people spent in them. Decoration in these great buildings *(see plan of La Trouille Baths p 69)* was lavish: columns and capitals picked out in bright colours, mosaic ornaments, coloured marble facings, richly coffered ceilings, mural paintings and statues.

Central heating. – The baths functioning demonstrated the Romans understanding of the canalisation of water and its subsequent heating. Water was brought from the mountains via aqueducts and placed into cisterns and then distributed by a lead-pipe and cement system of canals; evacuation was conducted through a network of drain pipes.

To heat air and water a number of underground furnaces (hypocausts) like bakers' ovens, in which roaring fires were kept going, were used. The hot gases circulated among the brick pillars supporting the stone floors of rooms and baths and rose through flues in the walls to escape from chimneys. In this way the rooms were heated from below and from the sides as in modern buildings. The warmest room, facing south or west, had large glazed windows and was used as a solarium. Water at three different temperatures, cold, lukewarm and hot, circulated automatically by thermo-siphon.

Bather's route. – The bather followed a medically designed route. From the changing room where he would have left his clothes and annointed his body with oil, he entered the *palestra* (a gymnasium of sorts) where he would warm up performing physical exercises; then the *tepidarium* (a luke-warm room) where he thoroughly cleaned himself scraping his skin with small curved metal spatulas *(strigiles)*, which prepared him for the *caldarium* (hot room) where he took a steam bath; he then proceeded into the hot swimming-pool. After having been massaged, he once again returned to the *tepidarium* before continuing onto the *frigidarium* (cold bath) to tone up the skin. Thoroughly revived he dressed and proceeded to take advantage of the baths' other activities (such as lectures, sports, gossip...). The private baths located in the wealthy urban dwellings and *villae* were not as spacious but did possess a comparable level of luxury.

Roman town house. – Excavations at Vaison-la-Romaine, Glanum or the Fountain quarter in Nîmes have uncovered Roman houses of various types: the small bourgeois house, a dwelling (several storeys high) for rent, shops open to the street and finally large, luxurious patrician mansions.

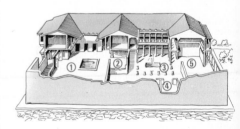

Roman House

The latter had a modest external appearance owing to their bare walls and few windows. But the interiors, adorned with mosaics, statues, paintings and marbles and sometimes including hot baths and a fish pond, revealed the riches of their owners. A vestibule and a corridor led to the *atrium.*

The **atrium** (1) which opened on the street through a vestibule containing the porter's lodge was a large rectangular court open, in the middle, to the sky *(compluvium)*; a basin called the *impluvium* under the open section, caught rainwater. Rooms opened off the *atrium:* reception room, private oratory, *tablinum* (2) or study and library of the head of the family.

The **peristyle** (3) was a court surrounded by a portico (a gallery with a roof supported by columns) in the centre of the part of the house reserved for the family. It was reached from the *atrium* along a corridor called the *fauces.* Here the peristyle was generally made into a garden with basins lined with mosaics, fountains and statues. The living quarters opened all around it: bedrooms, *triclinium* (dining room 4), and *oecus* (main drawing room 5).

The annexes included the kitchen with a sink and drain, baths, flush lavatory; other buildings housed slaves' quarters, attics, cellars, stables, etc.

Rural housing. – This kind of dwelling is just beginning to be examined. The towns must have been numerous and the settlement of these sites by Romans was done on pre-existing sites. The cadastral plan of Orange seems to show that the Romans tried to organise their territory into squared off lots called *centuries (pp 149 and 152)*. The most frequent type of house was the *villa,* forty of which have been discovered in Provence.

Aqueducts. – Grandiose like the Pont du Gard *(qv)* or more modest like Barbegal *(qv)*, aqueducts held an important role in daily life as they carried the water from their source to the town.

ROMANESQUE ART

The brilliant Gallo-Roman civilisation took a long time to disappear after the fall of the Western Empire *(p 22)*. The ancient public buildings remained standing and the architects of the Middle Ages took inspiration from them to build churches and monasteries.
A dark age followed (5-10C) when few buildings were erected, of which only isolated specimens now remain, such as the small baptistries at Aix and Venasque. Early Romanesque art, which developed from Catalonia to northern Italy in the 10 and 11C, did not leave significant examples, either.
In the 12C Provence went through one of its most outstanding historic periods and underwent a brilliant architectural renaissance. Churches, remarkable for the bonding of their evenly cut stones with fine mortar work, sprouted everywhere. Their style was closely linked to a school which had evolved in the area between the Rhône River, Drôme, Alps and the Mediterranean. This school was more original than innovative and knew how to capture the different influences: from Roman Antiquity came the use of vaults and especially decoration; from Languedoc came the carved portals; from Lombardy came the Lombard arcade or the lions adorning the base of the doors; from Auvergne came the dome on squinches over the nave and before the apse.
Given below are the essential characteristics of this style the best examples of which were the great sanctuaries in the Rhône Valley: Old La Major Cathedral in Marseilles, St-Trophime in Arles, St-Gilles, Notre-Dame-des-Doms Cathedral in Avignon, Former Cathedral of Notre-Dame in Orange and the church in Le Thor.

Churches and chapels

Plan. – Provençal Romanesque churches descended directly from the Roman basilica and Carolingian church. Their general appearance was of a solid mass. Transepts were rare and shallow. Often there was a single nave with side chapels hollowed out of the thickness of the walls. The east end took the form of an apse with two flanking apsidal chapels, where there were side aisles. Only the great pilgrimage churches of St-Gilles and St-Trophime, Arles, have ambulatories.

Plan of the former Cathedral of Notre-Dame-de-Nazareth in Vaison-la-Romaine

Minor buildings (Ste-Croix Chapel in Montmajour, St-Sépulcre in Peyrolles) present a quadrilobed plan.

Exterior

Bell towers. – The bell tower, an imposing most often square, sometimes octagonal structure, dominated the dome above the transept crossing.
It was sometimes placed above the bay preceding the apse or on the façade. It was decorated with blind arcading, Lombard arcades, or fluted pilasters in the Ancient style or sometimes both.

Side walls. – The walls were usually bare except for the cornice and the plain side doors. Massive buttresses, between which were set the windows of the nave, relieved the austere monotony of the exterior.

West fronts and doors. – The west front was generally plain opened by a door surmounted by an oculus as the main door was often located on the south side sheltered from the *mistral*.
The doors were most likely the architectural element most influenced by ancient Greek and Roman art; there were times when they were decorated with a fronton directly influenced by the ancient temples such as the porch at Notre-Dame-des-Doms and St-Gabriel's Chapel near Tarascon.
During the 12C, the façades became more ornate preceded at times by a porch: a large carved tympanum over a horizontal lintel began appearing. The doorways of St-Gilles and St-Trophime, superb carved examples, rivalled in quality, size and beauty the Gothic cathedral masterpieces of northern France.

Interior

Upon entering the Provençal Romanesque church one is struck by the simplicity and austerity of the inside structure enhanced only by some carved mouldings and cornices, barely visible in the dimly lit interior.

Chancel. – This is the part of the church reserved for the clergy. It was usually oven vaulted and linked to the transept crossing with rounded barrel vaulting.

Nave and vault. – The height – slight though it was – of the building's interior was remarkable for the purity of its lines.
The nave was roofed with pointed barrel vaulting in which the downward thrust was more direct than that of the rounded arches which tended to splay the wall outwards. The barrel vaulting had already been used in the Roman era having replaced the easily flammable wooden roofing, used from the 5-11C, which had caused the destruction of many buildings. It was buttressed by pointed arches, also called transverse arches, which came down on thick engaged pilasters in the side walls or down onto slender pillars lining the nave.
The nave was sometimes lined with aisles with quarter circle or pointed barrel vaulting, which acted as buttresses.

Owing to the height of the side aisles there were no tribunes but a decorative band of blind arcading, made of rounded arches, with three arches to each bay, the central arch being pierced by a lancet window, letting in very little light. Where the churches had but a single nave the side walls were quite thick in order to compensate the missing side walls and balance the whole structure.

Transept and dome. – The construction of the transept was a difficult problem for the architects in the Romanesque period. The groined vaulting made by the crossing of the nave and aisle vaulting had to be of great height in order to support the heavy weight of the central bell tower; the problem was solved by placing a dome on squinches over the crossing in the style of the Auvergne School.

Vertical section of a Provençal Romanesque church

Decoration. – Interior decoration was as austere as exterior decoration: decorated capitals usually ornamented with stylised leaves, friezes with interlacing and foliated scrolls, fluting and rope moulding.
The capital with leaves of the Romanesque style was an adaptation of the ancient Corinthian capital: it was formed by a group of leaves arranged according to the style of the Romanesque period (interlacing and stylised decoration). The most picturesque of these capitals were historiated, inspired by religious stories taken from the Old and New Testament. The cloisters offer the best examples: St-Trophime with its magnificent corner pillars adorned with statues of saints is remarkable. Fine capitals will also be found in the cloisters of Montmajour and St-Paul-de-Mausole (fantastic animals) and the apse of the church at Stes-Maries-de-la-Mer. There are also fragments of carved decoration worth seeing: in Avignon's cathedral there is the bishop's throne; in Apt's cathedral there is the altar.

Abbeys. – In Provence there are several fine abbeys. The Benedictine Abbey of Montmajour *(qv)* near Arles, founded in the 10C, forms a superb architectural ensemble illustrating the evolution of Romanesque forms from the 11 to 13C. It includes two churches (an upper church and crypt or lower church), two chapels, cloisters and its annexes in the characteristic Provençal style: simplicity in the monumental size, the volumes of which were inspired by the Antique style, carved decoration similar to St-Trophime and perfection in the stone bonding. Cistercian art was represented by three sister abbeys: Sénanque *(qv)*, Silvacane *(qv)* and Le Thoronet *(see Michelin Green Guide French Riviera)*.
Severely elegant, austere and unadorned were the required rules of the Cistercians, a reformed monastic order founded by St Bernard of Clairvaux. St Bernard had denounced the fanciful of Romanesque sculpture which could distract the monks at prayer. The Cistercians imposed everywhere an identical plan and they themselves directed the construction.

GOTHIC ART

Architecture. – The Gothic style is marked by the systematic use of quadripartite vaulting and pointed arches *(p 29; illustration VII)*. This innovative style, which originated in northern France, revolutionised construction by concentrating the weight of the structure on four pillars directed by stringers and transverse arches. Due to the absence of flying buttresses (characteristic of Northern Gothic) the thrust of the vaults was assured by the massive buttresses between which chapels were built.
Inside, the nave was relatively dark, almost as wide as it was high and ended by a narrower polygonal apse. Its width made it easier for the church, intended primarily for Dominican preaching. The wall surfaces required painted decoration.
St-Didier Church in Avignon is considered the best example of Southern Gothic in the region, whereas a building like the basilica in St-Maximin-la-Ste-Baume southern and northern influences appear; and the church of the Convent of the Celestines in Avignon which is entirely Northern Gothic in style. Religious edifices were not the only examples of Gothic art in Provence; civil and military buildings also held an important place. The Palace of the Popes in Avignon *(p 74)* was one of the finest and largest princely buildings in the 14C combining the demands of luxury and comfort with that of defence and security.

Evolution. – Romanesque art lasted longer in Provence than it did in the rest of France. Inspite of the relatively early appearance of Gothic, limited to two buildings (crypt of St-Gilles, porch of St-Victor in Marseilles) and quadripartite vaulting as early as pre-1150, Gothic art was late in taking hold in Provence.
In the early 13C the new vaulting was only used to cover buildings in the Romanesque style. The only edifices built entirely in the 13C Gothic style are found in Aix: central nave of St-Sauveur Cathedral and St-Jean-de-Malte Church, the former priory of the Knights of Malta. The Gothic style finally took hold under the influence of two historic factors: Capetian presence in the south, as a result of the Albigensian Crusade and the marriage of Charles of Anjou with Beatrice of Provence *(p 22)* and the settling of the mendicant orders in the towns.
In the mid-14C, there began a new step in Gothic evolution: a school of architecture called the Papal Gothic style began developing in Avignon. The popes attracted to their court artists from different regions of France, Germany, Flanders and Italy.

During the 15C the cardinals embellished Villeneuve-lès-Avignon with palaces *(livrée)* churches and cloisters; aisles and chapels were added to certain churches. St-Trophime was altered, the Romanesque apse was replaced by an ambulatory and radiating chapels.

The main Gothic churches include: Palace of the Popes (Clementine, Grand or Clement VI Chapel), St-Didier, St-Pierre, St-Agricol, Convent of the Celestines all in Avignon; St-Laurent in Salon-de-Provence, Old St-Siffrein Cathedral in Carpentras, basilica of St-Maximin-la-Ste-Baume, church in Roquemaure and especially charterhouse and church in Villeneuve-lès-Avignon.

Decoration. – The severe elegance of Provençal Gothic churches is confirmed by the lack of decoration.

Sculpture. – In the 14C sculpture consisted of recumbent figures (John XXII in Avignon's Notre-Dame-des-Doms, Innocent VI in Villeneuve-lès-Avignon's charterhouse and Cardinal Lagrange in the Petit Palais in Avignon), corbels, keystones and slender capitals; archaic in style they tended to derive from the Romanesque tradition. The reason for this penury was that mural painting was occupying a more and more important role in the interior decoration of churches.

Painting. – The Avignon region was for over two centuries (14-15C) the great centre of Provençal painting. Already in the 13C the frescoes of the Ferrande Tower recalled the miniatures painted during St Louis's reign. In the 14C the popes decorating the palace sought out the great Italian masters: Simone Martini from Siena and Matteo Giovanetti from Viterbo *(see Michelin Green Guide to Italy)*. The charterhouse in Villeneuve-lès-Avignon also contains fine works by Giovanetti. When the popes had left Avignon, Italian influence diminished, but artistic life underwent a renaissance in the mid-15C; Good King René *(qv)* was a patron of the arts and attracted master-craftsmen – artists and architects – to his court. Fresco painting disappeared before the Avignon School of panel painting. Artists from the north, Flanders and Burgundy painted splendid master-pieces such as the Triptych of the Annunciation (1443-5) in Aix's Ste-Marie-Madeleine Church and the Coronation of the Virgin (1453-4) by Enguerrand Quarton, which is exhibited in the Pierre de Luxembourg Museum in Villeneuve-lès-Avignon.

Nicolas Froment, King René's court painter from Languedoc, painted the famous *Triptych of the Burning Bush* (in Aix's St-Sauveur Cathedral). Avignon's Petit Palais contains a remarkable collection of lovely 14 and 15C paintings (Avignon and Italian Schools) worth admiring.

Annunciation by Taddeo di Bartolo

FROM THE RENAISSANCE TO THE PRESENT DAY

Renaissance. – Paradoxically when one is reminded that the Rhône Valley was the principal route by which personalities of the Italian Renaissance entered France, Provence remained virtually untouched by the movement. Such buildings as were erected in the 16C were after the Gothic style, except for a few chapels and chateaux.

Classical Period. – The 17 and 18C, by contrast, produced a large number of buildings. They were dignified and austere in design without distinctive regional characteristics. The so-called Jesuit style developed in the Comtat Venaissin churches, bringing with it Italian monumental features such as ornate retables or altarpieces, panelling and baldachins, often hiding the church's architectural lines. Avignon became the major centre, once more, with local artists such as the Mignards and Parrocels producing religious pictures and Bernus of Mazan carving for churches throughout the region.

In the Gard, an intense fever to rebuild churches mutilated during the Wars of Religion rose (St Gilles Abbey Church). An entirely novel element was the building of town houses by the old and new moneyed nobility, the magistracy and others: a few remain in Avignon and Nîmes but the finest line the streets of Aix. These well proportioned, dignified stone houses are distinguished by doorways coroneted with ironwork balconies often supported by robust caryatids or muscular atlantes. The artists of these works were the sculptor-decorators: Jean-Claude Rambot (1421-94) and Bernard Toro (1672-1731), both men contemporaries of Pierre Puget.

Puget (1620-94), an artist and architect from Marseilles, became one of the great baroque sculptors of 17C France. He began as a carver of ships' prows, was promoted by Colbert, but soon fell into disgrace through intrigue and devoted himself to urban decoration in his native south. Although he often sacrificed elegance for force, he knew how to bring to his works, sometimes of grandiose proportions, strength, movement and the feeling of pathos.

The 18C was the continuation of the towns' and cities' embellishment program which had begun the previous century: in Nîmes the engineer J.-P. Mareschal drew up the splendid Fountain Garden.

Doorway
of Hôtel de Maurel de Pontevès (17C)
in Aix-en-Provence

Doorway
of Hôtel de Panisse-Passis (18C)
in Aix-en-Provence

Among the painters of that period two stand out: Carle Van Loo, who was sensitive to the Provençal charm and Joseph Vernet, the painter of seascapes and ports.

Contemporary with the now domestic architecture was the work of local furniture and cabinet makers, fine chinaware, pottery from the works in Moustiers and Marseilles and the delicate wrought iron work preserved in the Calvet Museum in Avignon.

19C. – The art of architects and civil engineers was mostly executed in the Marseilles region where Espérandieu erected the new La Major Cathedral and Notre-Dame-de-la-Garde Basilica in the fashionable late 19C Romano-Byzantine style and Longchamp Palace.

Roquefavour Aqueduct is a superb civil engineering project which brings to mind the ancient Roman Pont du Gard. The Rove Underground Canal also represents an incredible feat.

At the same time painting knew an explosion of talented artists all fascinated by the luminous beauty of the Provençal countryside. Constantin Granet, Loubon, Guigou painted it as they saw it thereby preceding Van Gogh and Cézanne.

Van Gogh. – Vincent Van Gogh (1853-90), the son of a Dutch Calvinist pastor, admirer of Millet and Rubens, influenced by the art of Japanese prints, attracted to Impressionism, had nonetheless a strong personality.

In February 1888, he decided to settle in Arles *(p 64)* seeking a "different light". The two years he spent discovering the Provence (Arles, Stes-Maries, Les Baux, St-Rémy) correspond to an intense period of creativity: he sought to express with colours and dramatic forms the "terrible human passions" which tormented him and caused him to suffer. He painted intensely, with genius, the light and forms of Provence: landscapes *(View of Arles with Irises, The Alyscamps, The Starry Night, Crau Plain, Boats Along the Beach...)* and portraits *(Portrait of the Old Provençal Peasant, L'Arlésienne, Madame Ginoux...)*. His quarrel with Gauguin, who had joined him in October 1888, plunged him into dispair and madness; he was cared for at St-Paul-de-Mausole *(qv)* near St-Rémy-de-Provence and continued painting *(Wheatfields, Cypresses, Olive Trees, Self-portrait...)*. Having returned to Paris in May 1890, he committed suicide two months later. Precursor of the Fauves and Expressionism, Van Gogh left an intense work where his Provençal period is perhaps the most fascinating.

Cézanne. – Cézanne (1839-1904), contrary to Van Gogh, was from the Provence. Son of an Aix-en-Provence banker, he left his studies for painting *(p 53)*. Introduced to the Parisian Impressionists by his friend, the writer Émile Zola, he began as a Romantic studying Delacroix, whose theory of colours he adopted. Assimilating the Impressionist techniques, he rapidly went beyond them as early as 1879 and began his constructive period where large dabs of luminous colour and simplicity of form became vehicles of colour and geometrical form: "Everything in nature is modelled after the sphere, the cone and the cylinder", he wrote. He painted still-lifes and portraits where colour and form determined the painting's organisation.

After 1890, he hardly ever left his Provence and devoted his energy to Mount Ste-Victoire, which he painted some 60 times without ever being entirely satisfied with his work; his research continued until his death and brought on the beginning of Cubism.

20C. – Provence was now attracting many artists, the Fauves, with **Matisse** as their leader, found inspiration in the luminous Provençal framework. Their works played with colours and lines ignoring perspective and chiaroscuro. Matisse, Dufy, Derain, Camoin (born in Marseilles), all spent time in Provence. In around 1906-8, Estaque (Cézanne had painted views of it) became the privileged meeting place of those artists who were later named the Cubists. **Braque** and **Picasso** worked together closely in Sorgues; the product of this joint venture will be revolutionary pictorial compositions touching on abstraction. After World War II, a new generation was experimenting with new theories: expressionism, surrealism... **André Masson,** father of automatic drawing (a technique which enabled him to break off figurative conventions), settled in Aix region until his death in 1987 and drew a series titled *Provençal Landscapes*. Other prestigeous names were also linked to Provence: Max Ernst, Nicolas de Staël and **Vasarely,** who at Gordes has opened a foundation *(p 118)* destined to make known his research into optics and kinetics.

Presently, the Lumigny School of Art in Marseilles attracts and develops France's new talents.

TRADITIONAL RURAL ARCHITECTURE

The Provençal house in the country, whether a *mas,* a *bastide* or an *oustau,* will have the following characteristics:
– a shallow sloping roof of Roman style curved terracotta tiles, with a decorative frieze under the eaves, composed of a double or triple row of tiles embedded end-on in the wall and known as a **génoise**;
– stone walls, more or less smoothly rendered (pink or lavender), with no windows on the north side and those on the other three sides just large enough to let in light but keep out the summer heat;
– a north-south orientation, with sometimes a slight turn to the east to avoid the direct blast of the *mistral* and a serried row of cypresses to serve as a windbreak to the north, while plane and lotus trees provide shade to the south;
– floors covered with red or brown terracotta tiles *(mallons)*;
– vaulting in dried stone or masonry which completely replaced floor boards.

The **mas** *(see photograph below)* was a large low farmhouse rectangular in plan with a sprawling low roof covering the living quarters and annexes. The walls were made of stone taken from the fields or from Crau Plain, ashlar-stone, surrounded the openings. It was divided into two parts by a corridor, one for the master and the other for the farmer *(bayle),* this was repeated on the ground floor and on the upper storey. The kitchen was level with the courtyard, and was the centre of the house in spite of its small size; with little variation all Provençal *mas* kitchens were the same, the obvious sink, hearth and wall oven whereas the furnishings (tables, chairs, cupboards, shelves... and recepticles for the making and preserving of bread, *panetière,* a type of wooden cage at times beautifully worked) varied. On the upper floor were the tiled floor bedrooms and attic. The role of its outbuildings and its rooms varied according to the importance of the *mas* and the agricultural vocation of the region. The ground floor could have a vaulted cellar orientated to the north, stables, shed, store-room, sheeps pen (at times separated from the *mas*), bread oven and cistern; above were the attics containing the cocoonery, barn (above the sheeps pen) and a dovecote.

The **mas of the Lower Vivarais** was slightly different than the *mas* Provençal; it had an attractive pattern of stonework and had an added storey. The ground floor covered by solid vaulting contained the stables for the smaller animals and store-room for wine-making tools; in the cold-room were kept the harvested products as well as hams and sausages. A stone staircase which opened on to a **couradou,** a terrace, generally covered, led to the stone or terracotta tiled kitchen; the cocoonery was often off the *couradou* and was until *c*1850 an essential part of the Vivarais *mas* architectural conception. From the kitchen, off of which were the sleeping quarters, a small wooden staircase led to the attic. In the wealthier *mas* it became a spiral staircase in a turret and was visible from the exterior; it led to the sleeping quarters.
To the living quarters annexes were often added: bread oven, barn and in the chestnut region a chestnut dryer, **clède** (or *clédo*).

The **oustau,** was the typical Provençal farmhouse smaller in size than the *mas* but with the same layout. In the Upper Comtat it was called a *grange* and was progressively enlarged to house the family, which formed a clan and the workers; it constituted an intermediary type of building between the *mas* of the plain and the village house, small but compensating for the lack of surface area by adding on upper storeys.

The **bastide** was built of fine ashlar-stone and presented regular façades with symmetrical openings. Most often its layout was square in plan with a hipped roof. Unlike the *mas,* the *bastide* was not necessarily a farmhouse, thus its conception was more luxurious using decorative elements such as wrought-iron balconies, exterior staircase, sculpture etc...

The **gardian's cabin** *(photograph p 98),* the typical Camargue dwelling *(cabane)* was a small building (10 X 5m – 33 X 16 1/2ft) with a rounded apse at one end. The cob walls were low; only the front façade, with its entrance door, was built in rubble to hold a long ridge beam supported by another piece of wood sloped at a 45° angle and crossed by a piece of wood to form a cross. Thatched with marsh reeds, *sagnos,* the cabin consisted of two rooms divided by a wall of reeds; the dining room and bedroom.

Provençal mas

CHRISTMAS CRIBS

Christmas cribs (*crèche* means crib) have a long tradition in Provence although it was not until the late 18C that they became at all common and developed a typically local character – a few 18C groups, often highly original and beautifully modelled, may still be seen at a collectors or a few rare churches but most are now in museums (Museum of Old Aix, Old Marseilles, Museon Arlaten in Arles and Popular Arts and Traditions in Paris).

Church cribs. – Christmas was not an important festival in the early church nor did cribs form part of the medieval celebrations except for rare low reliefs of the adoration of the shepherds or the kings as in the St-Maximin crypt.
In 1545 the Council of Trent sought to advance the Counter Reformation through the encouragement of popular piety. The practice of setting up a crib in church arrived in Provence from Italy in the 17C. There is a particularly beautiful crib from this period in the church of St-Maximin; the carved figures, about 50cm – 20in high, are of gilded wood. In the 18C, bejewelled wax figures were introduced with glass eyes and wigs. Only the head, arms and legs were carved and attached to a richly dressed articulated frame. The 19C saw the employment of printed or painted cardboard cut-outs with gaily coloured clothing, or figures made from spun glass, cork or other materials.
In the 19C all the Provençal churches had adopted the Christmas crib of dressed figures; this kind of Christmas crib can still be seen today.

Live cribs. – At midnight mass in many churches today – Séguret, Allauch, Isle-sur-la-Sorgue and Marseilles – there is a virtual nativity play. In Gémenos, children in costume place the Infant Jesus in a straw-filled manger. In Les Baux *(p 87)*, a little cart, decorated with greenery and bearing a new-born lamb, is drawn into church by a ram and accompanied by shepherds. The procession is headed by angels and fife and tabor players while the congregation sing old Provençal carols. The lamb is offered to the church and the cart stands to one side in the aisle throughout the year.

Talking cribs. – The 18C passion for marionettes was adapted to produce talking cribs in which mechanical figures enacted the Nativity to a commentary and carols; people came from far and wide to see and hear the talking cribs of Marseilles and Aix. Characters were added to the already numerous cast and, as imagination ran wild, historical accuracy and relevance vanished: reindeer, giraffes and hippopotami joined the other animals, the pope arrived in a carriage to bless the Holy Family...
In the 19C, Napoleon, accompanied by his soldiers and a man of war firing salvoes brought the scene up to date! Another new idea came to those presenting a crib close to Marseilles station: the Three Kings travelled to the scene in a steam train!
Some of these talking cribs functioned until the late 19C.

Santon cribs. – The *santon* cribs are the most typical of the Provençe. They first appeared in 1789 at the time of the Revolution when the churches were closed and cribs, therefore, inaccessible. **Jean-Louis Lagnel,** a church statue maker from Marseilles, had the idea of making small figures which families could buy at little cost. Known in Provençal as **santouns**, little saints, the figurines had an immediate and wide appeal. They were modelled in clay, fired and naïvely painted in bright colours. Limited at first to Biblical personnages, they were soon joined by men and women from all walks of life, dressed, of course, in the local costume; the Holy Family, the shepherds and their sheep, the Three Kings, occupied the stage together with the knife grinder, the fife and tabor player, the smith, the blind man and his guide, the fishwife, wetnurse, milkmaid, the huntsman, fisherman and even the mayor!

So great was the figurines success, as virtually every family began to build up a collection, that a **Santons Fair** was inaugurated in Marseilles, which is still held on the Canebière from the last Sunday in November to Epiphany. Aubagne was also famous for its *santons*. Santon makers established workshops in towns throughout Provence while in the country men and women made figures in the long winter evenings. The craft reached its peak in 1820-30s which is why so many of the characters, now mass-produced, appear in the dress of that period.

Today the *santons* of Provence are known the world over and many a family seeks its own Christmas crib peopled with *santons*.

Christmas Crib

FOOD AND WINE IN PROVENCE

Provençal cooking is garlic and fried oil. Garlic was praised by poets: "the truffle of the Provence" the "divine condiment", this "friend of man". While oil – preferably olive oil – replaced butter in all the Provençal dishes. An old Provençal proverb says "A fish lives in water and dies in hot oil".

Bouillabaisse. – This most famous of Provençal dishes, traditionally comprises "the three fishes: the spiny, red hog fish, gurnet, and conger eel" *(rascasse, grondin, congre)*. To these are added as many others as are available – sea bass *(loup)*, turbot, sole, red mullet *(rouget)*, eel pout *(lotte)* – a selection of crustaceans: crabs, spider crabs *(araignées de mer)*, mussels *(moules)*, etc and, in very special cases, spiny lobsters *(langoustes)* or crawfish.
These are all cooked together very rapidly in a *bouillon*, emulsified with a small quantity of olive oil and seasoned with salt and pepper, onion, tomato, saffron, garlic, thyme, bay *(laurier)*, sage, fennel, orange peel, maybe a glass of white wine or cognac – in the seasoning lies the magic or not of the result.
A *rouille* or paste of Spanish peppers, served at the same time, sharpens the sauce and gives it colour.
In a restaurant one is usually presented with a soup plate and toast, with which to line it. Some people then spread some of the toast with the *rouille* paste, others mix it directly into the by now thickened bouillon soup which arrives in a tureen. To your plate full of toast, *rouille* and soup, you then add tit bits from the dish of assorted cooked fish and crustaceans. *Bouillabaisse* is a main dish. The fish must be fresh and the dish freshly prepared (it is not a stew – the actual cooking time is only some ten minutes).

Aïoli. – Aïoli (pronounced exactly as it is written), the other great Provençal speciality, is a mayonnaise made with freshly pounded, mild, Provençal garlic to which are added the usual egg yolks, olive oil and condiments.
It is served with *hors-d'œuvre,* asparagus and other vegetables, and also as a sauce with *bourride,* the fish soup made from angler fish *(baudroie),* sea bass *(loup),* whiting *(merlan)* etc and preferred by many to *bouillabaisse.*

Fish and crustaceans. – Local fish dishes include red mullet *(rouget)* cooked whole, sea bass *(loup)* grilled with fennel or vine shoots and *brandade de morue,* a heavy cream of pounded cod, olive oil and milk, seasoned with crushed garlic and slivers of truffle.
Fish specialities associated with individual towns, include, for Marseilles, in addition to *bouillabaisse,* clams *(clovisses),* ascidia or iodine tasting sea squirts *(violets),* mussels *(moules)* and edible sea urchins *(oursins)* – all to be found most easily in the small restaurants around the Old Port; in St-Rémy, the *catigau,* a dish of grilled or smoked Rhône eel in sauce; in the Camargue, *tellines* or sand crustaceans served with a pungent sauce.

Vegetables and fruit. – Raw onion and tomatoes, common favourites among vegetables, are followed closely by cardoons (served in white sauce), fennel, peppers, courgettes, aubergines, watermelons, and first class melons. The most popular fruit is the small green fig or Marseilles fig, a juicy sweet fruit. Peaches, apricots, strawberries, cherries and grapes are all top quality.
Local olives are the small, meaty green and black varieties which are left whole, pitted or stuffed; there is the early picked green olive, then marinated, which comes from Nîmes and the black olive of Nyons preserved in brine. Nyons and Carpentras are the main production centres.

Specialities. – Among the numerous Provençal specialities are the *pieds-paquets* (a kind of tripe) of Marseilles, Arles's sausages or *saucissons*; *Gardian* beef stew from Camargue; Avignon's preserved melons; Aix *calissons* or rice paper covered, almond paste sweets; Carpentras *berlingots* or caramels; Nîmes's *brandade de morue (see above)*, small almond cakes or *caladons* and crisp Villaret biscuits; Tarascon's *tartarinades* or special chocolates; the crystallised fruits of Apt; the *nougat* of Sault, the black olives of Nyons and Modane bread (bread split and stuffed with crystallised fruit...).

Wines. – Provence has been cultivating wine since Antiquity when it is said to have been planted by the Phocaeans.

Rosé wines, pink or rose-coloured wine, which comes from red grapes, which have fermented the juice on the skin giving its pink colour, are more and more appreciated for their pleasant and fruity taste served chilled and easily drunk with any dish.

White wines are generally dry with a fine aroma and are particularly appreciated with fish and shellfish.

Red wines are anything from full-bodied and fruity to light and supple depending upon their origin.
On the Rhone's east bank Châteauneuf-du-Pape is warm and full-bodied, its alcoholic content can be as high as 15°; it is one of France's great vintages. Gigondas is heady, Rasteau and Beaumes-de-Venise are sweet fortified wines best served with dessert. Cassis vineyards produce red – full bodied and fruity – and white – dry – wines; they are not to be confused with the black current liqueur *(cassis)*.
From the Rhone's west bank at the foot of the *garrigues*, Tavel produces a bright pink full-bodied rosé wine, while Lirac produces a fine robust red or rosé wine. Listel, near Aigues-Mortes, is a so-called *Rosé des sables* as it is a light delicate rosé wine produced from vines which grow in the sand *(sable* means sand).

The Michelin Guide France lists hotels and restaurants serving goods meals at moderate prices.
Use the current guide.

Key

Sights

★★★ **Worth a journey**
★★ **Worth a detour**
★ **Interesting**

Sightseeing route with departure point indicated
on the road   in town

⚔	⁂	Castle, Château – Ruins
⊥	◎	Wayside cross or calvary – Fountain
☀	♈	Panorama – View
⌖	✗	Lighthouse – Windmill
⌣	✿	Dam – Factory or power station
☆	∪	Fort – Quarry
▲		Miscellaneous sights

⬛✝ ⬛✝	Ecclesiastical building: Catholic – Protestant
⬛	Building with main entrance
⬤—⬤	Ramparts – Tower
⫶	Gateway
▪	Statue or small building
▒	Gardens, parks, woods
B	Letters giving the location of a place on the town plan

Other symbols

	Motorway (unclassified)	
◂▸ ▸ / ❶ ❷	Interchange complete, limited, number	
	Major through road	
	Dual carriageway	
	Stepped street – Footpath	
	Pedestrian street	
	Unsuitable for traffic	
→1429→←	Pass – Altitude	
🚂 🚌	Station – Coach station	
🚢	Ferry services: Passengers and cars	
⚓	Passengers only	
✈	Airport	
③	Reference number common to town plans and MICHELIN maps	

⬜	Public building
✛ ✉	Hospital – Covered market
🛡 ⚔	Police station – Barracks
⁒	Cemetery
✡	Synagogue
🏇 ⛳	Racecourse – Golf course
≋ ≋	Outdoor or indoor swimming pool
⛸ ⊤	Skating rink – Viewing table
⚓	Pleasure boat harbour
⌁	Telecommunications tower or mast
⬭ ⌂	Stadium – Water tower
B	Ferry (river and lake crossings)
△	Swing bridge
✉	Main post office (with poste restante)
ⓑ	Tourist information centre
��	Car park

MICHELIN maps and town plans are north orientated.

Main shopping streets are printed in a different colour in the list of streets.

Town plans: roads most used by traffic and those on which guide listed sights stand are fully drawn; the beginning only of lesser roads is indicated.
Local maps: only the primary and sightseeing routes are indicated.

Abbreviations

A	Local agricultural office (Chambre d'Agriculture)	J	Law Courts (Palais de Justice)	POL.	Police station
C	Chamber of Commerce (Chambre de Commerce)	M	Museum	T	Theatre
H	Town Hall (Hôtel de ville)	P	Préfecture Sous-préfecture	U	University

⊙ **Times and charges for admission are listed at the end of the guide**

Additional signs

⌒ Cave, Chasm	⌁ Rice Fields	⌁ Marshland
⌁ Refinery		⬤ Metro station

SIGHTS

listed alphabetically

Séguret

Michelin map 🔲🔲 fold 8 or 🔲🔲🔲 fold 27 – Local map p 96 – Facilities

Aigues-Mortes (from *Aquae Mortuae* meaning dead water), with its large towers and fortified curtain wall, stands erect in a melancholy landscape of ponds, sea marshes, and salt pans.
One never tires from admiring this solitary fortified city during the long sunsets of a summer's evening.

HISTORICAL NOTES

St Louis's creation. – In the early 13C the king of France, Louis IX (St Louis) possessed no Mediterranean seaport as such. As he was preparing to set out on a crusade to Palestine, Louis IX did not want to embark from a "foreign" seaport like Marseilles, for example (foreign, because Marseilles was ruled by the Counts of Provence and thus independent of the king's government); he was seeking a site on the coast where he could set up a port of embarkation and city which would serve to establish and confirm Capetian influence in the region.
In 1240 he obtained, from the monks of the Abbey of Psalmody, a tract of virgin land frequented only by fishermen; and, on which he rapidly had built the powerful Constance Tower *(p 46)*. In order to encourage people to settle on this rather desolate site, the king granted, in 1246, a charter which offered many advantages such as tax exemption and commercial privileges.
Like the southern *bastides (see Michelin Green Guide to Dordogne),* the new town was built on a regular grid plan within a rectangle (550m × 300m – 1 804ft × 984ft) cut by five straight streets which were also cut by five cross streets. Clusters of settlements developed in the vicinity of the three religious establishments (Notre-Dame des Sablons, Franciscan Monastery and the Psalmody monks' residence), which offered protection from the wind.

Setting off for the Crusades. – In 1248 a huge armada chartered from Venice and Genoa gathered at Aigues-Mortes, which at this time was linked to the sea by the channel of Grau Louis. Approximately 1 500 ships, carrying 35 000 men plus horses and equipment – the Seventh Crusade – set sail for Cyprus on 28 August. On the flagship, St Louis's suite included a spacious room with large port holes, the queen's chamber, as well as a room for her attendants and a chapel.
The ships' passengers were obliged to have a long chest which served as a trunk bed, and in case of death, as a casket, which was thrown into the ocean. They were also told to bring a small barrel of pure water as well as miscellaneous provisions. The crusaders arrived at Cyprus 23 days later; and met with some success before being defeated at al-Mansūrah; the king was captured in 1250.
In 1270 a sick St Louis embarked on a fleet from Marseilles which sailed to Tunis. It was there that he died of the plague (caught while attending to his sick crusaders).

The salted Burgundians. – In 1418, during the Hundred Years War, the Burgundians captured Aigues-Mortes by surprise. The Armagnacs lay siege to the town and were desperate to seize it. A handful of their partisans within the city walls succeeded, in the dead of night, to massacre the garrison attending one of

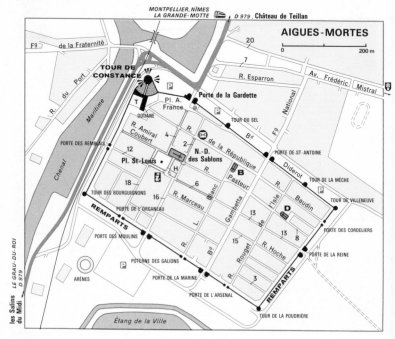

the gates; the city gates were opened to the besieging army. The Burgundians were decimated; so numerous were the dead that awaiting burial the corpses were thrown into a tower, since named the Burgundian Tower. To prevent putrefaction the cadavers were salted until the Armagnacs could bury them.

Decline. – Aigues-Mortes stayed prosperous until the mid-14C. It had a population of 15 000 and even Jacques Cœur (Charles VII's master of the mint) set up a counting-house. However, the sea withdrew and the channels silted up in spite of the dredging. Even the construction of a canal to the coast was unable to prevent the decline.

The town participated in the Wars of Religion and became a Protestant stronghold. In the 18C the founding of Sète dealt the port a final blow.

The town's activities now include wine growing, which extends over 3/4 of the town's land and extraction of salt *(pp 16 and 96)*.

★★FORTIFICATIONS *time: 1 1/2 hours*

★★**General view.** – To admire the site of Aigues-Mortes from the best approach, it is recommended, before beginning the tour, to drive along the road to Le Grau-du-Roi (D 979) to about 1 500m – 1 mile before the town (turn around just before a small bridge). As you return there are superb views of the ramparts on the south side.

Some modern buildings have unfortunately been built in front of the age old walls, which seem transfixed since medieval times, creating a rather astonishing contrast.

La Gardette Gate (Porte de la Gardette). – This, the town's northern gate, was used by travellers coming on the only road from the north through marshy country. 3km – 2 miles beyond, on this road stands the advanced barbican of Carbonnière Tower *(qv)*, the first defence encountered.

> Go through La Gardette Gate, turn right, cross Place Anatole-France and go to the ticket office at the foot of the tower.

★★**Constance Tower (Tour de Constance).** – A massive circular keep 22m – 72ft in ⓥ diameter and 40m – 131ft high (including the turret), this tower has walls 6m – 20ft thick.

Located northwest of town and isolated from it, the tower was built between 1240-9. The entrance fort and bridge, which connected the tower to the ramparts, date from the 16C. An elaborate defensive system protected the entrance; there remain the portcullis and the embrasures through which missles were hurled onto the assailants.

The lower room with fine pointed arches has kept its bread oven. The upper floors are approached by a spiral staircase: St Louis's Oratory, a minute chapel built into the wall and the upper room, which served as quarters for well-known prisoners; in a display case are various documents concerning these famous detainees, among whom, over a period of 500 years, included political contestants, Templars, rebel barons and Huguenots. Two Protestants held in the tower were **Abraham Mazel**, a leading Calvinist who escaped down knotted bedclothes with 16 co-religionists in 1705 and **Marie Durand**, whose indomitable courage finally secured her release together with 10 of her companions from the cell in which she had been incarcerated for 38 years (1730-68) – note her graffito: *Register* (*register* means to resist in Vivarais dialect).

Climb to the watch tower summit (53 steps) crowned by a wrought iron cage, which in the 13-16C protected a lantern, which served as a beacon. An immense **panorama**★★ extends over the town and its grid-like patterned streets, the surrounding plain punctuated right to left by the Cévennes, the Grande Motte "pyramids", Mount Sète and the Midi and Camargue salt marshes.

★★**Ramparts (Remparts).** – The ramparts were built after 1272 with stone quarried ⓥ from Beaucaire *(qv)* and Les Baux *(qv)*. Four-sided and of remarkable unity, the fortifications represent the best example of 13C military architecture. The walls, topped by a watchpath, are flanked by towers of different size and importance. The more massive towers defending the main gates contained two vaulted rooms with terraces.

Inside a wide street ran between the curtain wall and the town's houses allowing the garrison swift access to any point. Outside, the moat, now filled, was another element of defence. The curtain wall pierced by two rows of arrow slits included hoarding, traces of which are visible at the base of the crenellations.

The ramparts were opened by only two gates to the north whereas, to the south five gates or posterns offered access to the town from its loading docks. The towers, in order of approach are, Burgundians' Tower *(p 44)*, Organeau Gate (Porte de l'Organeau), an *organeau* being the great iron ring to which the ships were moored, Mill Gate (Porte des Moulins), where grain was ground for the garrison, Galleons' Postern (Porte des Galions), in front of which moored the galleys, Maritime Gate (Porte de la Marine), a ceremonial entrance, the magazine (Tour de la Poudrière), Villeneuve Tower, Wick Tower, (Tour de la Mèche), where a light was kept constantly burning to ignite fire arms, and Salt Tower (Tour du Sel).

ADDITIONAL SIGHTS

Place St-Louis. – On this lovely shaded square, the heart of town, stands the statue of St Louis (1849) by Pradier.

ⓥ **Notre-Dame-des-Sablons.** – This Gothic church was often rearranged. Inside, its timberworked nave adds to the simplicity of the décor: 14C Christ, altar table from the former Abbey of Psalmody and Chapel of St Louis.

Ⓥ **Chapel of White Penitents (Chapelle des Pénitents Blancs)** (B). – A service is held in this baroque chapel once a year on Palm Sunday. It houses a number of mementoes (liturgical vestments, penitents' attributes) of this brotherhood established at Aigues-Mortes in 1622.

Ⓥ **Chapel of Grey Penitents (Chapelle des Pénitents Gris)** (D). – This 17C chapel contains an imposing altarpiece (1687) carved by Sabatier.

EXCURSIONS

Ⓥ **Midi Salt Marshes (Les Salins du Midi).** – *3km – 2 miles southwest of Aigues-Mortes. The tour presents the different stages involved in the making of salt (p 16).*

Ⓥ **Château de Teillan.** – *13km – 8 miles northeast on the D 979, left on the D 34 then right on the D 265 in Marseillargues and just after the bridge a non-surfaced road on the right.*
Built on the site of a Gallo-Roman stronghold, this former priory of the Abbey of Psalmody was sold in the 17C and enlarged.
A watch tower (15C) surmounts the main part of the building. From the terrace a fine view embraces the Cévennes, Languedoc Plain, Aigues-Mortes and Camargue. On the ground floor, there is a large vaulted hall and 17 and 18C furnishings. The outbuildings, rebuilt in the 18C, house a vast dovecote, containing 1 500 nests; it has preserved its interior arrangement and especially a revolving ladder. In the park landscaped with a fine variety of plants and trees can be found a number of Roman altars and milliary columns; note as well a remarkable chain pump in a small vaulted outhouse.

★★ AIX-EN-PROVENCE   Pop 124 550

Michelin map 🟦 fold 3 or 🟦 fold 31 or 🟦 fold J – Local map p 173

This old capital of Provence has kept a great deal of the character imparted to it in the 17 and 18C. The sober elegance of its mansions, the graceful charm of its squares, the majesty of its avenues and the loveliness of its fountains are impressive.
Around old Aix a new town has developed, which is both a spa and an industrial complex – it is the largest centre in France and Europe for prepared almonds. A part of the production is used to make the cakes and confectionary of Aix, including the local speciality, a small almond cake, *calisson.*
In July and August the **International Music Festival** (festival international d'Art lyrique et de Musique), one of the most famous in Europe, is held in the open air in the courtyard of the archbishop's palace as well as the surrounding countryside.
Aix is also the home of the painter Paul Cézanne *(qv).*

HISTORICAL NOTES

Origins of Aix. – In 3C BC western Lower Provence was inhabited by the Celtic-Ligurian Confederation of the Salian Franks, whose capital, the *oppidum* of Entremont *(p 53)* crowned a plateau to the north of Aix, near the Puyricard road. Excavations, now being carried out, are uncovering traces of a fairly advanced urban civilisation, as is testified by the scope of the buildings and statuary exhibited at the Granet Museum *(p 52).*
These brutal peoples hindered the expansion of the merchants of Marseilles, who appealed to the Roman army to break their neighbours' resistance. In 124BC, the Consul Sextius seized and destroyed the town of Entremont; the inhabitants were condemned to slavery (900 of them were spared) and their king fled. To consolidate the conquered region, Sextius, the following year, set up an entrenched camp called Aquae Sextiae (the waters of Sextius) near the thermal springs (which were already known); this camp site was the origin of Aix.

Marius the First (2C BC). – Twenty years later the Teutons, on their march to Italy, arrived before Aix, where they encountered Marius at the head of a Roman army. The Barbarians, from the Baltic Coast, travelled with their families and animals, living in carts, covered with hide canopies; they were tough fighters.
It was in the environs of Aix, in the Arc Valley, perhaps, at the foot of the height which has since been known as Mount Ste-Victoire, that there was delivered, according to tradition, the stroke which stopped the invaders and which developed into a great Roman victory (102 BC). According to Plutarch *(qv),* Marius, entrenched, at first refused battle and allowed the Teutons to parade before his front for six days. Then, dividing his army into three corps, he opposed the enemy, opening a converging attack with devastating results: 100 000 Teutons killed, 100 000 prisoners taken. The last survivors of the Barbarians used their grouped chariots as a barricade; the women were massed there. They were of such fierce nature, that they themselves killed the warriors who fled. Just before their capture they strangled their children and then killed themselves.
In memory of the Roman general, first conqueror of the Teutonic hordes, many Provençal families adopted the custom of calling one of their children Marius.

Good King René (1409-80). – At the end of the 12C, the Counts of Provence held a both refined and literate court at Aix. The development of the town continued during the 13C and yet in the 14C its surface area diminished. In 1409 Louis II of Anjou founded the university but Aix's golden age occurred later in the second half of the 15C under Good King René's *(qv)* reign.

A city of 4 to 5 000 people, a bishopric and county seat, Aix's influence covered all of the neighbouring countryside settled by wealthy townspeople and enhanced by Italian craftsmen. Within the walls lived the bourgeois, aristocrats and farmers; included in this category were the shepherds responsible for ensuring a return on livestock investments made by a handful of powerful merchants.

Second son to Louis II and Yolanda of Aragon, René became Duke of Anjou, Count of Provence, titular King of Sicily and Naples at the death of his older brother, Louis III, in 1434. René knew Latin, Greek, Italian, Hebrew and Catalan; he played and composed music, painted illuminations with meticulous detail, wrote verses, understood mathematics, astrology and geology. To conclude, René possessed one of the most universal minds of his time. He was an enlightened patron of the arts surrounded by artists, Flemish painters in particular. Dating from his rule are the famous triptychs of the *Annunciation* (said to be by Barthélemy of Eyck – *qv*) and the *Burning Bush* painted by Nicolas Froment (of Languedoc origin, he studied in Flanders and Burgundy). By the end of the 15C some forty artists of quality lived

King René

and worked in Aix under contract with René and his nobles. They produced prestigious works of art as well as participating in the decoration of mystery plays and popular festivals (such as Corpus Christi, which underwent a brilliant revival). A man of arts and letters, René did not neglect his obligations as a ruler; he legislated, stimulated commerce and encouraged agriculture. He introduced the Muscat grape into Provence and on occasion cultivated his own vineyards. He was concerned with the health standards of his people and instituted a public service of doctors and surgeons, promulgated a sanitation law and ordained the cleaning up of the different quarters of the city. He was, however, criticised for his heavy taxation as well as his weak currency; the coinage he struck – coins were called *parpaillottes* – was of rather base alloy; thus, later, when the Catholics wished to use an abusive term to designate the Protestants, they called them *parpaillots* (or counterfeiters).

At the age of 12, René married Isabelle of Lorraine, who brought him as dowry the Duchy of Lorraine. Their younger daughter, Margaret of Anjou (1429-82), married the English King, Henry VI (1421-71) in 1445. Two years after the death of Isabelle (at 44) to whom he remained tenderly attached during the 33 years of their union, he married Jeanne of Laval, aged 21. This second marriage, which seemed a challenge to fortune, was as happy as the former. Queen Jeanne, who should not be confused with the 14C Queen Joan I of Sicily *(p 86)*, was as popular as her more elderly husband among the people of Provence.

Having lost both his son and two grandsons, King René sadly observed Louis XI annexe Anjou to the kingdom of France. Thereafter, instead of dividing his time between Angers *(see Michelin Green Guide Chateaux of the Loire)* and Provence, René no longer left the land of sunshine and died at Aix in 1480, aged 72. His nephew Charles of Maine, who had been chosen as his heir, died a year later.

A capital. – After the union of Provence to the crown in 1486, a governor appointed by the king lived in Aix. In 1501, the city became the seat of a newly created parliament (a royal court of justice); it was also where the Estates General met most often to vote taxes.

In contrast to René's golden age, the preceeding century, the 16C appeared quite gloomy, marked by incessant wars (repeated hostilities engaged by Charles V's army from 1524-43), and religious and political disputes (Mérindol Affair, *p 23*, commitment to the Holy League, etc...). And yet in the 17C, the city made great strides which radically changed its appearance. Inhabited by approximately 27 000 people, its population touched on all the social classes of which one, the men of law, became prominent.

The parliament, a strong advocate of local liberties, in face of the centralist trend of the monarchy, was a breeding ground of well-to-do judges and lawyers (the majority of these appointments were procured financially). These men of law led stimulating and active lives and consequently proceeded to build magnificent *hôtels* worthy of their name and rank. At the same time the urban landscape was transformed: new areas of the city mushroomed (notably the Mazarin Quarter, south of the city), the old ramparts were razed and replaced by an avenue for carriages, which later became Cours Mirabeau. Louis XIV, himself, during his stay in 1660 was able to admire the renovations.

In the 18C the city continued its transformations with its wide avenues, squares, fountains, and new buildings (the old county palace was demolished and a new law court was built in its place). The conception of the *hôtel* had changed, it tended to be more simplified, attention was paid more to comfort and less to decoration, although inventiveness was encouraged.

Parliament was living its last hours; the conflict of opinions and clan rivalry created a constant scene of dissent which nurtured gossip and epigrams. In 1763 it decreed that the Jesuits be banned from the land. This was its last great legal act as the parliament was dissolved in 1771 (reestablished in 1775) to no one's regret as stated in the couplet:

> Parliament, Mistral and Durance
> Are the scourges of Provence.

Marriage of Mirabeau (18C). – Aix played an important role in the life of Mirabeau. He married here in 1772 and was divorced here in 1783. It was here, too, that he was elected to the Estates General in 1789.

The volcanic Mirabeau, whose family called him "Mr Squall" or "Mr Hurricane", was only 23 when he married Mlle de Marignane. The bride was a rich heiress, and among her suitors figured the best of Provence nobility. Mirabeau, although a count, was ill-favoured: with a monstrous great head and a face disfigured by smallpox; he was penniless and had a scandalous reputation. But our man knew well the mysterious attraction he had for women. He entered the competition and swept off the prize like a Hussar. Cynically, he made a parade of his good fortune and left his coach at the door of the Marignane mansion *(p 51)* when he spent the night there. After this scandal, marriage had to take place. But Mirabeau's father-in-law showed his resentment by cutting off the young couple's allowance. Mirabeau displayed no embarrassment at this blow and promptly ran up 200 000 *livres* of debts with Aix merchants. Their complaints were such that a warrant was issued sending him to enforced residence at If Castle *(qv)* and subsequently Joux Fort. He published his *Essay on Despotism.*

No sooner was he liberated that he seduced the lovely young Mme Monnier and fled to Holland with her. Mirabeau returned to Aix in 1783 to answer a summons for separation instituted by his wife. "The Hurricane" presented his own defence. His prodigious eloquence secured him victory at a first hearing but he lost on appeal, although it is said that his pleading aroused such enthusiasm and the violence of his language was such that the opposing counsel fainted!

But 1789 dawned and with it the elections to the Estates General. The Count of Mirabeau, who had encountered only contempt and rebuff among his peers, decided to represent not the nobility but the Third Estate. His election was a triumph and his historic role as Tribune began; but it was also the beginning of Aix's downfall.

Decline and renaissance. – In the 19C as Marseilles developed, Aix declined: the provincial capital became a *sous-préfecture,* the parliament a court of appeal, the university a faculty of law and letters only.

In 1914 Aix's population counted 30 000 people. Today, however, the city has experienced an upsurge in population and has expanded considerably. Its industrial activities, spa and tourist attractions as well as its cultural brilliance (university and festival) maintain its rebirth and establish it as one of France's most popular cities.

★★OLD AIX *time: 4 hours – see plan p 50*

The circle of boulevards and squares which ring the old town mark the line of the ancient ramparts. North of Cours Mirabeau, the town's focal point, lies old Aix nestled between the cathedral and Place d'Albertas.

Start from Place du Général-de-Gaulle.

In the centre of this square stands a monumental fountain erected in 1860.

★★Cours Mirabeau (DY). – This wide avenue, shaded by fine plane trees, is the hub of Aix; a verdant tunnel of foliage protects against the hot Provençal sun.

Built in the 17C on the site of the medieval ramparts, the avenue, originally, had no shops or boutiques; yet now Aix's life revolves around it. Lining the north side of the street are cafés and shops; a number of bookshops show the intellectual and scholarly vocation of Aix. On the other side stand the aristocratic façades of the old *hôtels* with their finely carved doorways and wrought iron balconies supported by caryatids or atlantes from the Puget School *(qv).*

Walk up the avenue on the south side.

Hôtel d'Isoard de Vauvenargues. – *No 10.* This mansion was built *c*1710 with a wrought iron balcony and fluted lintel. The Marquess of Entrecasteaux, Angélique de Castellane was murdered here by her husband, the president of parliament.

Hôtel de Forbin. – *No 20.* Ornamenting the *hôtel's* (1656) façade is a balcony with lovely wrought iron work. Received in this *hôtel* were the Dukes of Berry and Burgundy, grandsons of Louis XIV, Pauline Borghese, the ill-favoured Fouché, the future Duchess of Berry and the Duke of Angoulême.

Fountain of 9 Cannons (Fontaine des 9 canons) (DY B). – Midway, at the junction with Rue Joseph-Cabassol, stands a fountain (1691).

Hot Water Fountain (Fontaine d'eau thermale) (DY D). – Further up Cours Mirabeau, at its junction with Rue Clemenceau, is a hot water fountain covered with moss dating from 1734. Its water, which gushes out at 34°C-93°F, was appreciated by the Romans some 2 000 years ago for its healing properties.

Hôtel de Maurel de Pontevès. – *No 38; illustration p 38.* Pierre Maurel, Diane de Pontevès's husband, is a good example of social ascension: an ordinary shopkeeper, he received confirmation of his hereditary peerage at the end of his life.

In 1660 the *hôtel* housed Anne-Marie Montpensier, known as La Grande Mademoiselle; it now contains the Department of Economics of Aix-Marseilles University.

King René's Fountain (Fontaine du Roi René) (EY E). – This fountain marks the end of the avenue. Carved by David d'Angers (19C), the fountain portrays René holding a bunch of Muscat grapes *(qv)*, which he had introduced into Provence.

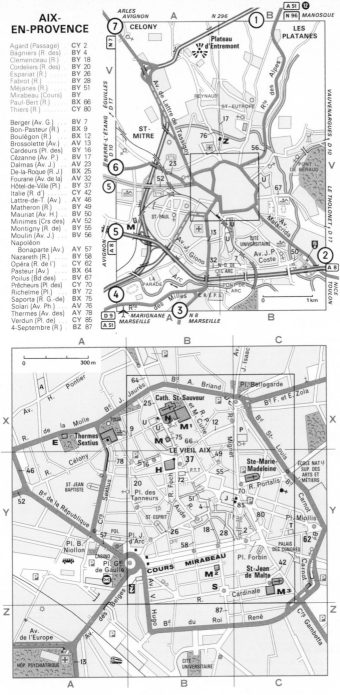

Cross the avenue.

Rue Fabrot *(first street on the left),* a pedestrian and shopping street leads to Place St-Honoré (on the corner of a house, a 19C statue of St Vincent).

Bear left on Rue Espariat.

Hôtel Boyer d'Eguilles. – *No 6.* Erected in 1675 and probably by Pierre Puget, the *hôtel* contains the Natural History Museum.

Natural History Museum (Muséum d'histoire naturelle). – Interesting collections of mineralogy and palaeontology. The palaeontology section includes general exhibits as well as exhibits from Provence, notably a collection of dinosaur eggs from the fluvial and lacustrine basin of Aix-en-Provence. In addition, the *hôtel* is embellished with fine 17C doors, paintings and interior panelling from the bedroom of Lucrèce de Forbin Solliès, the "Belle du Canet", as well as busts by Gassendi, Peiresc, Tournefort and Adanson.

Hôtel d'Albertas. – *No 10.* Built in 1707, this *hôtel* includes carvings by the sculptor Toro (from Toulon – *p 87*).

Place d'Albertas. – This square opened in 1745 and embellished by a fountain in 1912, is lined with lovely mansions. Each summer concerts are held here.

Bear right into Rue Aude.

AIX-EN-PROVENCE

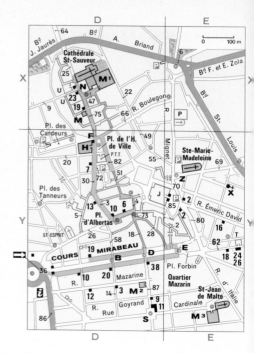

Hôtel Peyronetti. – *No 13.* Italian Renaissance in style, it dates from 1620.
Follow Rue du Maréchal-Foch.

Hôtel d'Arbaud. – *No 7.* Fine atlantes frame the doorway. Across the way, giving onto Place Richelme, note the corner statue.

Place de l'Hôtel-de-Ville (DY). – The flower market takes place here. The old grain market (now a post office and administrative centre) is decorated with a finely carved pediment by Chastel, the 18C sculptor, and native of Aix; a number of his works have been preserved.

Town Hall (Hôtel de Ville) (DY H). – Constructed between 1655-70, the town hall was designed by the Parisian architect Pierre Pavillon. Both the lovely wrought iron balcony and entrance gate are of the 17C. Around the splendid paved **courtyard★**, the buildings are divided by pilasters of the classical order *(p 33)*; there is a niche with scrolls on the inside façade.
The 1st floor contains the Méjanes Library and the Saint-John Perse Collection.

Saint-John Perse Collection (Fondation Saint-John Perse). – *Take the staircase on the left underneath the porch.* A collection of Mss, works and photographs illustrate the life (1887-1975) and work of this diplomat, who won the Noble Prize for Literature in 1960. In 1940 he went to the United States, where he worked in the Library of Congress.
Among his most famous works are *Anabase* (1925) a long poem translated by T.S. Eliot and *Seamarks* (1958).

Clock Tower (Tour de l'Horloge) (DY F). – *Beside the town hall.* The former city bell tower (16C); its bell in a wrought iron cage also dates from the 16C; a different person marks each season.
Continue into Rue Gaston-de-Saporta.

Museum of Old Aix (Musée du Vieil Aix) (DX M). – *No 17.* Located in the Hôtel d'Estienne de St-Jean (17C), attributed to Laurent Vallon, the museum presents local memorabilia. Displayed are a collection of marionettes evoking the talking cribs and the local Corpus Christi procession, porcelain from Moustiers, *santons...*
Admire the lovely wrought iron banister and the ceiling painted by Daret in the boudoir.

Hôtel de Châteaurenard. – *No 19.* Home of the Social Work Office. Just after the mansion's completion, Louis XIV was received here during his visit in 1660. The splendid staircase of views painted in *trompe l'œil* by Daret draws the attention.

Hôtel de Maynier d'Oppède. – *No 23.* Built in 1490 and remodelled in the 18C, the *hôtel's* wrought iron balcony is supported by a basket arch and pilasters crowned with acanthus leaves.
Rue Gaston-de-Saporta ends at Place des Martyrs-de-la-Résistance; at the end stands the Tapestry Museum, to the left St-Sauveur Cloisters.

★Tapestry Museum (Musée des Tapisseries) (DX M). – *Take the stairs on the left underneath the porch.* Housed in the former bishopric, built in the 17C and enlarged in the 18C, the museum exhibits collections found here in the 19C. The vast courtyard is the scene of the annual International Music Festival *(qv)*. Note 17 magnificent tapestries made in Beauvais in the 17 and 18C, 6 of which were composed after Bérain; 9 famous panels of the *Life of Don Quixote*, after cartoons by Natoire, preserved at the Château de Compiègne; and 4 panels of *Russian Games* produced after Leprince.

★ St-Sauveur Cloisters (Cloître St-Sauveur) (DX N). These Romanesque cloisters are a delight; they are roofed with tiles instead of being vaulted like the cloisters at Arles *(p 67)* and Montmajour *(p 141)*. Because the arcades are not buttressed, the cloisters seem delicate; the small paired columns and the capitals adorned with leaves or historiated, add a great deal of elegance to the construction. For the most part the carvings on the capitals are badly damaged, however, on a fine corner pillar stands a remarkably carved St Peter.

A door northwest of the cloisters gives onto the cathedral.

St-Sauveur Cathedral (DX). – St-Sauveur is a curious building where all styles from the 5-17C are to be seen side by side. The Romanesque nave into which you enter via the cloisters dates from the 12C. The furthest chapel to the west, transformed into a lapidary museum, contains the tomb, said to be of St Mitre, a 5C white marble sarcophagus. The two bays which follow open onto the **baptistry★** of the Merovingian period; it was built on the site of the old Roman forum in front of a basilica, of which 6 of the 8 Roman columns surrounding it have been used to hold up the Renaissance dome. On the east side are traces of the *cardo,* the old Roman street, orientated north-south. In the vast Gothic central nave hang two 15C triptychs. Of the first triptych, depicting the Passion, only the central panel is of the 15C. The second triptych, the **Triptych of the Burning Bush★★** is a masterpiece wrongly attributed to King René. In fact it is the work of his court painter Nicolas Froment *(qv)*. King René and Queen Jeanne are shown kneeling at either side of the Virgin. The Virgin holding the Infant Jesus is in the Burning Bush, from which the triptych takes its name. It was in a burning bush that God appeared to Moses; in the Middle Ages the Bush, which burned but was consumed, symbolised the virginity of Mary. In the 13C chancel are 16C stalls and fine tapestries (1511) made for Canterbury Cathedral, illustrating the life of Christ and Virgin Mary. Behind the altar, in the Chapel of St Mitre hangs a

Triptych of the Burning Bush
by Nicolas Froment (detail)
in St-Sauveur Cathedral

painting on wood (Martyrdom of St-Mitre) attributed to the school of Nicolas Froment. The north aisle was redone in the 17C.

The great doorway is closed by **panels★** *(masked by false doors)* in walnut; this masterpiece (1504) of sculpture in wood by Jean Guiramand of Toulon represents the 4 prophets of Israel and 12 pagan sibyls.

The cathedral's west face includes to the right a small door in the Romanesque Provençal style, in the middle a Flamboyant Gothic part (early 16C) and on the left a Gothic bell tower (14-15C). Only two of the statues are old: the lovely Virgin and Child on the pier and St Michael slaying the dragon above the main window.

Return to Cours Mirabeau via Place de l'Hôtel-de-Ville and Rues Vauvenargues, Méjanes, des Bagniers and Clemenceau.

Hôtel d'Arbaud-Jouques. – *19 Cours Mirabeau.* Built in 1700, this *hôtel* presents a finely decorated façade: a carved frieze underlines the 1st floor, a medallion on the impost underneath the balcony and carved oak doors.

MAZARIN QUARTER *time: 1 1/2 hours*

This quarter of orderly design was built (1646-51) by the Archbishop Michel Mazarin, brother of the famous cardinal of the same name, south of the old town.

Paul Arbaud Bibliographical and Archaeological Museum (Musée bibliographique et archéologique Paul-Arbaud) (DY M²). – *2a Rue du 4-Septembre.* The museum is located in the home of a collector; it was built at the end of the 18C on the site of a Feuillant Convent.

Exhibited are books concerning the Provence, a lovely collection of porcelain from the region (Moustiers, Marseilles, Allemagne-en-Provence), and some fine paintings and sculpture.

Hôtel de Marignane (DY). – *12 Rue Mazarine.* Late 17C. This *hôtel* was the scene of Mirabeau's scandalous behaviour towards Mlle de Marignane *(p 48)*.

Hôtel de Caumont (DY). – *3 Rue Joseph-Cabassol.* An elegant mansion built in 1720, it presents a lovely façade adorned with balconies and pediments. It houses the Darius Milhaud Music and Dance Conservatory.

Hôtel de Villeneuve d'Ansouis (DY). – *9 Rue du 4-Septembre.* Early 18C. Birthplace of Folco de Baroncelli, Marquis of Javon *(p 173)*, the *hôtel* is decorated with balconies and carved mascarons.

Hôtel de Boisgelin (DY). – *11 Rue du 4-Septembre*. A vast building built in 1650, designed by Pierre Pouillon and decorated by J.-C. Rambot.

★**Four Dolphin Fountain (Fontaine des Quatre Dauphins)** (DY S). – A delightful work (1667) by J.-C. Rambot.

⊙**St-Jean-de-Malte** (EY). – This church, dating from the late 13C, was the chapel of the former priory of the Knights of Malta, and was Aix's first Gothic building. The 67m – 220ft bell tower stands to the left of the austere looking façade. The **nave**★ presents the elegant simplicity of the Radiant Gothic with its wide arches, clerestory windows, without triforium, and its lovely sexpartite vaulting. In the past, the church housed the tombs of the Counts of Provence; they were destroyed in 1794 and partially rebuilt (1828) in the north arm of the transept.

★**Granet Museum (Fine Arts and Archaeology) (Musée Granet Beaux Arts et Archéologie)**
⊙(EY M³). – The museum is in the former priory of the Knights of Malta; it contains a fine collection of paintings acquired through various legacies including those of the Aix painter Granet (1775-1849).

Exhibited beside the Flemish, Italian and Avignon (panels of a triptych by Matteo Giovanetti) Primitives are the paintings characteristic of the great European schools and covering the 16-19C.

The French School is represented by a series of paintings by Clouet, Philippe de Champagne, Le Nain, Rigaud, Largillière, Van Loo, Greuze, David, Ingres... A number of works of the Provençal School are also on display; note in particular Granet, Constantin, Loubon, Parrocel, Emperaire.

The Italian (Bassano), Flemish (Rubens, Master of Flémalle) and Dutch (Rembrandt's studio, Frans Hals) are also worth admiring. Note the portrait of *Diane de Poitiers* by Jean Capassin.

A gallery devoted entirely to Cézanne *(qv)* presents 8 of his paintings and 3 of his watercolours: *Still Life* (1865), *Naked Woman Before a Mirror* (1872), *The Bathers* (1895)...

Another room contains works by contemporary artists such as Estève, Tal Coat, Masson (*Mount Ste-Victoire Emerging From the Fog* – 1949, *Young Chimera* – 1956) Lasne, Aubrun, Léger, Sorgue, Forat, Vasselin...

The archaeological galleries display objects found at the Entremont *(p 53)* and Aquae Sextiae (Archbishopric, Grassi Gardens and Pasteur Parking) sites. The statues unearthed at Entremont typify a unique native Celtic-Ligurian art although influenced by Greek and Etruscan forms. The statues represent, in general, effigies of people squatting, busts of warriors (a tunic clad torso showing a breast plate and buckle), male and female heads and low and high reliefs. It has been suggested that the squatting warrior held on his knees several severed heads (note the hand placed on some of them).

ADDITIONAL SIGHTS

Rue de l'Opéra (EY 62). – In this street houses of interest include: *no 18* Hôtel de Lestang-Parade built *c*1650 by Pavillon and Rambot and remodelled in 1830; *no 24* Hôtel de Bonnecorse (or Arlatan-Lauris) dates from the 18C; *no 26* Hôtel de Grimaldi was constructed in 1680 after drawings by Puget.

Hôtel de Panisse-Passis (EY). – *16 Rue Émeric-David. Illustration p 38*. Built in 1739, the façade is enhanced by fine wrought iron and corbelled balconies with fantastically carved heads.

Former Jesuit Chapel (Ancienne chapelle des Jésuites) (EY X). – Dating from the 17C, the chapel has an imposing façade pierced with five niches.

⊙**Ste-Marie-Madeleine** (EY). – The church's west front is modern although the church is 17C. At the end of the south aisle, in the 4th chapel, an 18C marble **Virgin**★ by Chastel can be seen. In the chapels hang 17 and 18C paintings. A massive picture attributed to Rubens is in the north transept.
The central panel of the 15C **Triptych of the Annunciation**★ in the north aisle, near the altar to Our Gracious Lady, is all that remains of the triptych (the other two panels are elsewhere). Ordered *c*1443-5 by Pierre Corpici, this work is attributed to Barthélemy of Eyck (a relative of the famous Van Eycks), an artist who used chiaroscuro effects subtly and inventively.

Preacher's Fountain (Fontaine des Prêcheurs) (EY Z). – An 18C work by Chastel.

Hôtel d'Agut (EY). – *2 Place des Prêcheurs*. – Ornamenting this *hôtel* erected in 1676 by Pierre d'Agut, a parliament counsellor, are two ships' figureheads, rustication, a corner statue and a sundial.

Hôtel de Roquesante (EY). – *2 Rue Thiers*. Dating from the first half of the 17C, the *hôtel's* façade presents friezes and pediments, which underline the different floors and a monumental doorway.

Sextius's Baths (Thermes Sextius) (AX). – The 18C spa complex stands close to the site of the Roman baths. The 34°C-93°F waters cure circulatory problems.
A tower from the 14C city walls has been preserved in the park.

⊙**Vendôme Pavilion (Pavillon de Vendôme)** (AX E). – *34 Rue Célony*. The mansion was built in 1667 from plans by A. Matisse and P. Pavillon, as Cardinal de Vendôme's country home. The façade, unfortunately heightened in the 18C, offers a dignified décor with the three classical orders represented: Ionic, Doric and Corinthian. The central balcony, supported by atlantes has kept its original wrought iron work. Displayed inside are Provençal furnishings and *objets d'art*. Note the staircase adorned with 17C wrought iron work.
A slide show recounts the history of this house and its residents.

★ Vasarely Foundation (Fondation Vasarely) (A V M). – *4km – 2 1/2 miles west.* On a hill, at the hamlet Jas de Bouffan, stands the Vasarely Foundation. A striking building, 87m – 285ft long composed of 8 cubicles, houses on the ground floor the works of Victor Vasarely (born in Hungary in 1908). Tapestries and wall paintings – geometric and abstract subjects – hang side by side. His research, as early as 1930 (also the year he left Hungary for Paris), led him to geometric abstractions via lines and graphics. In 1955 he evolved into a more kinetic field where by various optical means Vasarely was able to produce visual illusion with the use of movement (the viewer moves about the work and the subject depicted moves and changes). The 1st floor includes a succession of visual displays (22 screens containing 798 mobile documents; by pressing a button the works inside the case move), which unfold the works of this master of Optical Art.

Cézanne's Studio (Atelier Paul Cézanne) (B V Z). – *9 Avenue Paul Cézanne.* Paul Cézanne was born in Aix in 1839 and received a classical education at the Collège Bourbon where he became friends with Émile Zola. In accordance with his father's wishes he took up law at the university; at the same time he wrote verse and painted at Jas de Bouffan, a wooded family estate not far from Aix.

It was not in Paris, where he stayed frequently, that he met with success but in Aix, thanks to the respect of such artists as Monet, Manet, Sisley and especially Pissarro (under whom he later studied); they were to become the founders of the Impressionist School. During his early years with them his palette lightened; it was with his contact with the countryside around Aix that his colours were enriched. He sought, like his masters, to represent: diffused light, the shimmering of the reflected light and its shadows, the depth of the sky and the softening of the hues produced by the reflection of light.

The House in Aix-en-Provence by P. Cézanne

Cézanne rapidly broke with Impressionism. With large dabs of luminous colour – colours of the same intensity and blending of tone were used for the first time – and simplicity of form (the most familiar objects painted – apple, cup, mountain) became vehicles of colour and geometrical form (cone, sphere, cylinder). He was a major source of inspiration for the Fauves, cubists, and modern artists.

Nostalgia for his own countryside brought him frequently back to Aix. He often went to the banks of the Arc and the Pistachio Tree Courtyard of Château Noir, the country house with its sole cypress, overlooking Bibemus Plateau. He found constant inspiration in his beloved countryside and it became the main theme for his paintings *(Mount Ste-Victoire).*

Fleeing Paris in 1870, he settled at Estaque in his mother's house *(The Bay from l'Estaque).* When his mother died in 1897, he had built, some 500yds from the cathedral, a Provençal-style house called the "Lauves" surrounded by a garden; in the 1st floor studio he painted, among other works, *The Bathers.*

The studio has been left as it was at the painter's death in 1906 (memorabilia).

Entremont Plateau (Plateau d'Entremont) (A B V). – *2.5km – 1 1/2 miles then 1/4 hour on foot Rtn. Leave Aix going north by the D 14 uphill; after 2.5km – 1 1/2 miles, walk up the path on the right to the plateau.*

Excavations. – Entremont *(see Origins of Aix p 46)* in 2C BC was a veritable fortified town (surface area 3.5ha – 9 acres). It was naturally defended by steep slopes on one side and to the north by ramparts with strong curtain walls reinforced by regularly interspersed large round towers. The inside fortifications consisted of a wall dividing the upper town from the lower town. The former, an elevated area, was set to a regular grid pattern with a street network and sewage and drainage systems. The small dwellings made with walls of dried stone and unbaked brick, were built against the ramparts or grouped together to a pre-established plan. Between two towers stood a building in the form of a portico, it was probably a sanctuary where enemy skulls were hung.

The lower town seems to have been the quarter of artisans and tradesmen (ovens and oil presses have been uncovered).

The excavations have uncovered a great deal of objects and works of art proving that the *oppidum* possessed quite a high level of civilisation and explaining how the town fell (stone balls, buried treasures) under the Romans, Entremont statuary is of capital interest for history of art and may be seen at the Granet Museum *(p 52)*, the visit of which is complementary to the tour of the site.

The low relief carvings and statues displayed represent offering scenes, warriors riding horses or seated cross-legged, full-length figures or women with long veils.

Viewing Table. – From the plateau there is a wide view of Aix Basin, Mount Ste-Victoire, Ste-Baume Massif and the Étoile Chain.

EXCURSION

Arc Valley. – *Round tour of 43km – 26 1/2 miles – about 2 hours. Leave Aix-en-Provence southwest of the town plan on the D 9.*
The road offers lovely views of Étoile Chain, in particular the characteristic peak of Pilon du Roi and, further to the right, Grande Étoile.

ⓥ **Château de la Pioline.** – Set in Les Milles industrial zone, this manor-house dates partly from the 16C; it also received Charles V in 1536. Enlarged and embellished in the 17 and 18C, it served as the Aix parliamentarians' summer residence. A main building flanked by two wings opens onto a great courtyard decorated with a pool.

Inside, a vestibule precedes a succession of richly decorated and furnished rooms, especially the Louis XVI Room with its gilt work and columns. Across the drawing room, a vast hall of mirrors can but evoke its opulent past. In the back is a lovely park with a terrace.

Le Réaltor Reservoir (Réservoir du Réaltor). – This pleasant body of water (58ha – 143 acres) is surrounded by luxuriant foliage. This is the settling tank of the water which has come from the Grand Torrent (brought from the Arc River) and the Durance River (brought via the Marseilles Canal).

After the reservoir, bear right on the D 65ᴰ on its western shore skirting radio station buildings and crossing the Marseilles Canal.

After La Mérindolle turn right.

★**Roquefavour Aqueduct** (Aqueduc de Roquefavour). – This fine aqueduct was constructed to transport the Marseilles Canal across Arc Valley at a point 12km – 7 1/2 miles west of Aix-en-Provence. Built between 1842-7 under the direction of Montricher, the aqueduct is a spectacular example of a 19C civil engineering project. Made up of three stages – three tiers of arches – supporting the water channel, it is 375m – 1 230ft long and 83m – 272ft high (Pont du Gard: 275m – 902ft high and 49m – 161ft high). Its lower level counts 12 arches, the middle level 15 arches and the top level with its 53 smaller arches carries the canal which transports the waters of the Durance to Marseilles.

Follow the D 65 towards Salon-de-Provence and 328yds further on bear right on the D 64 uphill.

A lovely view opens out to the right of the aqueduct before entering a wooded area of pine and oak trees.

Top level of Roquefavour Aqueduct (Sommet de l'aqueduc de Roquefavour). – *After 2.1km – 1 mile bear right on a path towards Petit Rigouès and right again to the keeper's house located on the aqueduct's topmost level.* Drive past the ruins of Marius's *(qv)* Roman camp *(excavations underway)*. From the plateau's edge admire the lovely view of Aix Basin, Mount Ste-Victoire and Étoile Chain.

From the car park walk to the aqueduct's top level where the canal runs.

Return to the D 64 and bear right.

Ventabren. – Pop 2 717. Dominated by Queen Jeanne's castle, now in ruins, is this tiny village of picturesque streets. Via Rue du Cimetière, at the foot of the castle ruins, enjoy the splendid **view**★ of Berre Lagoon, Martigues and Caronte Gap and Vitrolles Chain.

Take the D 64ᴬ then right on the D 10 to Aix-en-Provence.

ALLAUCH   Pop 13 528

Michelin map 🔲 fold 13 or 🔲🔲🔲 folds 44 and 45 or 🔲🔲🔲 fold L

A large suburb of Marseilles, Allauch (pronounced Allau) rises in tiers up the foothills of Étoile Chain *(qv)*.

Esplanade des Moulins. – Appropriately named (*moulin* means mill), this esplanade, with its five windmills (one of which has been restored), offers a good **view**★ of Marseilles.

ⓥ **Museum of Old Allauch** (Musée du Vieil Allauch). – *Near the church.* It contains objects and documents pertaining to local history.

Notre-Dame du Château Chapel (Chapelle N.-D.-du-Château). – *1/2 hour on foot Rtn.* A relic of an 11 and 12C castle of which only some ramparts remain. From its terrace enjoy the fine view of Marseilles.

EXCURSION

Château-Gombert; Loubière Caves. – *7km – 4 miles northwest on D 44ᶠ. Description p 138.*

★★ ALPILLES Chain

Michelin maps 🗺️ fold 10 and 🗺️ fold 1 or 🗺️ fold 29

The limestone chain of the Alpilles, a geological extension of the Luberon Range, rises in the heart of Provence between Avignon and Arles.

From faraway these jagged crests, rising 300-400m – 984-1 312ft, appear like real mountains.

The arid, white peaks of these summits standing out against the blue sky remind us of some Greek landscape. At the mouth of the dry valleys, which cross the mountain chain, olive and almond trees spread their foliage over the lower slopes. Occasionally a dark line of cypress trees will break the landscape. In the mountains the gently sloping lower areas are covered with kermes oaks and pines but often the rock is bare and peppered with a few scraggy bushes covered by *maquis* or poor pasture only suitable for sheep.

Alpilles Chain

★★① BAUX ALPILLES
Round tour starting from St-Rémy-de-Provence
40km – 25 miles – about 4 hours – local map p 56

★ **St-Rémy-de-Provence.** – *Description p 166.*

Leave St-Rémy-de-Provence going southwest by the Chemin de la Combette; turn right into the Vieux Chemin d'Arles.

Cardinal's Tower (Tour du Cardinal). – This is, in fact, a 16C country house with an attractive Renaissance balcony and ornamental windows and friezes.

Turn left into the D 27.

The road winds between cypress enclosed fields before rising through a rock landscape in the heart of the Alpilles. Towards the end of the climb, the view extends to the left and behind over the Comtat Venaissin limited by Mount Ventoux.

Just before reaching the top of the hill turn left on a surfaced corniche road; after 1km – 1/2 mile park the car.

Les Baux Viewing Table (Table d'orientation des Baux). – *Description p 88.*

Return to the D 27; bear left on it.

The road winds through Hell Valley (Val d'Enfer – *p 88).*

★★★ **Les Baux-de-Provence.** – *Description p 86.*

Continue along the D 27 through Paradou to the D 78ᴱ.

The road winds through olive groves.

Barbegal Aqueducts (Aqueducs de Barbegal). – *1/4 hour on foot Rtn.* Note the impressive ruins (on the left in particular) of a pair of Gallo-Roman aqueducts. The one which branches off to the west supplied Arles with water from Eygalières some 50km – 31 miles away. The other one, after having cut through the rock, served a hydraulic flour mill built on the slope's south side. The ruins of this 4C flour mill is a rare example of Gallo-Roman mechanical engineering. This system comprised a triangular-shaped cistern feeding two channels which in turn activated eight successive mills with their water wheels and mill stones. The flour mill occupied 1 200m² – 12 900sq ft and could grind 300kg – 661lbs of flour an hour!

Continue along the D 78ᴱ then the D 82; turn right on the D 33.

Daudet's Mill. – *Description p 108.*

A lovely avenue of pines leads to Fontvieille.

Fontvieille. – Pop 3 432. Facilities. Tradition endures in this small town where Alphonse Daudet is remembered for his *Letters from My Mill* and where the chief industry for centuries has been the quarrying of Arles limestone.

In the 18C parish church, the old ceremony of the shepherds' bringing the offering of the lamb is celebrated on Christmas Eve.

Continue along the D 33.

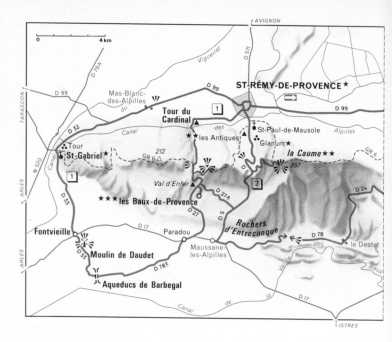

The road runs through a countryside of olive groves, pinewoods and fields of early vegetables cut by long files of poplars.

★St-Gabriel's Chapel (Chapelle St-Gabriel). – Located originally on the chapel's site was Ⓥ a Gallo-Roman town, Ernaginum. Surrounded by marshland, it was a port for rafts (called *utriculaires – qv*) as well as being the junction of commercial and military roads. The small, late 12C chapel, has a west doorway framed within a rounded arch by antique style columns and a pediment. The pediment and tympanum are richly, if somewhat naively carved with the Annunciation, the Visitation, Adam and Eve, and Daniel in the lions' den. The symbols of the four Evangelists frame the richly decorated oculus.
The interior, by contrast, is plain; it comprises a single aisle and three bays covered by broken barrel vaulting and an oven vaulted apse, resulting in a great unity of style. In the nave, to the right, note the cippus dating from Augustus's time.
Further on are the ruins of a 13C square tower, which belonged to the fortifications of a village long gone.

Via the D 32 and the D 99 return to St-Rémy-de-Provence.

After Mas-Blanc-des-Alpilles a fine view of Mount Ventoux can be had (on the left).

★★② EYGALIÈRES ALPILLES
Round tour from St-Rémy-de-Provence
73km – 45 miles – about 5 hours – local map above and p 57

★St-Rémy-de-Provence. – *Description p 166.*

Leave St-Rémy-de-Provence by ③, the D 5.

The road passes the old monastery of St-Paul-de-Mausole *(qv)* and Les Antiques *(qv)*, before continuing deep into the mountains where one can observe the regular lines of the rock strata.
From a bend, a wide view opens up onto the Montagnette and Durance Valley.

After 4km – 2 1/2 miles turn left into the road to La Caume (it may be closed in summer).

★★La Caume Panorama (Panorama de la Caume). – Alt 387m – 1 270ft. A television relay mast is located at the top. Walk to the southern edge of the plateau to enjoy a vast panorama of the surrounding countryside, including the Alpilles in the foreground and the Crau and Camargue Plains; from the northern edge, the view encompasses the Rhône Plain, the Guidon du Bouquet with its characteristic beak-like outline, Mount Ventoux and Durance Valley.

Return to the D 5 and turn left.

The road traverses a pinewood and several small gorges.

Entreconque Rocks (Rochers d'Entreconque). – Lying to the left of the road, the rocks are, in fact, former bauxite quarries *(p 16)* as can be seen from their characteristic dark red colour.
Suddenly, the road runs through olive, apricot, almond and cherry orchard country.

Turn right into the D 27ᴬ for Les Baux.

★★★Les Baux-de-Provence. – *Description p 86.*

Turn round and by way of the D 5 make for Maussane-les-Alpilles (facilities). At the town entrance bear left and immediately left again into the D 78.

The road runs through olive groves at the foot of the Alpilles before rising gently to a low pass from where there is a view of Les Opiès, a hillock crowned by a tower. At Le Destet, turn left into the D 24 which, as it rises, reveals the crest of La Caume. After 5km – 3 miles bear right into the D 25 which circles the Plaines Massif.

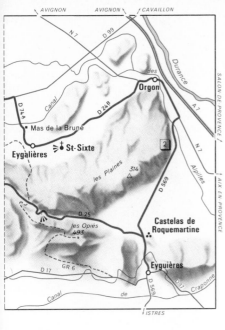

Roquemartine Castle (Castelas de Roquemartine). – It comprises a group of ruins of various ages perched on the hillside. At the end of the 14C the fortress was, with Les Baux, the hide-out of Raymond de Turenne's band of thieves *(p 86)*.

Eyguières. – Pop 4 171. *2km – 1 mile from Roquemartine Castle by the D 569*. At the limits of Salon Plain, this small Provençal town is made even more delightful by its many splashing fountains.

Turn left into the D 569, a picturesque stretch of road which goes through olive groves, to the N 7 which leads to Orgon.

Orgon. – *Description p 154*.

The D 24ᴮ skirts the north flank of the Plaines Massif.

St-Sixte Chapel (Chapelle St-Sixte). – This 12C chapel, crowning a stony hill, stands on the site of a pagan temple erected to the spirit of the local spring *(see Eygalières below)*. The arch, separating the nave from the fine oven vaulted apse, rests on boar's head consoles. A small 16C hermitage stands next to the chapel. Lovely view of Eygalières and Alpilles Chain.

Eygalières. – Pop 1 427. Facilities. The small town of narrow winding streets rises in tiers up the hill to an ancient castle keep. Once a neolithic settlement, it was later occupied by a Roman legion sent to divert the local spring waters to Arles. Park the car in the square and walk through Auro Gate up to the clock tower: 12C church surmounted by a 19C bell tower. From the top of the village a pleasant view opens out onto La Caume Mountains, Alpilles Chain and Durance Valley.

Take the D 74ᴬ, which near Mas-de-la-Brune (16C) crosses the Alpilles Canal.

Bear left on the D 99 for St-Rémy-de-Provence.

St-Sixte Chapel, Eygalières

ANSOUIS
Pop 612

Michelin map 🔢 fold 3 or 🔢🔢🔢 fold 31 – Local map p 125

Located between the Durance River and the Grand Luberon foothills, the town was built on the southern slope of a rocky spur crowned by a castle.

SIGHTS

★ Castle (Château). – The charm of this half-castle, half-country house, is that it has been in the Sabran family for centuries and each generation has left its imprint. From the north it looks like a fortress, but go up the stone steps and a ramp leading into a chestnut walk and one is greeted by a more welcoming Louis XIII façade. The grand staircase in the Henri IV style leads to the guard room embellished with 17-19C arms and armour. Note the 17C Flemish tapestries (*Aeneas* and *Dido*) in the dining room, a tester bed and credence table in the François I Room, St Eleazarius and St Dauphine de Sabran's room, the lords' room, with memorabilia of these two saints, the Provençal kitchen, the prison and the chapel.
The terrace affords a beautiful view of Durance Gap and Trévaresse Range.
The gardens are a delightful surprise: hanging gardens planted with boxwood and dark leafed trees fill every corner of the place; like the Garden of Paradise, cultivated during the Renaissance on the castle's former cemetery.

Church (Église). – This Romanesque building contains busts of the two saints.

Extraordinary Museum (Musée Extraordinaire). – 15C vaulted cellars house this small museum devoted to underwater life. Works of art by G. Mazoyer (1st floor: artist's workshop) are displayed. An underwater cave has been recreated. Provençal furniture also on exhibit.

Michelin map 🗺 fold 14 or 🗺 fold 31 – Local maps pp 59 and 125 – Facilities

Apt, a small bustling town in the Calavon Valley, is known for its crystallised fruit and preserves, lavender essence and truffles; it is the main centre of ochre mining *(p 16)* in France. The town is also considered a good excursion centre for trips to the Luberon Range *(qv)*. A colourful, animated market is held on Saturday mornings. The Roman colony of Julia Apt was a prosperous ancient city and a bishopric in the 3C.

The first sanctuary dedicated to St Anne in France, its cathedral holds the saint's reliquaries brought back from the Orient in the 3C and, according to legend, miraculously found by Charlemagne during a trip in 776. It is the scene of a traditional pilgrimage which takes place the last Sunday in July.

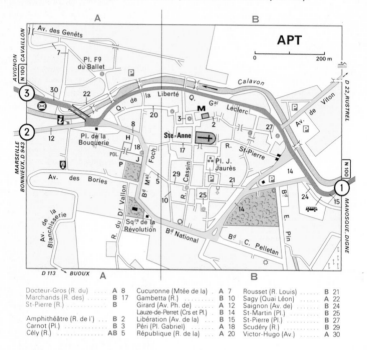

Docteur-Gros (R. du)	A 8	Cucuronne (Mtée de la)	A 7	Rousset (R. Louis)	B 21
Marchands (R. des)	B 17	Gambetta (R.)	B 10	Sagy (Quai Léon)	A 22
St-Pierre (R.)	B	Girard (Av. Ph. de)	A 12	Saignon (Av. de)	B 24
		Lauze-de-Perret (Crs et Pl.)	B 14	St-Martin (Pl.)	B 25
Amphithéâtre (R. de l')	B 2	Libération (Av. de la)	B 15	St-Pierre (Pl.)	B 27
Carnot (Pl.)	B 3	Péri (Pl. Gabriel)	A 18	Scudéry (R.)	B 29
Cély (R.)	AB 5	République (R. de la)	A 20	Victor-Hugo (Av.)	A 30

SIGHTS

ⓥ **Old St Anne's Cathedral** (Ancienne cathédrale Ste-Anne) (B). – The actual building was constructed in the 11 or 12C and was very often remodelled. The south aisle is Romanesque, north aisle is 14C Gothic and the nave was rebuilt in the 17C. Covering the transept crossing is a dome on squinches similar to the one at Notre-Dame-des-Doms Cathedral in Avignon *(p 77)*. At the end of the apse, a 14C stained glass window, given by Pope Urban V, depicts St Anne holding the Virgin and Child in her arms.

St Anne's Chapel or Royal Chapel (Chapelle Ste-Anne ou chapelle royale). – The first chapel off the north aisle was built in 1660, the same year that Anne of Austria came in pilgrimage. Note, above the wooden gilt altarpiece, a large reliquary bust of St Anne, left, under the dome, a marble group of St Anne and the Virgin by the Italian Benzoni, and across the way the family tomb of the Dukes of Sabran *(qv)*.

ⓥ **Treasury** (Trésor). – In the sacristy of St Anne's Chapel sacristy are displayed 11 and 12C liturgical Mss, shrines decorated with 12 and 13C Limoges enamels, 14C Florentine gilded wood caskets and St Anne's shroud and an 11C Arabian standard brought back from the First Crusade (1096-9). In the 2nd chapel off the north aisle, above the altar, held up by a 4C sarcophagus, hangs a painting from the Byzantine School portraying St John the Baptist against a gold background. In the Corpus Domini Chapel, south of the chancel, stands an elegant altar, the cathedral's former altar, with fine antique-style decoration.

Crypt (Crypte). – Composed of two floors: the upper crypt is Romanesque and contains an altar held up by a Romanesque capital and 13C sarcophagi; the lower crypt is Pre-Romanesque. At the back of the two crypts stand two tombstones.

ⓥ **Archaeological Museum** (Musée archéologique) (B M). – An 18C *hôtel* houses this interesting museum. Exhibited on the ground floor are displays covering prehistory (flint, stone implements), protohistory (arms and tools, large jar, earthenware) and Gallo-Roman carvings (funerary inscriptions, capitals, various fragments). The 1st floor includes displays of the Gallo-Roman period (mosaics, pottery, glassware, funerary furnishings, jewellery, coins) and items (tools, votive objects especially oil lamps dating back to 2C BC) excavated from the *oppidum* of Chastellard-de-Lardiers, near Banon in the Alpes-de-Haute-Provence *département*. The 2nd floor covers 17-19C ceramics (Apt, Moustiers, Allemagne-en-Provence, Castellet, some originally from the former hospice). Works of art by Léon Sagy (1863-1939), the ceramist from Apt, complete the collection. A number of 17-19C ex-votos are also exhibited.

EXCURSION

★★Ochre Drive. – *49km – 30 miles – about 3 1/2 hours. Leave Apt by ③ on the town plan, the N 100.*

Julien Bridge (Pont Julien). – Spanning the Coulon (or Calavon) River in the 3C BC, this 3-arched bridge was on the ancient Domitian Way linking Italy to Spain. It was mounted on 2 piers pierced to allow flood-waters to swiftly pass through them.

The D 108 and the D 149 on the right lead to Roussillon.

★Roussillon. – *Description p 159.*

D 227 offers fine views to the right onto the ochre cliffs and Luberon Range and to the left onto Vaucluse Plateau.

Cross the D 4, bear right on the D 2 and right again on the D 101.

In a field to the right of the road some twenty settling tanks used for the processing of ochre *(qv)*, extracted from neighbouring quarries, can be seen.

On entering Gargas bear left on the D 83 and left again on the D 943.

St-Saturnin-d'Apt. – Pop 1 741. The village, perched on the first foothills of the Vaucluse Plateau, is overlooked by old castle ruins and a Romanesque chapel. Take the alley left of the village church and climb to the chapel for a view of the Apt countryside and Luberon Range. The upper, Ayguier Gate (15C), still preserves some of its defences.

Return south along the D 943 and turn left along the D 179 towards Rustrel.

On the way, if it is the right season, you will see the many cherry orchards, which cover the plain, in blossom.

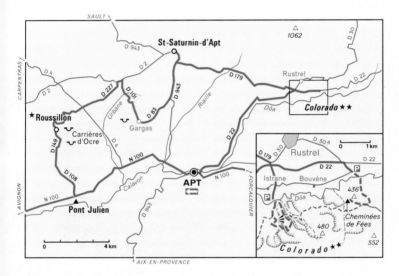

★★Rustrel Colorado (Colorado de Rustrel). – *3 hours on foot Rtn; steep paths.* The gigantic ochre quarry is a rare sight and can be explored in two walks.

– The canyon *(2 hours Rtn)*: at the D 179, 22, 30 crossroads, take the road opposite to Istrane (surfaced at the start); park the car beside the Dôa River, ford the Dôa and walk first between the settling tanks before bearing left immediately and following the stream to the floor of the quarry cirque. Climb gently to the right towards a ridge where there is a well-defined path to several natural viewpoints. Among the sights is a second quarry with entrances half-way up the cliff face to old underground workings. *Retrace your steps to the first cirque and return, bearing left all the way.*

– The belvederes *(1 hour Rtn)*: at the D 179, 22, 30 crossroads, turn left into the D 22; after 2.5km – 1 1/2 miles bear right, downhill, to a car park beside the Dôa. Ford the river and follow the yellow arrows. After the departure ramp and a curve to the right, the path cuts through a pinewood to come out at the natural viewpoints overlooking the old quarry workings, an ochre coloured landscape of cliff faces, clay capped earth pillars (Cheminées de Fées means fairies' chimneys)...

Return by the way you came. The D 22 takes you back to Apt.

Michelin map 🎛 folds 9 and 10 or 🎛🎛 folds 1, 2 14 and 15 or 🎛🎛 fold 23

The Ardèche Gorges, overlooked by an audaciously engineered road, rank among the most imposing natural sites in the south of France; part of the gorges are now a nature reserve.

A temperamental river. – The Ardèche River rises in the Mazan Massif (alt 1 467m – 4 813ft). After a 119km – 74 mile journey, it joins the Rhône, 1km – 1/2 mile upstream from Pont-St-Esprit *(qv)*. The river slope has a steep gradient and particularly so in the upper valley *(see Michelin Green Guide Vallée du Rhône, in French only)*; but it is in the lower valley that the most surprising examples of erosion can be observed as the river carved a passage through the limestone strata of the plateau, already hollowed out by underground rivers. The Ardèche's tributaries flowing down from the mountain accentuate its sporadic yet typically Mediterranean flow: autumn spates are followed by a shallow rivulet in winter, spring torrents, then subside to a comparative trickle during the summer. During the peak flow there is a formidable convergence of floodwaters at Vallon-Pont-d'Arc *(qv)*. A powerful wall of water advances down the valley at 15-20km – 9-12 miles an hour! The strength of these erratic floodwaters is such that the river pushes the flow of the Rhône eastwards and deposits a pile of rubble in its river bed. In 1877, the overflow of the Ardèche was so strong that it cut through the Rhône and broke the Lauzon breakwater on the opposite bank. Its drainage is as erratic.

FROM VALLON-PONT-D'ARC TO PONT-ST-ESPRIT

58km – 36 miles – allow 1 day – local map below and p 61

On leaving the Vallon Basin, the Ardèche reaches the lower Vivarais limestone plateau which it divides by its deep course into two plateaux: the Gras to the north and the Orgnac *(p 62)* to the south, covered with evergreen oak and scrub and riddled with caves.

A **panoramic road**, the D 290, overlooks (in corniche style) the gorge along the Gras Plateau side.

Vallon-Pont-d'Arc. – *Description p 189.*

Leave Vallon for Pont-d'Arc.

The road makes for the Ardèche, past the ruins of old Vallon (Vieux Vallon) and across Ibie River. On the left is the **Cave of Tunnels** (Grotte des Tunnels) which once had an underground stream.

★★**Pont-d'Arc.** – *Photograph p 63.* Leave the car in one of the car parks, on either side of the belvedere. The river flows under the natural arch (34m – 112ft high 59m – 194ft wide), which it once skirted (the road just taken in the car). Thousands of years ago the arch was most likely a narrow passage through which ran a subterranean stream. Infiltration and erosion isolated it and thus when the floodwaters caused the river to alter its course, it adopted the passage already made, which it has since been enlarging. *To reach the foot of Pont-d'Arc, there is a path on the Vallon side 164yds from the belvedere.*

The scenic splendour begins immediately after you leave Pont-d'Arc: the river flows in wide curves punctuated by rapids all in the framework of a 30km – 20 mile gorge enclosed by rock walls 300m – 984ft high in some places, dramatically coloured in tones of white, dark and light grey and overgrown with scrub oak and vegetation; the river is jade green. Beyond Chames, on the floor of Tiourre Valley, the road curves to the left creating a grandiose rocky **cirque★** before climbing to the plateau's edge.

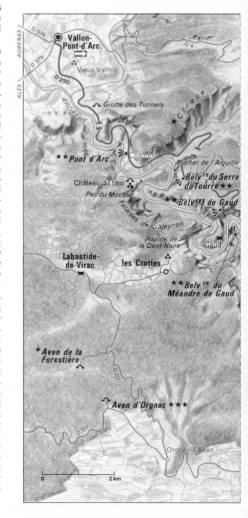

Serre de Tourre Belvedere (Belvédère du Serre de Tourre). – The viewpoint, poised almost vertically 200m – 656ft above the Ardèche, offers a superb **picture of the river winding round the **Pas du Mousse Rock** on which stand the few remaining ruins of the 16C Ebbo Castle (Château d'Ebbo). Also to be seen are the Saleyron Cliffs (Falaises de Saleyron). Standing out to the right, on the horizon, are Mount Lozère and the wide expanse of the Orgnac Plateau, to the left.

On the left bank, the tourist road adopts the tormented relief of its cliffs and passes through the evergreen oaks of Bouchas and Malbosc Woods (respectively Bois Bouchas and Bois Malbosc).

Gaud Belvederes (Belvédères de Gaud). – The **view is upstream towards the Gaud meander (Belvédère du Méandre de Gaud) and the turrets of its small 19C castle.

*Autridge Belvederes (Belvédères d'Autridge). – To reach the two viewpoints take the panoramic curve. There Morsanne Needle (Aiguille de Morsanne) advances above the gorges like the prow of a ship.

500m – 1/3 mile beyond the Agrimont Coomb (Combe d'Agrimont), new **vistas**** open up of the great bend in the river with the Morsanne Needle in the foreground.

**Le Gournier Belvederes (Belvédères de Gournier). – The viewpoints are well situated 200m – 656ft above the river. Below, Le Gournier farm lies in ruins in a small field bordering the Ardèche, which carves its course through the rocks of Gournier's Tourpine (*tourpine* means cooking pot).

*Madeleine Cave (Grotte de la Madeleine). – *Description p 126.*

Approach Marzal Chasm by the road running along Gras Plateau.

**Marzal Chasm. – *Description p 140.*

Return to La Madeleine crossroads and the carparks of Madeleine Belvedere.

***High Corniche (La Haute Corniche). – This, the most outstanding section of the drive, affords unrivalled views, in close succession, of the gorges.

Madeleine Belvedere (Belvédère de la Madeleine). – *1/4 hour on foot Rtn.* The viewpoint is admirable. Rock spikes rising in the foreground resemble the spires of a ruined cathedral (Rocher de la Cathédrale – *cathédrale* means cathedral) while downstream the Madeleine Fort (Rochers du Fort de la Madeleine) at 300m-984ft, the tallest cliffs in the gorges, appear to bar the defile.

Cathedral Belvedere (Belvédère de la Cathédrale). – The point commands Madeleine cirque (cirque de la Madeleine) and Cathedral Rock.

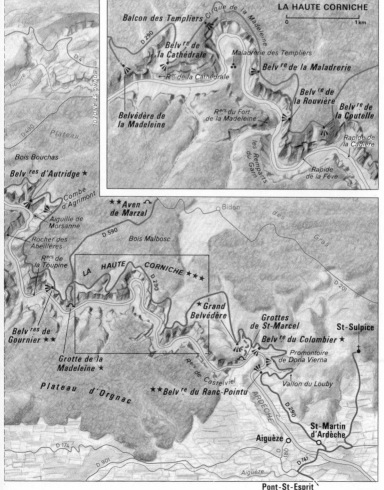

61

Templars' Belvedere (Balcon des Templiers). – The belvedere affords views of a tight loop in the river flanked by the high walls of a rock cirque. Down below, crowning a small spur are the ruins of a Templars' Leper Hospital.

Leper Hospital Belvedere (Belvédère de la Maladrerie). – View of the Cathedral Rock.

Rouvière Belvedere (Belvédère de la Rouvière). – Facing the Garn Ramparts (Remparts du Garn).

Coutelle Belvedere (Belvédère de la Coutelle). – The vertiginous viewpoint overlooks the river from a height of 180m – 590ft. To the right are the last of the Garn Ramparts; to the left the Castelviel Rocks (Rochers de Castelviel) and directly in the river's course, up and downstream the swift Fève and Cadière Rapids (respectively Rapide de la Fève and Rapide de la Cadière).

★**Grand Belvedere**. – View of the end of the gorges and the Ardèche's final bend.

★**Colombier Belvedere** (Belvédère du Colombier). – View down into the bend enclosed by rock strewn banks.

St-Marcel Caves (Grottes de St-Marcel). – *Description p 163.*

The road describes a loop along a dry valley, skirts the Dona Vierna promontory (Promontoire de Dona Vierna) and makes a wide detour around Louby Valley (Vallon du Louby) to reach the next viewpoint.

★★**Ranc-Pointu Belvedere** (Belvédère du Ranc-Pointu). – The belvedere, perched at the end of the Louby Valley slope, overlooks the Ardèche's last enclosed bend. Note the different types of erosion, striation, pot holes and caves.

As you come away from the gorge, the countryside changes completely: the bare defile is replaced by a cultivated valley opening ever more widely as it approaches the Rhône. On the far bank stands the village of **Aiguèze** *(see below).*

St-Martin-d'Ardèche. – Pop 380. The first village on the north bank since Vallon.

St-Sulpice Chapel (Chapelle St-Sulpice). – *4km – 2 1/2 miles via Trignan from St-Martin-d'Ardèche.* The dazzling white Romanesque chapel (12-17C) stands on a slight rise amid a sea of vines. The south wall is built of re-used stones carved with interlacing designs.

Cross the Ardèche by the St-Martin suspension bridge.

Take the D 901 on the left, which joins the N 86 slightly before the confluence of the Ardèche and the Rhône.

The N 86 goes to Pont-St-Esprit.

Pont-St-Esprit. – *Description p 157.*

ORGNAC PLATEAU (south bank)
Local map pp 60-61

Aiguèze. – Pop 182. The old fort's ramparts command a good **view★** of the river.

Les Crottes. – A village deserted since 3 March 1944, when all the villagers were shot by the Germans; a stele recalls this event.

★**Forestière Chasm** (Aven de la Forestière). – Explored by A. Sonzogni, this chasm ⊙ was opened to tourists in 1968. It is not far below ground and is easily accessible. The dramatically lit chambers are rich in attenuated concretions such as the cauliflower-like concretions, macaroni-like strips, which hang from the roof, variegated stalactite curtains, phantasmagoric and eccentric formations and floors bristling with stalagmites.
A small zoo has a variety of crustaceans, fish, frogs, toads and insects.

⊙**Labastide-de-Virac**. – Pop 184. North of this fortified village, located on the boundary line between Languedoc and Vivarais, stands the 15C **castle** belonging to the Roure family, which guarded the passage through the gorges at Pont-d'Arc. The two round towers were razed in 1629 during the Wars of Religion.
Since 1825 the castle belongs to the family of the sculptor James Pradier (1795-1825; he carved Lille and Strasbourg which are on the Place de la Concorde), whose descendants were tenant farmers to the Counts of Roure. During the visit note the Florentine-style courtyard, spiral staircase and great hall (1st floor) with its fine chimney. The watchpath overlooks the Ardèche and Gras Plateaux; during clear weather you can spot the Lozère Mountains and Mézenc Mount to the north. An active silkworm farm revives the tradition of silkworm cultivation.

★★**Gaud Bend Belvedere** (Belvédère du Méandre de Gaud). – It commands an excellent **view★★** of the river at the foot of the Gaud cirque.

★★★**Orgnac Chasm**. – *Description p 153.*

★★★DESCENDING THE GORGES BY BOAT OR CANOE
From Pont-d'Arc to St-Martin-d'Ardèche
Local map pp 60-61

⊙ The descent which can be made at any time between March and late November, is best in May-June.
After a long calm stretch, the river bends and one enters the gorges. To the right are Ebbo Cave and Pas du Mousse Rock, a narrow passage through the cliff to the plateau; the rock on the north bank is Aiguille Rock (Rocher de l'Aiguille). The first rapids, Dent Noire (Rapide de la Dent Noire), occur just below the immensely tall Saleyron Cliffs and are followed by the wide Gaud meander and cirque with its small château.
Rapids and smooth flowing stretches, overlooked by canyon-high cliffs, alternate as you pass landmarks such as Morsanne Needle on the north bank and Abeillères' jagged red and black spikes (Rocher des Abeillères) on the south bank.

After approximately 4 hours you should have negotiated the rocks of Gournier's Toupine lying strewn in the river's course, which in places is 18m – 60ft deep, and be in sight of Cathedral Rock in the distance. Before you actually reach Cathedral Rock you pass the mouth of Madeleine Cave, on the left. Just after, the river flows below the enormous Cathedral Rock.

The Madeleine Rocks are among the most spectacular on the trip, when seen from water level. Straits, rapids and smooth iridescent passages follow one another as the river continues downwards between sheer cliff walls, bare of all but occasional evergreen oaks. Below the Castelviel Rocks, the opening of the St-Marcel Caves can be seen on the left, and rounding the bend, the Dona Vierna Promontory and Ranc-Pointu Belvedere. The cliffs melt away, the valley widens out, Aiguèze's tower can be seen on the edge of the rock escarpment on the right.

Pont-d'Arc

★★★ ARLES   Pop 50 772

Michelin map 🎓 fold 10 or 🎓 fold 28 or 🎓 fold 26 – Local map p 97

Roman capital and a major religious centre in the Middle Ages, Arles preserves, from its glorious past, two fine Gallo-Roman antiquities, its amphitheatre and theatre and two gems of Romanesque art, the cloisters and doorway of St-Tromphime. The development of Camargue *(qv)* has placed Arles as the rice capital and yet the city does not depend only on its vocation as a central market for agricultural produce (market gardening, breeding and raising of Crau sheep and rice) but also on its diversified light industry and administrative and cultural functions. It is also the largest *commune* of France encompassing 77 000ha – 30sq miles.

The Arles Festival, which has now gained a solid reputation of quality and Provençal originality, holds folklore manifestations, concerts, opera, dance and theatre. In addition there are the traditional Camargue bull fighting festivals: Easter *féria* Gardian's *(qv)* Festival etc.

Annually the International Photography Meeting (Rencontres Internationales de la Photographie), founded by Lucien Clergue (a famous photographer born in Arles in 1934), takes place. It consists of a series of quality exhibitions and events. This, with the National School of Photography, founded in 1982, has made Arles one of the capitals of photography.

Arles women have inspired Mistral *(qv)*, Daudet *(qv)*, Gounod *(qv)* and Bizet, to praise them through their music and prose. Although the splendid costume can only be seen during the festivals, the beauty of these women still holds *(photograph p 27)*.

HISTORICAL NOTES

Arles and Marseilles. – The site of Arles, amidst the marshes, at the tip of Camargue, was originally an island-like rocky eminence, which overlooked the Rhône Delta. It controlled the navigation on the river, the course of which was not yet established. The excavations, undertaken in 1975 under the Jardin d'Hiver have revealed the existence of a Celtic-Ligurian town (known as Theline) colonised by the Greeks from Marseilles as early as 6C BC.

The town, which soon took the name of Arelate, met with new prosperity when the Consul Marius *(qv)*, in 104 BC, built a canal which joined the Rhône to the Fos Gulf, greatly facilitating navigation. And yet Arles stayed economically dependent of the Massalians who levied a toll on the ships using the canal. This situation continued until 49 BC when Caesar defeated Marseilles. Arles had provided Caesar with 12 ships for his campaign and Caesar, thus, transferred to the town Marseilles's possessions and ordered them to found a Roman colony. Thereafter, Arles supplanted its rival and developed its economy.

It possessed, on the Rhône, the southern most bridge *(see Julien Bridge p 59)* on the Domitian Way, the direct road between Italy and Spain. Other roads leaving from the city united the Mediterranean with northern Gaul and other western provinces. These land routes were complemented by a number of waterways. Arles, closer to the sea than now, became a sea and river port: the largest ships could dock there easily.

Roman Arles. – *Town plan p 32.* A colony of veterans of the 6th Legion, Arles was granted the privilege of building a fortified wall around the 40ha – 99 acres of the official city; on the Rhône side stood a triumphal arch razed in 1687. The town was divided into two main streets: the *cardo* (north-south axis; located Rue de l'Hôtel de Ville) and the *decumanus* (east-west axis; located in part Rue de la Calade) and included the forum (on the site of the Cryptoporticus, *p 67)*, most likely several temples, a basilica, baths (under Place de la République) and a theatre. The streets (4 to 7m – 13 to 23ft) wide dividing the town into a checkerboard pattern, were all paved and often lined with footpaths; while the *cardo* with a total width of 12m – 39ft (4m – 13ft of which were street), was lined with porticoes.

An aqueduct (vestiges near La Redoute Gate to the east) brought water in abundance from the Alpilles Chain *(qv)*. From a central cistern, water was distributed to three points: local fountains, baths and private houses. A remarkable drainage system (the masterpipe being 3.50m – 11ft in diameter) evacuated the used water: the public lavatories were built of white marble and equipped with running water. The town was spreading at the end of the 1C beyond the fortifications: part of the ramparts were destroyed to build the amphitheatre. To the south lay the Roquette shipyards and, beyond, the circus (the obelisk standing in front of St-Trophime originates from it); further to the east the Jardin d'Hiver Quarter and the Esplanade were residential (two villas were discovered); on the right bank of the Rhône, at Trinquetaille was the large bustling dockland frequented by sailors, boatmen and merchants. A bridge of boats joined the two banks of the river northeast of the town, level with the Bourg-Neuf quarter.

The expansion of Arles reached its maximum in the 4 and 5C. Under Constantine the northwest quarter was remodelled; an imperial palace and the La Trouille baths were built. The ground plan of the fortifications was hardly modified; the ramparts are still visible to the east where two towers from La Redoute Gate *(p 70)*, still stand.

Rome of the Gauls. – Trade was such that in the 5C it was written that: "All that the Orient, unguent Araby, luxuriant Assyria, fertile Africa, beautiful Spain and fecund Gaul produce, is to be found in Arles and in as great quantity as in their countries of origin".

The town was made up of five guilds of boatmen. Some sailed the Rhône, Durance, and the lagoons around Arles's hill using rafts carried on inflated goatskins called *utriculaires,* others sailed the Mediterranean.

It was an active industrial centre as well: textiles and gold and silver work were manufactured, ships were built, sarcophagi and arms were made. Imperial money was minted. Wheat, pork butcher's meat (already famous), olive oil, dark and thick wine from the Rhône hills, were all exported. Stonecarvers, masons and architects were reputed for the quality of their work.

Prosperity brought political importance: Emperor Constantine established himself followed by his sons. In 395 Arles became the political and administrative capital of the Gauls (made up of Spain, Gaul as such, Brittany) and obtained in 417, the primacy removed from Lyons. It was a great religious centre where 19 synods were held. The first bishop of Arles, Trophime, was most likely sent from Rome in c225 and legends rapidly grew around him *(p 66)*. From this period (mid-3C) dates Christianisation, illustrated by the martyrdom of St Genesius in c250. In the 4 and 5C the bishops were constantly acquiring importance under the protection of imperial rule and hoped to control all the other churches of the Gauls.

The decline. – Arles suffered from the Barbarian invasions at the end of the 5C, but rediscovered a certain illustriousness under the Ostrogoths between 508-36. More than the insignificant and temporarily re-established praetorian prefects, it was the brilliance of the bishops, notably St Caesarius who continued to make Arles a great religious centre where important synods were held, such as in 524. The Frank domination led to Arles's decline.

In the 8C the Franks and Saracens fought over the country and as result left much destruction. In the 9C Arles was but a shadow of its former self, when it became the capital of the kingdom of Arles, which included Burgundy and part of Provence. It was not until the 12C that the town experienced a political and economical revival with the foundation of the town as a commune governed by elected consuls. Its prestige was considerable as the Germanic Emperor Frederick Barbarossa came to the town in 1178 to be crowned king of Arles, in the just completed, superb Romanesque Cathedral of St-Trophime. In 1239 the bourgeois of Arles submitted to the count of Provence. From that time onwards, the town followed the fortunes of the province: political status was transferred to Aix and Marseilles took its revenge and acquired economic prosperity.

As long as the Rhône remained the main commercial route, Arles continued being relatively prosperous and even more so when the land was upgraded by the Crau irrigation project and drainage of the marshland. However, the arrival of the railway made river traffic obsolete and delt a severe blow to trade. In the past (some twenty years) it had been only the agricultural market centre of Camargue, Crau and Alpilles.

Van Gogh in Arles. – Vincent van Gogh (1853-90), a painter of Dutch origin, came to Arles from Paris on 21 February 1888. He first lived at the Hôtel-restaurant Carrel, Rue de la Cavalerie and then rented a small house, "Yellow House", on Place Lamartine: both buildings were destroyed during the war.

He adapted quickly and his health improved, he made friends and received Gauguin in October. His style changed as he moved away from Impressionism. He sought to find "Japan's equivalent", the engravings of which fascinated him. The Provençal countryside, and its luminosity answered his call. He painted non-stop: nature, working in the fields, portraits, views of Arles and his surroundings. In all, more than 200 paintings and 100 drawings. His Arles subjects including: *House of Vincent, The Alyscamps, L'Arlésienne, Crau Plain* and *Langlois Bridge* (this, the said Van Gogh bridge, was destroyed in 1926 and rebuilt on the Arles canal at the Fos-sur-Mer port) were some of the most exciting works of his Arles period. Stricken with mental disorder, made worse by his brutal break with Gauguin (24 December

Self-portrait with bandaged ear and pipe by Van Gogh (private collection)

1888, when he cut off part of his left ear *(Self-portrait)*, Van Gogh was hospitalised. There then began a trying period: Gauguin abandoned him, his friend Roulin, the postman, was sent to Marseilles and in February 1889 a petition circulated demanding that he be confined. He finally decided to leave Arles for the asylum at St-Rémy-de-Provence *(qv)*; he arrived 3 May 1889.

THE CENTRE'S PUBLIC BUILDINGS *time: 1 day*

★★**Amphitheatre** (Arènes) (YZ). – *See p 33*. It suggests, properly speaking, an amphitheatre dating most likely from the end of the 1C. Transformed into a fortress during the early Middle Ages, it constituted a system of defence. Later on, under the filled in arcades, in the galleries, on the tiers and arena itself developed a small town of 200 houses and 2 chapels. In order to carry out these transformations, the materials were taken from the building itself which was mutilated but saved from destruction. The excavation and restoration began in 1825. Three out of the 4 medieval watch towers remain.

The amphitheatre measured 136m × 107m (446ft × 351ft) and could seat more than 20 000 spectators. Two storeys, each made up of 60 arches, had a total height of 21m – 65 1/2ft. Corinthian half columns back to back adorned the pillars on the 1st floor. The 3rd floor, the attic storey, which was preserved at Nîmes *(p 144)*, has completely disappeared. The arena, as such, 69m × 40m (226ft × 131ft) was separated from the tiers by a protective wall; this wall was floored and underneath it were the machinery, animal cages and backstage.

To appreciate the grandeur of the building, climb to the platform of the tower dominating the entrance. From here enjoy an all around view of the amphitheatre's construction and an interesting view of Arles, the Rhône, Alpilles and Montmajour Abbey. Wander through the upper level of arches of half the amphitheatre in order to understand the building's construction; finally go around the arena at the lower level of arches. This allows you to grasp the strength of this ancient construction and the originality of the trabeated form of construc-

Amphitheatre in Arles

tion where in fact the circular galleries are covered with enormous flat slabs which replaced the traditional Roman vault and prove Greek influence in Arles.

★★**Roman Theatre** (Théâtre antique) (Z). – This theatre, built under Augustus's reign *c*27-5BC, was much more mutilated than the amphitheatre. As early as the 5C it was used as a quarry for the construction of churches and in the 9C was transformed into a redoubt before disappearing completely under houses and gardens. Rediscovered in the 17C, it was excavated from 1827-55.

Smaller in size than the one in Autun or Lyons, the theatre measured 102m – 335ft in diameter and had a seating capacity of 12 000. Contrary to the one in Orange *(p 150)*, which was built onto a natural height, this theatre was backed up by a 27-arched portico made up of 3 levels of arcades, of which only one bay (part of the medieval ramparts, Roland Tower) remains.

All that is preserved of the stage wall are two columns in African breccia and Italian marble standing whole amidst the ruins, as a reminder of the theatre's great past. The scene, curtain slit, orchestra and part of the tiers are still visible. The tiers of seats went up to and were level with the Roland Tower; the attic level was added on to the top most rows. In 1651 excavations in the pit unearthed the famous Venus of Arles (a cast is in the Museum of Pagan Art – *p 67*) given to Louis XIV. One hundred years later, a naked torso, part of a colossal statue of Augustus, was discovered; it was most likely set in the large niche of the stage wall; in 1834 its head was uncovered (now in the Museum of Pagan Art).

★ **St-Trophime** (Z). – Around St Trophime, perhaps the first bishop of Arles in the early 3C, were born a number of legends: sent by St Peter, cousin and disciple of St Paul, received the St Marys when they landed *(p 171)*, and Christ, Himself, appeared before him at the Alyscamps, etc.

The early cathedral was first consecrated to St Stephen, destroyed and then rebuilt during the Carolingean era (part of the façade built of rubble remains). It was again rebuilt at the end of the 11C (transept) and in the first half of the 12C (nave) in order to house the relics of St Trophime, to whom it was then consecrated. In *c*1190 the building was enhanced by a magnificently carved doorway, set against the façade and raised, which necessitated the uplifting of the nave. The construction was completed just after the bell tower. The former bell tower was replaced by a square tower of bands and arcades and fluted pilasters, the last storey of which was remodelled in the 17C, St-Trophime, thus, presents a masterpiece of the late Provençal Romanesque style *(qv)*. In the 15C the cathedral underwent massive transformations: the chancel with its ambulatory and radiating chapels was redone, enlarging the church by one-third. In the 17C two classical doors were opened on either side of the main doorway, two windows illuminated the transept crossing and galleries were added.

★★ **Doorway** (Portail). – Due to the beauty of its carved decoration, this doorway can be compared to the one at St-Gilles. It presents an ancient classical ordonnance, suggesting the form of a triumphal arch, often used in 12C Provence. Its archaic appearance recalling the Roman tradition has not evolved in comparison with the main French Romanesque works of art, especially those works from the north.

1) Tympanum of the Last Judgment, Christ crowned, in glory, holding the book of the Evangelists in one hand and raising the other in benediction; his physiognomy suggests a great deal of formalism. He is surrounded by the attributes of the four Evangelists – the winged man (St Matthew), the eagle (St John), the ox (St Luke), the lion (St Mark). Crowding the recessed arches are a procession of angels with at the top, the three angels of the Last Judgment.
2) The elected, clothed, advance towards Christ.
3) An angel receives the elected and drops their souls in the aprons of Abraham, Isaac and Jacob.
4) Joseph's vision and the Annunciation.
5) Twelve Apostles.
6) Christ's birth and the bathing of the newborn child.
7) An angel guards the Gates to Paradise from where a group of sinners (prelates, men, women) are refused admission.
8) The condemned, naked, held closely by one chain, carried by a demon, are led to hell.
9) St Bartholomew.
10) St James the Lesser.
11) St Trophime (in bishop's robes) two angels are placing the mitre on his head.

12) St John the Evangelist, unbearded.
13) St Peter with his keys.
14) St Paul. This statue with its deeply cut and closely set folds was inspired by the central doorway of St-Gilles *(p 161)*.
15) St Andrew.
16) The stoning of St Stephen: two angels bear off his soul (represented by a child) and take it to Paradise.
17) St James the Greater.
18) St Philippe.

On the sides near the side doors: on the left St Michael weighing souls; on the right some hellish demons.

Interior. – Inside the main body of the building is surprisingly high and the aisles very narrow. The nave, lit by a rounded clerestory, is roofed with pointed barrel vaulting; the aisles have half-barrel vaulting. The Romanesque severity contrasts with the rib and moulding work of the Gothic chancel. Among the works of art of particular interest:
– in the 2nd bay of the north aisle: 4C Christian sarcophagus with two carved registers, some of which are in high relief.
– in the north arm of the transept an admirable Annunciation by Finsonius; in the transept chapel, called Chapel of Grignan, another sarcophagus which served as an altar and represents the crossing of the Red Sea.
– in the Chapel of St Sepulchre (right of the axial chapel) the sarcophagus of Geminus, who died *c*400, surmounted by a 16C Entombment.
– in the south arm of the transept a long painted panel (16C) shows a synod assembled around the Virgin.
– in the Kings' Chapel (south side aisle) Adoration of the Magi by Finsonius *(p 138)*.
– on the wall of the north aisle Aubusson tapestries illustrate the Virgin's life.
– in the nave above the triumphal arch the Stoning of St Stephen by Finsonius.

★★St-Trophime Cloisters (Cloître St-Trophime) (Z). – These cloisters, the most famous ones of the Provence by the elegance and richness of their carved decoration, may have been carved with the collaboration of the craftsmen of St-Gilles *(p 161)*. Developed for the cathedral's canons at the same time as the surrounding conventual buildings, its construction occurred in several stages:

Northwest Pillar
1. St Peter – 2. Resurrection of Christ – 3. St Trophime – 4. Holy Women (above) and perfume merchants (below) – 5. St John

the Romanesque north and east galleries in the last third of the 12C, the Gothic south and west galleries in the 14C.

The best work is to be found in the north gallery (on the left on entering) particularly on the magnificent corner pillars decorated with large statues and low relief. The capitals are adorned with scenes from the Resurrection and the origins of Christian Arles and foliage. Note especially on the northeast pillar, the statue of St Paul, with the deeply incised folds, very long under the elbows, the work of a craftsman who was familiar with St-

Northeast Pillar
1. St Andrew – 2. Stoning of St Stephen; above Christ blessing – 3. St Stephen – 4. Ascension of Christ – 5. St Paul

Gilles's central doorway. Of a later period the east gallery's capitals and pillars recount the major episodes of Christ's life. The south gallery tells of the life of St Trophime and the west gallery concentrates on typically Provençal subjects such as St Martha and the Tarasque *(qv)*. From the south gallery can be seen the cloisters and, above, the former chapter premises, the church nave. Dominating the whole stands the stout plain bell tower. Above the gallery runs a walk.

The chapterhouse, opening onto the north gallery, vaulted with pointed barrel vaulting, houses, on the ground floor, Flemish and Aubusson (17C) tapestries and upstairs some Romanesque capitals and various lapidary fragments. Along the east gallery the refectory, and dormitory display temporary exhibitions.

Town Hall (Hôtel de Ville) (Z H). – The town hall was rebuilt between 1673-5 with the plans of Hardouin-Mansart and by the architect Peytret from Arles. It includes the **Clock Tower,** a vestige of the original building, which was built between 1543-53 and inspired by the Glanum mausoleum. The vestibule's (which gives onto Plan de la Cour, *see below*), flat vaulting is a masterpiece; at one time it was studied by the craftsmen touring France (before they became master craftsmen). The setting is completed by the town hall's Versailles-like classical façade overlooking Place de la République and the fountain, in the middle of which stands a fine **obelisk** from the Arles's Roman circus and moved here in the 17C.

The Plan de la Cour, access via the vestibule, is an unusual small square lined with old buildings, one of the buildings of which is the 12-15C Hôtel des Podestats. Leaning against one of the walls is the judgment bench from where the magistrates pronounced sentence.

★Museum of Pagan Art (Musée d'Art païen) (Z M²). – This fine museum of ancient art has been located since 1805 in the former church of Ste-Anne (17C). Several admirable objects were discovered during the excavations of the theatre *(p 65)*: the colossal mutilated statue of Augustus, two statues of dancers, Apollo's altar and a cast of the famous Venus of Arles, which was the copy of a masterpiece of Hellenistic statuary. When the Venus was uncovered, it was broken in three places and armless. The city of Arles offered it to Louis XIV, who had it restored by Girardon (1628-1715); it is now in the Louvre. Discovered during the excavations of the Cryptoporticus *(see below)* are: the bearded head of Octavius (39BC), the votive shield of Augustus (26BC) and the head of Tiberius (whose father was the founder of the colony of Arles).

Note also the white marble sarcophagus the so-called Phaedra and Hippolytus (2-3C) sarcophagus and several 4C mosaics found in a Gallo-Roman villa in Trinquetaille.

★★Museum of Christian Art (Musée d'Art chrétien) (Z M¹). – Located in a former Jesuit chapel (17C), this museum, with that of the Vatican *(see Michelin Green Guide to Rome)*, is one of the richest in the world in paleochristian sarcophagi. These splendid works, all of the 4C, were carved in marble by craftsmen from Arles and exalted the new triumphant Christian faith. For the most part the scenes recounted are from the Old and New Testament: the passage of the Red Sea, Jonah and the whale, etc. The other sarcophagi are adorned with pastoral scenes. In the middle of the nave are three sarcophagi discovered during the 1974 excavations of the Trinquetaille, note especially the one of the Trinity or spouses with three carved registers.

★Cryptoporticus. – *Enter via the museum.* The Cryptoporticus, the forum's substructure, is a double, horseshoe-shaped, underground gallery, 90m – 295ft long and 60m – 197ft wide. The two rounded arched corridors were divided by a line of massive rectangular pillars; ancient air shafts let the light in. The north corridor cut in the 2C by a temple, the ruins of which can be seen on the Forum Square *(p 69)*, was flush with and opened onto the *decumanus* by two doors; it was doubled in the 4C by a new covered gallery.

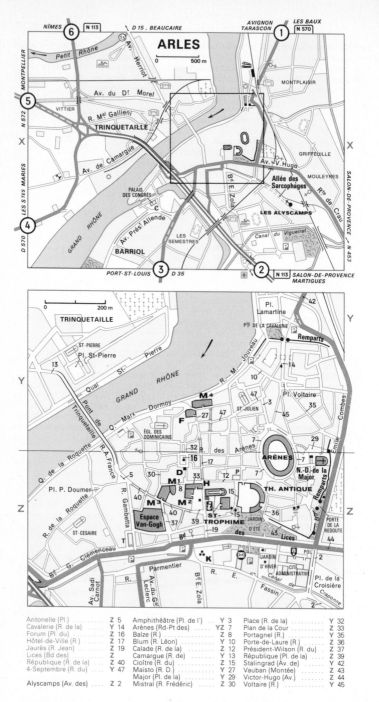

The use of the Cryptoporticus is not well-known, apart from the fact that they enhanced and assured the stability of the forum's monuments. The specialists have often imagined that they were huge graineries or more prosaically just walkways. During its excavations were found several fine sculptures now exposed in the Museum of Pagan Art *(p 67)* especially the bearded head of Octavius and a votive shield, a marble copy of the gold shield offered to Augustus by the Senate in 27BC.

★Museon Arlaten (Z M³). – This fascinating Provençal ethnographic museum was created by Frédéric Mistral *(qv)* in 1896 and installed, from 1906-9, in the 16C Hôtel de Castellane-Laval, which was bought by Mistral with the prize money he was given when awarded the Nobel Prize for Literature in 1904. Worried by the evident loss of Provençal indentity before the national policy of centralisatiuon and uniformity, Mistral wanted to preserve, for future generations, the details of Provençal daily life. On entering the courtyard is a small tiled forum with *exedra* which led to a small 2C basilica.

The Museon, with its attendant in traditional Arles costume, as Mistral had wished, consists of some thirty rooms devoted of first importance to the Arles country and organised according to theme or scene. Furnishings, costumes, ceramics evoking local customs, crafts and music, items of popular devotion, documents on the Félibrige *(qv)* and the history of Arles and its surroundings make this museum the most complete of its kind in Provence.

Not to be missed are the reconstructed interiors (delivery room, *mas (qv)* dining room) displayed in a delightful atmosphere of days past...

Also noteworthy is the Frédéric Mistral Room containing a moving display of the poet's personal items (cradle, hat, cane, clothes).

Place du Forum (Z 16). – The actual Place du Forum is not on the site of the ancient forum; it borders it. Left of the Hôtel Nord-Pinus, two Corinthian columns (D) surmounted by a fragment of pediment, are what remains of a 2C temple which straddled the north corridor of the Cryptoporticus *(p 67)*. Augustus's forum lay more to the south.

On this very animated square, lined with cafés, stands a statue of Mistral surrounded by a railing of Camargue *gardians'* pitchforks.

★**Réattu Museum (Musée Réattu)** (Y M⁴). – The museum is located in the former Grand Priory of the Order of the Hospital of St John of Jerusalem (15C). The façade, overlooking the Rhône, was once part of the medieval walls. Before becoming the property of Arles in 1867, the priory belonged to the painter Réattu (1760-1833). Three of the museum's galleries exhibit his work. There are also works from the Italian (16 and 17C), French (17C), Dutch (18C) and Provençal (18C) Schools.

The other galleries contain a large collection of modern and contemporary art. Displayed are watercolours, engravings and paintings by Gauguin, Dufy, Prassinos, Léger, Marchand, Vlaminck, Vasarely, Singier, Sarthou, Marquet, Rousseau and Degottex; sculpture by César, G. Richier, Zadkine, Bury and Toni Grand.

The **Picasso Donation★** is exhibited in 3 galleries: 57 drawings done in 1971 show the variety of techniques (pen, pencil, felt-tip pen, chalk and wash drawing) mastered by Picasso.

The 2nd floor houses a permanent photographic art collection by the most important photographers (Karsh, Izis, Lartigue, Man Ray, Klein, etc.). Photography is represented here not as a technique but as an image of the present.

The Hospitallers have their own gallery.

★**Constantine's Palace (La Trouille Baths)** (Palais Constantin – Thermes de la Trouille) (Y F). – *Read p 34 for details on baths and how they work.*

The baths of Arles are the largest (98 × 45m – 322 × 148ft) remaining in Provence. They date from Constantine's era, 4C.

The plan opposite shows the lay-out and specifies the location of the non-excavated part in relation to present-day Arles. Enter by the *tepidarium,* through to the *caldarium,* which still has its hypocaust. The oven-vaulted wall and apse, completing the building towards the Rhône, are made of alternate courses of brick and stone.

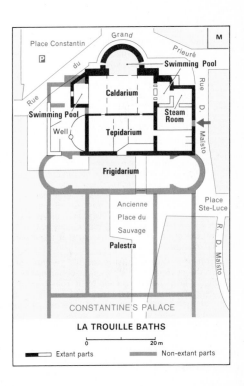

LA TROUILLE BATHS

0   20 m

■ Extant parts   ▬ Non-extant parts

★**THE ALYSCAMPS** (X) *time: 1 hour*

From Roman times to the late Middle Ages, the Alyscamps was one of the most famous necropolises of the western world.

In ancient times, when a traveller arrived by the Aurelian Way to the gates of Arles, he was accompanied to the city's entrance by a long line of tombs and mausoleums, the inscriptions of which beckoned him. And yet the Alyscamps's great expansion occurred during the Christianisation of the necropolis around the tomb of St Genesius. Genesius was a Roman civil servant, who was beheaded in 250 for having refused to write down an imperial edict persecuting the Christians. Miracles began to happen on this site and the faithful, more and more numerous asked to be buried here; added to that was the legend of St Trophime, which confirmed that he too was buried here. As early as the 4C the tombs began to accumulate by the thousands and sarcophagi piled up on several levels (three to be exact: 4-5C, 9-10C and 12-13C). The religious buildings multiplied, too, and in the 13C there were 19 churches and chapels.

From far and wide, recount the chroniclers, the coffins were sent down the Rhône, with a coin for the gravediggers, who stopped them at the Trinquetaille Bridge and from there they were delivered to the Alyscamps. In the 10C the legend stating that the knights of Roncevaux were buried here stepped up its popularity. The transfer of St Trophime's relics to the cathedral in 1152 removed part of the prestige of this immense necropolis.

The Alyscamps, Arles

From the time of the Renaissance the necropolis was desecrated. The city councillors took to offering their honoured guests one or several of the better carved sarcophagi as presents; monks in charge of the necropolis took funerary stones to build churches and convents and enclose monastery grounds.

Thanks to the Museum of Christian Art (p 67) some of the admirable sarcophagi, which enable us to get an idea of the splendour of the Alyscamps in the past, were saved and are exhibited. Finally, the remaining tombs – empty and artistically null – were assembled into an avenue but even this has not survived unscathed; the railway cuts through the approach, housing projects line the right side and on the left the canal and workshops are barely hidden by trees.

Sarcophagus Avenue (L'Allée des Sarcophages) (X). – The visitor cannot help but be awestruck, when he realises that he is walking where for over 2 000 years 80 generations have been buried. This funerary alley is bordered by tall trees interspersed with two rows of sarcophagi and St-Honorat in the background.

A 12C porch, all that remains of the Abbey of St Caesarius, opens onto the avenue also lined by several chapels. A large number of the sarcophagi are Greek in style: double pitched roof with four raised corners; the Roman style ones are identified by the flat top. Some of them are carved with the three symbols: a plumb line and a mason's level signifying the equality of man before death and a trowel, a tool used to mix sand and lime, meaning that the protection of the sarcophagi from robbers is assured.

St-Honorat (X). – Rebuilt in the 12C by the monks of St-Victor of Marseilles, keepers of the necropolis, this church is dominated by a powerful 2 storey bell tower (13C), or lantern tower, opened by 8 round arched bays. Besides the bell tower, the chancel, several chapels added on later on, and a carved doorway remain. Sarcophagi have been placed to show the former location of the nave and aisles, since disappeared. In the apse are 3 Carolingean sarcophagi adorned with "S"-shaped fluting. Across from the entrance is a 4C white marble sarcophagus and in the south chapels are a group of 5 sarcophagi. Note, also, the powerful round 16C pillars in the transept crossing.

ADDITIONAL SIGHTS

Ramparts (Remparts) (YZ). – Across from the cemetery are the Redoute Gate, also known as the Augustus Gate, and the southeast corner of the stronghold, with the ruins of a paleo-Christian church.

Ramparts from the barbarian period can be seen near the public gardens; near the 16C Cavalerie Gate the fortifications are medieval.

Notre-Dame-de-la-Major Collegiate Church (Collégiale N.-D.-de-la-Major) (Z). – This Romanesque church was built on the site of a Roman temple dedicated to Cybelius. It was enlargened in the 14C (aisles), 16C (chancel) and 17C (façade).

Boulevard des Lices (Z). – The favourite promenade of the local people, this broad avenue lined with cafés and their plane tree-shaded terraces, presents the characteristic Provençal avenue (see Cours Mirabeau at Aix-en-Provence, for example).

Esplanade Excavations (Fouilles de l'Esplanade) (Z K). – Skirting Boulevard des Lices, a Gallo-Roman quarter – baths, shops, houses (in one of which a lovely mosaic, illustrating Leda and the Swan) – has been uncovered. Also discovered is the southern continuation of the *cardo,* which crossed town following the present day Rue Hôtel-de-Ville and Rue de la République. Destroyed in the late 3C, this quarter was only partially rebuilt in the 4 and 5C.

ⓥ **Van-Gogh Cultural Centre** (Espace Van-Gogh) (Z). – This is the former hospital where Van Gogh *(qv)* was treated and where he painted; the courtyard is lined with arcades. A large multipurpose cultural centre is being installed.

Michelin map 🄫 folds 13 and 14 or 🄫 fold 45 or 🄫 fold L

In the Huveaune Valley, Aubagne lies in a verdant basin, dominated to the northwest by Étoile Massif. Its location is favourable to industrial expansion and local food production (important agricultural market centre). The once fortified town has preserved some of its old ramparts and a 12C church remodelled in the 17C.
Traditional local art is perpetuated by the production of ceramics and the numerous **Santon workshops.** The local santon makers have created a **Panoramic Christmas Crib** and **The Small World of Marcel Pagnol,** in the latter a group of santons illustrate the popular characters of Pagnol's work. Born in Aubagne (birthplace: 16 Cours Barthélemy), **Marcel Pagnol** (1895-1974 – *qv*) was at the same time a writer of novels, poems, short stories and scenarios; he was also elected to the French Academy.
Since 1962, the town is the home of the French Foreign Legion.
French Foreign Legion (Légion Étrangère). – Founded by King Louis-Philippe on 10 March 1931, the legion was to be a light infantry regiment that accepted all foreigners on the verge of receiving their naturalisation papers. For more than a century the legion has been in continuous combat. On 30 April, the legion celebrates the heroic stand of one of its regiments in **Camaron,** Mexico in 1863. In this village, 64 men under the orders of Captain Danjou resisted, without hope, against 2 000 Mexicains for more than 9 hours. On this day of celebration tradition has it that the youngest officer reads before the other legionnaires the account of this battle.

★**Museum of the French Foreign Legion** (Le musée de la Légion Étrangère). – *Access via the D 2 towards Marseilles, turn right on the D 44ᴬ.*
On the ground floor, opening onto the main hall, is the **great hall,** which exhibits memorabilia belonging to the legion's great leaders; prolonging it, the crypt contains a touching list of the dead. The **museum,** on the 1st floor, presents numerous historical documents, photographs, arms and uniforms.
In the honour's court, the Sacred Way (Voie Sacré) from the Viénot Quarter in Sidi-Bel-Abbès (Algerian headquarters) has been recreated; the way ends at the monument to the legion's dead, brought back from Algeria.

EXCURSIONS

★**Ok Corral Amusement Park** (Parc d'attractions Ok Corral). – *16km – 10 miles east on the N 8.*
Below the N 8, in the centre of a pine forest clearing with Ste-Baume Massif serving as a backdrop lies this exceptional amusement park (loop-the-loops roller coaster, Titanic, Tokaïdo Express, scenic railways, looping star, chairlift, little train). Snack bars, *crêperies* and picnic areas have been set up.

St-Jean-de-Garguier Chapel (Chapelle de St-Jean-de-Garguier). – *5.5km – 3 miles northeast on the D 2, turn left on the D 43ᶜ and right on the D 43ᴰ.*
Rebuilt in the 17C, this chapel, consecrated to St John the Baptist, is the object of an annual pilgrimage on 24 June. More than 300 ex-votos (painted on wood, canvas or zinc), dating for the most part from the 18 and 19C, although some date from the 15C, hang on the chapel walls. A small museum, off the chapel, displays documents relating to this small priory's history (17C missals, 18C religious art, 2 carved low reliefs).

Michelin map 🄫 fold 8 or 🄫 fold 1 or 🄫 fold 22

On the plateau separating the lower Chassezac Valley from the Beaume Gorges, not far from Auriolles, stands the isolated Languedoc *mas*, the Mas de la Vignasse which contains Alphonse Daudet *(qv)* memorabilia.

Mas de la Vignasse. – *When level with the church in Auriolles, bear right on the uphill road from Ruoms; about 500m – 1/4 mile further on an effigy of the author announces the* mas *entrance.*
Restored and transformed into a museum (**Lou Museon dou Bas-Vivarès**), this farmhouse belonged to the Reynauds, Alphonse Daudet's cousins on his mother's side, who were sericulturists and merchants.
In the cocoonery and courtyard is housed the **Museum of Popular Arts and Traditions** (musée des Arts et Traditions populaires) which displays thousands of objects (17C olive oil press, 18C still, wine press, ploughs 1700-1900, bread and lime ovens, tools used in chestnut cultivation, 16C loom, farmers' lace, workshop for wool, hemp and silk spinning, sericultural tools...) evoking daily life in an important *mas* of yesteryear.
The sericulturist's home (1714) contains the **Alphonse Daudet Museum** (musée d'Alphonse Daudet), which revives the author's epoch (1840-97). It is here that Daudet wrote his only book of poems *Les Amoureuses* (1858). Mss, documents and newspaper cuttings are exhibited alongside family portraits. Note the photograph of Henri Reynaud, Daudet's cousin, whose hunting stories served as inspiration for the famous Tartarin in *The New Don Quixote or the Wonderful Adventures of Tarascon.* The kitchen dates back to the end of Louis XIV's reign.

★**Walk to Labeaume.** – *1/2 hour on foot Rtn. On leaving the Mas de Vignasse turn right and 800m – 1/2 mile further on leave the car near a group of houses (Chantressac quarter). At the main crossroad take (on foot) the path on the left and 500m – 1/4 mile further on a path through a pine forest and acacia copse. On descending, the path opens facing Labeaume. Description p 121.*

Michelin map 🔳 folds 11 and 12 or 🔳 fold 16 or 🔳 fold 25 – Local map p 112
Plan of built-up area in the Michelin Red Guide France

A resplendent Avignon. – City of art and culture, the metropolis of the Vaucluse region spreads along the banks of the Rhône River. Peppered with bell towers emerging amidst a carpet of pink roofs, the city is surrounded by ramparts and dominated by Doms Rock, on which lies, majestically, the cathedral and Palace of the Popes. It is from the City of the Cardinals, Villeneuve-lès-Avignon, across the way, that Avignon should be admired, especially at sunset.

The bustling atmosphere, which pervades the city, is due, for the most part, to the annual **Dramatic Arts Festival** (festival annuel d'Art dramatique) founded in 1947 by Jean Vilar (1912-71; actor and director). Attracting a cosmopolitan crowd flocking here from the whole of Europe, the festival is the source of a cultural explosion to which other Provençal towns modelled themselves after. Aside from the great theatrical events, a number of manifestations, which tend to recall the popular pageants of the Middle Ages, illustrate the different art mediums (dance, music, films...). They make use of the enchanting historical monuments, which are a hive of activity, and overflow into the street, where a festive atmosphere is much in evidence. The city has adapted and acquired appropriate cultural facilities: Conference Centre (in the Palace of the Popes), Petit Palais, Livrée Ceccano...

Due to its administrative (*Préfecture* of Vaucluse) and cultural functions, Avignon is essentially concerned with tertiary activities. Already placed at the head of an important agricultural region – Comtat Venaissin – the city is equally developing a number of commercial and industrial activities (chemicals, fertilisers, ceramics, foodstuffs) concentrated east of town (Le Pontet, Montfavet and airport).

19C Avignon

HISTORICAL NOTES

Before the popes. – The presence of man has been noted on and around Doms Rock since the Neolithic Era (4000BC). In the 6 or 5C BC; the Massalians *(qv)* founded a settlement establishing Avignon as a river port; it began to flourish. On becoming a Gallo-Roman settlement with a Gallic then Roman code of law, the town developed and prospered; unfortunately there remain but a few ruins of the monuments which embellished ·it (in the area around Place de l'Horloge, which covers the forum).

Following the invasions of the 5C, Avignon fell into obscurity through the early Middle Ages. We do know, however, that Avignon took sides with the Arabs and that it was, thus, pillaged by Charles Martel's soldiers in 737. The rebirth occurred in the 11C and more so in the 12C. Avignon profited from the feudal rivalries taking place between the Houses of Toulouse and Barcelona to protect and reinforce its independence: like its Italian counterparts, Avignon formed a small city state. Its commitment in favour of the Albigensians brought about royal reprisals: in 1226, Louis VIII seized the town ordering it to raze its defences. Nevertheless, Avignon rose again quite quickly, and, inspite of losing its independence, acquired prosperity once again under the rule of the House of Anjou.

The popes at Avignon. – Avignon's destiny changed in the early 14C with the exile of the pontifical court in France which brought it a century of brilliance.

The court in Rome had become more or less impossible for the popes, who were incessantly the object of political differences. The Frenchman Bertrand de Got (former archbishop of Bordeaux), elected pope under the name of **Clement V** (1305) decided under pressure by Philip the Fair (who thought that he would make the pope a docile instrument of his wishes) to establish the court in France, where the Holy Seat possessed (since 1274) the Comtat Venaissin *(qv)*. Clement V solemnly entered Avignon – belonging to the Count of Provence – on 9 March 1309. However, he did not reside here permanently as he preferred the calm of Groseau Priory, near Malaucène or Monteux Castle, not far from Carpentras. He died in 1314 and the conclave was unable to find a successor.

Finally in 1316, the former bishop of Avignon, Jacques Duèse, an old man of 72 was elected. Pope **John XXII** settled in the episcopal palace located south of the cathedral; **Benedict XII**, a former Cistercian monk, established the court in a place worthy of it. **Clement VI** purchased Avignon from Queen Joan I of Sicily *(qv)*, countess of Provence in 1348 for 80 000 florins.

Babylonian captivity. – From 1309-77, seven French popes succeeded each other at Avignon: Clement V (1304-14), John XXII (1316-35), Benedict XII (1335-42), Clement VI (1342-52), Innocent VI (1352-62), Urban V (1362-70) and Gregory XI (1370-8).

The pontifical and cardinal courts lived on a grand scale; in their wake evolved a crowd of foreigners, ecclesiastics, artists, pilgrims, litigants and merchants. The university, founded in 1303 by Boniface VIII, counted thousands of students. The town was transformed: everywhere sprouted convents, churches and chapels, not to mention the splendid cardinals' palaces, *livrées (p 193)*, while the pontifical palace was always being enlarged and embellished. Avignon looked like a vast construction site. The pope wanted to be considered like the most powerful ruler in the world. His wealth and munificence shone brilliantly attracting the notice of the envious, which was why he lived in a fortress and established a line of fortifications to protect the town from the mercenary soldiers, who pillaged the country under war. These soldiers descended upon the city several times; each time the pope had to buy their departure for a very large sum of money: 40 000 écus in 1310, 100 000 écus in 1365. And yet life in Avignon remained pleasant: liberty and prosperity existed and a sign that never failed, the population increased from 5 000 to 40 000. An asylum for political refugees like Petrarch *(qv)*, the pontifical city also housed a Jewish community. But this tolerance extended, unfortunately, to adventurers, escaped criminals, smugglers and counterfeiters, who frequented taverns and brothels, which cropped up everywhere, working their way through itinerant merchants and onlookers. The Italians vituperated against the court at Avignon and declared the pontifical court's years of exile as the Second Babylonian Captivity. The poet **Petrarch** exclaimed passionately for the return of the Holy Seat to Rome and launched violent abuse against Avignon.

Tottering under the mass of criticisms and scourges of time (marauding soldiers, plague), the popes thought of returning to Rome. **Urban V** left for the eternal city in 1367 but had to return after 3 years due to the hostilities occurring in Italy. **Gregory XI**, convinced by St Catherine of Siena, finally left Avignon in September 1376 displeasing the king of France. His death in 1378 created the Great Schism of the West.

Popes and anti-popes. – The cardinals (majority French) of the Sacred College hostile to the reforms of the Italian Pope Urban VI, successor to Gregory XI, elected another pope **Clement VII** (1378-94) who returned to Avignon. The Great Schism divided the Christian world; the Avignon pope was recognised mainly in France. Popes and anti-popes mutually excommunicated each other and attempted by any means possible to down the other. They vied with each other for the papacy's vast resources of wealth, which included parts of shares of money collected from various benefices and tithes, taxes paid by the litigants to the pontifical court, sale of position, bulls, etc. and finally, on a scale which expanded daily, the traffic of indulgences. **Benedict XIII** (1394-1409) succeeded Clement VII, however, he no longer had the support of the king of France. He fled Avignon in 1403, yet his followers resisted in the palace until 1411. The Great Schism finally ended in 1417 with the election of Martin V.

At the same time life continued in Avignon as suggests the presentation of the *mystère* (mystery plays dramatised an episode in the Scriptures) during Whitsun in 1400 with huge tableaux vivants and processions which went on for 3 days and dramatised the Passion of Christ. The modern festivals *(see Principal Festivals pp 199-200)* preponderent in and around Avignon recall this medieval tradition.

The city of penitent brotherhoods. – Appearing as early as the 13C, the penitent brotherhoods were at their peak in the 16 and 17C. The brothers were to help each other mutually, do public penitence and perform good deeds. The brotherhood they belonged to was identified by the colour of their sackcloth and the hood which covered their heads during processions. Avignon was a city where many different brotherhoods – grey, white, blue, black, purple and red – existed. The White Penitents were the most aristocratic and included among their brothers Charles IX and Henri III. Each brotherhood had assets and a chapel: a number of these chapels are still standing (the most interesting are those of the Grey Penitents and Black Penitents). During the Revolution they were disbanded and yet several brotherhoods did survive.

Avignon at the time of the legates. – Until the Revolution, Avignon was governed by a legate and a vice-legate of the pope. It was a period of ease, of liberty which became licence. This friendly, hospitable city remained a centre of art and culture: publishing was flourishing in the 18C, during the time when the now famous Aubanel *(qv)* dynasty appeared. Tolerance toward the Jews was respected even though some persecution occurred. Located in a ghetto, which was locked every night, the Jews of the pope had to wear a yellow cap, pay dues, listen to sermons preached to convert them, were not allowed to mix with Christians, and only occupy certain jobs; even more they were watched.

Avignon society was a society of contrast: the gulf between the wealthy and poor was as great as was the confrontation which occurred between them from 1652-9. When the Revolution broke out Avignon was split between the partisans wanting to belong to France and those who wanted the pontifical state maintained. The former won and on 14 September 1791, the constitutional assembly voted the union of the Comtat Venaissin to France.

★★★THE PALACE OF THE POPES (Le Palais des Papes) (BY) *time: 1 hour*

Ⓥ The palace is a veritable maze of galleries, chambers, chapels and passages, today empty and deserted. That is why the visitor must try to imagine what it was like at the time of the popes... Its luxurious furnishings, sumptuously painted decoration, the soundless coming and goings of the prelates and servants, the changing of the guards in dress uniform, the cardinals, princes and ambassadors arriving and departing, the pilgrims gathered in the courtyard waiting to receive the pope's benediction or to see him leave on his white mule; the litigants and magistrates creating commotion around the pontifical court...

The construction. – This princely residence counts among the largest of its time with an area of 15 000m² – 2.6 acres. Fortress and palace at the same time, it is made up of two buildings joined together: the Old Palace to the north and the New Palace to the south; its construction lasted 30 years. The Cistercian, Benedict XII, brought up in contempt of luxury, had the old episcopal palace razed and entrusted to his compatriot Pierre Poisson, from Mirepoix, the task of building a vast residence which would lend itself to prayer and be well-defended: the Old Palace, thus acquired the appearance of an austere fortress.

Planned around cloisters, its four wings are flanked by towers, the most powerful of which, the north tower, Trouillas Tower (Tour de Trouillas) was used as a keep and prison. Clement VI, a great prince of the church, artist and prodigy, ordered Jean de Louvres, an architect from Ile de France to carry out the expansion of the palace. The Wardrobe Tower and two new buildings closed off the Great Courtyard, which preceded Benedict XII's palace.

The exterior was not modified. However, inside a team of artists directed by Simone Martini and then Matteo Giovanetti sumptuously decorated the different rooms and notably the pope's private apartments. The works continued under Clement VI's successors: Innocent VI had St Lawrence Tower to the south and La Gache Tower to the west built and the decorating completed (fresco on the vault in the Great Audience Chamber); Urban V had the Great Courtyard with its well arranged and had constructed several buildings linking the palace to the gardens, created behind the Angels' Tower. In 1398 and again from 1410-1, the palace was under siege resulting in the deterioration of the buildings. Allocated to the legates in 1433, it was restored in 1516 but continued to deteriorate. In a bad state when the Revolution broke out, it was pillaged: furniture dispersed, statues and sculptures broken. In 1791 the Latrines Tower (or Ice-House Tower) was the scene of a bloody episode: 60 imprisoned counter-revolutionaries were massacred and the bodies hurled to the bottom of the tower. The palace owes its survival only to its transformation into a prison and barracks (1810). Occupied by the military engineers, it was again mistreated: at least the statutory wash on the walls protected some of the mural paintings. Unfortunately, in many places, this safeguard was too late: the soldiers had the time to cut the protective coating off these frescoes and to sell the pieces to collectors or antique dealers from Avignon. Evacuated in 1906 the palace has been under restoration ever since.

Exterior. – The Palace of the Popes, from the outside, has the appearance of a citadel built straight out of the living rock. Its walls, flanked by 10 large square towers, some of which are more than 50m – 164ft high, are buttressed by huge depressed arches holding up the machicolations: this is one of the first known examples of such military architecture. Built into the living rock, it was naturally sheltered from sapping and mining.

A better idea of the palace's height can be had from the narrow and picturesque Rue Peyrollerie, which begins at the southwest corner of the palace and passes under the enormous buttress which supports the Clementine Chapel.

Enter the palace through the Champeaux Gate.

Ground floor (Old Palace)

Go through the Champeaux Gate, topped by two turrets (rebuilt in 1933), and the modern coat of arms of Clement VI and enter the former guard room (waiting room), the walls of which are decorated with 17C paintings (1). Skirt the Conclave Wing (**A**), which now holds the Conference Centre, and enter the Old Palace as far as the Consistory.

Consistory. – To debate the great theories of Christianity, the pope and his cardinals met in council in this vast rectangular hall which burned down in 1413. It was here that the pope announced the name of the newly appointed cardinals, received in great pomp the sovereigns and their ambassadors, the Papal Nuncios reported on their mission and where the cases proposed for canonisation were examined. Exhibited in here are the **frescoes** of **Simone Martini** which were brought from the porch of Notre-Dame-des-Doms Cathedral *(p 77)*. Native of Siena, Simone Martini is considered the most illustrious of the 14C Italian painters, with Giotto.

St John's or Consistory Chapel. – This oratory is adorned with lovely frescoes painted by Matteo Giovanetti from 1346-8 and depicting the lives of the two Saint Johns': Saint John the Baptist and Saint John the Evangelist. From Viterbo in Latium, Matteo Giovanetti can be considered Clement VI's official court painter.

Adjacent to the Consistory was Jesus's Room, under which was the very important Treasury. There, and in the basement of the Angels' Tower, were kept the sacks of gold and silver, gold pieces and the prize ornaments; in closets fixed to the walls were stored the account books, the archives. The wealth of the popes was considerable; a building like the Avignon palace, built in less than 20 years proves it. John XXII, from Cahors *(see Michelin Green Guide to Dordogne)* willed to his inheritors, after 19 years of papal reign, 24 million ducats.

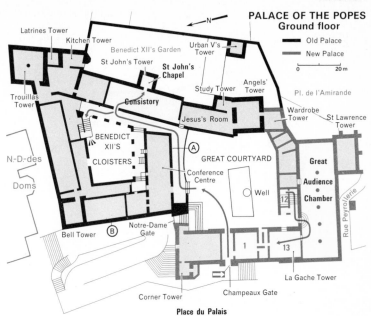

PALACE OF THE POPES
Ground floor

■■ Old Palace
■■ New Palace

0   20 m

Place du Palais

The importance of the pope's income explains why the highest dignitary of the court was the chamberlain, Minister of Finance, who was seconded only by the treasurer, the other very important person.

Next to the Angels' Tower, which housed the library on the 4th floor, was the Wardrobe Tower (New Palace), built by Clement VI because the austerity of Benedict XII's (his predecessor) apartments displeased him. On the ground floor was the bathroom; and the upper two storeys, adorned with coats of arms, contained the pontifical wardrobe.

The gardens planted in terraces on the palace's east side allowed the pope to take some air without leaving the palace.

First floor (Old and New Palace)

On leaving the Consistory, follow the lower gallery of Benedict XII's cloisters and take the staircase to the banqueting hall. Fine view of the Staff Wing **(B)** – where the staff (persons in charge of various functions) and the main servants, were lodged – the Bell Tower and Benedict XII's Chapel.

Banqueting Hall or Grand Tinel. – In this hall, one of the largest in the palace (48m – 157ft long and 10.25m – 33ft wide) is exhibited a superb series of 18C Gobelins **tapestries**. The immense panelled keel vaulted roof (in the form of a ship's hull) was restored. Continue into the upper kitchen (2) with its huge chimney in the form of an octagonal pyramid, located on the topmost floor of the Kitchen Tower. This tower was also used as the pantry and provisions store room. Next to it, the Latrines Tower (or Ice-House Tower) offered on each floor common latrines for the soldiers and staff. It included a 22m – 72ft pit where rainwater and used kitchen water were also directed; a main drain pipe took all the waste to a river which flowed into the Rhône. During a siege, the soldiers courageously went up the drain pipe, crossed the pit and appeared suddenly amidst the camp of defending soldiers.

In the Latrines Tower's pit, buried under a blanket of quick-lime for one month, were the bodies of the 60 political prisoners, who were imprisoned in the castle and killed in 1791. The bodies were pulled out by a crack made at the pit's bottom. As from the Consistory you go into St John's Chapel, here from the Banqueting Hall (which is above it) you go into St Martial's Chapel.

St Martial's Chapel. – This oratory is named after the **frescoes** of St Martial (apostle from the Limousin, Clement VI's native land) painted in 1344-5 by Matteo Giovanetti. They recount the life of the saint using a harmony of blues, greys and browns.

Robing Room. – Next to his room, this, the pope's antechamber, was used as a small audience chamber where those who had been accorded a private interview with the pope waited. Two 18C Gobelin tapestries hang on the walls.

Beside the Robing Room stands the Study Tower: on its 1st floor is Benedict XII's personal study (3) with magnificent tiles. Along the west wall of the Robing Room was the pope's personal dining room (4) or Petit Tinel and along side it was the kitchen (or secret kitchen) (5); these rooms were entirely destroyed in 1810.

Papal Bedchamber (6). – The walls of this room were richly painted against a blue background: birds entwined in vines and squirrels climbing oak trees. Designed in the window embrasures were exotic birdcages with open doors. The floor tiles of medieval inspiration have been recently restored. The decoration of this room dates most likely from the reign of Clement VI, replacing the more severe decoration of Benedict XII.

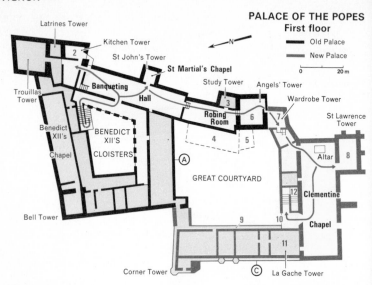

PALACE OF THE POPES
First floor

Latrines Tower
Kitchen Tower
St John's Tower
St Martial's Chapel
Study Tower
Angels' Tower
Wardrobe Tower
Banqueting Hall
Trouillas Tower
Robing Room
St Lawrence Tower
Benedict XII's Chapel
BENEDICT XII'S CLOISTERS
Altar
GREAT COURTYARD
Clementine
Bell Tower
Chapel
Corner Tower
La Gache Tower

■ Old Palace
■ New Palace
0   20 m

Stag Room (7). – This room is Clement VI's study, decorated with elegant **frescoes** painted in 1343 probably by Robin de Romans but under the direction of Matteo Giovanetti. The subjects illustrated are profane against a verdant background: hunting, fishing, fruit and flower picking and bathing scenes. The ceiling in larch wood is wonderfully ornate. This intimate and gay room had two windows: one offered a fine view of Avignon and the other overlooked the gardens. Above it was St Michael's Oratory, which at one time had been adorned with frescoes by Matteo Giovanetti; there remain but a few traces in red chalk.

Clementine, Grand or Clement VI Chapel. – It contains a pontifical altar which was largely restored (a part of it is authentic). The flat proportions of the nave – 15m – 49ft wide, 52m – 171ft long and only 19m – 62ft high – are due to the fact that the chapel's construction was decided afterwards: the architect had to cover the whole width of the Great Audience chamber without exceeding the average height of the castle.

South of the pontifical altar, the St Lawrence Tower contains the south sacristy (8) or Re-Robing, where the pope changed vestments when officiating a high mass. It contains the castings of the popes' recumbent figures: Clement V, Clement VI, Innocent VI and Urban V.

In this chapel, the Conclave of cardinals came to hear the Mass of the Holy Spirit before returning to the Conclave wing **(A)** via a narrow passageway called Conclave Gallery (9), the vaulting of which is a masterpiece. The doors closed behind them and did not open again until they had elected a pope with a 2/3 majority vote. The **Conclave** was made up of the college of cardinals, who met 10 days after the death of the pope, to elect a successor. To receive the cardinals the 1st floor of the Old Palace was used; and to isolate them from the rest of the world all the doors and windows were blocked up 8m – 26ft high. Some of the rooms were divided into individual cells for the cardinals; others housed the numerous domestics who assisted them. This tradition goes back to the 13C when at the death of Pope Clement IV in 1268 the cardinals were unable to decide upon a successor. Three years later the pope had still not been elected. The people, locked them up in an area reserved for the vote and freed them only after the election of the new pope had taken place. Thus the word *conclave* means under lock and key.

From the loggia window, Indulgence Window (10), which is across from the chapel's main door, the pope would bless the crowds, below. To the left of this window is a wing of the palace (the façade of which gives onto the court), the said High Dignitaries wing **(C)** where the chamberlain (11) and treasurer resided.

Ground floor (New Palace)

Go down the Great Staircase (12) the right flight of stairs is covered with pointed vaulting, which suggests a daring architectural feat for the time.

Great Audience Chamber. – This is a magnificent room with two naves divided by a line of columns upon which fall the pointed arches of the vaulting. This is also called the Palace of the Great Causes as it was here that the 13 ecclesiastical judges formed the Tribunal de la Rota – *rota* comes from the circular bench (*rota* means wheel) on which they throned and which is located in the room's last east bay. Around the judges sat the lawyers and the papal court's public servants. The rest of the room was for the public; seating ran along the whole of the room's wall. On the vaulting against a dark blue background sprinkled with stars is the fresco of the Prophets painted in 1352 by Matteo Giovanetti.

Small Audience Chamber (13). – Held in the Small Audience Chamber or contradictions was a law court made up of one judge. Before this one judge, the lawyers presented their "contradictions" or causes that arose during the Tribunal de la Rota. In the 17C, when this room was used as the arsenal, the vaulting was adorned with grisaille paintings, representing military trophies. Cross through the guard room to leave the palace by Champeaux Gate.

PLACE DU PALAIS (BY 38) *time: 2 hours*

Mint (Hôtel des Monnaies) (B). – This 17C *hôtel* (now the Conservatory of Music), with its crowning balustrade, presents an ornately carved **façade★** of dragons, eagles, Borghese coat of arms, cherubs and swags of fruit.

Notre-Dame-des-Doms Cathedral (Cathédrale N.-D.-des-Doms). – Built in the mid-12C, the cathedral was damaged many times and each time rebuilt and altered. Pillaged during the Revolution, it began worship services again in 1822.
In the 15C the large bell tower was rebuilt from the 1st floor and since 1859 a very tall statue of the Virgin crowns it. A plain lantern tower crowns the bay preceding the chancel.
Added in the late 12C in the Ancient style, the porch shelters two tympana (a semi-circular one surmounted by a triangular one) once magnificently decorated with frescoes by Simone Martini and now located in the Palace of the Popes *(p 74)*. On the north side, on entering, the 15C St John the Baptist Chapel contains a fine 16C Christ (Ecce Homo) in painted stone.
The sole nave with five bays is roofed with pointed barrel vaulting; the Romanesque appearance of the building was tempered by the addition of side chapels (14-17C), the reconstruction of the apse and the construction of baroque galleries in the 17C. The Romanesque **dome★** that covers the transept crossing is remarkable: to reduce the area, the master craftsman created a series of projections upon which were supported the dome and its elegant columned lantern.
On entering the chancel, on the left, stands a fine 12C white marble episcopal throne; on its sides, are carved animals symbolising St Mark (lion) and St Luke (ox). In the chapel adjoining the sacristy is set the Flamboyant Gothic tomb of Pope John XXII, the recumbent figure of which was lost during the Revolution and replaced by a bishop.

★★**Doms Rock (Rocher des Doms)**. – An elegantly planted garden of different species has been arranged on this bluff. From the terraces superb **views★★** can be had of the Rhône and St-Bénézet Bridge, Villeneuve-lès-Avignon with Philip the Fair's Tower and St-André Fort, the Dentelles de Montmirail, Mount Ventoux, Vaucluse Plateau, Luberon Range and the Alpilles. Viewing table.

★★**Petit Palais**. – This was formerly Cardinal Arnaud de Via's *livrée* before being Ⓥ bought by the pope in 1335 to install the bishopric. The building deteriorated during the different sieges brought upon the Palace of the Popes, had to be repaired and transformed in the late 15C, especially by Cardinal della Rovere, who subsequently became Pope Julius II.
Famous guests resided here: Cesare Borgia in 1498, François I in 1533, Anne of Austria and duke of Orléans in 1660 during Louis XIV's visit to Avignon.

Gallery 1. – This vast pointed barrel vaulted chamber contains **Romanesque and Gothic sculpture** (capitals, statues, etc...); 15C chimney. On the walls there are parts of 14C **frescoes** originally from a cardinal's palace.

Gallery 2. – This, the former bishops' chapel, with pointed vaulting, presents a sculpture collection which comes from the monumental **tomb of Cardinal de Lagrange** built in the late 14C in the chancel of St-Martial d'Avignon Collegiate Church. Note especially the carved figure (at the back of the room) which formed the tomb's base; the realism of the emaciated cadaver anticipates the macabre representations of the 15 and 16C.
Galleries 3 to 16 house an exceptional group of Italian paintings (13-16C) which were part of the collection of the 19C Italian, Gian Pietro, Marquess **Campana di Cavelli**, whose interest became an aquisitive obsession to which he sacrificed his personal fortune. Bankrupt, he was tried, convicted of embezzlement and sentenced to 20 years in the galleys. Napoleon III came to his rescue by buying the entire collection amounting to some 15 000 objects to form the nucleus of a museum he was planning in Paris on the model of the newly founded Victoria and Albert Museum in London. Nothing came of the idea; the collection was dispersed throughout the different French museums after 1870 and only now have the early paintings been reunited. Campana lived out the rest of his life in exile from Italy (d 1880).

Gallery 3. – Tuscany, Rimini, Bologna, Venice 1310-70. The works of the 13C betray the Byzantine influence still very acute (fragment of a Crucifix by **Berlinghieri** and Last Supper by the **Master of the Madeleine**). The intense artistic activity of the 14C is illustrated by the works of the **Master of 1310** (a large *Virgin in Majesty* in the centre of the room), the **Master of Figline** *(God the Father Blessing)*, **Taddeo Gaddi** *(Virgin and Child)* and **Paolo Veneziano** *(Virgin and Child)*.
These paintings adorned church altars; the polyptychs were assembled in a richly gilt decoration of Gothic architecture.

Gallery 4. – Tuscany (Siena, Pisa, Lucca) and Liguria (Genoa) 1350-1420. The Siennese School (to which belonged Simone Martini, the painter of the Palace of the Popes) shines by the wealth of ornamental decoration, its finely executed graphics and the beauty of its models, especially visible, for example, in the works of **Taddeo di Bartolo** *(Virgin and Child)*. It influenced the neighbouring cities, notably Pisa with **Cecco di Pietro** *(St Peter, St John the Baptist, St Nicholas and St Bartholomew)*.

Galleries 5 and 6. – Florence 1370-1420. The Florentine School was very prolific and was inspired by Giotto, as suggests the work of the **Master of St Verdiana** (triptych of the *Virgin and Child* between several saints). The international Gothic style, characterised by a certain realistic naturalism is represented by **Lorenzo Monaco** and **Gherardo Starnina** (Angel and Virgin of the Annunciation).

Gallery 7. – Venice 1370-1470.

Gallery 8. – 15C Italy: Bologna, Umbria, Marches, Lombardy, Siena. The works of art exhibited in this room offer different facets of the international Gothic style outside of Tuscany and Venice; **Pietro di Domenico da Montepulciano's** *Virgin of Mercy,* **Antonio Alberti's** *Virgin and Child between St Dominic and St Madeleine* and **Giovanni di Paolo's** triptych of the Nativity.

Gallery 9. – Florence and Tuscany, Perugia 1420-90.

Gallery 10. – This room contains documents on the history of the museum and the Campana collection.

Gallery 11. – Florence, Umbria 1450-1500. Florence, capital of the Renaissance, stays attentive to the form of the drawing in the balanced compositions where perspective plays an important role, especially with **Bartolomeo della Gatta** *(Annunciation).* **Botticelli,** the master, introduces, in the late 15C, a new dimension at the same time lyrical and mystical; *Virgin and Child* is a masterpiece.

Gallery 12. – Padua, Venice, Marches 1440-90. Note the violently expressionist *Calvary,* attributed to **Ludovico Urbani** and the four figures of saints by **Carlo Crivelli.**

Gallery 13. – Italy mid-15 to early 16C. Assembled in this room are varied works of differing style and inspiration: *Abduction of Helen of Troy* by **Liberale da Verona** and the altarpiece by **Giovanni Massone** ordered by Della Rovere and works by **Louis Bréa,** the painter from Nice.

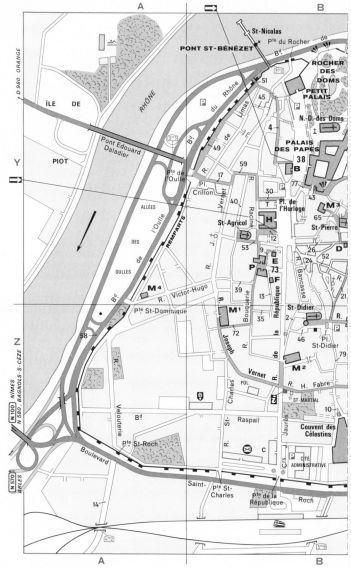

AVIGNON

Gallery 14. – Florence and Lucca 1470-1500.

Gallery 15. – Florence and its surroundings *c*1500. The Renaissance rediscovers Antiquity exemplified by the **Master of the Cassoni Campana's** four panels depicting episodes of Greek mythology.

Gallery 16. – Italy 15-16C. Of note are: the large Florentine altarpiece of the Crowning of the Virgin by **Ridolfo Ghirlandaio,** an *Adoration of the Magi* by **Johannes Hispanus** in which an eleborate landscape of trees and castles appears and a *Calvary with St Jerome* by **Marco Palmezzo**.

Galeries 17, 18 and 19. – These galleries are devoted to the painting and sculpture of the Avignon School. The Avignon School, because of its monumental simplicity of composition, its sculptural force and the importance of light played in these compositions can be placed mid-way between the realism of the Flemish School and the stylisation of the Italian Schools. **Enguerrand Quarton,** painter of the *Coronation of the Virgin* preserved in the Municipal Museum *(p 195)* in Villeneuve-lès-Avignon and the *Pietà* in the Louvre, is represented here by the significant Requin altarpiece (1450-5). **Josse Lieferinxe** (panels of the altarpiece of the Virgin) is later, at the end of the 15C. From the early 16C, note the two anonymous works: *Deposition of the Cross* from Barbentane *(qv)* and an admirable *Adoration of the Child*. On either side of a remarkable *Virgin of Pity* (1457) stand the works of **Jean de la Huerta** *(St Lazarus and St Marthe)* and **Antoine le Moiturier** *(Angels)*.

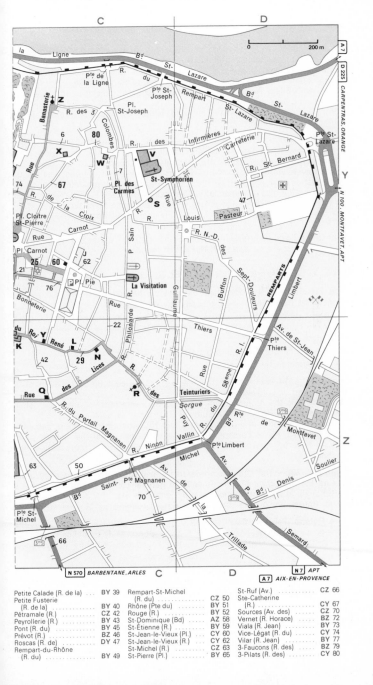

BALANCE QUARTER (BY) *time: 3/4 hour*

The gipsies lived in this area in the 19C and it was completely renovated in the 1970s. It descends as far as the ramparts and the bridge of the French song: *Pont d'Avignon.*

Start at Place du Palais, on level with the Mint, and take Rue de la Balance.

Rue de la Balance (4). – This is the Balance Quarter's main street. Lined up on one side are old restored *hôtels* with elegant façades, decorated with mullioned windows; while on the other side are modern buildings Mediterranean in style, with small flower-decked patios above arcaded luxury shops.

★★St-Bénézet Bridge (Pont St-Bénézet). – In reality St-Bénézet's Bridge was a narrow bridge – a bridge for people on foot or on horseback; it was never one on which one could dance in a ring *(tous en rond)* – the dancing took place on the island in midstream (*sur* means on; *sous* means underneath), in other words not:

Sur le pont d'Avignon
but *Sous le pont d'Avignon*
On y danse, tous en rond

Spanning over two arms of the Rhône to Villeneuve-lès-Avignon at the base of Philip the Fair's Tower, the bridge was 900m – 2 953ft long and composed of 22 arches. Another gatehouse guarded the bridge on the Avignon side but surrounded by modern buildings it is barely visible: on one of the bridge's piers stands the **Chapel of St-Nicolas** consisting of two superimposed sanctuaries one Romanesque and the other Gothic.

Legend has it that in 1177, a young shepherd boy, Bénézet, was commanded by voices from heaven to build a bridge across the river at a spot indicated by an angel. Everyone thought him crazy until he "proved" that he was inspired by miraculously lifting a huge block of stone. Volunteers appeared, and formed themselves into a **Bridge Brotherhood** (Frères Pontifes) funds flowed in and in eleven years construction was complete.

Rebuilt from 1234-7, the bridge was restored in the 15C and then broken by the flooded Rhône in the mid-17C.

★Ramparts (Remparts). – 4.3km – 2 3/4 miles long the actual fortifications were built in the 14C by the popes. From a military standpoint this is not a first class work. It was backwards in comparison with the defence procedures of the preceding century: the towers were open to the town, part of the walls had no machicolations. In fact the popes had not built an ultimate defence but a preliminary obstacle against attack on the palace. Viollet-le-Duc last century restored the southern section but was unable to re-establish the moats where the Sorgue River branched off. In any case the most interesting part is along the Rue du Rempart-du-Rhône to the pleasant Place Crillon.

Return to the Place de l'Horloge via Rue St-Etienne bordered by old town houses, Rue Racine to the right and Rue Molière to the left.

CHURCHES, MUSEUMS, HÔTELS... *time: 3 hours*

Place de l'Horloge (BY). – The theatre and town hall overlook this vast square shaded by plane trees and in part occupied by open-air cafés.

Town hall (Hôtel de Ville) (BY H). – Built in the 19C, it includes the 14 and 15C **Clock Tower** (Tour de l'Horloge). This former belfry, all that remains of the Gothic period, contains a Jack.

Take the Rue Félicien-David and go around St-Agricol's east end.
Note the Gallo-Roman rampart ruins.

St-Agricol (BY). – 14-16C. A large staircase leads to the church's parvis overlooked by a finely carved 15C façade.

In the tympanum is the Annunciation: the kneeling Virgin receives the angel while God the Father sends her the Holy Spirit. A 15C Virgin is on the pier.

Inside there are a number of works of art: a mid-15C white marble stoup, paintings by Nicolas Mignard, Pierre Parrocel and in the south aisle, near the sacristy door, the Doni altarpiece, a work in stone by Boachon (1525) representing the Annunciation.

Rue Viala (BY 73). – The street is bordered by two 18C *hôtels* facing each other and housing the *Préfecture* (P) offices and the general council of the *département* (Conseil Général): to the north is the Hôtel de Forbin de Ste-Croix, formerly a school (Collège du Roure), and to the south is the Hôtel Desmarez de Montdevergues.

Le Roure Palace (Palais du Roure) (BY E). – *3 Rue du Collège-du-Roure.* This is the former residence of Baroncelli-Javon *(qv).* A decoration of leafy branches frames the doorway. It houses the Flandreysy-Espérandieu Foundation, a centre of Provençal studies.

Hôtel de Sade (BY F). – *5 Rue Dorée.* This 16C mansion contains the offices of the Vaucluse *département.* Elegant mullioned windows overlook the street. In the courtyard a fine pentagonal turreted staircase.

To get to the Calvet Museum use Rues Bouquerie and Horace-Vernet.

★Calvet Museum (Musée Calvet) (BZ M¹). – The museum, the product of Esprit Calvet, a doctor, who bequeathed his collections and library to his native town, is in a fine 18C mansion with 3 rooms, an entrance hall, stairwell and small room, the so-called *méridienne.*

The charming decoration includes original woodwork and stucco as well as old furnishings. Aside from the German, Spanish, Flemish, Dutch and Italian Schools, there is a fine selection of paintings from the 16-19C French and Avignon Schools: Corneille de Lyon, Simon de Châlons, Nicolas Mignard, Pierre Parrocel, Le Nain, Subleyras, Joseph Vernet (Seascapes), Hubert Robert (the follow-up of the 4 Seasons), David, Géricault, Chassériau *(Sleeping Nymph)*, Corot, Daumier, Manet, Toulouse-Lautrec *(Manon, Here is the Sun)*.

In the modern art gallery note the works of Utrillo *(The Lapin Agile)*, Vlaminck, Dufy, Soutine *(Old Man, Provençal Landscape)*, Modigliani, Gleizes and Baboulène.

On the left, there is a room which contains a number of **wrought-iron pieces,** some of which, from the 14 and 15C, previously ornamented some Avignon houses. In the room adjoining are a remarkable **collection of Greek sculpture** (funerary stelae, votive reliefs) as well as Greek and Italiot vases. Also included are an interesting series of Etruscan funerary urns; Roman and Greco-Roman antiquities, statues and reliefs.

On the next floor two levels of attractively presented galleries display a large **collection of local prehistory** grouped according to their site; note the tools and bones excavated from the Vallonet site (1 million years) and the anthropomorphic stelae (Copper Age).

Requien Museum (Muséum Requien). – Located next to the Calvet Museum. This museum was named after the great Avignon naturalist Esprit Requien (1788-1851). It contains a very important natural history library, a herbarium with more than 200 000 specimens brought from the world over, and a local geological, zoological and botanical collection.

Rue Joseph-Vernet (BYZ). – This long street, established on the site of the 13C ramparts (razed after the siege of 1226), is lined with a number of fine 17 and 18C *hôtels* (nos 58, 83 and 87). It opens out across from the tourist information centre and the public gardens and runs into Cours Jean-Jaurès to the south and Rue de la République to the north.

Rue de la République (BYZ). – Very animated and commercial main street.

★**Lapidary Museum (Musée lapidaire)** (BZ M²). – Located in the former chapel of the 17C Jesuit College, this building with its unique nave, flanked by side galleries, presents a fine baroque façade. It contains sculpture and stone carvings representing the different civilisations which have left their mark on the region: a Celtic-Ligurain bestiary, particularly the Tarasque monster *(qv)* from Noves, the ruins of a triumphal arch (from Avignon), fragments of mosaics, numerous Greco-Roman (Bacchus), Gallic (warriors from Vachères and Mondragon) and Roman (Venus of Pourrières) statuary. Several portraits of emperors (Marcus Aurelius, Tiberius), people and low reliefs (relief of Cabrières d'Aigues representing a towing scene), sarcophagi and a remarkable series of masks from Vaison are also worth noting.

> *Go backs towards the tourist information centre bear left on Rue Henri-Fabre which goes into Rue des Lices.*

In Rue Henri-Fabre stands the former Abbey of St-Martial built from 1378-88.

Rue des Lices (BCZ). – As its name indicates *(lice* means ward or bailey), this street traces the 13C curtain wall. On the left are the 18C buildings of the former almshouse (CZ **Q**) with its façade divided into galleried storeys; it houses the Fine Arts School. Next to it is the Chapel of the Verbe-Incarné by J.-B. Franque.

> *At the end of the street bear right on Rue des Teinturiers.*

Rue des Teinturiers (CDZ). – The picturesque cobbled street shaded with plane trees follows the course of the Sorgue River, the waters of which were used by the clothdyers (after whom the street is named). Several of the large paddle-wheels, which were used by the printed calico manufacturers to make fine shawls until the end of the 19C, can still be seen. On the right is located the Franciscan's bell tower all that remains of a convent where Petrarch's Laura *(qv)* may have been buried.

Grey Penitents Chapel (Chapelle des Pénitents Gris) **(R)**. – *No 8.* A small bridge leads to this 16C chapel rearranged in the 19C. It contains paintings by Nicolas Mignard, Pierre Parrocel and Simon de Chalons. Above the altar is a fine 17C gold glory from Peru.

A 15C house at no 26 has kept its crenellations and battlemented corner turret.

> *Turn around and walk back as far as Rue de la Masse.*

Rue de la Masse (CZ 29). – At no 36 is the Hôtel de Salvan Isoard **(N)**, a 17C mansion with ornately carved window surrounds; and at no 19 Hôtel Salvador **(L)** is an impressive 18C square mansion.

Rue du Roi-René (BCZ). – At the corner of Rue Grirolas stands the **house of King René** (CZ **Y**), where the king lived during his visits to Avignon; it has since been subjected to numerous transformations.

Further on four 17 and 18C *hôtels* form a remarkable **group★ (K)**.

The Hôtels d'Honorati (no 10) and de Jonquerettes (no 12) are bare of decoration except for their pediments which are triangular or basket handle.

The Hôtel Berton de Crillon (no 7) is emblasoned with portrait medallions, masks, flower, garlands and adorned with a wrought iron balcony; in the inner courtyard is a grand staircase with a stone balustrade.

Across from it at no 8 is the Hôtel de Fortia de Montréal, less ornate with pediments over grotesques.

St-Didier (BZ). – This 14C church is in the purest Provençal style *(qv)* with a pentagonal apse and single nave lined with chapels. Located in the first chapel on the south side is the dramatic 15C **altarpiece★** of the Carrying of the Cross by a Dalmatian artist François Laurana.

The baptismal font chapel at the left north end is adorned with a group of **frescoes★** belonging to the second half of the 14C and attributed to Italian artists belonging to the School of Siena. Illustrated are the Deposition of the Cross, the Virgin and the Annunciation, St Gregory, St John the Baptist and the prophets.

Livrée Ceccano. – Across from St-Didier's south side rises the powerful tower of the *hôtel* (or *livrée*) built by the Cardinal of Ceccano in the 14C and later incorporated into the Jesuit College. The building now houses the **media centre.**

Take Rue des Fourbisseurs and then bear right onto Rue du Vieux-Sextier.

Place St-Jean-le-Vieux (CY 60). – Set at one corner of the square is a tall square tower (14C), all that remains of the Commandery of the Knights of St John of Jerusalem destroyed in the 19C.
On the small Place Jérusalem (**25**) is the synagogue, which until the 19C, was the heart of the Jewish Quarter, also known as the Carrière.

Hôtel de Rascas (BY D). – *At the corner of Rue des Marchands and Rue des Fourbisseurs.* This is a fine 15C corbelled mansion.

Ⓥ **St-Pierre** (BCY). – 14-16C. On the church's west façade open two doors adorned with fine richly decorated Renaissance **panels★**. Carved in perspective in 1551 by Antoine Valard, the subjects treated illustrate on the right the Virgin and the angel of the Annunciation and on the left Saints Michael and Jerome.
Inside, in the chancel, elegant 17C **woodwork** frames painted panels. North of the chancel, the first chapel contains a 16C altarpiece carved by Boachon, the third chapel a 14C dalmatic; south of the chancel the first chapel contains a 15C stone Entombment. A fine late 15C throne can also be seen.

Ⓥ **Théodore Aubanel Museum (Musée Théodore Aubanel)** (BY M³). – This museum is located on the ground floor of the Aubanel family home, a family of printers and publishers since 1744. In the first room are assembled mementos belonging to Théodore Aubanel, a founder of the Félibrige *(qv)* as well as paintings by Grivolas, Fromentin and a remarkable sailor's cross. The second room is especially concerned with old printing methods (hand press, fount case (boxes containing characters), gilt stamp machine, etc.). In the display cases are exhibited rare editions and numerous documents relating to life in Avignon (13-20C).

Rue Banasterie (CY). – This street is named for the basket makers guild (*banastiers* in Provençal). At no 13 the 17C Hôtel de Madon de Châteaublanc has a façade adorned with garlands of fruit, eagles and masks.
As you continue along the street there are glimpses of the cathedral's east end and of the Palace of the Popes.

Ⓥ **Black Penitents' Chapel** (Chapelle des Pénitents Noirs) (CY Z). – On the chapel's façade, remodelled in the 18C, two angels, in the middle of a very large glory surrounded by cherubs, carry, in a dish, St John the Baptist's head (the brotherhood's emblem is the beheading). The baroque interior presents a handsome group of woodwork and marble, paintings by Levieux, Nicolas Mignard and Pierre Parrocel. In the chancel the roof was painted by Pierre Courtois; note the Apotheosis of St John the Baptist.

Turn around; via Rue du Vice-Légat and Rue Peyrollerie go back to Place du Palais.

ADDITIONAL SIGHTS

Ⓥ **Louis Vouland Museum (Musée Louis Vouland)** (AY M⁴). – The museum contains a decorative arts collection which concentrates especially on 18C French **furnishings:** a commode signed by Migeon, an inlaid backgammon table, a money changers desk and an amusing travelling table service stamped with the Countess Du Barry's coat of arms.
A fine collection of porcelain and **faience★** are displayed in two rooms; there is a predominance of Moustiers and Marseilles wares. A number of Flemish and Gobelins *(Pastoral Scene)* tapestries hang on the walls. Among the paintings exhibited is the small canvas of a *Child Eating Cherries* by Jan Gossaert called Mabuse. The Far Eastern Art collection consists of a number of vases and Chinese plates and a series of ivory polychrome statues.

Convent of the Celestines (Couvent des Célestins) (BZ). – 15C. Founded in 1393 on the tomb of Cardinal Pierre de Luxembourg, the convent was built in the Northern Gothic style. Its church, presenting a fine east end and the cloisters were restored.

Church of the Visitation (Église de la Visitation) (CY). – This former convent chapel (17C) offers a finely carved façade adorned with a pediment.

Place des Carmes (CY). – The square is named after the former monastery of the Barefoot Carmelites of which the church and 14C cloisters (CY V) still remain. A wrought iron gate by the church's north wall marks the entrance to the cloisters.

Ⓥ **St-Symphorien (or Carmelites Church)** (CY). – 15C façade. In the first north chapel admire the three fine 16C statues in painted wood: Christ, Virgin and St John; in the succeeding chapels hang paintings by Pierre Parrocel (Holy Family), Nicolas Mignard (St Eligius) and Guillaume Grève (Adoration of the Magi).

Augustinian Bell Tower (Clocher des Augustins) (CY S). – This is all that remains of the convent founded in 1261. Built between 1372-7, the bell tower stands at the corner of the Place des Carmes. The bell cage *(qv)* was added later (16C).

Rue des 3-Pilats (CY 80). – At no 16 stands a 17C *hôtel* (CY W) with a triangular pediment.

Rue Ste-Catherine (CY 67). – At no 17, the Hôtel de Fonseca (CY X) built in 1600 is adorned with mullioned windows. It has a fine courtyard with an old well.

EXCURSIONS

★ **Villeneuve-lès-Avignon.** – *On the Rhone's south bank. Description p 193.*

Montfavet. – *6km – 3 1/2 miles on the D 100* (DY) *and the N 7ᶠ to the right.*
ⓥ This small town possesses an imposing **church**, the remains of a monastery built in the 14C by the Cardinal Bertrand de Montfavet. There remain two crenellated towers. An openworked bell tower, capping the church, balances out against the massive flying buttresses. Interesting carvings adorn the doorway's lintel. The nave, vast and very austere is covered by elegant Gothic vaulting and flanked by side chapels.

Barbentane. – *9.5km – 5 3/4 miles on the N 570* (CZ), *then right on the D 35. Description p 85.*

BAGNOLS-SUR-CÈZE   Pop 17 777

Michelin map 80 folds 10 and 20 or 245 fold 15 or 246 fold 24 – Facilities

To the old town of Bagnols, ringed by boulevards, on the site of the former ramparts, has been added the new city accommodating the workers of the Marcoule Atomic works *(p 126)*. The town was also the home of the 18C French journalist and writer Antoine Rivarol (1753-1801), whose works upheld the monarchy and traditions; among the other works he wrote a treatise *On the Universality of the French Language.*

BAGNOLS-SUR-CÈZE

André (R. A.)	2
Avignon (Rte d')	3
Boissin (Pl. Bertin)	5
Château (Pl. du)	6
Gentil (R.)	7
Horloge (R. de l')	9
Lacombe (Bd Th.)	10
Mallet (Pl. V.)	13
Mayre (Av. de la)	14
Pasterlon (Pl.)	15
Richard (R. U.)	17
Rivarol (R. A.-de)	18
Roc (R. du)	20
Verrerie (R. J.)	21

The main through routes are clearly indicated on all town plans.

★ **Modern Art Museum (Musée d'Art moderne)** (H). – The museum shares the same
ⓥ building as the town hall (2nd floor), a fine 17C mansion. It exhibits contemporary works collected by the painter Albert André, curator from 1918-54, with the help of Renoir. In addition there are works by the 19C Lyonnais School, faience from Moustiers and Marseilles and commemorative portrait medals of painters and sculptors. The museum has also been endowed with the private collection of George and Adèle Besson. It is made up of artists' signed works – oils, watercolours, drawings, sculpture (Renoir, Valadon, Bonnard, Matisse, Marquet, Van Dongen).

ⓥ **Archaeology Museum (Musée d'Archéologie)** (M). – The museum's collections originate from the Rhône Valley and illustrate the different periods of Antiquity. Two rooms evoke the Celtic-Ligurian civilisation and Greek influence from the 6C BC-1C BC: pottery, bronze wares, cult objects and sculpture (a ram's head). Along one gallery are assembled various Gallo-Roman remains: ceramics, amphorae, glassware, everyday objects and cinerary urns. Note the fine shop sign of a stone carver with its mason's level, hammer and two scissors.
One room is devoted to the site of the St-Vincent de Gaujac *oppidum (p 84).* A reconstructed hypocaust, small pool originally from the baths, pottery and documents (photographs and plans).

Old houses. – In **Rue Crémieux,** left of the town hall, note the classical doorways of nos 10, 25 and 29 and the large façade at no 15 adorned with overflowing cornices and huge gargoyles.

EXCURSIONS

Round tour of 153km – 95 miles in the Lower Vivarais. – *Allow 1 day. Leave Bagnols-sur-Cèze on the N 86 to the north and turn left into the D 980.*

★ **La Roque-sur-Cèze.** – *2km – 1 mile on the D 166. Description p 158.*

Valbonne Charterhouse. – *5km – 3 miles on the D 23, then take the road to the left. Description p 188.*

Goudargues. – Pop 680. The village, ringed by massive plane trees, is dominated by its church. This former abbey church, partly rebuilt in the 17 and 19C, is interesting for its tall Romanesque apse, decorated inside by two storeys of arcading.

Continue along the D 980.

Note on the right the old perched village of Cornillon.

Montclus. – Pop 139. At the junction of the D 980 and the D 901, there is a lovely **view★** of this old village dominated by a tower.

Bear left on the D 901 and then right on the D 712 and the D 417.

★★★ Orgnac Chasm. – *Description p 153.*

Return to the D 901, bear left on the D 980 and just before St-André-de-Roquepertuis bear right on the D 167.

The road winds through a desolate plateau. Turn right into the D 979 which, as it descends, offers fine views onto the deserted **Cèze Gorges★**.

Leave to the right the village of Tharaux and take the road towards Rochegude. Then via the D 16 and the D 7 go to Brouzet-lès-Alès.

★★ Guidon du Bouquet. – The highest point of the Bouquet Range, is a beakshaped rock which dominates the vast horizon extending between the Gard and Ardèche Rivers. From the steep approach road the ruins of Bouquet Castle (Château de Bouquet) are visible through the clumps of holm oaks. The **panorama★★** from the summit extends across the Cévennes Causses to the west, the irregular crests of the Lower Vivarais Range to the north, Mount Ventoux and the Alpilles Chain to the east. From the statue of the Virgin there is a vertiginous view of the immense *garrigue* surrounding Uzès and to the rear of the television mast a view of the Bouquet Range itself.

Return to Brouzet-les-Alès, take the D 7 and turn right into the D 37.

The road rises offering a good view of the **ruins★** of Allègre Castle (Château d'Allègre). It continues through the *garrigue* to the perched village of **Lussan**.

At Lussan take the D 143, then bear right on the D 643.

★★ Concluses Gorges. – *Description p 107.*

Once on the D 143 turn left. Return to Bagnols-sur-Cèze via St-André-d'Olérargues.

Sabran. – Pop 1 243. This old town is perched on a rock spike. From the foot of the giant statue of the Virgin, in the castle ruins, a vast **panorama★** unfolds before you.

Round tour of 50km – 31 miles through the garrigues and the Côtes du Rhône vineyards. – *Allow 3 hours. Leave Bagnols-sur-Cèze on the N 86 southwards to Gaujac, turn right onto the D 310 which passes below the village. Take a dirt road (signposted) which climbs (unsuitable for automobiles).*

St-Vincent-de-Gaujac Oppidum (Oppidum de St-Vincent-de-Gaujac). – Perched on a height amidst a forest, this site was occupied intermittingly 5C BC-6C AD and then again 10-14C. During the Gallo-Roman era it was a rural sanctuary with temples and baths. Go through a fortified gate (the vestiges of a curtain wall and peribolus) to discover the ruins of the medieval fortified stronghold with its cistern and the Gallo-Roman excavations. The latter dates from the Upper Empire (1-3C).

Above are the remains of a *fanum*, a small Roman temple; below are the **baths** *(qv)*, the arrangement of which can be seen with the remains of the hypocaust and drains. The sanctuary was abandoned in the 3C for no apparent reason.

Return to the N 86 and 4km – 2 1/2 miles south, after Pouzilhac, turn left into the D 101.

The narrow and winding road crosses a landscape of *garrigues* and forest; shortly before St-Victor-la-Coste, there is a good view of the ruins of an imposing feudal castle dismantled during the Albigensian Wars.

St-Victor-la-Coste. – Pop 1 143. On the border of the *garrigues* and vineyards, this picturesque old village *(under restoration)* huddles at the foot of its castle.

Continue along the D 101.

On the left a narrow road leads to an isolated chapel. The countryside is now covered by the Côtes du Rhône vineyards. These wines are made from selected grapes and naturally have different names; the most well-known of which are Lirac and Tavel.

St-Laurent-des-Arbres. – Pop 1 403. In the past this village belonged to the bishops of Avignon. It has preserved some interesting medieval ruins. The Romanesque ⓥ church was fortified in the 14C: the walls were raised and a crenellated parapet was added; inside the domes on squinches are adorned with symbols of the Evangelists. Near the church stands a rectangular keep from the Lords of Sabran's castle. The base dates from the late 12C; it was raised in the 14C with a storey set-back with crenellated arcades, battlemented turrets at the corners and a small square watch-tower. Not far from the keep, above the village is located another 12C square tower, subsequently remodelled.

Via the D 26 go to Lirac and Tavel.

These two wine-growing villages have given their names to excellent wines *(p 41)*.

Return to St-Laurent-des-Arbres and then take the N 580 back to Bagnols-sur-Cèze.

★ LA BARBEN Castle

Michelin map 🅈🄳 fold 2 or 🄉🄴🄵 fold 30 or 🄉🄴🄶 south of fold 12 – 10km – 6 miles east of Salon-de-Provence

La Barben Castle occupies a precipitous position in the small Touloubre Valley. The access ramp to the castle offers a plunging view onto the formal French gardens.

★Castle (Château). – The present castle was originally a medieval fortress, built before 1000 belonging to the Abbey of St-Victor from Marseilles and then King René, who sold it to the powerful Forbin family. This family owned it for some 500 years and remodelled and enlarged it several times, especially in the 14 and 17C, when it was transformed into a stately home. Its round tower was recently rebuilt after an earthquake. In front of a noble 17C façade is the terrace (Henri IV staircase with double flight of stairs), from where there is a good view of the gardens designed by Le Nôtre and the Provençal countryside.

Inside, note the painted ceilings, 16-17C Aubusson, Flemish and Brussels tapestries, and a fine painting by Largillière. The great drawing room is covered by a Second Empire Aubusson carpet. The reception hall is decorated with **Cordoban leather★** made near Avignon in 1680. On the second floor the Empire-style bedroom of Pauline Borghese, Napoleon's sister, and her boudoir ornamented with paper, painted by Granet, and representing the Four Seasons are also worth noticing.

Vivarium. – In the castle's former vaulted sheeps' pen is a display of reptiles and tropical and European fresh water fish. The aviary contains birds from the five continents.

Zoo (Parc zoologique). – Opposite side of the road. A stairway (112 steps) leads to the heart of the zoo (400 animals in 30ha – 12 acres).

BARBENTANE   Pop 3 249

Michelin map 🄸🄸 fold 11 or 🄉🄴🄵 fold 29 or 🄉🄴🄶 fold 25 – Facilities

Built against the north slope of the Montagnette (p 141), Barbentane overlooks the plain of market garden produce positioned near the confluence of the Rhône and Durance. It is an important dispatching centre for fruit and vegetables.

Château in Barbentane

Château. – This elegant 17C château recalls, by its architecture, the stately homes of Ile-de-France. A cornice surmounted by flame ornaments and pediments adorn the finely ordered façades. Terraces lined with stone railings decorated with lions and flower filled urns open over the formal gardens.

The interior, which is enhanced by the mementos belonging to the Marquis of Barbentane, presents rich 18C **decoration★** of Italian influence. The vaulting, which used a particular stone carving technique, plasterwork, painted medallions, coloured marble, Louis XV and XVI furnishings, Chinese porcelain and Moustiers faience all add to the charm of this delightful château.

Old village. – Remaining from the fortifications are the Calendale Gateway which opens onto the Cours and Séquier Gateway above the village.

House of the Knights (Maison des Chevaliers). – A lovely Renaissance façade composed of a turret and two basket arches topped by a columned gallery. Across the street is a 12C church, often remodelled, with its 15C bell tower (badly damaged).

Anglica Tower (Tour Anglica). – Overlooking the village, the tower is the keep of the former castle, built in the 14C by the brother of Pope Urban V, Cardinal Anglic de Grimoard. From the terrace there is a good view of Avignon, Châteaurenard and in the distance Mount Ventoux.

A short walk through the pines, leads to the nicely conserved 18C **Bretoul Mill** (Moulin de Bretoul – qv), from where there is a lovely view of the Rhône Plain. Near the cemetery, ruins of the old Roman way have been discovered.

Michelin map 🟦🟦 fold 10 or 🟧🟧🟧 fold 29 or 🟨🟨🟨 fold 26 – Local map p 56 – Facilities

Detached from the Alpilles, this bare rock spur – 900m-2 953ft long and 200m-656ft wide – with vertical ravines on either side, a fortified castle lying in ruins, and old desolate houses, compose the spectacular **site★★★** of the village of Les Baux, once a proud fief.

The village gave its name to a mineral discovered on its land in 1822, **bauxite** *(qv)*, the commercial source of aluminium. North of the village are quarries of soft stone used essentially for statuary. Gigantic regular blocks of stone are cut out of the cliff face, and once removed, create huge Cyclopean galleries.

HISTORICAL NOTES

A warrior line. – The lords of Baux were renowned in the Middle Ages and as Mistral described them were "warriors all – vassals never"; vaingloriously they traced their genealogy back to the Magi king, Balthazar, and, so as no one could ignore, boldly placed the star of Bethlehem on their arms!

From the 11C the lords were among the strongest in the south of France, having in their control 79 towns and villages. From 1145-62 they warred against the House of Barcelona, whose rights on Provence they contested; backed for a while by the German emperor, they had finally to submit after having succumbed to a siege at Les Baux itself.

They won titles: members of different branches became variously Princes of Orange, Viscounts of Marseilles, Counts of Avellino and Dukes of Andria (having followed the Capetian Princes of Anjou who were campaigning in southern Italy).

One of them married Marie of Anjou, sister of Joan I, Queen of Sicily and Countess of Provence, a lovely woman much loved by the people of Provence. She was destined to tragedy – 3 times a widow she died in 1382 smothered by an ambitious cousin.

Courts of Love. – Les Baux was famous as a court of love in the 13C. To become a member the women were of noble birth, well read and beautiful. Before this court, the questions of galantry and chivalry were raised and discussed. Troubadours *(p 24)*, often great lords, came from all the southern provinces composing passionate verses in praise of these ladies. The prize awarded to the best poet was a crown of peacock feathers and a kiss from the lady in question.

Turenne, the brigand. – The house of Turenne, from the Limousin, was a large family: two of its members were popes at Avignon, one of whom was the famous Clement VI. Another one of its members was the Viscount Raymond De Turenne, nephew of Gregory XI, who became guardian of his niece, Alix of Baux, in 1372. His ambitions caused civil war in the region. His pillaging and cruelty terrorised the countryside and he was appropriately named the "Scourge of Provence". His chief delight was to force his unransomed prisoners to jump off the castle walls.

The pope and the Lord of Provence hired mercenaries to get rid of the brigands, but the mercenaries equally ravaged both the enemy territories as well as the territories to be protected; as a result their contract was broken and these soldiers were given 80 000 *livres* to leave the area. A truce with Turenne was obtained in 1391 costing 30 000 *livres*. Peace was short-lived and pillaging and fighting broke out quite soon. The King of France joined Turenne's enemies; in 1399 the "scourge" was surrounded at Les Baux, however, he escaped and fled into France.

The end. – Alix was Baux's last princess, and at her death in 1426, the suzerain state, incorporated into Provence, became simply a barony. King René granted it to his second wife Jeanne de Laval. Joined with Provence to the French crown, the barony revolted against Louis XI, in 1483, who subsequently had the fortress dismantled.

As of 1528 the Constable Anne De Montmorency, who was titular of Les Baux, undertook a large restoration project on the town which once again enjoyed a prosperous period.

Les Baux then became a centre of Protestantism under the Manville family who administered it for the crown.

However, in 1632, Richelieu tired of this troublesome fief had the castle and ramparts demolished and the inhabitants were fined 100 000 *livres* plus the cost of the demolition!

Les Baux was then placed as a marquisate under the Grimaldis, Princes of Monaco. And what was once a proud town of 4 000, fell to pieces...

THE LIVING VILLAGE *time: 1 hour*

Arriving in the town on the D 27 has the advantage of plunging the visitor more quickly into the atmosphere of Les Baux.

Ⓥ *Leave the car at the car park located at the town's entrance and follow the itinerary marked on the town plan.*

Mentioned below are the main sights to be seen on this itinerary, and yet while touring, the visitor will discover other, less important ones (signposted). Enter through the Magi Gate (Porte Mage) pierced in 1866.

Ⓥ **Former Town Hall** (Ancien hôtel de ville) (**B**). – 17C. It has three rooms with pointed vaulting. Christmas cribs and Provençal *santons* are displayed.

Eyguières Gate (Porte Eyguières) (**D**). – This was once the only entrance.

Ⓥ **Museum of Contemporary Art** (Musée d'Art contemporain). – Located in the 16C **Hôtel des Porcelets** (**E**). The ground floor vaulting has 18C frescoes depicting the Four Seasons. Seven rooms house contemporary works of art by such artists as Gleizes, Carzou, Buffet; or works illustrating the surrounding countryside (Brayer, Thuiller).

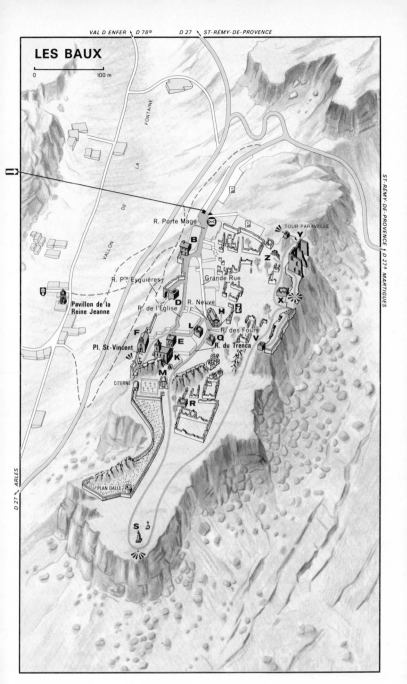

★Place St-Vincent. – This charming square shaded by elms and lotus trees offers a lovely view of the small Fontaine Valley and Val d'Enfer.

White Penitents' Chapel (Chapelle des Pénitents Blancs) **(F)**. – Built in the 17C the chapel was restored in 1936; inside, the wall frescoes are by Yves Brayer.

St-Vincent (K). – This 12C building, is flanked on its north side by a graceful campanile, the so-called lantern of the dead. Inside the pointed barrel vaulted nave, was enlarged in the 17C by one bay (at the east). On its south side the nave is bordered by a wide aisle covered with rounded vaulting and upon which open three 16C monolithic chapels.

Note the 15C knight's tombstone, a baptismal font carved out of the living rock, windows by Max Ingrand and the lamb's cart, the centrepiece of the **Shepherds Festival★★** celebrated at Christmas midnight mass *(p 200)*. The shepherds dressed in their long capes, lead to the altar a newborn lamb in a small cart.

Former Protestant Chapel (Ancien temple protestant) **(L)**. – The chapel was once part of the Manville's *(see below)* mansion and the ruins of a 1571 house. On one of its fine window lintel's is the Calvinist watchword: *Post tenebras lux.*

Ⓥ **Hôtel de Manville (H)**. – The 16C façade is decorated with lovely Renaissance windows. It now houses the town hall.

Former manorial bread ovens (Ancien fours banaux) **(Q)**. – The townspeople came here to cook their bread.

★Rue du Trencat. – The street has been carved into the living rock; note on the right the ridges and cavities created by rain and wind.

THE DESERTED VILLAGE *time: 1/2 hour*

○ **Lapidary Museum** (Musée lapidaire) (**M**). – Located in the former 14C Tour-de-Brau House, the museum displays articles excavated in the village's surrounding area.

> *On the outskirts of the village, at the end of Rue Trencat, follow the path leaving the ruins of the 14C Chapel of St-Claude-et-St-Blaise (**R**) on the left and cross the plateau to join the cross and monument to the Provençal poet Charloun Rieu.*

On the plateau's right slope can be seen large paved sections which serve as a rainwater catchment which then drains into a cistern (1 000 m³-35 315ft³) carved into the rock.

Charloun Rieu Monument (Monument Charloun Rieu) (**S**). – From this monument erected to honour the poet Charloun Rieu *(qv)*, there is an all embracing **view★★** of Montmajour Abbey, Arles, the Crau and Camargue Plains; in clear weather Ste-Maries-de-la-Mer and Aigues-Mortes can be seen.

> *Go towards the castle, pass beneath the Saracen Tower (**V**), perched on the right, a couple of hundred yards after the tower take the path to the left. The path to the right leads to a difficult staircase which goes up to the rock and tower from the top of which there is a good view of the village and castle.*

After having passed by Ste-Catherine's Chapel (**X**), restored in the 16C; go to the Paravelle Tower from where there is a lovely **view★** of Les Baux, Val d'Enfer and the castle ruins.

Castle (Château) (**Y**). – From the 13C keep, there is a magnificent **panorama★★** similar to the one from the Charloun Rieu Monument.

After the old columbarium (**Z**) return to the Lapidary Museum.

ADDITIONAL SIGHTS

★**Picture Palace** (Cathédrale d'Images). – *On the side of the road (D 27); 500m –*
○ *1/3 mile north of the village.*
The remarkable site of the bauxite quarries, its colossal decoration evoking an Egyptian temple, were "discovered" by Albert Plécy (1914-77), the photographer, who established a research centre in the quarries. In the semi-darkness the limestone surfaces of the huge rooms and pillars are used as 3-dimensional screens. This giant **audio-visual show★** changes theme annually.

Viewing Table (Table d'orientation). – *Continue along the D 27 for about 1km – 1/2 mile and bear right on a steep road.*
A rocky promontory offers a far-reaching **panorama★★★** *(signposted car park):* Arles and Camargue, Rhône Valley, Cévennes Mountains, Aix-en-Provence, Luberon and Mount Ventoux.

Val d'Enfer. – *Access from the D 27 and the D 78G.*
A path *(1/4 hour on foot Rtn)* crosses this jagged and irregular gorge aptly named Hell Valley. The caves used to be lived in and are still the source of many legends as the place where witches, fairies and sprites reign.

Queen Jeanne's Pavilion (Pavillon de la reine Jeanne). – *On the D 78G. A path leads down to the pavilion from Eyguières Gate (**D**).*
The small Renaissance building, built by Jeanne of Les Baux *c*1581, was beloved by the Provençal poets of the Félibrige *(qv)*. Mistral had a copy made for his tomb at Maillane *(qv)*.

*With this guide use the **Michelin Maps** (scale 1:200 000) shown on p 3.*

★ **BEAUCAIRE**   Pop 13 015

Michelin map 🖽 fold 10 or 🖽 fold 28 or 🖽 fold 26

At the point where the Domitian Way linked Italy to Spain, Ugernum was an important Gallo-Roman city, where in 455 an assembly of senators from Gaul selected the Emperor Avitus from Arverne. A royal seneschalship in 1229, Beaucaire watched Tarascon, across the river, which was part of the Holy Roman Empire. The Vallabrègues project in 1970 demonstrates a recent phase in the hydro-electric
○ works of the Compagnie Nationale du Rhône. The **Beaucaire Power Station** *(via ⑥ on the town plan)* located on the last branch of the river before flowing into the sea, has an average annual production of more than 1 thousand million kWh.

Beaucaire Fair. – Created in 1217 by Raymond VI of Toulouse, the fair lasted originally one week beginning on 22 July. Throughout the Middle Ages it became one of those great medieval fairs to which people came from all parts – as many as 300 000, it was said, gathered to do business, roister and celebrate in the town every year in the month of July. Streets were decorated, houses beflagged and crammed with visitors and their merchandise; those who could not get a room on land, slept aboard the ships gathered from all corners of the Mediterranean, Brittany and Gascony and moored in the river. Streets specialised in single commodities after which many were named: Beaujolais was a wine street, Bijoutiers – a jeweller's row; the Rue des Marseillais was where oil and soap were sold; elsewhere there were wool, silk, linen, cotton, lace, coloured woven cloth, clothing, weapons, hardware, rope and saddlery shops and harness makers. On the quayside and on board, traders proffered dried fish, sugar, cocoa, coffee, cinnamon, vanilla, lemons, oranges, dates...

BEAUCAIRE

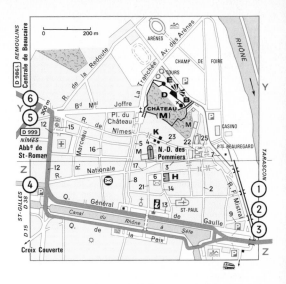

The fairground, on the large flat expanse between the castle cliff and the river, was set with stalls offering everything from games to perfume, pipes to pottery. It was of course, also a horse fair. Tumblers and jugglers, acrobats and clowns entertained the crowds; bearded women, giants and dwarfs, monkeys, performing dogs, lions, bears and elephants amazed. There were even dioramas of Paris, Constantinople and Versailles to be viewed through magnifying lenses.

The fair died in the 19C, killed by the railway which brought about a completely different way of life. Only the riverside quays remain, still trading in wine.

★CASTLE (Y) – time: 1 hour

⊙ *Start at Place du Château, take the steps up to the pine and cypress walk flowered with irises and broom (absolutely no smoking).*

Built in the 11C on the site of a Roman camp remodelled in the 13C, the castle was dismantled in the 17C on the orders of Cardinal Richelieu. It stood on the crown of the hill surrounded by ramparts (imposing ruins).

Romanesque chapel (Chapelle romane) (Y B). – This small chapel (restored in the 19C) has a twin bayed bell tower and carved tympanum.

Polygonal Tower (Tour polygonale) (Y D). – 104 steps. Of rare design the tower is also called the triangular tower.

The very narrow staircase in the thickness of the walls goes up to two floors which have unusual heavy pointed vaulting. From the platform there is a **panorama★★** of the Montagnette and Alpilles Chain, Rhône Valley, Beaucaire and Tarascon.

Round Tower (Tour ronde) (Y E). – A fine corner tower.

Curtain wall (Les courtines). – A short walk enables the visitor to admire the sheer curtain wall, the barbican defending a castle entrance, and the rocky spur on which stands the Polygonal Tower *(see above)*.

⊙ **Vignasse Museum (Musée de la Vignasse).** – Located within the castle walls, the museum contains the collections once exhibited in the Museum of old Beaucaire and the Lapidary Museum.

It is essentially a local collection (costumes, furnishings and Provençal utensils) with notably documents on the Beaucaire Fair (the oldest dates back to 1651).

The archaeological section consists of Gallo-Roman finds (pottery, lamps, cinerary tombs).

ADDITIONAL SIGHTS

Town Hall (Hôtel de ville) (Z H). – The town hall is a late 17C mansion by Mansart with a central block flanked by wings outlined by a high, balustraded wall; carved flower garlands surround the windows and the grand staircase (courtyard) rises behind a double portico of Ionic columns.

⊙ **Notre-Dame-des-Pommiers (Y).** – Rebuilt from 1734-44 by the architect J.-B. Franque *(qv)* in the Jesuit style, this church presents an elegant façade adorned with two superimposed orders: Ionic and Corinthian; a low relief of the Assumption crowns the great doorway.

All that remains of the early Romanesque church is the frieze imbedded in the upper part of the eastern wall which can be seen from Rue Charlier. It depicts the Last Supper, Kiss in the Garden, Flagellation, Carrying of the Cross and Resurrection. The inside is majestic; on the transept crossing is a fine dome on pendentives.

House of the Caryatids (Maison des cariatides) (Y K). – *23 Rue de la République.* This 17C house with its lovely carved façade (restored) is known for the caryatids flanking the porch.

Covered Cross (Croix couverte). – *1.5km – 3/4 mile southwest at the junction formed by the D 15 (Z) and the first road to the right.* This small triangular shaped oratory (early 15C) is decorated at the top by a delicately pierced railing.

EXCURSION

ⓥ **St-Roman Abbey** (Abbaye de St-Roman). – *4.5km – 2 1/2 miles by ⑤ on the town plan and the D 999 and the road to the right, then 1/2 hour on foot Rtn.*
Park the car and take the path which winds through the garrigue *of cistus and kermes oaks.*
Located on a limestone peak, the abbey, which is now being excavated, depended in the 12C, on the Abbey of Psalmody near Aigues-Mortes. It was abandoned by the monks in the 16C; gradually transformed into a fortress and then enlarged by the construction of a castle on the upper terrace; stone for both fortress and castle was quarried from the abbey and in turn disappeared from the castle when this was dismantled in 1850.
The chapel, built into the rock, contains, at the transept crossing, the tomb of Romanus, a 12C abbot's chair and, on the north side over tombs sunk into the floor, a lantern to the dead with recesses for oil watching lights.
The **view**★ from the terrace extends to the Rhône and the Vallabrègues Dam, Avignon, Mount Ventoux, the Luberon, the Alpilles Chain and, in the foreground, Tarascon and its castle. Note the graves hollowed out of the rock, the basin from which rainwater was channelled to a collecting tank, the monks' cells and a vast hall three storeys high.

The times indicated in this guide
when given with the distance allow one to enjoy the scenery
when given for sightseeing are intended to give an idea
of the possible length or brevity of a visit.

★ **BERRE Lagoon** (Étang de BERRE)

Michelin map 𝟾𝟺 folds 1, 2, 11 and 12 or 𝟤𝟦𝟻 folds 30 and 43 or 𝟤𝟦𝟼 folds 13 and 14

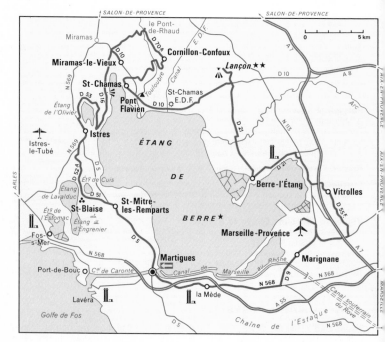

The Berre Lagoon, 15 530ha – 60sq miles in extent and nowhere more than 9m – 30ft deep, has been France's principal **petroleum port** for the last 70 odd years. The Caronte Canal, dredged out where there was once a lagoon of the same name, provides a passage to the Mediterranean, as does the underground Rove section of the Marseilles-Rhône Canal.
The lagoon is fed fresh water by the Rivers Arc and Touloubre and the EDF Canal (Électricité de France) and is ringed around its 50 mile perimeter by limestone hills: the Lançon Chain (alt 195m – 640ft) to the north, the Vitrolles (alt 271m – 890ft) to the east, the Estaque (alt 201m – 660ft) to the south, and the St-Mitre (alt 142m – 465ft) to the west.
The modern installations are but the latest of man's constructions in the area: buildings still above ground and excavations reveal the presence of earlier inhabitants at St-Blaise, Flavian's Bridge *(qv)*, built by the Romans, the medieval town of Miramas-le-Vieux and the 17C walls of Port-de-Bouc *(qv)*.
The region, nevertheless, was still largely uninhabited when in 1920, under the San Remo Agreement, France obtained the right to purchase the major part of Iraq's annual crude oil production.

The lagoon was transformed into an ideal port for shallow draft oil tankers; at the same time harbours also began to be developed on the Gulf of Fos – the French BP company at Lavéra in 1922-4, Shell-Berre at the Pointe de Berre in 1928, the Compagnie Française de Raffinage at La Mède in 1934...

The growth in demand for oil, apparent even in 1938, brought about the transformation, soon after the war, of **Lavéra,** to enable 80 000 ton tankers to dock and pump their cargoes directly into onshore installations. Finally in the 1960s a completely new port was constructed at Martigues.

The lagoon complex is also the terminal of the **South European Oil Pipeline.** This line, inaugurated in 1962, supplies four refineries around the lagoon and eleven in regions as distant as Feyzin, Cressier in Switzerland, Baden and Bavaria in Germany; the total amount of oil piped a year is 65.2 million tons.

Between the Second World War and 1973 the refineries had considerably expanded; since, however, their distillation capacity (40 000 000 metric tons – for the 2 refineries around the lagoon as well as at Lavera and Fos) has been reduced. The very modern equipment permits the treatment of crude oil as well as a wide range of oil related products.

Petrochemicals have considerably developed in the last 10 years with Shell's construction of steam cracking facilities, rubber-making units and plastics.

Dependant on the docks and refineries which ring the lagoon shore and coast around the Gulf of Fos are petrochemical factory complexes extending far inland, so that from the air or from one of the heights overlooking the bay, one sees an irregular mass of silver aluminium storage tanks, tall factory chimneys belching smoke, petroleum gas flares, vast metal warehouses and concrete works and office blocks.

Aviation centre. – At the turn of the century the peaceful lagoons and deserted Crau Plain were an ideal testing ground for pioneer aviators.

At **Istres** before the First World War, a military aerodrome was established which exists today. Since then it has expanded considerably and now occupies 2 031ha – 5 017 acres.

Berre was until 1940 the most important hydroplane base of the National Marines with Bizerte. When a civil airport was required for Marseilles, the **Marseille-Provence** airport was sited at the east end of the Berre Lagoon at **Marignane.**

ROUND TOUR STARTING FROM MARTIGUES
113km – 70 miles – allow 1 day – local map p 90

Martigues. – *Description p 138.*

> *Leave Martigues by ① on the town plan (p 139), the D 5.*

The road undulates through vineyards, orchards and pinewoods.

St-Mitre-les-Remparts. – Pop 4 299. The old town, encircled by 15C ramparts still pierced by only two gateways, stands just off the road.
A network of small streets and alleys leads to the church where there is a view of the Engrenier Lagoon.

> *Leave St-Mitre-les-Remparts by the D 51 across the D 5.*

Good view on the right of Berre Lagoon; the road skirts Citis Lagoon in a cultivated site before passing the foot of the hill on which stands St-Blaise Chapel, the east end of which is just visible among the pine trees.

St-Blaise Archaeological Site. – *Description p 160.*

Istres. – Pop 30 360. The town beside Olivier Lagoon is a military airport base *(p 92).*
The small **museum** is devoted to local history (prehistory, Gallo-Roman archaeology – underwater objects from the Gulf of Fos), contemporary economic life, flora, fauna and folklore.
To the north lies the Greco-Ligurian town of Castellan also on the banks of Olivier Lagoon; a surfaced path leads to the edge of the rocky advancement from where there is a fine view.

> *Circle the lagoon by way of the D 53 and then turn left into the D 16.*

The road offers good views of Berre Lagoon to which it returns.

Miramas-le-Vieux. – The small town on a flat ledge of rock, is characterised by medieval ramparts, the ruins of the 13C castle and the 15C parish church which replaced the even smaller 12C church still standing in the churchyard. Good view of the Berre Lagoon.

> *Return to the D 10 and take the D 16 across the way and then the D 70ᴰ.*

The road goes through pastureland (sheep herding).

> *At Le Pont-de-Rhaud bear right into the D 70ᴬ.*

The road ascends a height overlooking the Touloubre on the right.

Cornillon-Confoux. – Pop 980. At the centre of the perched village stands a small Romanesque church with a bell gable and modern stained glass windows by Frédérique Duran *(qv).*
There are good local **views★** from the walk which starts at the church and circles the village.

> *Take the D 70 and a tourist road on the right to St-Chamas.*

St-Chamas. – Pop 5 045. The town is unique in being dominated by a small, triple arched, aqueduct. The **church,** which is 17C with a baroque west front, contains a marble high altar and a 16C altarpiece to St Anne (third south chapel).

Flavian's Bridge (Pont Flavien). – The bridge is named after the patrician who in 1C ordered its construction at what is now the south approach to St-Chamas. It crosses the Touloubre in a single span and celebrates the feat in triumphal arches at either end, surmounted by small lions.

Continue along the D 10 which passes the **St-Chamas Power Station**, the EDF Canal's final project which has an annual production capacity of 610 million kWh.

Turn left into the D 21 and left again after 1.7km – 1 mile into an unsurfaced road. Park the car.

★★ **Lançon Viewing Table** (Table d'orientation de Lançon). – *1/4 hour on foot Rtn.* Steps (48) lead to the top of a rock from where there is a **view★★** over the lagoon to the surrounding hills.

Turn round and once on the D 21 continue to Berre-L'Étang.

Berre-l'Étang. – Pop 12 562. The town lives by fishing and its chemical factories. The chapel, Notre-Dame-de-Caderot displays at the altar, a 16C polychrome wood retable and, in a recess opposite the door, a Roman crystal vessel known as the Caderot Vase, said to have contained a lock of the Virgin's hair.

Flavian's Bridge

Continue first along the D 21, then the N 113 on the right; finally turn left for Vitrolles.

Vitrolles. – *Description p 195.*

Leave Vitrolles by the D 55ᶠ. At the N 113 crossroads, cross into the D 9 then right into the D 20.

Marseille-Provence Airport (Aéroport de Marseille-Provence). – The airport, France's second after Paris, sprawled over 550ha – 1 235 acres beside Berre Lagoon, is equipped with two runways. There is a new control tower which is 50m – 164ft high.

Marignane. – Pop 31 213. The town possesses two interesting buildings – the château, known as Mirabeau's Castle and the church.

⊙ One wing of the castle is now the **town hall.** The decoration in the bathroom, the registry office formerly the marquess' bedroom and the mayor's parlour once the marchioness's boudoir are well conserved. Beautiful painted ceilings with floral decoration can be seen.

The church nave, which is late 11C, has pointed barrel vaulting but is entirely lacking in windows; the pointed vaulted aisles and high altar are 16C.

Follow the D 9; and turn right on the N 568.

The road crosses the Rove or Marseilles-Rhône Canal and passes through acres of market gardens; fine views of the lagoon and the site of **La Mède** marked by two peculiar rocks at the harbour entrance.

The N 568 returns to Martigues (p 138).

For a peaceful night
*the **Michelin Red Guide France** revises annually*
its choice of pleasant, quiet and well situated hotels.

BOLLÈNE
Pop 12 690

Michelin map 🔢 fold 10 or 🔢 fold 16 or 🔢 fold 23 – Facilities

The town, which stands on a hillside, has been an agricultural marketing centre since the days of the Avignon popes, when it was one of the popes' richest possessions. A few houses and fine doorways remain as mementoes of the past in what is now a typical Provençal town with wide shaded boulevards marking the line of the ancient ramparts and a web of narrow streets at the centre.

From the terraces overlooking the Rhône can be seen the Donzère-Mondragon Canal, the Bollène hydro-electric power station and the vast Tricastin Nuclear Power Station; beyond in the distance are the mountains of the Ardèche and Lower Vivarais.

Pasteur Garden (Belvédère Pasteur). – From this small public garden, set around the former Romanesque Chapel des Trois-Croix (now a museum, *see below*), there is a pleasant view of the town and its surrounding countryside.

A bust of Pasteur memorialises that when the scientist stayed in Bollène in 1882, he discovered an inoculation against swine fever.

⊙ **Museum** (Musée) (**M**). – The museum contains drawings by Picasso and Chagall besides a selection of local artists' paintings and sculpture and Greco-Roman coins.

BOLLÈNE

Chabrières (R. des) ... 5
Cimetière (Rue Gd) ... 6
Fabre (R. Henri) ... 7
Gambetta (Bd) ... 9
Giono (A. Jean) ... 10
Louis (R. Auguste) ... 12
Paroisse (Montée de la) ... 13
Puy (R. du) ... 15
Récollets (Pl. des) ... 16
République (Cours de la) ... 17
Réservoirs (Montée des) ... 19
Reynaud-de-la-Gardette (Pl.) ... 20
Tour (R. de la) ... 21
Zola (R. Émile) ... 22

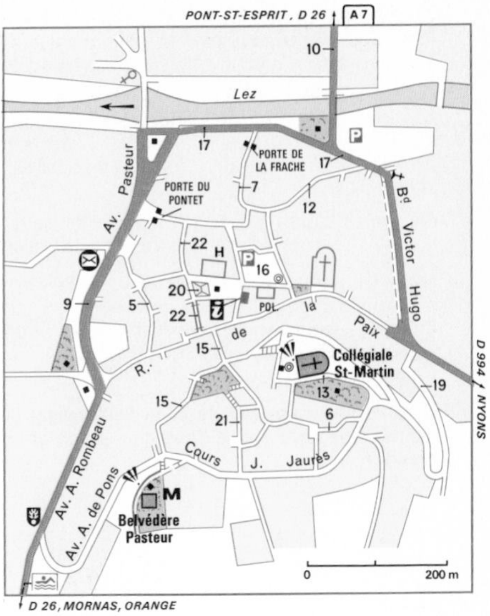

All symbols on the town plans are explained in the key p 42.

St-Martin Collegiate Church (Collégiale St-Martin). – The former parish church (12-16C) is now used for exhibitions. Its robust bell tower stands atop the hill overlooking the town's roof tops from the east. Go through the lovely Renaissance doorway to admire the size of the nave covered with a vast timberwork saddleback roof.

From the east end, there is a lovely view of old Bollène's roof tops, the Tricastin hills, the Barry site and the Rhône Valley.

EXCURSION

Mornas. – Pop 1 737. Facilities. *11km – 7 miles south via the D 26 and the N 7.*
The D 26 crosses Mondragon dominated by the ruins of its castle, and joins the N 7.

The old village of Mornas clings to the foot of a sheer cliff (137m – 449ft) on which lies the ruins of a powerful fortress; with the fortified gates and old houses a medieval atmosphere pervades... *Access by a steep alleyway (car park) and path.* Near the cemetery stands the small, pretty, Romanesque Church of Notre-Dame-du-Val-Romigier.

The **castle** has a vast curtain wall 2km – 1 mile long which is flanked either by semi-circular or square towers. At the top are ruins of the keep and chapel. Belonging to the bishops' of Arles, it was enfeoffed to the count of Toulouse in 1197 and entirely rebuilt by him.

The castle was also the scene of a terrible episode during the Wars of Religion: it was held by the Catholics, fell into the hands of the sinister Baron des Ardets, who in reprisal had all the inhabitants jump off the top of the cliff.

★ BONNIEUX — Pop 1 385

Michelin map 81 fold 13 or 245 fold 31 or 446 fold 11 – Local map p 124 – Facilities

This large attractively terraced village situated on a Luberon promontory has preserved its rampart ruins.

BONNIEUX

Ancien-Presbytère (R. de l') ... 2
Aurard (R. J.-B.) ... 3
Carnot (Pl.) ... 4
Gare (Av. de la) ... 5
Hugues (Av. Clovis) ... 7
Liberté (Pl. de la) ... 8
Mairie (R. de la) ... 9
République (R. de la) ... 12
Victor-Hugo (R.) ... 13
Voltaire (R.) ... 14
4-Septembre (Pl. du) ... 16

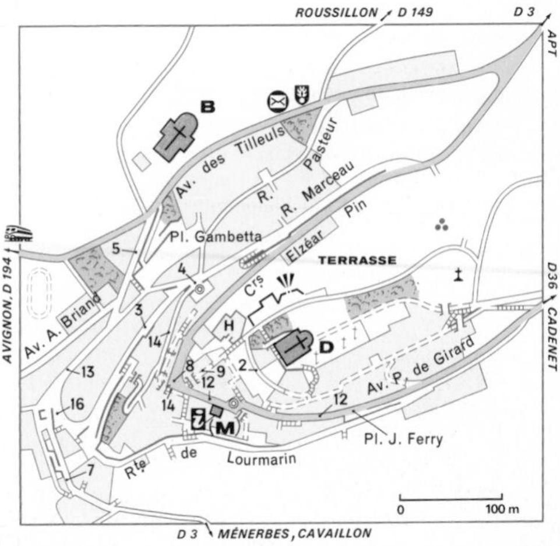

Street names either appear on the town plan or are listed with a reference number.

Upper Bonnieux. – *Start from Place de la Liberté by the steep vaulted passageway, Rue de la Mairie, to reach the terrace situated below the former church. By car take the road to Cadenet and a steep surfaced path on the left.*

Terrace (Terrasse). – From here there is a lovely **view★** of Calavon Valley, all the way to the left of the perched village of Lacoste, further to the right on the edge of the Vaucluse Plateau to which cling the villages of Gordes, on a hill and Roussillon blending into its red cliffs. In the background Mount Ventoux stands out.

Ⓥ **Old Church** (Église Vieille) (**D**). – From the terrace, take the stairs to the former parish church (12C) remodelled in the 15C and surrounded by fine cedars.

Ⓥ **New Church** (Église Neuve) (**B**). – This vast building dating from the second half of the 19C contains **four paintings★** belonging to the Old Church. These 15C Primitives from the German School are brightly painted on wood and illustrate St Veronica wiping Jesus's face, an Ecce Homo, the Crowning of Thorns and a Flagellation.

Ⓥ **Bakery Museum** (Musée de la Boulangerie) (**M**). – Located in the tourist information centre, the museum evokes the work of the baker (utensils, different kinds of bread).

CADENET
Pop 2 640

Michelin map 🔢 fold 3 or 🔢 fold 31 or 🔢 fold 12 – Local map p 113 – Facilities

The small town is perched on a spur below the ruins of an 11C castle now half hidden by pine trees.

The Drummer Boy. – In the main square, is a statue of André Estienne born in Cadenet in 1777, the town's famous **drummer boy**. It was he who served in Napoleon's north Italy campaign of 1796, and in the midst of the battle against the Austrians and Italians for the Arcole Bridge, swam the river and beat such a tattoo that the Austrians mistook it for artillery fire; as they retreated, the French advanced to capture the bridge and win the battle.

It is also the birthplace of Félicien David (1810-76), whose travels to the Orient brought to his music, an Oriental exoticism (*Le Désert*, 1844).

Church (Église). – The 14C structure, remodelled in the 16 and 17C, has a fine square bell tower.

Inside the church the north aisle holds a beautiful **baptismal font★** made from a 3C Roman sarcophagus decorated with low reliefs illustrating the Triumph of Ariadne.

Drummer Boy

CALÈS Caves (Grottes de CALÈS)

Michelin map 🔢 folds 1 and 2 or 🔢 fold 30 or 🔢 fold 12 – 10km – 6 miles north of Salon-de-Provence

Carved out of the side of Défends Mountain, the Calès Caves are dominated by a statue of Our Lady of the Watch.

Access. – *3/4 hour on foot Rtn. Bear right up a street, then a path which then becomes a paved way. After about 400m – 1/4 mile turn right onto a rocky path.*

Caves (Grottes). – On either side of the arch are the caves carved out of the rock by the Ligurians, occupied by the Saracens and inhabited until the Middle Ages. Brief climbs enable the visitor to see the disposition of these troglodyte dwellings : partitions, stairs, defensive arrangements, as well as silos dug out of the rock and used to store food.

Follow the path which skirts the rocky hill to the top where the statue of Our Lady of the Watch stands.

From the edge of the terrace **views** can be had through the pine forest : northwards of the Durance Valley and the Luberon ; eastwards on these troglodyte dwellings ; and southwards of the Lamanon Gap, where the Durance used to flow, Salon Plain, Estaque Chain, Crau Plain and Berre Lagoon.

Go back down, keeping to the left.

Looking for a pleasant hotel or camping site
in peaceful surroundings?
you couldn't do better than look in the current
Michelin Guides
FRANCE
and
CAMPING CARAVANING FRANCE

** CAMARGUE

Michelin map ▨▨ fold 8 to 10 and 18 to 20 or ▨▨▨ folds 40 to 42 or ▨▨▨ folds 26 to 28

Camargue, the most original and romantic region of Provence and possibly of France, has been largely preserved in its natural state through its designation in 1928 and 1970 as a botanical and zoological nature reserve. Late spring or early autumn are the best times for a visit: horses and bulls are easily seen and birds abound, the sun shines (but not overpoweringly) and there are the famous pilgrimages to Stes-Maries-de-la-Mer *(p 171).*

Camargue Regional Nature Park (Parc Naturel Régional de Camargue). – Covering 85 000ha – 328sq miles including the *communes* of Arles and Stes-Maries-de-la-Mer, the regional nature park has been set up to help and encourage the inhabitants in their surroundings and to protect the flora and fauna by preserving farms, controlling water power and tourism.

Camargue Nature Reserve (Réserve Nationale de Camargue). – The National Society for the Protection of Nature has established, in the area around the Vaccarès Lagoon, a vast reserve of 13 500ha – 52sq miles for the protection of flora and fauna.

GEOGRAPHICAL NOTES

The Rhône Delta. – Camargue, an immense alluvial plain of 95 000ha – 367sq miles (75 000ha – 289sq miles for the delta's island) is the product of the interaction of the Rhône and Mediterranean and the winds.

During the end of the Tertiary Era and the beginning of the Quaternary Period while the sea was receding, water ways transported huge quantities of shingle which piled up along the shore creating a shingle bar some 10m – 33ft wide. On top of this rocky base marine sediment was deposited after the last glacial period (some 10 000 years ago): the sea then extended to the north shore of Vaccarès Lagoon. However, the landscape had been constantly, changing due to the conflicting forces of the fresh water Rhône and the sea. The powerful Rhône has shifted its course over the centuries – it has occupied the two present arms of its bed only since the 15C – transporting enormous amounts of alluvial deposits: barriers were formed which isolated the marshes; sandbanks created by the coastal currents closed off lagoons. Every year the Grand Rhône, which comprises 9/10 of the flow hollows

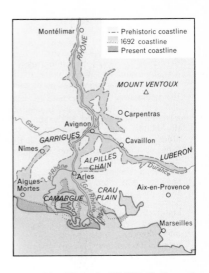

out from its banks and sweeps towards the sea 20 million m³ – 26 157yd³ of gravel, sand and mud – enough to cover Paris in a silt blanket 25cm or 10 1/2in thick. A part of the deposit is moved on by currents to the Lower Languedoc coast; some used to form sandbanks across the Gulf of Fos and thus blocking the access to Berre Lagoon.

The construction of the **seawall** and the Rhône dykes have partially helped to curb these phenomena. And yet the encroachment of the shore line 10-50m – 33-164ft a year continues in several places (l'Espiguette and Sablon Points); Aigues-Mortes where St Louis embarked is now 5km – 3 miles inland.

While elsewhere, owing to continental subsidence, the sea is invading the shore: the Vieux Rhône and Petit Rhône promontories have been swept away by southeasterly storms; **Faraman Lighthouse,** 700m – 1/2 mile inland in 1840 was swallowed by the sea in 1917 so that a new one had to be built; Stes-Maries-de-la-Mer once an inland town, is now protected by breakwaters...

The country of Camargue. – Although Camargue is one vast plain, it is divided into three distinct regions.

The cultivated region. – North of the delta and along the two arms of its river bed, the Rhône has created banks of fine alluvium – *lônes* – which make up the best soil and where the *mas (qv)* have been built. This area, the Upper Camargue, dry and useful, started being improved during the Middle Ages. Man had to battle against water and salt, the level of salt in the soil was heightened by an intense heat in summer causing evaporation.

Since the last war great drainage and irrigation projects have been undertaken and have brought satisfactory results. After having drained the marshes by dumping their waters into Vaccarès Lagoon, expulsing salt, the soil's sterilising element, by washing down the soil, the Rhône's fertile water is then pumped through; after being used the water is then drained into Vaccarès Lagoon. This operation is a very difficult one as it requires a constant surveillance because the irrigation can cause the water table to rise and thus the problem of evaporation and increase of salt in the soil begins the process all over again.

Vaccarès Lagoon near Méjanes

The extent of arable land has considerably increased and everywhere large farming units are predominant. Wheat, vineyards, fruit orchards, market gardening, maize, rape and forage alternate annually on this productive soil.

After a very large expansion in the 1960s, rice cultivation has distinctly dropped: the 33 000ha – 127sq miles in 1961 have now become 4 to 5 000ha – 9 880 to 12 350 acres. Rice is sown directly in perfectly levelled 3ha – 7 acre plots separated by banks of earth and submerged from April to September. The harvesting starts late September early October and includes the milling, processing and application of a glossy finish; the rice can then be pretreated or parboiled. Here and there appear small clumps of white oak, ash, elm, poplar, robinia and willows.

The saltmarshes. – They extend to near Salin-de-Giraud (11 000ha – 27 181 acres) and west of Petit Rhône and present a checkerboard of evaporation pans and huge glistening mounds. The cultivation of salt goes back to Antiquity and made, during the Middle Ages, the wealth of the salt abbeys like Ulmet and Psalmody; industrialisation of salt occurred in the 19C. The global annual production of the Provence-Côte d'Azur region is evaluated at 1 023 000 metric tons.

Between March and September a shallow flow of seawater (not more than a foot deep) is pumped across large "tables" for about 20 miles until a saturated solution of sodium chloride has been formed. This is then passed into 9ha – 22 acre crystallising pans, 12cm-5in deep, divided by dykes *(cairels)*. Between late August and early October, when evaporation is complete the salt crystals are raked to the edge, washed and piled into huge white glistening mounds *(camelles)*, some 21m-70ft high. After further washing, drying and crushing, the salt crystals are ready for use in industry to feed to animals or for human consumption.

The Midi Salt marshes *(qv)* is today the most powerful company of salt harvesting as well as being the largest owner of vineyards (Listel) on the coast.

The natural region. – The wild southern delta comprises a sterile plain dappled by lagoons and smaller pools which are linked to the sea by a number of channels. A desert of sand and marsh lined with small dunes along the coast forms a fascinating nature reserve.

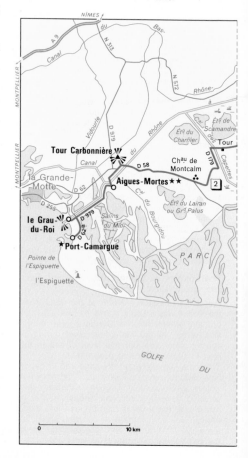

Traditional Camargue. – The Camargue preserves the tradition of the herds *(manades)* of sheep, horses and bulls and herdsmen *(gardians)* and has conserved an ecosystem protected from human encroachment. Roads cross Camargue but for a better idea of this nature reserve, walk along the paths established by the Regional Nature Park or Nature Reserve.

Flora and fauna. – *If you are interested in bird watching, admiring the flora or spotting animals bring binoculars and one of the books on the area listed in the books to read section p 198.* These flat expanses, cracked by draught and whitened by the efflorescence of salt are covered with (sparse vegetation known as *sansouire*). Halophilous plants (liking salt), sea lavender and glasswort, green in the spring, grey in the summer and red in the winter proliferate and are food for the herds of wild bulls. Water willows and gorse supply the reeds *(sagno)* with which baskets, chair covers and roofs of **gardians' cabins** *(cabanes – photograph p 98)* are made. The only shrubbery is tamarisks.

The **Rièges Islands** which lie at the south end of Vaccarès Lagoon, have a lush vegetation, a kaleidoscope of colour in the spring, of blue thistles, tamarisk, wild daisies and zinerarias, junipers, wild daffodils and narcissi...

The fauna is of an exceptional variety and quantity. Beside the racoons, otters and beavers, difficult to find, birds reign supreme in this vast marshy land. There are some 400 different species of which 160 are migratory. The bird population changes according to the season due to the migratory birds. Other kinds to be spotted are: the cattle egret, which follows the *manades* so as to feed off the insects which the cattle put into flight: the greater flamingo which feeds on shellfish, the egret, seagull, herring gull, cormorant, lark, tit...

The water abounds with fish: pike perch, carp, bream and especially eel found in the fresh water canals *(roubines)* which are fished by long nets *(trabacs)* composed of three pockets sectioned by passages which get narrower. In the past the people lived from their catch.

The cistudo (small aquatic tortoise) and common snake are equally happy in this aquatic zone.

The manades and gardians. – The *manade* designates livestock and all that relates to it: herdsmen, pastureland, horses, etc. It is given the name of its owner *(manadier)*. The *mas (qv),* the large farm of several hundred acres, resembles the ranch of the Far West. It is managed by a steward *(bayle-gardian)* and groups an average of 200 horned cattle plus the horses. The *manades,* which contribute to the ecological balance of the Camargue tend to retreat before agriculture and salt production.

The *gardian* is the soul of the *manades;* the cowboy of Camargue, a man of pride and character, in a large felt hat, carrying a long, three pronged stick watches over his herd (checking the sick animals, caring for them, selecting the bulls for the *cocarde*)...

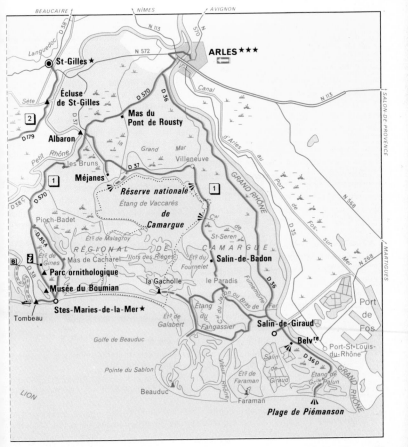

CAMARGUE★★

Although the hat and three pronged stick are kept more and more for traditional fairs, the horse stays the *gardian's* – an excellent horseman – faithful companion. Camargue horses descend from the prehistoric animal, the skeletons of which were discovered in a vast horse cemetery at Solutré (north-northwest of Lyons). Small (not more than 10 hands) they possess stamina, sureness of foot and quick intelligence; the

Gardian's cabin

foals are born brown and turn white only in their fourth or fifth year. The *gardian's* saddle specially made by a saddle-maker of the region, must offer a maximum of comfort and security: padding, fenders which fall along the horses flanks, cage-like stirrups, pommel in front and cantle in back.

The bulls, black, lithe and agile, with horns aloft, are the heroes of the Provençal, or *cocarde*, bullfights where the bull survives the fight (as opposed to the Spanish-style bull fight which ends with the bull's death); some Spanish bulls with low horns are also raised. In the spring the roundup *(ferrade)* is a colourful event; the young calves (1 year old) are separated from the herd by the *gardians* in order to be branded. They are roped, thrown on their side and branded on their left thigh with the mark of their owner – the excitement, crush of beasts, smell of burning leather all combine to create a very festive occasion.

The herd of sheep which attain 80 000 heads graze in Camargue during the winter and go up to the Alps over the summer; they too seem to be affected by the encroachment of farm land and salt cultivation.

There are a large number of owners who hire out horses for cowboy accompanied, **organised rides** amongst the animals on the plain, in the marshes or on the beach *(see Practical Information pp 196-198)*.

★★① THE RHÔNE DELTA
Round tour starting from Arles
160km – 99 miles – allow 1 day, tour of Arles not included – local map p 97

★★★**Arles.** – *Tour: time: 1/2 day. Description p 63.*

Leave Arles by ④ on the town plan (p 68), the D 570.

Ⓥ **Mas du Pont de Rousty.** – Within the Camargue Regional Nature Park, the sheepfold of this *mas* contains a local **museum** (musée camarguais) which recounts the history of Camargue through the years (especially the 19C). A signposted trail *(time: 1 1/2 hours)* winds through the surrounding countryside.

Continue along the D 570 through a seemingly infinite cultivated area.

Albaron. – Albaron, once a stronghold, as can be seen from its fine 13-16C tower, is now an important pumping and desalination station.

Continue again along the D 570 through Les Bruns and Pioch-Badet.

Ⓥ **Ginès.** – The **Camargue information centre** has been set up at Pont-de-Gau along the banks of Ginès Lagoon. A presentation of slides, photographs and documents illustrates traditional Camargue and Camargue at work, its flora and fauna. Large bay windows look out over the lagoon and its animal life.

Ⓥ **Pont-de-Gau Bird Sanctuary** (Parc ornithologique du Pont-de-Gau). – The sanctuary contains most of the birds living or passing through Camargue. Huge aviaries contain birds difficult to spot. There are 12ha – 30 acres of signposted paths.

Ⓥ **Boumian Museum** (Musée du Boumian). – Camargue life is depicted in 18 tableaux peopled by wax figures. There is also an ornithological collection and a display of shot guns.

★**Stes-Maries-de-la-Mer.** – *Description p 171.*

Leave west on the D 38 and after 1km – 1/2 mile, turn left into a surfaced road.

On the left is the tomb of Folco de Baroncelli-Javon *(qv)*; it was set up in 1951 on the site of his property, the Mas du Simbeu.

★**Boat trip on the Petit Rhône.** – The trip, which goes upstream to the Petit Sauvage
Ⓥ Ferry, takes you to the grazing pastures on the plain where you may see wild horses and bulls, and, from the tamarisk-covered river banks fish, osprey, grey heron, duck and occasionally flamingoes.

Return to Stes-Maries-de-la-Mer and take the D 85ᴬ.

The road crosses Couvin Marsh, a saltwater landscape of stunted plants and swamp. Mas de Cacherel stands to the right, Stes-Maries to the rear.

At Pioch-Badet, turn right into the D 570; at the entrance to Albaron, turn right again into the D 37 which winds through rice fields. 4.5km – 2 1/2 miles further on bear right to Méjanes.

Ⓥ **Méjanes.** – The amusement centre includes a bull ring, pony trekking and horse-drawn carriages; an electric railway runs 3.5km – 2 miles along the Vaccarès.

Continue along the D 37.

The road crosses an expanse relieved by the occasional clump of trees, reeds and isolated *mas*.

Viewpoint over Vaccarès Lagoon. – *3/4 hour on foot Rtn. Turn right into an unsurfaced road and park the car.*

The footpath, which skirts an irrigation canal, ends at a small belvedere which looks out over the lagoon towards Rièges Islands *(qv)*.

Return to the D 37 where you bear right; in Villeneuve turn right towards Vaccarès Lagoon.

To the right is the lagoon, to the left, on St-Seren Marsh, a typical *gardian's* cabin. The road skirts Fournelet Pool.

Salin-de-Badon. – Offices of the Camargue Nature Reserve are located here.
From Le Paradis two excursions *(traffic tolerated, drive at your own risk)* can be undertaken in dry weather enabling the tourist to discover the birds of the Camargue and particularly the pink flamingoes.
– one goes to **Gacholle Lighthouse** (Phare de la Gacholle) where there is a telescope in a cabin *(traffic prohibited from Perthuis de la Comtesse, do the last 1/2 mile on foot)*.
– the other is along the causeway between the **Fangassier** and **Galabert Pools.**

The D 36ᶜ and the D 36 on the right, bring you to Salin-de-Giraud.

Salin-de-Giraud. – In salt country, the small town on the south bank of the Rhône with its grid pattern of streets shaded by plane trees, acacias and catalpas, is a chemical manufacturing centre – note how each quarter is named after a firm (Péchiney, Solvay). The surrounding countryside lives from cattle-rearing and mixed farming (rice, lucerne, asparagus).

Follow the road which skirts the Grand Rhône.

Viewpoint. – The viewpoint beside a salt heap looks out over the Giraud pans and workings *(pp 16 and 96)*.

Continue towards Piémanson Beach.

The Rhône and Port-St-Louis can be seen at intervals before you cross the causeway between lakes white with salt.

Piémanson Beach (Plage de Piémanson). – The vast sweep of fine sand *(25km – 15 1/2 miles)* is bordered by low dunes; to the east can be seen the Estaque Mountains, the Marseilleveyre and Étoile Massifs and due north, in the far distance, the Alpilles.

Return to Arles through Salin-de-Giraud and along the D 36 and the D 570 on the right.

The road crosses an area of cultivated fields cut by rows of poplars.

★★ ② AIGUES-MORTES PLAIN
From St-Gilles to Port-Camargue
43km – 26 1/2 miles – about 5 hours – local map pp 96-97

★**St-Gilles.** – *Description p 161.*

Leave St-Gilles by the N 572 going southeast; turn right into the D 179.
Vineyards, pinewoods and fields edged with rushes border the road.

St-Gilles Lock (Écluse de St-Gilles). – The lock controls the canal between the Petit Rhône and the Rhône-Sète Canal – go on to the bridge for a good view of the works.
Continue along the D 179.

Rice fields extend to the hills on the horizon where the dominant Puech de Dardaillon is all of 146m – 479ft high! On the left is an old watch tower.

The road bears left to skirt the Capettes Canal.

The ruins before the junction with the D 58, where you turn right, are those of the early 18C château of the Marquess of Montcalm who lived here before travelling to Canada. The chapel in the vineyards on the right is also 18C.

Continue along the D 58, which crosses the Rhône-Sète Canal, and shortly afterwards turn right into the D 46.

Carbonnière Tower (Tour Carbonnière). – 14C tower, complete with gates, portcullisses and battlements, this was the advanced barbican of Aigues-Mortes *(qv)* on the old salt road. A small garrison was quartered in the first floor room which was equipped with a big fireplace and a bread oven.
The platform (66 steps) commands a **panorama★** of Aigues-Mortes and the saltmarshes to the south, the Cévennes foothills to the northwest and the Lesser Camargue to the east.

Return to the D 58 and turn right.

★★**Aigues-Mortes.** – *Description p 44.*

Take the D 979 southwest.

The road passes between the Grande Roubine and the Midi Saltmarshes.

Le Grau-du-Roi. – Pop 4 204. Facilities. The small fishing village at the mouth of the channel connecting the saltmarshes and the sea, has developed into a picturesque resort. From the end of the jetty, there is a view of the Grande Motte highrises and the new resort of Port-Camargue.

Return to the entrance to Le Grau-du-Roi, to take the D 62ᴮ on the right.

★**Port-Camargue.** – *Description p 158.*

Michelin map 🎆 folds 12 and 13 or 🎆 fold 17 or 🎆 fold 10 – Facilities

Carpentras, well-known for its special caramel sweets, *berlingots* and thrush hunting, is a town with an ancient past. Market centre for a Celtic-Ligurian tribe, Gallo-Roman city, bishopric which was temporarily moved to Venasque, the town blossomed when the popes came to Provence.

Pope Clement V stayed here frequently between 1309-14; as did the cardinals. Even a conclave met here in 1314, although it moved to Lyons where it elected John XXII. Capital of the Comtat Venaissin in 1320, the town profited from papal munificence; it expanded and protected itself, under Innocent VI with powerful ramparts consisting of 32 towers and 4 gates, demolished in the 19C. With Avignon, Cavaillon and Isle-sur-la-Sorgue it had, until the Revolution, a Jewish ghetto.

The famous sons of Carpentras include the 18C Bishop Malachie d'Inguimbert, benefactor and founder of the hospital (Hôtel-Dieu) who also founded, in 1745, the famous library named after him, Inguimbertine Library (west of town). The 19C can account for F. Raspail (1794-1878) and A. Naquet (1834-1916) both doctors and republican political figures and in the 20C E. Daladier (1884-1970), President of the Council and one of the signers of the 1938 Treaty of Munich.

Although Carpentras profited from the expansion of madder, a plant introduced in 1768, the surrounding plain turned into a fertile garden when in the 19C a canal, a branch of the Durance, enabled the area to be irrigated. At the same time the railway arrived. The town continues as an active agricultural centre. The old tradition of making decoys, which the Provençal hunter uses to attract game also continues. Each year Carpentras is the centre of a **festival** *(p 200)* of great diversity : theatre, opera, dance, folklore events etc.

OLD ST-SIFFREIN CATHEDRAL PRECINCTS *time : 3/4 hour*

★**Old St-Siffrein Cathedral** (Ancienne cathédrale St-Siffrein) (Z). – Started in 1404 by the archbishop of Arles, in the name of Pope Benedict XIII of Avignon, the cathedral is a good example of the southern Gothic style. Finished in the early 16C, its façade was completed in the 17C with the classical doorway. The bell tower is recent.

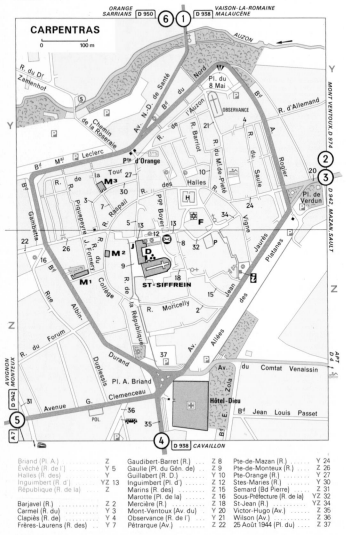

Briand (Pl. A.)	Z	Gaudibert-Barret (R.)	Z 8	Pte-de-Mazan (R.)	Y 24
Évêché (R. de l')	Y 5	Gaulle (Pl. du Gén. de)	Z 9	Pte-de-Monteux (R.)	Z 26
Halles (R. des)	Y	Guillabert (R. D.)	Y 10	Pte-Orange (R.)	Y 27
Inguimbert (R. d')	YZ 13	Inguimbert (Pl. d')	Z 12	Stes-Maries (R.)	Y 30
République (R. de la)	Z	Marins (R. des)	Z 15	Semard (Bd Pierre)	Z 31
		Marotte (Pl. de la)	Z 16	Sous-Préfecture (R. de la)	YZ 32
Barjavel (R.)	Z 2	Mercière (R.)	Z 18	St-Jean (R.)	YZ 34
Carmel (R. du)	Y 3	Mont-Ventoux (Av. du)	Y 20	Victor-Hugo (Av.)	Z 35
Clapiès (R. de)	Y 4	Observance (R. de l')	Y 21	Wilson (Av.)	Z 36
Frères-Laurens (R. des)	Y 7	Pétrarque (Av.)	Z 22	25 Août 1944 (Pl. du)	Z 37

Enter the cathedral by the Flamboyant Gothic south door (late 15C), known as the Jewish Door after the Jewish converts who passed through it to be baptised. Inside, note the balcony on the nave's end wall which connects with the bishops' apartments, and the small room above the first bay from which he could follow services. There are paintings in the north chapels by Mignard and Parrocel and sculptures, including a gilded wood glory, by the Provençal, Bernus *(qv)* in the chancel; to the left is a 15C painting of the Virgin surrounded by the Holy Trinity, St Siffrein and St Michael.

★**Treasury** (Trésor d'Art sacré). – Displayed in a chapel north of the chancel. Ⓥ Among the exhibits are 14-16C wooden statues (14C Virgin and Child, 15C Prophet Daniel), sacerdotal ornaments, gold and silver plate (18-19C), sculpture by Bernus and a Limoges enamel cross.

Ⓥ **Law Courts (Palais de Justice)** (Z J). – The former episcopal palace dates from the 17C. The interior is decorated with paintings (17C), especially worth noting in the Assize Gallery and Sitting Room.

Triumphal Arch (Arc de triomphe) (Z D). – The Roman municipal arch behind the Law Courts was built most likely during the same period as the arch in Orange *(p 151)*. Its decorations (mutilated) are particularly interesting on the east face where two prisoners are chained to a tree hung with military trophies.
Amid ruins of the old Romanesque cathedral, located near the actual church's east end is a richly decorated dome.

ADDITIONAL SIGHTS

Circular tour of town. – Follow the boulevards, laid out on the site of the old ramparts; start at Place A. Briand and drive along Boulevards Albin-Durand, Gambetta, Maréchal-Leclerc, du Nord, Alfred-Rogier and Avenue Jean-Jaurès and back to Place A. Briand. Fine **views** of the Dentelles de Montmirail and Mount Ventoux; the best view is from the terrace at Place du 8-Mai.

Orange Gate (Porte d'Orange) (Y). – From the 14C, it is the only remaining part of the city wall.

Ⓥ **Museums (Musées).** – Four museums have assembled collections of essentially regional interest.

Comtat Venaissin (Musée Comtadin) (Z **M¹**). – *Ground floor.* Regional mementos include coins and seals, local head-dresses and bells for cattle and sheep driven through the town to summer and winter pastures.

Duplessis Museum (Musée Duplessis) (Z **M¹**). – *First floor.* Paintings by local Primitive artists, Parrocel, Rigaud, the Carpentras artist, Duplessis and J. Laurens.

Sobirats Museum (Musée Sobirats) (Z **M²**). – 18C house with contemporary interior.

Lapidary Museum (Musée Lapidaire) (Y **M³**). – The building was formerly the Chapel of the Grey Penitents (former Convent of the Visitation), consecrated in 1717. In the 2nd south chapel note several columns and capitals from the cathedral's Romanesque cloisters.

Ⓥ **Hospital (Hôtel-Dieu)** (Z). – Going through the 18C building one sees the pharmacy, (cupboard doors decorated with pastoral scenes and cartoons including monkey apothecaries; Moustiers ware jars) the chapel (Mignard and Parrocel paintings; the tomb – north of the chancel – of Bishop Inguimbert, founder of the hospital; wrought iron altar grill) and the grand staircase with a delicate iron banister.

Ⓥ **Synagogue** (Y F). – The synagogue, dating from the 15C, rebuilt in the 18C and restored in 1929 and 1958, is the oldest in France and the last relic of a Jewish ghetto, which before the Revolution numbered 1 200 people. On the first floor is the panelled sanctuary with lamps and candlesticks; below are the oven for baking unleavened bread and the temple annexes and in the basement the *piscina*.

EXCURSIONS

Mazan. – Pop 3 729. *7km – 4 miles by ③, on the town plan, the D 942.* The small town in the Auzon Valley is close to Mormoiron, the largest gypsum deposit and quarry in Europe.
The village was the birthplace of the Comtat Venaissin's most reputed sculptor, Jacques Bernus (1650-1728) *(qv)*.
Sixty-two Gallo-Roman sarcophagi, which once lined the Roman road from Carpentras to Sault, now a wall in the **churchyard** of the 12C Notre-Dame-de-Pareloup, which is half-underground. From here there is a fine **view★** of the mountains.
Ⓥ Near the church, the 17C Chapel of White Penitents houses a **local museum** (parchments, costumes, furnishings, agricultural implements). Note the vestiges from the Stone Age found during the excavations on the south face of Mount Ventoux, a carving by Jacques Bernus. In the courtyard is a 14C bread oven.

Sarrians. – Pop 5 030. *8km – 5 miles by ⑥ on the town plan by the D 950.* The partly hidden **church,** of this small town of the Comtat Venaissin, on a rock bluff, is a former Benedictine priory. The interior has an unusually attractive chancel and is remarkable for the great age (11C) of its squinch supported dome.

Monteux. – Pop 7 552. *4.5km – 2 1/2 miles by ⑤ on the town plan, the D 942.* This small market-garden centre knew a moment of glory, in the early 14C when Pope Clement V came here to rest; a tower remains from the castle in which he stayed. Also standing are two gates from the old 14C ramparts.
Monteux is also the birthplace of St Gentius, patron saint of the Provençal farmers, who had the ability to bring on rain. A pilgrimage *(p 200)* is held annually in his honour in Beaucet.

★ CASSIS

Pop 6 318

Michelin map 🆄 fold 13 or 🆄 fold 45 or 🆄 fold M – Local map p 103 – Facilities

Cassis, a bustling, small fishing port, lies in an attractive **setting★** at the end of a bay where the valley, between the arid Puget heights (to the west) and the wooded escarpments of Cape Canaille (to the east) comes down to the sea. It is justly reputed for the quality of its fish, shellfish and other seafood; the eating of sea-urchins *(oursins)* with Cassis white wine is very popular. It is also a popular summer resort which has three small beaches, two of sand one of shingle, each sheltered by rocks with a fairly steep slope. Cassis became known in 1867 with a mention of the village by Mistral in his poem *Calendal* and again at the turn of the century, when it became the chosen summer resort of the artists Derain, Vlaminck, Matisse and Dufy.

The quarries not far from the village, notably by Port-Miou Inlet, produce a hard white stone which has been used for quaysides and gateways as the Rove Tunnel and as far away as the Suez Canal and the Campo Santo in Genoa.

Climbing at En-Vau Inlet

Regattas and watersports celebrate the feast day of the patron saint of fishermen, St Peter, on 29 June and other special days throughout the summer.

Ⓥ **Local Museum (Musée municipal) (H)**. – Located on the first floor of an 18C town house (restored), Maison de Cassis, this small museum of popular arts and traditions contains archaeological finds from the area (1C cippus, Roman and Greek coins, pottery...), Mss and paintings and sculpture by local artists.

Promenade des Lombards. – This pleasant walk along the beach continues
Ⓥ round the foot of the rock spike crowned by the restored **castle** of Les Baux.

★★INLETS (Calanques)

The valleys of the Marseilleveyre and Puget limestone ranges, west of Cassis, continue under the sea, forming as they dip below the water, a shoreline of deep inlets (known locally as *calanques*), between high ridges.

The scenic attraction lies in the brilliant limpidity of the deep blue or, sometimes, bluegreen water below tall, rough white cliffs.

Tour. – The pleasantest way to make the excursion is by boat. With a motor-boat *(vedette)* one can go as far En Vau visiting the three inlets of Port-Miou, Port-Pin and En-Vau.

By car you can go to the end of Port-Miou Inlet *(1.5km – 3/4 mile)*, and yet it is preferable to park at the top of the slope and do the last 1/2 mile to the harbour on foot. Continue on foot along the marked paths – Port-Pin *(1 hour Rtn)*, En-Vau *(2 1/2 hours Rtn)*. Take the D 559 *(6.5km – 3 3/4 miles from Cassis, 17km – 10 1/2 miles from Marseilles)* and turn off down a narrow road along a gorge, then through Gardiole Forest, to the Gardiole Pass *(Col de la Gardiole 3.2km – 2 miles)*.

CASSIS

Abbé-Mouton (R.)	2
Arène (R. de l')	4
Autheman (R. V.)	5
Baragnon (Pl.)	6
Barthélémy (Bd)	7
Barthélémy (Quai J.-J.)	8
Baux (Quai des)	9
Ciotat (R. de la)	10
Clemenceau (Pl.)	12
Jaurès (Av. J.)	16
Leriche (Av. Professeur)	17
Mirabeau (Pl.)	22
Moulins (Q. des)	23
République (Pl.)	25
Revestel (Av. du)	26
St-Michel (Pl.)	27
Thiers (R. Adolphe)	29
Victor-Hugo (Av.)	32

The maps and plans are orientated with north at the top.

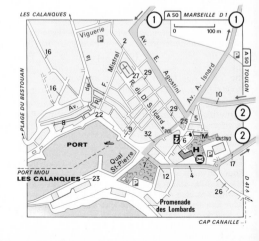

Park the car and continue on foot: En-Vau *(2 hours Rtn)*; Port-Pin *(3 hours Rtn)*.

⊘ **Port-Miou Inlet (Calanque de Port-Miou).** – The 1km – 1/2 mile long inlet shelters a small village of the same name.

★ **Port-Pin Inlet (Calanque de Port-Pin).** – Tucked away at the end of the inlet, with its high rock walls plumed by occasional pines, is a small, shady, beach.

★★ **En-Vau Inlet (Calanque d'En-Vau).** – The best known and prettiest inlet has high white cliffs and tall needle rocks rising out of the sea with a beach of fine sand at the end.

Sormiou and Sugiton Inlets. – *Description p 138.*

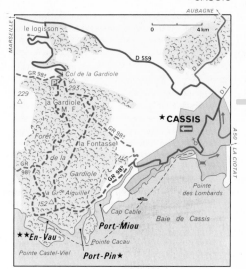

CAVAILLON
Pop 20 830

Michelin map 🟦 fold 12 or 🟦 fold 30 or 🟦 fold 11 – Local maps pp 112 and 124 – Facilities

The name Cavaillon, to the French, conjures up fragrant melons and the sweet vegetables of early spring. The melons are sweet and rose pink inside; the harvest begins in May; the vegetables come from the mile upon mile of market gardens which surround the town and make it France's largest designated "national market" with an annual turnover of nearly 800 000 metric tons.
Oppidum of the Celtic-Ligurian people, the Cavares, ancient Cabellio located on St-Jacques Hill was under Marseilles's jurisdiction until the latters downfall. The town then left its hilltop site and became a prosperous Roman colony.
During the Middle Ages it had two famous bishops: in the 6C St Veranus, patron saint of shepherds and in the 14C Philippe de Cabassole, friend of Petrarch's *(qv)*.

SIGHTS

⊘ **Chapel of St-Jacques (Chapelle St-Jacques).** – *3/4 hour on foot Rtn. Start from Place François-Tourel.* On this square lie the ruins of a small delicately carved **Roman arch,** re-erected here in 1880.

Left of the arch, at the end of the square, take the picturesque stepped path.

Carved into the rock at the second bend is an inscription to Mistral *(qv)*. From the viewing table placed in front of the Calvary, the **view★** embraces Cavaillon Plain, Mount Ventoux; Coulon Valley, Vaucluse Plateau, the Luberon (quite near), Durance Valley and the Alpilles Chain.
Continue to the **Chapel of St-Jacques,** a 12C chapel remodelled in the 16 and 17C. It stands among cypresses, pines and almond trees, near a small hermitage occupied from the 14C to the beginning of this century.
Accessible also by car *(5.5km – 3 miles)* by way of the D 938 going north; 50m beyond the crossroad turn left uphill (views of the Montagnette and the Rhône).

CAVAILLON

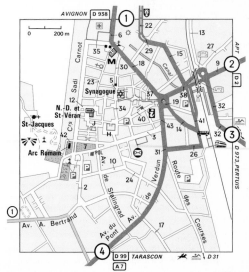

◯ **Old Notre-Dame-et-St-Véran Cathedral** (Ancienne cathédrale Notre-Dame-et-St-Véran). – To the original Romanesque structure, side chapels were added from the 14-18C. The façade was almost entirely rebuilt in the 18C and the east end holds a fine pentagonal apse.

Enter on the south side.

Cross the small Romanesque **cloisters.**
Inside, despite the darkness, one can glimpse gilded 17C panelling in the chancel and side chapels (paintings by Pierre and Nicolas Mignard, Parrocel and Daret) and choirstalls which date back to 1585.

◯ **Synagogue.** – The synagogue, built in 1772 on a small scale – the Jewish community never exceeded 200 – is decorated with Louis XV style panelling and wrought iron balustrades.
A small **Jewish Comtat Venaissin Museum,** located in the old bakery, includes the large grey marble tablet and oven for unleavened bread, prayer books, torahic ornaments and relics of the first synagogue (14C) built on the same site.

◯ **Museum** (Musée) (M). – The museum is located in the old hospital chapel and outhouses. The chapel contains a lapidary section (prehistoric cup-shaped stones, cippi and Gallo-Roman columns, 6C tabular altar); the André Dumoulin Gallery (ground floor) is devoted to prehistory in the Luberon.
An important **archaeological collection★** (1st floor) includes objects for the most part found on St-Jacques Hill in wells or ditches, which were used for storage and dating from the 2 and 1C BC, pottery (5C BC-6C AD), coins, utensils, funerary urns and food. On the 2nd floor a room exhibits mementoes of the hospital itself (books of 17-18C remedies, a 1773 mortar, Moustiers faience).

Avoid visiting a church during a service.

CHÂTEAU-BAS

Michelin map 🔢 fold 2 or 🔢 fold 30 or 🔢 fold 12 – 8km – 5 miles northwest of Lambesc

At the far end of the castle (16-18C) park, in a charming site, stand the fascinating ruins of a Roman temple and chapel.

1km – 1/2 mile southwest of Cazan a road (marked) goes off the D 22 in the direction of Pélissanne; car park at the end.

◯ **Roman Temple** (Temple romain). – The temple probably dates from the late 1C BC, contemporary with the Commemorative Arch at St-Rémy-de-Provence *(p 166)* or the Maison Carrée in Nîmes *(p 145)*. The remains include part of the foundations, the left side wall, a wall ending in a square pilaster, surmounted by a beautiful Corinthian capital and a 7m – 23ft fluted column still standing intact.
Among the surrounding ruins are a second temple and a semi-circular precinct (Roman) probably the ruins of a sanctuary.

◯ **Chapel of St-Césaire** (Chapelle St-Césaire). – The 12C chapel, abutting the left wall of the temple, is barrel vaulted, with an oven vaulted apse and a 16C doorway and niche.

CHÂTEAUNEUF-DU-PAPE   Pop 2 060

Michelin map 🔢 fold 12 or 🔢 fold 16 or 🔢 fold 24 – Facilities

The town is the source of the most heady of all the Rhône wines. The original vineyard was planted in the 14C on land belonging to the Avignon popes, who summered here, and the wine was consumed locally until the mid-18C when its renown began to spread. For a long time the wine was sent in barrels to Burgundy for improvement. In *c*1880 phylloxera ravaged the vineyards resulting in its ruin; the vineyard was replanted.
In 1923 the winegrowers' association laid down strict rules defining the area, the management of the vineyards, harvest dates, the selection of grapes, the thirteen acceptable wine types, vinification and vintage labelling. The strict control has brought about a highly refined and often superb product: a wine known for its finesse and nose – Châteauneuf-du-Pape.

Popes' Castle (Château des Papes). – All that remains of the fortress built by the Avignon popes in the 14C and burned down during the Wars of Religion, is one tower and stretch of wall. The ruins, however, still command a splendid **view★★**: the Valley of the Rhône, Roquemaure and the ruins of Hers Castle, Avignon with Notre-Dame-des-Doms and the Palace of the Popes clearly outlined against the more distant Alpilles Chain, the Luberon and the Vaucluse Plateau, the Dentelles de Montmirail and, farther off, Mount Ventoux, the Baronnies and Lance Mountain.

◯ **Winegrowers Museum** (Musée des outils de vignerons). – Located in Father Anselme's wine cellar, this museum treats the world of wine. The tour is conducted in the order that wine is produced: from the work in the vineyard (plough, hoes, pruning clippers), its treatment (copper sulphate spraying machines), harvesting (baskets, wine press), the work in the cellar (funnel, 16C press, huge 14C barrel) and its related activities such as cooperage, grafting, weights and measures, phylloxera, bottling, corking...
In one room the vineyards presentday 3 300ha – 8 151 acres are illustrated; it includes 300 winegrowers. In the courtyard is a display of old ploughs.

EXCURSION

Roquemaure. – Pop 4 054. *10km – 6 miles on the D 17 and the D 976.*
The road drives through beautifully kept vineyards. On the left some 2km – 1 mile later appear the ruins of Hers Castle, the machicolated tower of which seems to hover protectively over its precious vineyard. Across from it, on the opposite bank of the Rhône, is Roquemaure Castle where Pope Clement V died 20 April 1314. Cross the Rhône, which the road borders, for a couple more miles, and continue to Roquemaure which has preserved several old houses (notably the one belonging to Cardinal Bertrand, near the church). The 13C church has a fine 17C organ.

CHÂTEAURENARD   Pop 11 072

Michelin map 🔳 fold 12 or 🔳🔳 fold 29 or 🔳🔳 fold 25 – Local map p 112 – Facilities

The town, at the foot of a hill beneath medieval twin towers, has become a national market with a designated site of 150 000m² – 35 acres, handling the produce (350 000 to 400 000 metric tons annually) harvested from the market gardens and fruit farms in the neighbouring plain.
In Mistral's work *Nerte,* a 15C lord from Châteaurenard, sold his daughter's soul to the devil.

ⓥ **Feudal Castle (Château féodal).** – *Access: on foot by taking the staircase to the right of the church, by car 1km – 1/2 mile via Avenue Marx-Dormoy and a signposted road on the right.*
Of the feudal castle, ruined during the Revolution, there remain but two towers. From the top of the said Griffon Tower a fine **panorama★** can be had of the town and surrounding countryside, the Montagnette, Avignon and Villeneuve-lès-Avignon, the Dentelles de Montmirail, Mount Ventoux and the Alpilles Chain.

LA CIOTAT   Pop 31 727

Michelin map 🔳 fold 14 or 🔳🔳 fold 45 or 🔳🔳 fold M – Facilities – See plan of built-up-area in the current Michelin Red Guide France

La Ciotat, where the houses rise in tiers above the bay of the same name, has been a port since ancient times when, as Citharista, it was an outpost of Marseilles. Roman occupation, barbarian invasion and devastation were followed by a revival in the Middle Ages, and from the 16C the provision of a merchant fleet in the eastern Mediterranean.
The city's mainstay, today, is still the port where there are shipyards which build oil and methane gas tankers, and docks for ships up to 300 000 metric tons; there is also a boilers and industrial hollow-ware factory.
The Lumière brothers, cinema and photographic inventors, brought fame to this town when, in September 1895, the first private showing of a short motion picture occurred, two months before Paris.

SIGHTS

Old Harbour (Vieux port). – Dominated by the massive bulks of the ships under construction, the harbour, nevertheless, retains the charm of a small fishing port.

ⓥ **Notre-Dame-de-l'Assomption (B)**. – This 17C church's lovely pink baroque façade, overlooks the harbour. Inside, the modern looking interior is notable for a *Descent from the Cross* by André Gaudion painted in 1616 (south aisle) and a modern frieze (22m – 72ft long) by Gilbert Ganteaume of scenes from the Gospels. At the end of the nave are paintings by Tony Roux representing man and woman.

ⓥ **Local Museum (Musée ciotaden) (M).** – Inside are mementoes and documents on this seafaring town and its past.

La Ciotat-Plage. – The quarter has been created just north of the new harbour (Nouveau Port: 700 berths) as a resort with hotels and seaside villas lining the beach. A thalassotherapy centre has been established. Marking one of the squares open to the sea is a monument to the Lumière brothers *(see above).*

ⓥ **Mugel Gardens (Parc du Mugel).** – *Access by Quai Stalingrad, south of the town plan.* Located at the tip of Aigle Point (Cap de l'Aigle), this natural protected area with pudding stone soil (reddish conglomerate of shingles and sand) grows abundant and varied vegetation (cork trees, mimosa, arbutus, etc). A marked trail amidst the identified plants enhances the walk. At the top *(steep path)* at 155m – 509ft lovely view of La Ciotat and its surroundings.

LA CIOTAT

Foch (R. Mar.)	16
Poilus (R. des)	
Anatole-France (Bd)	2
Bartolucci (Bd)	6
Clemenceau (Bd G.)	13
Gallieni (Av. Mar.)	18
Ganteaume (Quai)	19
Gaulle (Quai Gén. de)	21
Kennedy (Av. J.F.)	23
Lamartine (Bd)	24
Prés. Wilson (Av.)	31

★**Verte Island (Ile Verte).** – *1/2 hour by boat Rtn.* The rock at Aigle Point, so
ⓥ clearly a bird of prey (*aigle* means eagle), when seen from the small fort on Verte
Island is what gave the point its name.

Inlets (Calanques). – *1.5km – 3/4 mile.* Leave La Ciotat via Quai Stalingrad and
Avenue des Calanques and bear left into Avenue du Mugel.

Mugel Inlet (Calanque du Mugel). – The inlet is dominated by the rock of Aigle Point.
Good view of Verte Island.

Take Avenue des Calanques and bear left into Avenue de Figuerolles.

★**Figuerolles Inlet** (Calanque de Figuerolles). – *1/4 hour on foot Rtn.* A short green
valley leads to the small clear water inlet marked by strangely eroded rocks.

Notre-Dame-de-la-Garde Chapel. – *2.5km – 1 1/2 miles – plus 1/4 hour on foot
Rtn.* Leave La Ciotat by Boulevards Bertolucci and Narvik, Rue du Cardinal-Maurin
and Chemin-de-la-Garde, on the right, after 500m – 1/3 mile turn left towards a
built-up area and park the car.
At the chapel, bear right into a path which leads to a terrace above the chapel (85
steps cut out of the rock). The **view★★** embraces the full extent of La Ciotat Bay.

★ COCALIÈRE Cave (Grotte de la COCALIÈRE)

Michelin map 🎴 fold 8

This cave, northwest of St-Ambroix on the Gard Plateau, contains a network of
explored caves (14 ºC-57 ºF inside temperature) running 46km-29 miles underground. In addition the site of La Cocalière has revealed a very populated prehistoric
settlement which was occupied from the Mousterian period (45 000 BC) to the Iron
Age (400BC).

From Les Vans bear left on a road which branches off the D 904 on the left,
not far after, the road to the right goes off to Courry.

ⓥ **TOUR** time: 1 1/4 hours

At the bottom of the tunnel, a path follows along (about 1 200m – 1 312yds) the
bottom of a horizontal gallery which communicates with each of the other galleries.
The cave is rich in its variety of concretions which reflect in the pools of water fed
by small waterfalls. As you travel underground you will see discs – huge concretions
with a wide diameter which specialists have not yet been able to explain – fine
stalactites: white (if charged with calcite) or multi-coloured (if charged with metallic
oxide and gours (natural dams).
After the speleologists camping site, via the Chaos Chamber, where the roof is
covered with stalagmites and other forms of erosion, you enter the land of frozen
falls and eccentrics and overlook an imposing sparkling **waterfall** and wells linked
to the lower stages where underground rivers flow.
Pass through a prehistoric deposit before returning to the entrance area on a small
train.
Outside, the cave's immediate surroundings note: a dolmen, tumuli, small
constructions of dried stones much like the *bories (qv)* from Provence, prehistoric
shelters and varied karstic phenomena (caves, sinkholes, faults).

COMTAT VENAISSIN

Michelin map 🎴 folds 2, 3,
12 and 13 or 🎴 folds 16
to 18 and 30 and 31 or 🎴
folds 9 to 11

Located between the Rhône
and Durance Rivers and
Mount Ventoux, the territory
comprising this old county,
owes its name to its first
capital, Venasque. It was
designated the name Comtat
Venaissin when it was an-
nexed by the Holy See in
1274. The Comtat Venaissin
is an important notion for
the French in the history of
their country. It had previously been included in the
marquisate of Provence and
was under the county of
Toulouse's rule; and like all
the county's other possessions was affected by the
Albigensian heresy and the
Treaty of Paris (1229).
United under the crown in
1271 it was ceded three
years later to Pope Gre-
gory X by Philip III, the Bold

After July 1745 map

and remained under papal authority until 1791 when it once again became part of France.

This enclave had its own administration; its law courts were located at Carpentras, capital of the Comtat, having superseded Pernes-les-Fontaines *(qv)* in 1320. Made up of the rich Vaucluse Plain, Comtat Venaissin occupies the largest and most southerly basin of the Rhône Valley. Its rich calcareous soil, benefiting from irrigation, has brought upon the creation of vast gardens specialising in the production of market garden vegetables and fruit distributed nationwide *(p 14)*. Cultivation occurs within a framework of scattered habitats and a mosaic of scientifically exploited small farms.

The Rivers Ouvèze, Sorgue and Durance have created vast fertile alluvial plains upon which market-towns – Orange, Avignon, Cavaillon and Carpentras – have profited; some of these same towns have become very large dispatching centres.

★★ CONCLUSES Gorges

Michelin map 🔠 south of fold 9 or 🔢 fold 14 or 🔢 fold 24 – 8km – 5 miles northeast of Lussan

The D 643, lined by clipped boxwood, crosses a *garrigues* of holm oak *(qv)* to the Aiguillon Gorges, also known as the Concluses Gorges.

The **Aiguillon** torrent, dry in summer, has hollowed out of the calcareous grey white rock a rocky defile some 1km – 1/2 mile long and opened upstream by a fine natural phenomenon: the Gateway (Portail).

TOUR *time: 1 hour on foot Rtn*

Leave the car at the road's end, preferably in the second of the two car parks, a lay-by halfway down. From here there is a **view★** upstream of the giant holes in the riverbed.

> *Take the path on the right signposted: Portail (meaning gateway).*

As you descend you see the caves on the opposite bank, most notably the Baume de Biou or Bulls' Cave, and come to the promontory and Beauquier Pool, a widening of the stream fringed by trees at the feet of majestic rock escarpments. Note on the cliff face three abandonned eagles' eyries. The path ends at the gateway where the rock overhang finally meets above the river's course; the bottom forms a narrow gorge by which the Aiguillon flows when in spate. Pass under the gateway, then walk through the rocky **straits** following the river bed about 200m – 219yds. *(This walk is possible only in summer.)*

On the return, experienced walkers may enjoy climbing back to the car park by way of the river bed upstream as far as Bull's Cave and from there a very rough path *(allow an extra 1/4 hour)*.

CRAU Plain (Plaine de la CRAU)

Michelin maps 🔠 fold 10 and 🔠 fold 1 or 🔢 folds 29 and 42 or 🔢 folds 12, 13, 26 and 27

The Crau Plain, which extends for 50 000ha–200sq miles between the Rhône, Alpilles Chain, St-Mitre Hills and the sea, is a grey white desert of shingle and gravel which, in places, reaches a depth of 15m – 50ft. For centuries the only sign of man's existence were the roads going north up the Rhône Valley towards Lyons. Since the construction of the Craponne Canal in 1554 which brought the waters of the Durance to their original delta on the Berre Lagoon, and the subsequent development of a network of irrigation channels, the cultivation of the **Petite Crau** in the north has steadily extended until it now covers half the plain. From Arles in the west to Salon in the east, windbreaks of poplar and cypress shelter fields of fruit and vegetables (follow the N 113). There are four crops a year of the famous Crau hay (annual crop approximately 100 000 metric tons) – the last of which is grazed in the fields by sheep which winter in the plain.

The **Grande Crau** to the south, remains the symbolic Provençal desert, a region which fires the imagination and inspired a legendary origin: Hercules, the tale goes, finding his way to Spain barred by the Ligurians, against whom he exhausted his stock of arrows, called on Jupiter for help; the god sent down a hail of stones and rocks which became the plain. More prosaically, geologists attribute the presence of the stones to the Durance, which originally flowed directly into the sea through the Lamanon Gap *(see map p 13)*. The rocks and stones brought down by the stream accumulated into a vast delta which eventually dried out when the river changed course and became a tributary of the Rhône.

The Grande Crau, resembling a huge steppe is devoted entirely to **sheep raising.** The traditional breed is the fine wooled Merino. About 100 000 head graze on *coussous* (tufts of grass which grow between the stones) between mid-October and early June. The shepherd (grouped with the Union of Arles Breeders) owns only his flock, they settle each year on the grazing land (which they rent) which includes a sheep-fold and a well. All the sheepfolds, which amount to forty, were built between 1830-80 on an identical plan: a rectangle (40m × 10m – 131ft × 33ft) opened on each side and covered by stones placed like fish scales. Sometimes the shepherd lives nearby in a one room hut. The well is made up of Alpilles stone carved in one piece.

During the autumn and winter, the flock grazes on *coussous,* hay and the second growth of the irrigated plain; at the end of the winter they eat the grass (lucern, sainfoin...) bought by the shepherd; starting mid-April the flock once again grazes on *coussous.*

They move to summer pastures at a much higher altitude. The transportation of the flock from its summer pastures to its winter pastures (and visa-versa) is done with trucks.

The flocks, although well integrated into the local rural economy, pose a number of problems: the Merino is not sufficiently profitable, shepherds are hard to find, and the area of sheep-grazing land is diminishing.

Starting from St-Hippolyte *(12km – 7 1/2 miles southeast of Arles on the N 453)* and driving southeast along the N 568 one gets a good idea of the special atmosphere of the Grande Cau. The green countryside gives way to a progressively more barren landscape, devoid of artefacts, of man and beast, except for the very occasional sheepfold and cabin near a well reminding us of the decline of such pastoral activities as sheep raising.

In addition to the encroachment of agriculture from the north, the continued expansion of the Fos Complex *(qv)* implies incursion from the south for industrial development, but for the moment the heart of one of France's most fertile regions remains a semi-desert, the Crau Plain.

★★ CRESTS' CORNICHE (Corniche des CRÊTES)

Michelin map 245 fold M

The stretch of coast road between Cassis and La Ciotat skirts the Canaille, a short limestone range which rises from the sea in towering white cliffs, which are among the tallest in France – 362m – 1 188ft at Cape Canaille, 399m – 1 310ft at the Grande Tête. The tourist road and its viewpoints present superb views.

FROM CASSIS TO LA CIOTAT *19km – 11 1/2 miles – 4 hours*

★**Cassis.** – *Description p 102.*

Leave Cassis by ② on the town plan, the road to Toulon and during the ascent take a signposted road to the right. At Pas de la Colle turn left.

Saoupe Mountain (Mont de la Saoupe). – The **panorama★★** from the television mast includes Cassis, Riou Island, Marseilleveyre Massif and St-Cyr Chain to the west, the Étoile Chain, Garlaban Mountain and Ste-Baume Massif to the north, La Ciotat and Capes Aigle and Sicié to the southeast.

Return to Pas de la Colle and continue uphill.

Bends and belvederes reveal an ever wider view of Cassis and La Ciotat.

★★★**Cape Canaille** (Cap Canaille). – From the guard rail there is an outstanding **view★★★** of the cliff face, Puget Massif and the inlets and Marseilleveyre Massif.

Beyond Grande Tête, turn right to the semaphore.

Semaphore. – The **view★★★** embraces La Ciotat and its shipyards, Aigle Point, the Embiez Islands, and Capes Sicié and Canaille *(telescope)*.

Return to the corniche road; bear right for La Ciotat.

The descent into town passes quarries, recently planted pinewoods and a "natural" arch of limestone standing on a puddingstone base.

La Ciotat. – *Description p 105.*

DAUDET'S Mill (Moulin de DAUDET)

Michelin map 83 fold 10 or 245 fold 29 or 246 fold 26 – Local map p 56

Between Arles and Les Baux-de-Provence, the admirers of **Alphonse Daudet's** *(qv)* works can make a literary pilgrimage to his **mill** where he wrote his famous *Letters from My Mill*. A lovely avenue of pines leads from Font-vieille to the mill.

Alphonse Daudet, the son of a silk manufacturer was born at Nîmes on 13 May 1840 (d 1897). An outstanding author of tales of Provençal life, member of Goncourt Academy, Daudet was also a contemporary of such important 19C literary figures as Zola and Mistral. He often stayed with friends at the Château de Montauban, at the foot of the hill but it was in Paris that he wrote. And yet he enjoyed ambling through the countryside, seeking inspiration, listening to the miller or daydreaming. The **view★** embraces the Alpilles Chain, Beaucaire and Tarascon Castles, the vast Rhône Valley and Montmajour Abbey.

Daudet's Mill

⊙ **Tour.** – Inside the mill, the 1st floor presents different kinds of millstones used in the grinding of grain. Note at roof level the names of the local winds, positioned according to their source.

The small **museum** contains memorabilia of this author remembered for the humour and sentiment with which he described the life and characters of Provence (*Letters from My Mill,* 1869; *The New Don Quixote or the Wonderful Adventures of Tarascon,* 1872; *Froment the Younger and Risler the Elder,* 1874 which won an award from the Académie Française; *Sapho,* 1884; *Notes sur la Vie,* 1899).

★ DENTELLES DE MONTMIRAIL

Michelin map 🔲 folds 2, 3 and 12 or 🔲 fold 17 or 🔲 folds 9 and 10

The pine and oak clad heights, sometimes blanketed with vines, are the final foothills of the Ventoux Range overlooking the Rhône and owe their lace point name (*dentelle* means lace) to the unique sharpness of the peaks. The geological cause of this special outline lies in the upper strata of Jurassic limestone having been forced upright by the folding of the earth's crust and then eroded by wind and weather into needle thin spikes and ridges. Although not very high in altitude (St-Amand: 734m – 2 409ft), the Dentelles have a more alpine appearance than their taller neighbour (Mount Ventoux: 1 909m – 6 263ft). The hills, broom-covered in May and June, attract painters and naturalists as well as walkers, who either come for a short stroll or a long hike.

Dentelles de Montmirail

ROUND TOUR FROM VAISON-LA-ROMAINE
60km – 37 miles – about 1/2 day – local map p 110

★★**Vaison-la-Romaine.** – *Description p 185.*

> Leave Vaison-la-Romaine by the D 977, the road towards Avignon; turn left after 5.5km – 3 3/4 miles into the D 88.

The road climbs into the mountains, disclosing views of the Ouvèze Valley to the west.

Séguret. – Pop 714. The village *(photograph p 43),* built against the side of a steep hill, is worth a brief visit. At the village entrance walk through the covered passage into the main street and continue past the 15C Mascarons Fountain and the 14C belfry to the 12C St-Denis Church. From the square *(viewing table)* the **view** embraces the Dentelles, the Comtat Venaissin and, to the far north, the line of the Massif Central.

A ruined castle and network of steep streets, lined with old houses, all add character.

> On leaving Séguret turn left into the D 23 for Sablet and then the D 7 and the D 79 for Gigondas.

Gigondas. – Pop 648. The village is know for the locally produced red Grenache wine, to which it has given its name.

> By way of Les Florets, where there is an alpine club hut, drive to Cayron Pass.

Cayron Pass (Col du Cayron). – Alt 396m – 1 299ft. The pass is at the centre of the Dentelles's principal peaks which, with faces rearing nearly 100m – 300ft high, offer all the complexity of feature relished by rock climbers.

> Park the car and bear right (1 hour on foot Rtn) on the unsurfaced road which winds through the Dentelles.

There are splendid **views**★ of the Rhône Plain blocked by the Cévennes, Vaucluse Plateau and Mount Ventoux. The road passes below a ruined Saracen tower.

Return to the car and take the D 7, then turn left towards Vacqueyras.

Chapel of Notre-Dame d'Aubune (Chapelle N.-D.-d'Aubune). – *Near the Fontenouilles Farm.* The Romanesque chapel at the foot of the mountain stands on a small terrace from which a good view of the Comtat Plain can be had. It is surmounted by an elegant **bell tower★** ornamented on each of its four sides by tall antique style pilasters and rounded bays between larger and smaller pillars – note the decoration of columns and capitals (straight or twisted fluting, grapes, acanthus leaves...).

Continue left along the D 81.

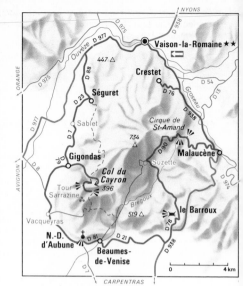

The road winds through vineyards and olive groves.

Beaumes-de-Venise. – Pop 1 721. A terraced village, on the southernmost foothills of the Dentelles, known for the sweet fortified wine it produces *(p 41).*

Leave Beaumes-de-Venise eastwards on the D 21 bear left on the D 938 and left again on the D 78.

Le Barroux. – Pop 437. Overlooking the village is the lofty restored Renaissance château.
From the château's **terrace** the **view★** extends over the Dentelles de Montmirail, Carpentras Plain, Vaucluse Plateau and Mount Ventoux.

Leave Le Barroux northwards towards Suzette and meet up with the D 90.

After Suzette the road enters the vertical walled St-Amand rock circus (Cirque de St-Amand).
The road rises to a small pass from where there is a good **view★** on one side of the Dentelles and on the other of Mount Ventoux, Ouvèze Valley and the Baronnies.

Malaucène. – Pop 2 096. Facilities. This large Provençal town is for the most part surrounded by a large avenue shaded by huge plane trees.
Rebuilt in the 14C, on the site of the former Romanesque church, the church was part of the ramparts which explains its fortified appearance: the façade is surmounted by corbelled machicolations. Inside the Provençal Romanesque nave is covered with fine pointed barrel vaulting and the south side chapels with pointed vaulting and the apse by a dome with flat ribs. Note the 18C organ with finely carved wood musical instruments and a pulpit carved out of oak.
Go through Soubeyran Gate, near the church, into the old village where reigns a confusion of small streets, old houses, fountains, wash-houses and oratories with at its centre an old belfry. A path along the church's north wall leads to a Calvary from where there is a view of the Drôme Mountains and Mount Ventoux.
The D 938 northwest climbs the fertile Groseau Valley.

Turn left into the D 76.

Crestet. – Pop 326. *Leave the car in the castle car park.* The village is one of the most typical of Vaucluse, with the 14C church standing in a minute square lined by an arcade and decorated at the centre with a fountain. Narrow streets between Renaissance houses, climb the hill crowned by a 12C **castle** from where there is a good view of the village, the Ouvèze, Mount Ventoux and the Baronnies.

Return to the D 938 and turn left for Vaison-la-Romaine.

DURANCE, Lower Valley of the

Michelin map 📖 folds 1 to 4 or 📖 folds 29 to 32 or 📖 folds 11, 12 and 25

The Durance, the great fluctuating river of the southern Alps, known for its bursting, unheralded floodwaters and long periods of low ebb, has, at last, been harnessed to serve the local economy; it supplies hydraulic power and a constant flow of water for irrigation for most of the fruit and vegetable growing area.

The Durance's hydraulic undertakings. – The river rises close to the Italian border (Genèvre Mountain, near Briançon), pours through a wide gap which it has cut in the mountains and continues on an irregular 324km – 201 mile course to join the Rhône as its final east tributary, at Avignon.

Above Sisteron. – *See Michelin Green Guide Alpes du Sud, in French only.* A number of small mountain streams, such as the Ubaye, give the river its torrential, alpine appearance, with shallows in winter.
The Serre-Ponçon Reservoir, with a capacity of 1 030 million m^3 – 36 373 million ft^3 – collected when the river is in spate, maintains regular irrigation (it can hold 200 million m^3 – 7 074 million ft^3 when the river is low.

From Sisteron to Manosque. – *See Michelin Green Guide Alpes du Sud in French only.* The river enters the Mediterranean basin, the slope of its bed, which is less steep reaches 3 to 1000 between Mées and Manosque; yet the river widens and flows between pebbly shores which are rarely flooded. The flow stays irregular.

At Cardache, 175km – 109 miles from the sea, the Durance remains at an altitude of 256m – 840ft. To reach the same altitude with the Rhône, the river flows 490km – 304 1/2 miles inland (at Génissiat Dam). These two figures clearly reveal the hydro-electric potential of the Durance.

Downstream from Manosque. – The river runs approximately parallel to the coast until it enters the Rhône, but once, when the ice cap melted at the end of the last ice age, the swollen waters burst through the Lamanon Gap on a more direct route to the sea, depositing a huge mass of rock and stone over the wide expanse of what is now the Crau Plain *(qv)*.

The violence of the rain showers provokes floodwaters, the power of which has no relationship with the Durance's average flow.

Upstream from the Verdon River (its last great tributary) at Mirabeau Bridge (Pont-de-Mirabeau), the flow is reduced in August to less than 45m³–9 900 gallons per second – the river in spate flowed in November 1886 6 000m³–1 320 000 gallons per second. This flooding raises the water level only slightly – it sprawls over a vast pebbly bed which slows the speed of the flow before being absorbed, for the most part, by sandy soil.

The Lower Provence's canal network. – It is rare for any one region to be so well served by canals, as is Provence between the Durance and the sea. Each was constructed for one of the three purposes: irrigation, the provision of town water and the production of electricity.

Craponne Canal. – The 16C course, one of the oldest in Provence, which is now decaying in its upper reaches, has contributed most, through irrigation, to the transformation of the Crau Plain.

Marseilles and Verdon Canals. – Each in its time – both date from the 19C – has increased the fertility of the countryside around Aix and Marseilles, but with the immense development in market gardening neither is now sufficient. The Marseilles, 90km – 60 miles long, begins at St-Estève-Janson and on its course serves the St-Christophe *(qv)* and Réaltor *(qv)* Reservoirs and crosses Arc Valley by means of the Roquefavour Aqueduct *(qv)*. To supplement supplies it is to be paralleled by the Provence Canal *(see below)*, which in its final course has been diverted to serve the industrial zone of the Berre Lagoon *(qv)*.

The Verdon, which starts at the industrial canal at Vinon, waters the area around Aix and, augmented by the spring floodwaters of the Verdon, flows through the underground Campane Canal to supply the Bimont Dam Reservoir. It is being rebuilt in part, the better to complement the new Provence Canal.

The EDF (Électricité de France) Canal. –The drop in water level between Cadarache and the Rhône was utilised to supply an 85km – 53 mile long canal, beginning at the Cadarache Dam and running parallel to the Durance before following the river's original course through the Lamanon Gap to the Berre Lagoon. Five major power stations (Jouques, St-Estève-Janson, Mallemort, Salon and St-Chamas) are served by the canal which goes on to supplement the Craponne, supplying fifteen other channels which irrigate some 75 000ha – 185 000 acres of Lower Provence including the Crau Plain *(qv)*.

Provence Canal. –The completion of the Serre-Ponçon Dam and the construction of the EDF Canal have removed the need for the Verdon Canal to act as a regulator of the Durance; its waters have, therefore, been diverted into the new Provence Canal which, with an annual flow of 700 million m³ – 154 000 million gallons drawn from a 3 000km – 1 865 mile catchment network, supplies town water to Aix, Marseilles and Toulon, irrigates some 60 000ha – 148 000 acres and tops up the Bimont Dam.

FROM MANOSQUE TO AVIGNON

145km – 90 miles – allow 1/2 day (tour of Avignon not included) – local map pp 112-113

★**Manosque.** – *Description in the Michelin Green Guide Alpes du Sud in French only.*
Leave Manosque on Avenue Jean-Giono, the D 907, southwest of the town plan.

At Ste-Tulle the two hydroelectric power stations have an annual production yield of 370 million kWh. The road nears the Durance at its confluence with the Verdon; the joined rivers are held back by Cadarache Dam.

Cadarache Dam (Barrage de Cadarache). – This small dam feeds by a canal the Jouques Power Station (a couple of miles south).

⊙ **Cadarache Centre on Nuclear Studies** (Centre d'Études Nucléaires de Cadarache). – Set at a distance from the villages, this centre lies on the north bank of the Durance in a large valley which opens onto a plateau wooded with oak. The centre produces experimental prototype reactors for power stations and carries out research into controlled fusion, radio ecology, radio agronomy, biotechnology etc...

Mirabeau Defile (Défilé de Mirabeau). – The river bends sharply to the west and emerges from Upper Provence through a dramatic narrow channel cut out by the action of the water.

Mirabeau Bridge (Pont-de-Mirabeau). – It spans the Durance at Mirabeau Defile.

Jouques Power Station (Centrale de Jouques). – The station was built against the cliff face on the EDF Canal which runs underground right up to the entrance. Average annual production 385 million kWh.

Follow the N 96 which skirts the EDF Canal.

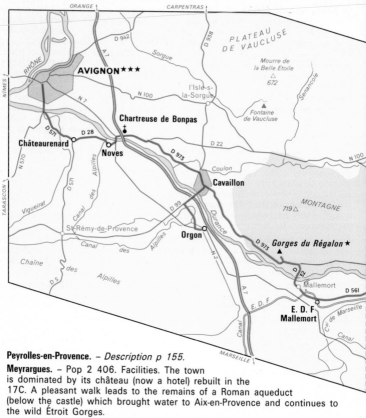

Peyrolles-en-Provence. – *Description p 155.*

Meyrargues. – Pop 2 406. Facilities. The town is dominated by its château (now a hotel) rebuilt in the 17C. A pleasant walk leads to the remains of a Roman aqueduct (below the castle) which brought water to Aix-en-Provence and continues to the wild Étroit Gorges.

> *On leaving, take the D 561 and after 3km – 2 miles, the D 556, on the right.*

Pertuis. – Pop 12 430. Facilities. Capital of Aigues Country and birthplace of Mirabeau's *(qv)* father, the town retains, as reminders of its past, a 14C battlemented St-Jacques Tower, 13C clock tower, a castle ruin and St-Nicolas. The church, rebuilt in the 16C contains a 16C triptych and two 17C marble statues.

La Tour-d'Aigues. – Pop 2 479. *6km – 3 1/2 miles from Pertuis by the D 956. Description p 182.*

> *Return to the D 956, to go Cadenet via the D 973 which parallels Cadenet Canal.*

Cadenet. – *Description p 94.*

> *The D 943 goes south to cross the Durance; turn left into the D 561 and after 2.7km – 1 1/2 miles, right towards the power station.*

St-Estève-Janson Power Station (Centrale de St-Estève-Janson). – Balcony and explanatory panel *(in French)* at the base of the building. Annual production 635 million kWh.

St-Christophe Reservoir (Bassin de St-Christophe). – The reservoir waters covering 22ha – 54 acres at the foot of Côtes Chain, derive from the Durance and tributary EDF Canal and are destined to supply Marseilles.

Rognes. – Pop 2 216. Rognes is located on the north face of Trévaresse Chain. The well-known Rognes stone is extracted from quarries found on the D 15 going to Lambesc *(qv).*

The **church** built in the early 17C is decorated with a remarkable group of 10 **altarpieces★** (17-18C). Note especially those at the high altar and along the chancel's north side which is decorated with three people in low relief.

> *Return to the reservoir: skirt it to the left until you come to the D 561.*

★★ Silvacane Abbey. – *Description p 178.*

La Roque-d'Anthéron. – Pop 3 759. At the centre of the town stands the 17C Château de Florans flanked by round towers (now a convalescent home).

> *Continue along the D 561 to the D 23 on the right.*

Mallemort Power Station (Centrale de Mallemort). – The power station, on the left, produces an average 420 million kWh annually.

> *Beyond Mallemort town turn into the D 32 to cross the river; turn left into the D 973. Continue for 2km – 1 mile and just before a bridge, bear right into a small road which skirts a quarry.*

★ Régalon Gorges (Gorges du Régalon). – *1 1/4 hours on foot Rtn. Some yards further on bear right, ignoring the uphill road on the left. Leave the car in the parking area; take the path opposite which skirts the stream; cross the olive grove on your left and go through a narrow gap to enter the gorges. Note: (a) it will be colder, (b) the rocks are often wet and slippery – go suitably clad and shod therefore; (c) on showery-rainy days the stream becomes a rushing torrent and the expedition should not be attempted.*

The route follows the bed of the stream, beneath a huge rock caught fast between the sides of the gorges, and over a rock and sometimes slippery section before coming to a cave. The tunnel bends sharply into a passage 100m – 328ft long and 30m – 98ft high but only 80cm – 30in wide in places. The cave and passage are the most remarkable part of the gorges. *At the end retrace your steps.*

Continue once more along the D 973 as it skirts the Luberon Range (qv).

Cavaillon. – *Description p 103.*

Orgon. – *Description p 154.*

Leave Cavaillon by ① of the town plan, the D 938; turn left into the D 973.

ⓥ **Bonpas Charterhouse** (Chartreuse de Bonpas). – *Enter through a fortified gate; the porter's lodge opens (under a vault) on the right.*
Next to a small chapel the Templars built, in the 13C, a church and monastery which took the name of Bonpas. It enjoyed a period of prosperity in the 17C when the chapterhouse was constructed. At the Revolution it was abandoned and it gradually fell into ruins. The charterhouse has recently been restored, the remaining conventual buildings were transformed into a house. The old Romanesque chapel has an elevated altar. The formal French gardens are well kept. From the terrace there is a clear view of the Alpilles Chain, which stands out in the distance, and the Durance spanned by a 500m – 1/3 mile long bridge.

Pass under the motorway and turn right into the N 7 and right again into the D 28.

Noves. – Pop 3 693. Noves is an old town with a network of narrow winding streets, ⓥ two medieval gateways (Gates Agel and Aurose) and a 12C stone roofed **church.** It is covered by a dome on squinches and its apse is enhanced by an arcade (restored); the aisles were added in the 14C.

Châteaurenard. – *Description p 105.*

The D 571 and the N 570 continue to Avignon.

From the bridge a fine view can be had of the wooded banks of the Durance.

★★★ **Avignon.** – *Tour: allow 1 day. Description p 72.*

*The **Michelin Sectional Map Series** at a scale of 1:200 000 (1cm:2km)*
covers the whole of France.

For the maps to use with this guide see p 3.

You may pick out at a glance
*   the motorways and major roads for a quick journey*
*   the secondary or alternative roads for a traffic free run*
*   the country lanes for a leisurely drive*

These maps are a must for your holidays.

113

★ ESTAQUE Chain (Chaîne de l'ESTAQUE)

Michelin map 245 folds P and Q

Estaque Chain, which divides the Berre Lagoon from the Mediterranean, is an unusual limestone formation, arid in appearance and almost uninhabited. Deep inlets *(calanques – qv),* in the steep coastline, shelter a few small fishing villages which scrape a meagre living from the exhausted Mediterranean but now hope to profit from the expansion of the port of Marseilles, the increasing industrialisation of the area and the tourist trade.

FROM MARTIGUES TO MARSEILLES
74km – 46 miles – about 4 hours not including the tour of Marseilles

Martigues. – *Description p 138.*

Leave Martigues by ③ of the town plan on the D 5.

On the left are views of the Berre Lagoon and Martigues.

After Les Ventrons continue along the D 5 to St-Julien.

St-Julien. – A path (on the left) from the village leads to a chapel where embedded in the north wall, there is a Gallo-Roman relief (1C) of a group of eight people in a funeral scene.

From St-Julien, return to Les Ventrons and bear left onto the D 49.

The road climbs through an arid landscape of dark pines against the white limestone and, at 120m – 394ft, looks back (observation tower) over the industrial harbour complex of Lavéra, Port-de-Bouc and Fos.

4km – 2 1/2 miles further on, bear right for Carro.

Carro. – The attractive small fishing village and resort lies well protected at the back of a rock strewn bay.

Make for La Couronne by way of the D 49ᴮ, turn right before the church.

Cape Couronne (Cap Couronne). – From the lighthouse on the point there is a view right round to Marseilles, with the Estaque Chain in the foreground, the Étoile Range and the Marseilleveyre.

On leaving the point, turn right onto the D 49.

The road winds through the hills before dropping down to follow the coastline.

Sausset-les-Pins. – Pop 3 876. Facilities. The fishing village and seaside resort, as well, has a fine promenade from where one can look across the sea to Marseilles.

Carry-le-Rouet. – Pop 4 570. Facilities. The onetime fishing village is now a seaside resort. Summer residences can be seen in the woods which line the bay.

Le Rouet-Plage. – An attractive inlet with a good beach and small harbour, and, half-hidden among the pine trees, some elegant houses.

The road up **Aigle Valley** is bordered by pines and holm oaks.

Ensuès-la-Redonne. – Pop 2 204. A village at the centre of vineyards and olive groves.

On leaving Ensuès, turn right onto the D 48.

A rapid descent, through a pinewood, goes to La Madrague-de-Gignac.

La Madrague-de-Gignac. – The village, set in a lovely site, lines a creek, which faces Marseilles across the water.

Return to the D 5 and turn right.

The road crosses an arid, treeless stretch of countryside.

Bear right on the D 48 to Niolon.

The road plunges into a bleak countryside where only a few pines resist the wind.

Niolon. – The village clings to the hillside above an inlet of the same name. There is deep-sea diving.

From the D 5, there is a clear view of the Étoile and Estaque Chains.

Turn right into the N 568.

As you emerge from the tunnel there is a glimpse of Marseilles before the road goes under the railway bridge and over the entrance to the Rove Canal.

★**Rove Underground Canal** (Canal Souterrain du Rove). – *Access: take the Chagnaud Quarry (Carrière Chagnaud) road – pass under the railway before turning down the slope to the entrance.*
The tunnel was cut in the 1920s beneath the Estaque Mountains to link the Marseilles docks and the Berre Lagoon, and was used regularly by 1 200 metric ton barges until obstructed by a rock fall in 1963. It is more than 7km – 4 miles long and dead straight – one can still see daylight at the far end. Height, width and water depth respectively are 15.4, 22 and 4.5m (50, 72 and 14ft).

L'Estaque. – This Marseilles suburb attracted many contemporary artists who admired the countryside: Cézanne, Braque, Dufy and Derain. The Marseilles fishing fleet and private yachts now fill the harbour.

The road continues through the industrial suburbs to the tunnel beneath the Old Port into the heart of Marseilles.

★★★**Marseilles.** – *Tour: allow 1 day. Description p 127.*

For historical notes on the region see pp 20-23.

★ ÉTOILE Chain (Chaîne de l'ÉTOILE)

Michelin map 245 folds K and L

This chain of mountains, which belongs to the category small Alps of Provence and is a result of the Pyrennean fold, separates the Arc Basin, to the north and that of the Huveaune to the east; it prolongs, beyond the shelf of St-Antoine, the Estaque Mountains. Inspite of the low altitude of its mountain tops, the chain dominates in an amazing way the Marseilles Plain. Its central crest which spreads out like a fan ends at 781m – 2 562ft at the Tête du Grand Puche. Julien Mountain, the Pilon du Roi and Étoile Peak also dominate the landscape bare to the south.

FROM GARDANNE TO AUBAGNE

61km – 38 miles – about 3 1/2 hours not including the climb to Étoile Peak.

Gardanne. – Pop 15 374. This important industrial town with its bauxite *(qv)* and cement works and coal mining lies between the Étoile Chain and Mount Ste-Victoire.

Leave Gardanne by the D 58 going south which becomes the D 8. After 7km – 4 miles turn right to Mimet.

Mimet. – Pop 2 531. This small perched village has encountered considerable expansion. From its terrace there is a fine **view★** of Luynes Valley, Gardanne and its furnaces.

Return to the D 8 and bear right.

The picturesque D 7 and the D 908 skirt the Étoile Chain.

At Le Logis-Neuf turn left to Allauch.

Allauch. – *Description p 54.*

Take the D 44ᶠ northwest of Allauch.

Château-Gombert. – *Description p 138.*

Leave Château-Gombert towards Marseilles and turn right into Traverse de la Baume Loubière.

Loubière Caves. – *Description p 138.*

Park the car at the caves; continue uphill (4 hours on foot Rtn). Bear right before the intersection of surfaced roads.

After a winding trail through a rocky passage you reach the **Grande Étoile** (alt 590m – 1 936ft), where a telecommunications tower stands, and then **Étoile Peak** (alt 651m – 2 136ft). From the shelf separating these last two summits there is a splendid **panorama★★** over Gardanne Basin to the north and the thresholds which cut the chain's southern slopes.

Return to Allauch by the same way you came. Continue south on the D 4ᴬ; at Les 4-Saisons bear left and soon after left again.

Camoins-les-Bains. – This small spa enjoys picturesque greenery.

La Treille. – Marcel Pagnol *(qv)* (1895-1974) writer and film director who was born in Aubagne is buried in La Treille cemetery at the town's entrance.

Return to Camoins-les-Bains and take the D 44ᴬ to Aubagne.

Aubagne. – *Description p 71.*

FONTAINE-DE-VAUCLUSE   Pop 606

Michelin map 81 fold 13 or 245 south of fold 17 or 246 fold 11 – Facilities

This small town is best known for its fountain, the famous resurgent spring which rises in a picturesque site dear to Petrarch and is the source of the Sorgue River. It is especially in the winter or spring, during the floods, that the stream is at its most dramatic when the water level rises 150m³ – 32 985 gallons – per second while in the summer or fall the flow is reduced to a mere 4.5m³ – 159ft³ – per second.

Petrarch. – The great poet and humanist, who was a familiar member of the pontifical court in Avignon, met in an Avignon church, on 6 April 1327, the lovely **Laura**, with whom he fell passionately in love with. And yet this love remained ideal – Laura was married and virtuous – inspiring many of the poet's works throughout his life and was the origin of his best works. Ten years after his first meeting with her, Petrarch, who was but 33 years old, retired to Vaucluse. He remained here 16 years seeking peace in the tranquil Sorgue Valley; during his stay Laura died of the plague in Avignon in 1348.

The poet died 20 years later in Arquà Petrarca near Padua, having never forgotten her...

★★★ VAUCLUSE FOUNTAIN (FONTAINE DE VAUCLUSE)

time: 1/2 hour on foot Rtn

Leave the car in the car park. From Place de la Colonne, where there stands a commemorative column of the fifth centenary (1304-1804) of Petrarch's birth, take Chemin de la Fontaine.

Vaucluse Fountain is one of the most powerful resurgent springs in the world and is the opening of an important underwater river fed by rainwater draining through the Vaucluse Plateau *(qv)* pitted with numerous *avens* (chasms) through which the speleologists have searched in vain the underground Sorgue. The exploration of the fountain's chasm began as early as the 19C (in 1878 a diver descended 23m – 75ft) and continues actively. The last record was 315m – 1 033ft deep which was achieved in August 1985 with the help of a small remote controlled submarine equipped with cameras.

A Son et Lumière takes place in summer.

The cave from where the Sorgue River emerges is at the foot of a rock cirque formed by high cliffs. Before it stands a pile of rocks through which the waters usually infiltrate.

During heavy flooding the water reaches the level of the fig trees growing in the rock above the cave mouth before racing away over the rocks in a vivid green fury of tumbling foaming water. It is a magnificent spectacle.

ADDITIONAL SIGHTS

Ⓥ **Underground World of Norbert Casteret** (Le Monde Souterrain de Norbert Casteret). – *On the fountain's path.* The underground museum presents the **Casteret collection**★ of limestone concretions (calcite, gypsum, aragonite) assembled over 30 years of underground exploration by the speleologist. Different sites have been reconstituted: stalagtite and stalagmite caves, *aven* and rubble, rivers, waterfalls, natural dams and caves with human imprints. A detailed documentation presents the visitor to Vaucluse speleology; a permanent display (documents, photos, models) explains the discoveries made on Vaucluse Fountain through the years.

Vallis Clausa. – *Near the underground museum.* In this craft centre is a **paper mill** where paper is made according to traditional methods.

Ⓥ **Museum (Musée).** – The museum is located on the site, it is said, of the house where Petrarch lived. The 1st floor exhibits rare editions of the poet's works (note the first edition edited in Basle in 1496), as well as books evoking his memory and that of Laura's.

Ⓥ **St-Véran.** – This small Romanesque church has rounded vaulting over its nave and an oven vaulted apse flanked by Antique fluted columns. To the right of the chancel opens the crypt containing the sarcophagus of St Veranus, 6C Bishop of Cavaillon, credited with having dispatched Coulobre, the local monster.

Castle (Château). – *1/2 hour on foot Rtn.* Set on a rock overlooking the village, the castle, now in ruins, belonged to the Bishop of Cavaillon, a friend of Petrarch's. It commands a lovely view of Fontaine-de-Vaucluse and its site.

★ FOS Complex (Bassins de FOS)

Michelin map 🆃🆃 fold 11 or 🆃🆃🆃 folds 42 and 43 or 🆃🆃🆃 folds 13, 14, 27 and 28

The development of the new complex, which complements the port of Marseilles, was begun in 1965 on Fos Bay. The advantages of the site, some 10 000ha – 24 700 acres, are a deep water channel, a low tidal range and the extensive stoney surface of Crau Plain *(qv)* which makes an ideal foundation on which to build an industrial estate.

The port. – With its approximately 90 million metric tons of traffic per year, of which Fos handles two-thirds, the combined Marseilles-Fos complex is the largest port in France and second only to Rotterdam in Europe.

Fos is equipped to handle two types of traffic: Dock 1 with its two basins can accommodate vessels up to 400 000 metric tons carrying bulk cargoes such as oil, gas and minerals; Docks 2 and 3 (Gloria Basin) handle commercial traffic such as containers, vehicles and wood. The South Dock is reserved for steel and petrol exports.

Dock 1 was linked to the Rhône and the Berre Lagoon by a canal built to European standards and capable of carrying 4 400 metric ton barge convoys.

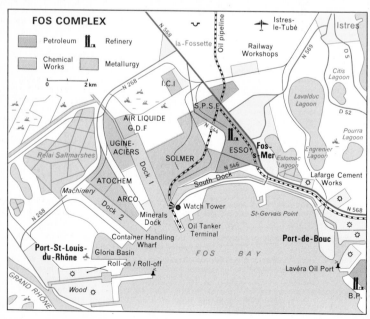

ⓥ **Tour of the port.** – Boat trips start from the watch tower, which gives a good overall view of the harbour, and include tours of the factories and major basins.

The industrial zone. – More than half the available land is given over to factories, some with their own quays, accommodating basic processing and first stage industries such as steel (Solmer – sheet and laminates: 4 million tons p.a., Ugine Aciers – production and lamination of special steels: 200 000 metric tons); metal construction; petrol (Esso: 8 million metric tons); chemicals (ATOCHEM: 150 000 metric tons of chloride, MCV Fos Company 200 000 metric tons of MVC; ARCO: 150 000 metric tons of propylene oxide); petrochemicals (ICI: 100 000 metric tons of polyethylene). Approximately 3 000 milliard m³ – 105 942 milliard ft³ of liquid natural gas are treated each year by Gaz de France and distributed after conversion. Crude oil and refined products supply the South European Oil Pipeline *(p 91)* and the Mediterranean-Rhône Oil Pipeline respectively.

ⓥ **Fos Community Information Centre (Le Centre de Vie).** – On the spot known as La Fossette, an exhibition and information centre displays a model of the area and shows films. Next to it is an arboretum.

Fos-sur-Mer. – Pop 9 446. *To the northeast.* The town is named after the Fosses Mariennes, a canal dug at the mouth of the Rhône by Marius's *(qv)* legions in 102BC *(fosse: hole, pit, canal)*. Medieval rather than Roman remains are evident in sections of the 14C ramparts and castle ruins. The chief attraction, however, are the **views** from the terrace and rampart garden of the new town of Fos, the harbour, Port-de-Bouc, Lavalduc Lagoon and the St-Blaise Heights.

EXCURSIONS

Port-St-Louis-du-Rhône. – Pop 10 378. *15km – 10 miles southwest.* A town and port have developed around the St-Louis Tower built to defend the mouth of the Grand Rhône in the 18C. The dock, constructed in 1863 and now part of the Marseilles complex, is used both by seagoing ships and Rhône barges, and handles products as diverse as hydrocarbons, liquid chemicals, timber and wine.

Port-de-Bouc. – *Description p 139.*

GARRIGUES

Michelin map 🔳 fold 19 or 🔳 folds 14 and 15 or 🔳 fold 25

The *garrigues (qv)* are a limestone formation which sweep like sea surf along the foot of the more ancient Massif Central. The low hills rise 200m – 300m – 656ft – 984ft in the area which is covered by this guide. This area had once been covered with holm oaks and Aleppo pines but the forest was razed almost everywhere by man. Rain, frost, draught and wind have in many places weathered and carried away the thin layer of soil. There where the rock has not been completely uncovered scrub oak, cistus, gorse, asphodel and wild aromatic plants carpet the land. Rivers have sometimes carved picturesque gorges in these arid, scorched hills.

FROM UZÈS TO REMOULINS *51km – 31 miles – about 6 hours*

★ **Uzès.** – *Description p 182.*

Leave Uzès by ②, the D 979.

The road winds through the countryside offering views of Uzès and its environs.

St-Nicolas Bridge (Pont St-Nicolas). – The nine-arched bridge, built in the 13C by the Bridge Brotherhood *(qv)*, spans the River Gardon in a particularly beautiful spot. The D 979 climbs in corniche fashion affording good views of the Gardon; in the right bend at the top *(car park)* look at the spectacular **view★** along the course of the Gardon Gorges.

Turn left into the D 135 and, just before Poulx, left again into the D 127.

★ **Gardon Gorges (Gorges du Gardon).** – *Poor surfaced road, passing difficult, sometimes impossible except in lay-byes hewn out of the rock: at the final bend, park the car.* A path *(1 hour on foot Rtn)* ends at the bottom of the gorges in a picturesque spot, facing the opening of the Baume Cave in the cliff on the far bank of the river.

Poulx. – Pop 725. Village with a small, single aisled, Romanesque church.

Continue along the D 427.

The road crosses the *garrigues* interspersed with vineyards and orchards.

In Cabrières turn left into the D 3.

Fine views open out onto the Rhône Plain and the Alpilles Chain; the road rises in a corniche at the end of the run before descending into the Gardon Valley.

On entering Collias bear right on the D 3, which climbs the large and cultivated Alzon Valley; bear right again onto the D 981.

ⓥ **Château de Castille.** – A small Romanesque chapel and a funerary chapel surrounded by columns stand to the right of the avenue of yew trees which leads to the château which was built in the 16C and remodelled in the 18C. Two low wings on either side, surrounded by a colonnade, are preceded by a vast balustered, horseshoe-shaped peristyle. The château itself, is also columned and balustered.

Continue along the D 981.

★★★ **Pont du Gard.** – *Description p 156.*

Remoulins. – Pop 1 866. Facilities. The village set amidst cherry and other fruit orchards, is protected in places by its medieval wall. A small Romanesque church with a bell gable houses the town hall.

Michelin map 🔢 fold 13 or 🔢 south of fold 17 or 🔢 fold 11 – Facilities

The houses of Gordes *(photograph p 11)* rise in picturesque tiers above Imergue Valley on the edge of the Vaucluse Plateau.
The walk through town along the *calades* – small paved, sometimes stepped alleyways lined with gutters defined by two rows of stone – vaulted passageways, arcades of the old, tall houses and rampart ruins, is full of charm; the shops, craftshops and market add to the bustle.

Viewpoint. – The site★ can best be seen from a rock platform belvedere (no barrier) about 1km – 1/2 mile short of the village on the Cavaillon road, the D 15.

Ⓥ **Château.** – The Renaissance château stands on the village's highest point. It was rebuilt by Bertrand de Simiane on the site of a 12C fortress. The north face flanked by round machicolated towers is austere, the south monumental, relieved by mullioned windows and small turrets. In the courtyard note the fine Renaissance door (the soft limestone has been worn away by erosion). Inside, in the great hall (1st floor) two flanking doorways show off a splendid **chimneypiece★** (1541) ornate with pediments and pilasters, shells and flowers. Five rooms and the stairwell have been remodelled as a **Vasarely Museum★**; Vasarely's *(p 53)* geometrically influenced work includes painting, sculpture and decorative panels. Among his works displayed are several figurative portraits *(The Chinese),* two self-portraits different in style to his other works *(The Blindman).*

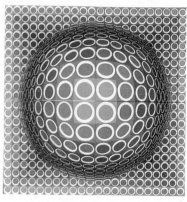

Heet by Vasarely

EXCURSION

Round tour of 12km – 7 1/2 miles. – *About 2 hours. Leave Gordes on the D 15 towards Cavaillon; just beyond the fork with the D 2 turn right into a tarred road and park the car.*

Ⓥ **Bories Village** (Village des Bories). – A path *(1/4 hour on foot Rtn)* leads to this village now a museum of rural life. Twenty restored *bories (p 122 and photograph p 123),* between 200-500 years old, are grouped around a communal bread oven. The larger *bories* served as dwellings, the others were either sheep-folds or various outbuildings. They were inhabited until the early 19C but their origin remains a mystery.

> *Return to the D 2 and bear right; bear left on the D 103 towards Beaumettes and left again onto the D 148 towards St-Pantaléon; continue along this road about 110yds to the place called Moulin des Bouillons.*

Ⓥ **Stained Glass Museum** (Musée du Vitrail). – The modern museum building houses an exhibition on the history of stained glass making (tools and documents) and presents reconstituted ovens, Middle East glassware, period stained glass and works by Frédérique Duran, contemporary painter and glassmaker, with her own distinctive technique for obtaining jewelled results.

Weathervane and stained glass (F. Duran) from Stained Glass Museum

ⓥ **Museum of Oil Mills** (Musée des Moulins à huile). – Located in the same park as the Stained Glass Window Museum, this *bastide*, the Moulin des Bouillons (16-18C) was transformed into a museum. The outstanding piece is the giant **press★** for olives made from a whole oak tree trunk weighing 7 tons! It is Gallo-Roman in aspect and it is the oldest and the only one preserved with its tools.

The history of lighting over the past 5 000 years is recounted with the help of oil lamps, tools for the cultivation of olives, vessels, and weights and measures. The use of olive oil through the ages is also explained.

Continue along the D 148.

St-Pantaléon. – Pop 91. The small village occupies a dominant position in the
ⓥ countryside. Its small Romanesque **church** is built out of the living rock and consists of three naves; the central part dates back to the 5C.

Surrounding the church is a rock necropolis, most of the tombs of which are the size of a child. This necropolis was most likely a sanctuary of grace, there are other examples like it in Provence. Children who died before they were baptised, were brought here by their parents, they resuscitated – according to the beliefs of the period – for the duration of a mass in which they were baptised, they then died again and were buried here.

Leave St-Pantaléon from the north and join the D 104ᴬ, then the D 2 which returns to Gordes.

The practical information chapter, at the end of the guide, regroups:
– a list of the local or national organisations supplying additional information
– a section on times and charges.

★ GRIGNAN   Pop 1 147

Michelin map ▨▨ fold 2 or ▨▨▨ fold 3 or ▨▨▨ folds 8 and 22 – Facilities

Located on an isolated rocky hillock, the imposing château, belonging to Adhémar de Monteil overlooks the old town of Tricastin and owes its fame to the delightful letters written in the last years of the 17C by **Mme de Sévigné** to her daughter, Mme de Grignan, wherein she recounts with a keen eye and nice turn of phrase, life at the court of Louis XIV and Paris society, visits to the country and day-to-day domestic matters.

A good marriage. – When in 1669 Mme de Sévigné's daughter married the Count of Grignan, Lieutenant-General of Provence, she commented: "the prettiest girl in France, is marrying not the most handsome of young men – the count was very ugly! – but one of the most honest in the kingdom".

The good Provençal life. – Madame de Sévigné spent several long stays at the château. She enjoyed her visits and described the château as "very fine and magnificent" adding characteristically "one eats well and there are masses of visitors".

Madame de Sévigné by C. Lefebvre
(Musée Carnavalet, Paris)

She gives a mouth-watering description of how the partridges were fed on thyme, marjoram and herbs to give them flavour, how the quail had fat and tender legs, the doves were succulent and the melons, figs and Muscat grapes perfect...

Although she admired the view from the terrace, she preferred the cool fragrance of the nearby grotto to write in; her only hate, and that a perpetual one, was the *mistral,* which she described as "that bitter, freezing wind which cuts one's being to the quick".

The misplaced curiosity of 18C phrenologists. – Mme de Sévigné died at the château in 1696 aged 69 from over fatigue after nursing her sick daughter. She was buried in the château's chapel, but during the Revolution her coffin was stripped of its lead lining and her head dispatched to Paris for examination by avid phrenologists. It has since disappeared.

The literary pilgrims. – "I am so proud to be here that I feel inclined to sit up all night and write letters if for no other reason than that they might bear the château's address. My imagination is so filled with Mme de Sévigné that at every moment I expect to see her before me!". So wrote an English noble woman in 1770; nicely expressing a sentiment felt by those who still relish the letters and come on a literary pilgrimage.

SIGHTS

★★**Château.** – The château was built from 1545-58 by Louis Adhémar, General of the Galleys and Governor of Provence.

The south façade is Renaissance (rebuilt in 1913) and looks onto Mount Ventoux; the courtyard opens onto a terrace which is enclosed on the left by a transitional Gothic pavilion and on the right by a Renaissance building.

To be visited are: the grand staircase, drawing rooms, audience chamber, Gothic staircase, the lovely panelled Adhémar Gallery, the Count de Grignan's apartments, Mme de Sévigné's bedroom and the state room. The **furnishings★** evoke an atmosphere of the past: Louis XIII furniture, Italian writing desk in the audience chamber; Régence style and Louis XV period furnishings in the Grignan's apartments where the parquets are lovely. The walls are hung with Aubusson **tapestries** (17C mythological scene).

From the terrace, constructed over St-Sauveur Church *(see below)*, there is a vast **panorama★** including Mount

Rachas and the long ridge of the Lance (northeast), Mount Ventoux and the Dentelles de Montmirail (southeast), the Comtat Venaissin Plain, the Alpilles Chain, Suze-la-Rousse and the Chamaret belfry (southwest), Grignan Woods and the Vivarais Mountains beyond the Rhône (northwest).

St-Sauveur (B). – 16C. The west front, the portico of which was destroyed by the Protestants and which was rebuilt in 1554, is opened by a Flamboyant Gothic rose window.

Inside the features of interest are the small gallery beneath the roof which communicated directly with the castle until the Revolution when the door was bricked up; 17C **organ loft,** 17C altarpiece and fine chancel panelling. On the north side is the marble funerary stone to Mme de Sévigné.

Belfry (Beffroi). – The belfry, the 12C town gateway, was transformed in the 17C.

Rochecourbière Cave (Grotte de Rochecourbière). – *1km – 1/2 mile. Take the D 541 south out of Grignan, at a Calvary take the road that branches off; after about 1km – 1/2 mile from the D 541 park the car and walk back to the stone steps on the right.* The grotto was one of Mme de Sévigné's favourite places to sit and write.

EXCURSION

Taulignan. – Pop 1 446. *7km – 4 miles northeast by the D 14 and the D 24.* On the boundary between Dauphiné and Provence, this old agricultural town remains ensconced within its medieval fortifications. An almost uninterrupted circle, it has preserved eleven towers (nine round and two square) joined by a curtain wall (machicolations remain in several places) into which dwellings are integrated.

Walk along the old streets and admire the ancient façades with their ogee arched doorways and mullioned windows (Rue des Fontaines) and go through (to the northeast) Anguille Gate (Porte d'Anguille), the only fortified gate flanked by two towers still standing. The Romanesque church was disfigured in the 19C.

On leaving town on the D 14, there stands a small Protestant church built in 1868.

L'ISLE-SUR-LA-SORGUE   Pop 13 205

Michelin map 🔟 fold 12 or 🔢 folds 17 and 30 or 🔢 fold 11 – Local map p 112 – Facilities

L'Isle-sur-la-Sorgue is set at the foot of the Vaucluse Plâteau *(qv)*. The arms of the Sorgue River and the avenues lined with plane trees add to this charming fresh site. For a long time the town was a very active industrial centre: weaving, dyeing, tanning as well as paper, grain and oil mills functioned; some ten wheels turned to the beat of this bustling town.

The town is also the birthplace (1907) of René Char (d 1988), the poet.

Church (Église) (B). – Rebuilt in the 17C, the church presents a lovely façade made up of two superimposed orders, Doric on the ground floor, Ionic above.

The interior's fascination is due to its very ornate 17C **decoration★** recalling Italian church interiors.

The single nave is adorned on the back of the west face with an immense gilded wood glory attributed to Jean Péru, as are the figures of the Virtues placed in the spandrels underneath the balustrades. The side chapels are decorated with fine woodwork and paintings by Mignard, Sauvan, Simon Vouet and Parrocel. In the chancel a large altarpiece includes a work by Reynaud Levieux representing the Assumption; 17C organ.

Map legend

CREST \ D 4

GRIGNAN

0   100 m

Artaudes (Ch. des)	2
Château (R. du)	3
Commune (R. de la)	4
Glacière (Pl. de la)	6
Grand-Faubourg (R. du)	7
Hôpital (R' de l')	8
La Planette	9
Montant-au-Chât. (R.)	12
Or (R. d')	13
Petit-Faubourg (R. du)	14

Grotte de Rochecourbière

St-Jean (R.)	15
St-Sauveur (R.)	16
Salle-Verte (R. de la)	17
Tranchat (Pl. du)	20

Anatole-France (Cours)	2	Égalité (Av. de l')	8	Monition (R. Paul)	18
Briand (Av. Aristide)	3	Gaulle (Av. du Gén. de)	12	Reboutade (R.)	20
Chalier (Pl. Marcel)	4	Goudard (Pl. Rose)	13	République (R. de la)	22
Char (Pl. Emile)	5	Guigne (Av. Julien)	15	Rouget-de-l'Isle (Quai)	24
Charmasson (Av. Jean)	6	Liberté (Pl. de la)	16	Théophile (R. Jean)	25
Dr.-Tallet (R. du)	7	Lices Berthelot	17	Victor-Hugo (Pl.)	26

Hospital (Hôpital). – The hospital's entrance is on Rue Jean-Théophile parallel to an arm of the Sorgue River. Admire in the hall the gilded wood Virgin, the grand staircase, embellished by an 18C wrought iron banister, a chapel with 18C woodwork, and pharmacy with Moustiers pottery jars and a huge 17C mortar. An additional attraction is the peaceful garden, ornamented by an 18C fountain.

Water wheels (Roues à eau). – Near the Place Gambetta at the corner of the Caisse d'Épargne's garden is a **wheel** (**D**), similar to those which worked the silk factories and oil mills. Five other old wheels still exist: one (**E**) Place Émile-Char, two others (**F**) Boulevard Victor-Hugo and two Rue Jean-Théophile.

★ LABEAUME   Pop 405

Michelin map **80** east of fold 8 or **245** south of fold 1

The aged village situated on the bank of Beaume Gorges, an affluent of the Ardèche, merges almost totally into the rock face. At the village's foot, a low level bridge, with no parapet walls but stout piers' protected by cutwaters, spans the river, a perfect artifact in such surroundings.

Leave the car on the large square at the village's entrance.

Church (Église). – The very high belfry-porch rests on two large round columns.

Take, to the left of the church, an alleyway which ends at the river bank and a shaded esplanade. For a better overall view of the village cross the bridge and follow the uphill path for a couple of hundred yards.

★**Beaume Gorges (Gorges de la Beaume).** – The walk upstream along the river's north bank, beside the clear waters, across from the fascinating eroded limestone cliff, is worth while.

Village. – As you return to the car amble along the uphill streets admiring the covered passageways and balconied houses along them.

EXCURSIONS

★**Ruoms Defile (Défilé de Ruoms).** – *5km – 3 miles. Leave Labeaume on the D 245 and bear left on the D 4.* The road goes through picturesque rock tunnels offering plunging views. Following the Ruoms Defile are the Ligne Gorges; from the confluence of the two rivers (Ardèche and Ligne) framed by 100m – 329ft high cliffs striped by the rock strata, opens a good **view** upstream. On the return, at the end of the tunnels, the silhouette of Sampzon Rock *(see below)* appears at the end of the valley.

★**Sampzon Rock via Ruoms.** – *8km – 5 miles. Leave Labeaume and cross the Ardèche towards Ruoms.*

Ruoms. – Pop 1 839. Facilities. The old walled centre of the small commercial town is unexpected – a quadrilateral of ramparts flanked by seven round towers. At the heart of the old town is a small Romanesque church with an unusual arcaded belfry faced with motifs worked in volcanic rock. The view is best from Ruelle St-Roch opening onto the parvis.

Leave Ruoms by the D 579 towards Vallon.

★**Sampzon Rock** (Rocher de Sampzon). – *On the Ardèche's south bank by a narrow road which climbs steeply through many bends. Park below Sampzon Church and walk to the top (3/4 hour Rtn) first by the tarred path and then by the path level with the turning place.* From the top (television relay mast) there is a **panorama**★★ including the Vallon Basin, the Orgnac Plateau and the serpentines of the Ardèche.

LOURMARIN
Pop 858

Michelin map **84** fold 3 or **245** fold 31 or **246** fold 12 – Local map p 125

The village at the foot of the Luberon Range and at the south end of the coomb of the same name, is dominated by its château built high on a rock bluff.
In the cemetery Albert Camus (1913-60), the author of *The Stranger* and *The Plague*, is buried.

★**Château.** – The château includes a 15C part, the old château, and a Renaissance
ⓥ part, the new château.
The Renaissance wing has remarkable stylistic unity and contains large chimneypieces ornamented with caryatids or Corinthian columns. The grand staircase ends dramatically with a slender pillar supporting a stone cupola. The 15C wing, now the library and students' rooms, overlooks arcaded courtyards.
Fifty-six steps in the hexagonal turret lead to a platform which commands a **view** of the coomb, the Luberon, the Durance Plain and Mount Ste-Victoire.

★ **LUBERON Range** (Montagne du **LUBERON**)

Michelin map **81** folds 12 to 15 or **245** folds 30 to 32

Mid-way between the Alps and the Mediterranean lies the mountainous Luberon Range. This region is full of charm: striking solitary woods and rocky countryside and picturesque, old perched villages and dry rock huts.

ⓥ **Luberon Regional Nature Park (Parc Naturel Régional du Luberon).** – Founded in 1977, the park includes some 50 communes covering 120 000ha – 463sq miles including the *départements* of Vaucluse and Alpes-de-Haute-Provence (or from Manosque to Cavaillon and the Coulon – or Calavon – Valley to the Durance Valley). Its goal is to preserve the natural balance of the region with the aim of improving the living conditions of the village folk, the promotion of agricultural activity through irrigation mechanisation and the reorganisation of the holdings.

The main improvements in the tourist industry are: the opening of tourist information centres and museums at Apt and at La Tour d'Aigues, the creation of nature trails (in the cedar forest at Bonnieux and the cliffs of Roussillon), the setting up of bicycle path itineraries between Cavaillon and Apt (40km – 25 miles) and between Apt and La Bégude (12km – 7 1/2 miles).

Natural habitat and man's imprint. – The Luberon Range is a gigantic anticlinal fold of calcareous rock of the Tertiary Era running east-west. The range is divided from north to south by Lourmarin Coomb into two unequal parts; to the west the Petit Luberon forms a plateau carved by gorges and ravines where the altitude rarely exceeds 700m – 2 297ft, whereas to the east, the Grand Luberon, raises its massive summits up to 1 125m – 3 691ft at Mourre Nègre.
The contrast between the north and south slopes is no less important. The northern face, steep and ravined, is cooler, more humid and wears a fine forest of downy oaks. The southern face, turned towards Aix, more Mediterranean in its vegetation (oak groves, rosemary filled *garrigues*), with its sunny slopes, crops and cypresses, announces the smiling countryside along the Durance River.
The diversity of the vegetation is a delight to nature lovers: oak forests, Atlas cedar (planted in 1862) on the heights of the Petit Luberon, beech, scots pine... The moors of broom and boxwood, *garrigues*, the extraordinary variety of aromatic plants (herbs of Provence), cling here and there to the rocky slopes. The *mistral (qv)* contributes provoking local unheard of changes: holm oaks are blown onto the northern exposed slopes and downy oaks onto the southern exposed slopes. In winter the contrast between the evergreens and deciduous trees is striking. The fauna is equally rich: snakes (seven different varieties), lizards, warblers, blue rock thrushes, owls, eagles... The Luberon has always been inhabited by man. Since prehistoric times, it has served as hiding place during periods of insecurity and political and religious persecutions: the memory of the Vaud tragedy *(qv)* still echos...
Villages appeared during the Middle Ages and clung to the rock face near a water hole. The tall houses, with their imposing walls huddled close together at the foot of a castle or church; most of them had rooms cut out of the rock. The men left their homes to work in the surrounding countryside and when necessary they lived in drystone huts called *bories (see below)*. Their livelihood was obtained mostly from sheep, olives, grain and vineyards as well as lavender and silkworms. Each parcel of cultivated land was carefully cleared of stones – the stones were grouped into piles called *clapiers* – and bordered by low walls which served to protect the land from soil erosion. The flocks were also contained within a close of drystone. Traces of these arrangements are still visible in the rural landscape.
This traditional economy was swept away by the agricultural improvements of the 19 and 20C: villages lost their inhabitants and fell into ruins. Today they seem more like open-air museums. However, the villages on the southern slopes, which were at all times preferred because of their rich land, have adapted to the requirements of the modern rural economy: market gardening, fruit growing and vineyards from Aigues have enabled the native population to survive.

The bories. – On the slopes of the Luberon and the Vaucluse Plateau stand these curious drystone huts, one or two floors high, called *bories*. They are either alone or in groups forming a very picturesque unit; there are about 3 000 of them. They were sometimes just tool sheds or sheep pens but many were inhabited over the different periods from the Iron Age until the 18C, for the most recent, which in fact are better constructed.

122

The bories of Gordes

The *bories* were built with materials found on the spot: thin slabs of limestone, which have become detached from the rock or slabs picked when clearing the fields. These stones called *lauzes* average 10cm – 3 3/4in thick. Specialised masons knew how to select the *lauzes* and assemble them without either mortar or water. The thickness of the walls obtained by the juxtaposition of several rows of slabs varied from .80m – 31 1/2in to 1.60m – 4 1/2ft; it was always reinforced at the base. The bonding whether from the outside or inside was remarkably regular. The technique used for the roofing of the *borie* consisted of a type of false corbelled vaulting: as the walls were raised each stone course was carefully made to overhang the preceding one so that at a height of 3 or 4m – 10-13ft – the diameter diminished to the point of being reduced to a small opening which could be closed simply by placing one slab. To avoid the infiltration of water the different layers of stone were slightly inclined towards the exterior. Inside the vaulting appeared as a hemispheric dome on pendentives which allowed the plan to pass from a square or a circle or a cone.

The *bories* offered a variety of forms. The simplest, round, ovoid or square consisted of one room (1-8m – 3-26ft in diameter) and one opening set east or southeast. The interior arrangement was rudimentary limited to hollow niches used for storage. The temperature of the *borie* remained constant inspite of the season. Larger dwellings exist, especially at Gordes *(qv)*. They are rectangular, have a few narrow openings and the roof had double or quadruple pitch using the technique of false vaulting either rounded, pointed barrel or an inverted ship's hull (Gordes).

Their organisation was similar to that of a traditional farm: disposed around a courtyard encircled by a high wall were the living quarters (tiled floors, benches, and chimney for the most comfortable ones), bread oven and outbuildings.

These villages of *bories* produce numerous suppositions: were these places of refuge during troubled times, and if so occupied permanently? But then why have neither a burial place nor place of worship been discovered near them? Were they then perhaps just temporary places to live, for example, seasonal?

★★① GRAND LUBERON
Round tour from Apt

119km – 74 miles – allow 1/2 day not including the climb to Mourre Nègre – local map p 125

Apt. – *Description p 58.*

Leave Apt by the D 48 going southeast on Avenue de Saignon.

As the road climbs, the perched site of Saignon, Apt Basin, Vaucluse Plateau and Mount Ventoux come into view.

Saignon. – Pop 967. The village, close to a tall rock, contains a Romanesque church with a west front rebuilt in the 16C to include beautiful, trilobed blind arcading.

Continue along the D 48.

The road skirts Claparèdes Plateau, with its scattered *bories*.

Leave the car at Auribeau; exit from town northwards and bear left on the unsurfaced road towards Mourre Nègre. The GR 92 leads to the summit.

★★★**Mourre Nègre.** – *1/2 day on foot Rtn.* Mourre Nègre at 1 125m – 3 691ft is the highest point of the Luberon Range and the site of the Paris-Nice television relay mast. The **panorama**★★★ embraces four points of the compass: Lure Mountain and Digne Pre-Alps (northeast), Durance Valley with Mount Ste-Victoire in the background (southeast), Berre Lagoon and Alpilles Chain (southwest), Apt Basin, Vaucluse Plateau and Mount Ventoux (northwest).

Return to the D 48 and continue through Auribeau.

Castellet. – Pop 72. The minute stepped hamlet is today a lavender distillery centre.

The road crosses a *garrigues* landscape before reaching Calavon Valley.

Turn right on the N 100.

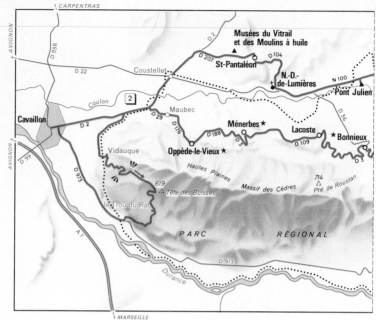

Céreste. – Pop 862. *Description in the Michelin Green Guide Alpes du Sud, in French only.*

Southeast of Céreste take the D 31.

The road winds up the north slope of the Grand Luberon from where one can see over Calavon Valley to Vaucluse Plateau. The road then descends the southern slope passing through Vitrolles down into the plain; turn right into the D 42; continue along the D 27, which skirts Bonde Lagoon.

⊙ **Cucuron.** – Pop 1 409. Inside the **church** which has a Romanesque nave and Gothic apse and chapels, are an early 18C marble altarpiece, a multicoloured marble pulpit and a 16C painted wood *Christ Seated and Chained* in the baptismal chapel.

⊙ Opposite the church, on the 1st floor of the 17C Hôtel de Bouliers is a small **Luberon Museum**: local prehistory, Gallo-Roman period, and later local traditions.

From the pavement below the keep you can see how the belfry was once a gateway in the old walls and a look-out over the Cucuron Basin to Mount Ste-Victoire on the horizon.

Ansouis. – *4.5km – 2 1/2 miles from Cucuron on the D 56 going southeast. Description p 57.*

Lourmarin. – *Description p 122.*

The D 943 travels northwest up the Lourmarin Coomb.

The Aigue Brun River has cut narrow gorges through the rock. The road crosses a children's holiday camp (old 16-18C château) before crossing a bridge and reaching a group of houses.

Just before these houses turn right to the car park.

⊙ **Buoux Fort** (Fort de Buoux). – *1/2 hour on foot Rtn, plus 3/4 hour tour. Go through the gate and follow the path beneath a vertical rock wall to the porter's lodge.* The rock spur on which the fort stands is a natural defence which has, in consequence, been occupied by Ligurians, Romans, Catholics and Protestants. Louis XIV ordered its demolition in 1660 – there, nevertheless, remain three defensive walls, a Romanesque chapel, houses, silos hewn out of the rock, a keep, a Ligurian sacrificial altar and a concealed staircase.

From the rock spur, where there stood a medieval keep, there is a fine view of the Upper Aigue Brun Valley.

Return to the holiday camp and turn right into the D 113.

Beyond Buoux village the road returns to Apt by a picturesque route.

★② PETIT LUBERON
Round tour from Apt

101km – 62 1/2 miles – about 6 hours – local map pp 124-125

Apt. – *Description p 58.*

Leave Apt by ② on the D 943. After Pointu Pass, turn right into the D 232.

The road crosses the Claparèdes Plateau, studded with *bories* among oak trees and truffle beds *(p 16).*

Bear right into the D 36.

★**Bonnieux.** – *Description p 93.*

Leave Bonnieux south on the D 3 then bear right on the D 109.

The road winds along the slope of the Petit Luberon, behind you Bonnieux appears picturesquely.

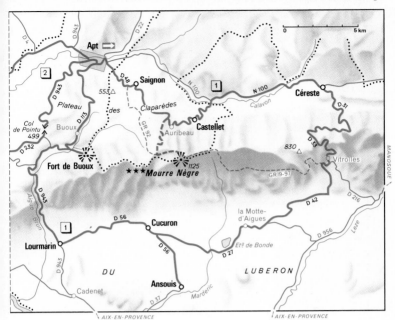

Lacoste. – Pop 309. This perched village has a small elegant 17C belfry and is dominated by the imposing ruins (partially rebuilt) of a château which belonged to the Sade family and included 42 rooms. The Marquis de Sade (1740-1814), author of erotic works *(The Adversities of Virtue, Justine, or the Misfortunes of Virtue),* was the lord of Lacoste for some 30 years; several times condemned, he escaped and hid here; but in 1778 he was imprisoned.

Continue to Ménerbes via the D 109; note the quarries which extract a well-known freestone in the area near Lacoste.

★**Ménerbes.** – *Description p 140.*

Go south along the D 3 and then take the D 188.

The road offers attractive views of the Vaucluse Plateau and Mount Ventoux.

★**Oppède-le-Vieux.** – Pop 1 015. The terraced **site★** of the village on its picturesque rocky spur, once partially abandoned, has come to life again through its restoration.

Leave the car in the new car park.

The old village square is surrounded by restored houses. An old gateway in the walls leads to the upper village crowned by its 13C church (remodelled in the 16 and 19C) and ruined castle (founded by the Counts of Toulouse and rebuilt in the 15 and 16C).

The fine **view★** from the church terrace is of Coulon Valley and Vaucluse Plateau, Ménerbes *(qv)* and, from the rear of the castle, of the ravined north face of the Luberon.

Cross the Maubec wine region (D 176, D 29) and bear left on the D 2.

On leaving Robion bear left on the D 31 to the intersection with the Vidauque road, which you take to the left.

This very steep and winding road (one-way road; speed limit 30kph – 20mph), skirts the wild Vidauque Coomb and offers magnificent plunging **views★★** of the surrounding countryside: tip of Vaucluse Plateau and Coulon Valley (north), Alpilles Chain and Durance Valley (south and west) and below Cavaillon Plain with its market-gardens hemmed in by cypresses and reeds.

Level with the television relay mast the road branches off to the right on the said Trou-du-Rat road which leads to the D 973 which you take to the right.

Cavaillon. – *Description p 103.*

Leave the town by ② on the town plan (p 103).

The D 2 climbs the fertile Coulon Valley.

3km – 2 miles after Coustellet bear right on the D 207 towards Moulin des Bouillons.

Stained Glass Window Museum and Museum of Oil Mills. – *Description pp 118-119.*

St-Pantaléon. – *Description p 119.*

The D 104 and the D 60 to the right lead to Notre-Dame-de-Lumières.

Notre-Dame-de-Lumières. – The statue of Our Lady in the crypt of this 17C sanctuary is the object of a popular Provençal pilgrimage; in the chapel above, on the third south altar is a 17C Pietà in carved and gilded wood. An important ex-voto collection is on display. A pleasant walk in the park around the conventual buildings is worthwhile.

The N 100 climbs the Coulon Valley. On the left is ochre country *(p 16).*

Julien Bridge. – *Description p 59.*

The N 100 returns to Apt.

★ MADELEINE Cave (Grotte de la MADELEINE)

Michelin map 80 fold 9 or 245 north of fold 15 or 246 fold 23 – Local map p 61

This cave opens onto the north face of the cliff, hollowed out by the Ardèche Gorges.

The downhill road to the cave branches onto the D 290, the road of the Ardèche Gorges, and leads to the entrance (car park).

⊘ TOUR

The cave discovered in 1887 was carved out by a former underwater river which once drained part of Gras Plateau. Enter through the Obscure Cave (Grotte Obscure), then a tunnel hewn out of the rock (steep staircase) takes the visitor to the Chaos Cave (Salle du Chaos).

Beyond this chamber, divided into two parts by a mass of columns detached from the vault, extends a vast gallery full of richly decorated concretions: draperies, organs 30m – 987ft high, eccentrics in the shape of horns etc. Note in particular a magnificent white flow, between two formations of red draperies evoking frozen falls by their fluidity and concretions in the form of gypsum flowers. The sides of the chamber are covered with small crystallisations resembling coral.

MAILLANE   Pop 1 430

Michelin map 81 folds 11 and 12 or 245 fold 29 or 246 fold 25 – 16km – 10 miles south of Avignon

In the fertile countryside named Petite Crau de St-Rémy, Maillane offers the charm typical of a Provençal town with its small squares shaded with plane trees and white houses roofed with tiles. Its renown is due largely to the fame of Frédéric Mistral, the Provençal poet and one of the founders of the Félibrige movement *(qv)*.

Frédéric Mistral. – Mistral was born 8 September 1830 (d 1914) and spent his
⊘ childhood at the **Mas du Juge** *(1km – 1/2 mile from town on the road to Graveson)*. From schooling in Maillane, he went to boarding school at St-Michel-de-Frigolet then studied at the Collège Royal in Avignon where he met Roumanille. After having studied law at Aix (in 1851), he returned to the family home more attracted to the charm of the Provençal language than the quibbling of the *Code Napoleon*. At the death of his father, he had to leave the Mas du Juge for the Lézard House (Maison du Lézard: *facing the museum*) a small family home at the village's entrance, where he lived with his mother and finished writing *Mirèio* (1859). He married in 1876 and moved to a new house which has religiously safeguarded his memory *(see below)*. In 1904 he was awarded the Nobel Prize for Literature.

In the cemetery, down the main path, level with the war memorial stands, on the left, Mistral's mausoleum which he copied from Queen Jeanne's pavilion near Les Baux *(p 88)*.

⊘ **Museon Mistral.** – The museum is located in the house which Mistral had built and lived in from 1876-1914. Mistral's memory is evoked throughout the different rooms – office, living room, dining room, bedroom – which have been kept as they were at his death.

★ MARCOULE

Michelin map 80 north of fold 20 or 246 fold 24

The nuclear power centre, which can be identified from afar by its two 80 and 100m (262 and 328ft) tall chimneys, is surrounded by vineyards and *garrigues (qv)*. Two organisations are active here: COGEMA (Compagnie Générale des Matières Premières – Raw Materials Company) and CEA (Commissariat à l'Énergie Atomique – Atomic Energy Commission). The main purpose of COGEMA is the industrial processing of nuclear wastes (natural uranium-graphite-gas) coming from nuclear reactors. An industrial workshop, complementary to the chemical factory, started in 1978 the French process of vitrification of radio-active wastes.

The CEA, which is more a centre of research than a producer of energy, works on different aspects of research and development in the processing of wastes from fast breeder reactors.

For this purpose the Phénix Nuclear Power Centre, a prototype fast reactor, north of the Marcoule site, between the Rhône River and the D 138 has functioned since 1973; it has an electrical power of 250 MW.

★★**Viewing platform.** – *Access via the D 138 east of Chusclan.*

View. – A panel on the raised area between the two exhibition halls identifies the main installations. From the platform there is also an extensive scenic view of the Rhône, Orange and its Roman Theatre, Mount Ventoux, the Comtat Plain, the Alpilles Chain, the Ardoise iron and metalworks and the Lower Gard Valley.

⊘ **Exhibition.** – The first gallery presents the world of the atom, fission, nuclear energy and fuel and radio-activity; the second illustrates the function of the Marcoule plant.

Join us in our never ending task of keeping up to date.
Send us your comments and suggestions, please.

Michelin Tyre Public Limited Company
Tourism Department
Davy House-Lyon Road-HARROW-Middlesex HA1 2DQ

Michelin map 🄼🄸 fold 13 or 🄼🄸🄵 fold 44 or 🄼🄸🄶 folds, K, L and M

Marseilles (spelt without an "s" in French) is admirably situated at the end of a wide bay, which is surrounded by the limestone ranges of the Estaque and the Étoile. The animation that reigns in the centre of the town, principally in the celebrated Canebière and around the Old Port *(p 130)*, is a well-known Marseilles attraction.

It is when the sun is setting that one can admire, from Notre-Dame-de-la-Garde *(p 134)*, Marseilles and the Mediterranean.

The Old Port and Notre-Dame-de-la-Garde, Marseilles

Twenty-six centuries of history have gone to make Marseilles the oldest of the great French cities.

Jealous of its independence, the city has always been on its own, resulting in its isolation from the regional and national community until the 19C. Even today, although proud to be the second most populated city in France, it has preserved a distinct personality: a combination of authenticity and old clichés (the stories about Marius and César, the cries of the fishmongers on the Old Port, the boule *(p 10)* players, or the sombre judicial affairs).

And yet Marseilles does not survive on its folklore, it is a city which has progressed with the times: modernising constantly and developing ambitious projects especially cultural ones (eleven museums to which have been added the Old Charity Cultural Centre, the dynamic Luminy School of Art, a group of young artists, etc.).

Marseilles's economic activity. – France's first seaport, Marseilles owes everything to the sea. It has always depended on international commerce and its crowds of sailors, dockers and immigrants of all nationalities have left their mark. The traditional gate to the Orient, its fortune was established on the 19C colonial possessions, which offered immense possibilities of trade: imported products were treated then re-exported at an advantageous price. But this system regressed in the 20C: the end of free exchange, the two world wars, the closing of the Suez Canal and decolonisation felled it a heavy blow.

Reconversion and modernisation, aimed mainly at petrol and chemicals, have brought the geographical move of the great industrial activities to the area around the Berre Lagoon *(qv)* and the Golf of Fos *(qv)*. These new installations are administered by one organisation, the port authority, making Marseilles the second port of Europe, known also as Europort-Sud. It has, nevertheless, kept several traditional processing industries: oil refineries, soap works, flour mills, semolina works and metallurgical factories. *For more details on the port of Marseilles see p 136.*

To make soap, olive oil was, for a long time, one of the raw materials used. In the 19C olive oil was replaced by oils of tropical origin. Marseilles in the past a great production centre of peanut, coconut and palm oils and their related products such as stearin had lost its top position in the French industry of oil products to the regions which were closer to the stock rearing areas and with better transportation facilities like the north of France, Seine-Maritime or the Paris region.

Household soap or Marseilles soap (savon de Marseille) represents about 20% of the French consumption of the washing products market.

In the field of communications Marseilles confirms its role as an international crossroads with its network of motorways, which link it to Paris, Spain and Italy, and its air (Marseilles-Provence airport) and shipping routes (Joliette Port) which supply the African and Far Eastern countries.

Annually in the **Amable-Chanot** (BCZ) Park, where the conference centre (Palais des Congrès) is located, the Marseilles Spring Fair (Printemps-Marseille – late March-early April) and the great Marseilles International Fair (Foire Internationale de Marseille – last fortnight in September) take place. Beside the park stands the Radio and Television Building.

HISTORICAL NOTES

The founding of Massalia. – Before the official founding of the city a settlement, a sort of trading-post, existed used by the Greeks. In 620 or 600BC a few galleys manned by Phocaeans (Greeks from Asia Minor) in search of fortune landed on the coast in the inlet (Lacydon Creek) which today is the Old Port.

According to legend, their leader, Protis, visited the Ligurian tribe which occupied the country. It was the day on which the king was giving a great banquet for the warriors seeking the hand of his daughter, Gyptis. According to the Ligurian custom, at the end of the meal, the young girl was to enter with a cup full of wine which she would present to the man of her choice. Protis, invited to the banquet, mixed with the crowd of suitors: Gyptis entered. She stopped in front of the handsome Greek and offered him the ritual cup. The marriage was celebrated and the young woman brought as her dowry the hill on which Notre-Dame-de-la-Garde now stands and the land around it. Soon, a little town grew up. This was Massalia (or Massilia), the mother of Marseilles.

After the destruction of Phocaea by the Persians (540BC). Massalia was at the head of a number of additional possessions. The Greeks, who were expert traders, quickly made the city prosperous. They set up busy trading-posts at Arles, Nice, Antibes, Agde, Le Brusc, Hyères Islands, and inland at Glanon, Cavaillon, Avignon and perhaps St-Blaise on Berre Lagoon. With the Celto-Ligurians, relations were limited to the trade of pewter, amber, arms, foodstuffs, most likely slaves, wine and pottery. The Provençal coast was cleared and planted with fruit and olive trees and vineyards. The Greek sailors pushed farther south as far as Senegal and to the north as far as Iceland. Administered as a republic, Massilia was famous for the wisdom of its laws.

That it was a centre of civilisation is evidenced by the excavations of the Old Port and around the Centre Bourse shopping centre quarter. These discoveries have enabled the historians to specify the ordonnance of the town; it covered 50ha – 124 acres and was built facing the sea on the hills of St-Laurent, Moulins and Carmes and on the north bank of Lacydon Creek (forming a peninsula). It was surrounded by ramparts, which protected the town, two temples (one to Artemis and the other to Apollo), a theatre and most likely other monuments.

Rome comes to Massalia's aid. – An ally of Rome during the Second Punic War (154BC), Massalia asked for its help against the Salian Franks a tribe (which grouped the majority of the local peoples) less than 30 years later. The Romans fearing a break in the balance of their power in Gaul, took this event as an occasion to acquire more influence, and entered Provence in 125BC, rescued Massalia and began the conquest of the area. During three years battles raged as the Salian Frank tribe harassed the land from entrenched camps. But Roman tenacity triumphed; Transalpine Gaul was founded with Aix and Narbonne as colonies. Massalia remained an independent republic allied to Rome; it kept a strip of territory along the coast.

Roman Marseilles. – At the moment when the rivalry between Caesar and Pompey was at its height, Marseilles was forced to decide for one or the other of the two Roman generals. It backed Pompey – the wrong horse. Besieged for six months, the town at last fell in 49BC; Caesar took away its fleet, its treasures and its trade. Arles, Narbonne and Fréjus were enriched with its spoils. Nevertheless, Marseilles remained a free city and maintained a brilliant university, the last refuge of Greek teaching in the West.

The excavations of the old quarter have uncovered maritime warehouses (Roman dockyards) from 1C proving that the town stayed commercially active in spite of the fact that most of the trade with the Far East and Italy was with Arles. In the 3C Marseilles lost its municipal autonomy and became a town like the others; the town seemed to vegetate. And yet Christianity came early to the town as is shown by: the catacombs on the slopes of La Garde Hill, the martyrdom of a Roman officer c915, the two monasteries (among the first in the West) founded in the 5C and the treatises (c450) written by a priest.

After the invasions and subsequent looting, Marseilles seemed to remain an active port which continued to trade with the Far East; it was the object of violent rivalry between the barbarian leaders.

In 453 the plague arrived in Gaul for the first time. The definite decline began in the 7C. The pillaging by the Saracens and Franks pushed the town back behind the fortifications of the bishopric on St-Laurent Hill.

Maritime development. – As early as the 11C the old Phocaean city mobilised all its shipping resources and put its shipyards to work. In 1214 Marseilles became an independent republic; it lasted a short time, as in 1252 it had to submit to the rule of Charles of Anjou. During this prosperous period (12-14C) which was marked by the Crusades, Marseilles competed with Genoa for the rich supply trade in war material and food to the Crusaders. Not only did the city reap great profit from this, but it was granted ownership of a section of Jerusalem with its own church.

Marseilles, now rich again, sought new outlets. Its sailors began to trade along the Catalan coast, competed in their own waters with the men of Pisa and Genoa, and often sailed as far as the Levant, Egypt and North Africa. In the early 15C prosperity was overtaken by crises and a weakening which was confirmed in 1423 when the fleet from Aragon pillaged the city. But this was just temporary because under the influence of two clever merchants, the Forbin brothers, trade started up again.

Good King René *(qv)* also discovered this world of trade and commerce during his long stay in the city during the summer of 1447.

In 1481 the town was united under the French crown at the same time as Provence. But there was hardly a reign in which the turbulent people of Marseilles were not in rebellion, especially during the Wars of Religion.

The great plague. – In the early 18C Marseilles's population was at about 90 000. It was a great port which had profited from an edict of franchise since 1669 and from a monopoly of levantine trade. It subsequently became a huge warehouse of imported products (textiles, food products, drugs and miscellaneous items); and was preparing to launch into trade with the West Indies and the New World, when in May 1720 the imprudence and greed of a shipowner stopped everything.

A ship coming from Syria had several cases of plague during its journey; the captain informed the port authorities. But since the cargo was destined for powerful merchants of the town, who did not want to miss the Beaucaire Fair *(qv),* quarantine was suppressed. A few days later the epidemic broke out and ravaged the city. The hospitals were full; the sick, often driven from their homes by their families, died in the streets; thousands of corpses lay on the ground, for there were not enough galley slaves to carry the bodies to the mass graves.

Three persons distinguished themselves by their unselfish devotion during this dark period: Bishop Xavier of Belsunce, the Chevalier Rose and the Squadron Commander Langeron.

The Parliament at Aix forbade all communication between Marseilles and the rest of Provence under penalty of death. But this did not stop the plague from spreading to Aix, Apt, Arles and Toulon. In two years 100 000 people died, 50 000 of whom were from Marseilles.

Rapidly Marseilles recovered: in but a couple of years the city had re-established its incredible demographic and economic energy. In 1765 the city had returned to the demographic level it had in 1720 with 85 to 90 000 inhabitants. Trade found new openings with Latin America and especially the West Indies; Marseilles began importing sugar, coffee and cacao. Industrialisation began: soap and glass making, sugar refining, glazed earthenware and textiles etc.

Huge fortunes developed: ship owners and merchants, the number of which doubled in the century, displayed their wealth amidst the artisans and workers who lived directly from the cargo brought off the docks.

The landscape painter Claude Vernet evokes beautifully in his pictures of the port of Marseilles the bustling, electric atmosphere which reigned here in the 18C.

The Marseillaise. – The city welcomed the Revolution with enthusiasm. It elected Mirabeau *(qv)* as representative to the States General. The Tribune, however, opted for Aix, which had also chosen him.

In 1792 a young sapper officer from the Engineers, Rouget de Lisle, composed at Strasbourg the *Chant de guerre de l'Armée du Rhin* (the war-song of the Army of the Rhine).

This battle song was published and reached Marseilles. The town was sending 500 volunteers to Paris and at a banquet in their honour someone sang the new song that had come from Alsace. It was an immediate success and everyone present sang it in unison.

Before the departure of Marseilles's volunteers, each of them was given a copy of the song. They sang it at every stopping place, arousing constant enthusiasm. By the time they reached Paris, the volunteers had become something of an expert choir; as they marched through the streets they electrified the crowds as they sang the stirring words at the top of their warm southern voices. The new hymn was quickly given a name: it was *La Marseillaise.*

But the heavy hand of the Convention soon became unbearable for Marseilles, federalist at heart. It rebelled. Taken by assault, Marseilles became "the city without a name". A guillotine was permanently set up on La Canebière.

The **Aix Gateway** (Porte d'Aix – ES V) is a triumphal arch erected in 1833 to commemorate the Revolutionary and First Empire Wars.

The 19C. – Under the Empire, Marseilles became royalist. It must be said that the city's trade had been hard hit by the British fleet and the continental blockade. When Napoleon returned from Elba, the authorities of Marseilles pursued him and he only just escaped arrest. The city supported the Bourbons against the Orléans family. Blood ran in 1848. Under the Second Empire, Marseilles became Republican; important urban projects were undertaken (the opening of the actual Rue de la République, construction of Longchamp Palace, Notre-Dame-de-la-Garde, the cathedral, Pharo Palace and park etc).

The conquest of Algeria, which put an end to the Barbary pirates, had already stimulated the economic activity of Marseilles.

The opening of the Suez Canal in 1869 was another step forward in its development.

The events of 1940-4. – The German-Italian bombing of 1940 and that of the Allies in 1943-4 to prepare for their landing in Provence caused great damage and many victims in the town.

In January 1943, under the pretext of public health, the Germans forcibly evacuated 40 000 inhabitants from the old quarter in order to raze the densely populated little streets, often ill-famed but at least picturesque, between Rue Caisserie *(p 133)* and the Old Port. They left merely a façade of old houses along the quayside.

After the war. – As with most towns damaged by the war, Marseilles has been rebuilt. In the place of the old quarter that was destroyed, a new quarter has been planned and built. In addition, a whole series of new buildings have gone up on Boulevard Michelet, including the first "Unité d'Habitation" by Le Corbusier who, since 1952, has made his mark with his audacious and original designs.

Several large projects of urban reorganisation have followed especially in the stock exchange quarter (Centre Bouse).

Since November 1977 a subway line has linked the northeast suburb, the Rose, to the city centre; an extension to the east is expected. A second line, northwest-southeast was opened in 1987.

★★ OLD PORT (VIEUX PORT) (DETU) *time: 2 1/2 hours*

The port opens from the west between the St-Jean and St-Nicolas Forts, which can be reached on foot and from where lovely views can be had.

In this creek the Phocaeans landed in 600BC. It was here that, until the 19C, all Marseilles's maritime life was concentrated. In the Middle Ages, the marshes bordering the head of the harbour were converted into hempfields or *chenevières* (whence the name Canebière). The hemp was used for rigging and was woven on the spot *(p 134)*.

The quays were constructed under Louis XII and Louis XIII.

In the 19C, the depth of two fathoms was found to be insufficient for steamships of large tonnage; new basins were built.

After the Second World War, the buildings around the old port were rebuilt after the plans of Fernand Pouillon (1912-86).

Today the old port contains only yachts, pleasure boats or motorboats for excursions creating a picturesque scene.

Every morning on Quai des Belges (ET **5**) the **fish market** is held – a colourful animated scene where the thick Marseilles accent can be heard at its best.

Follow on foot the itinerary indicated on the town plan; it corresponds for the most part with the itinerary posted.

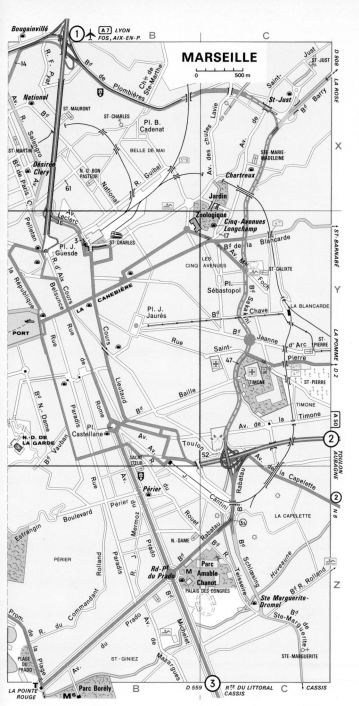

MARSEILLE

0   500 m

Garden of Ruins (Jardin des Vestiges) (ET **K**). – Excavated behind the stock exchange, the fortifications of the Greek town, the docks of the ancient port (1C AD) and an entrance way into the town (4C AD) make up this archaeological garden. During the Phocaean period, this site was located beside a swamp (the sea went further inland than it does today) which was slowly drained and dried up in the 3 and 2C BC thanks to the installation of drainage pipes.

In the second half of the 2C BC a new wall was built, of which interesting ruins remain: square towers, bastions and stepped curtain walls. Note the construction of the blocks of stone hewn out of pink limestone from Couronne Cape. Coming from the port, in the shape of a horn, a road entered the town through a gate which opened into a convex wall, flanked by two large towers. An underground aqueduct carried spring water from the east; a canal brought water to a square tank (extra-muros). In order to have a good idea of the town plan (opposite the ancient town) stand in front of the Historical Museum of Marseilles which is at the end of the Roman road.

⊙ **Historical Museum of Marseilles** (Musée d'Histoire de Marseille) (**M¹**). – The museum is located at the end of the Garden of Ruins, on the ground floor of the Centre Bourse shopping centre. It traces the history of Marseilles in its Provençal context from prehistorical to Gallo-Roman times through archaeological finds (a number of moulds), documents and models.

131

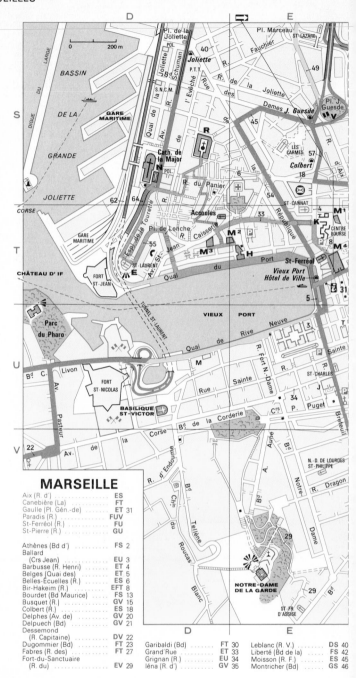

MARSEILLE

A didactic exhibit revolving around a **Roman merchant vessel** (19m – 62ft long and 8m – 26ft wide, discovered in 1974 and entirely freeze-dry – ridding the vessel of all moisture) treats different archaeological themes: Celto-Ligurian customs (reconstruction of the Roquepertuse portico), funerary customs, food storage (large urn), metallurgy, ship building etc. A panorama of the ramparts, with a model, enable the visitor to understand their plan.

★**Museum of Old Marseilles** (Musée du Vieux Marseille) (DET M²). – The museum is in the 16C Maison Diamantée (*diamant* means diamond) so-called because of the faceted stones used in its construction.
The ground floor contains 18C Provençal furniture and domestic objects.
The fine staircase with its coffered ceiling goes up to the 1st floor where a number of 18C cribs in spun glass or resin-and-bread-crumbs and a large collection of *santons* (1830-early 1900s) are exhibited. Another room is devoted to Marseilles's old quarter, with a relief model of the town in 1848, while another room contains miscellaneous items concerning the great plague of 1720 *(p 129)*.
On the 2nd floor displays of costumes, engravings and paintings illustrate 19C Marseilles life. Also worth noting is the large Camoin (Marseilles cardmakers since the 18C) donation, which includes the appropriate material needed for the making of playing cards and the different techniques used.

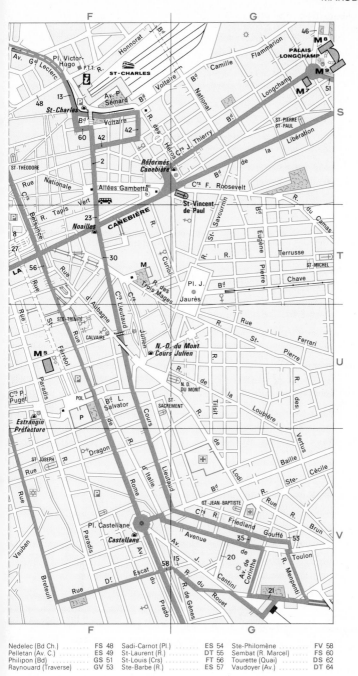

★Roman Docks Museum (Musée des Docks romains) (DT M³). – During the rebuilding of the old quarter, Roman docks dating from the second half of 1C AD were unearthed. The docks included warehouses opening onto the quayside and an upper storey communicating with the Roman town's main road, the *decumanus*, now Rue Caisserie. The ground floor contained enormous urns for storing grain, wine and oil. The museum retraces Marseilles's commercial history (documents). Uncovered during the underwater excavations were enormous urns, pottery and ships' frames.

Accoules Bell Tower (Clocher des Accoules) (DT). – This 12C bell tower is all that remains of one of Marseilles's oldest churches.

Via the Accoules stairs, and the Rues des Muettes, du Refuge and Rodillat, you reach the Old Charity Cultural Centre.

Old Charity Cultural Centre (Centre de la Vieille Charité) (DS R). – This recently restored former hospice constituted a fine architectural unit built from 1671-1749 on the plans of Pierre and Jean Puget. The buildings, created originally to shelter the deprived, stand around the central chapel, a fine baroque building by Pierre Puget *(qv)* with an ovoid dome. The façades looking onto the courtyard present three storeys of arcaded galleries in elegant pink and yellow tinted Couronne stone.

The hospice transformed into a cultural centre *(expected transfer of the Borély Castle collections)* houses the large Marseilles's exhibitions.

Ⓥ **La Major Cathedral (Cathédrale de la Major)** (DS). – Built between 1852-93 in the Romano-Byzantine style, this is a huge and sumptuous edifice 140m – 459ft long and 70m – 230ft high (under the dome).

★**Old La Major Cathedral** (Ancienne cathédrale de la Major) (DS N). – The "Old Major"
Ⓥ in stout contrast, is a fine example of mid-11C Romanesque, truncated in the 19C to make space for the building of the new cathedral. Only the chancel, transept and one bay of the nave and side aisles remain. The contents include a reliquary altar of 1073, a ceramic relief of the Deposition by Luca della Robbia and a 15C altar to St Lazarus by Francesco Laurana.

Via Esplanade de la Tourette go to St-Laurent's parvis.

St-Laurent Belvedere (Belvédère St-Laurent) (DT E). – 92 steps. Located on St-Laurent's (12C) parvis above a road tunnel, the belvedere offers a fine **view**★ of the Old Port; the entrance to the Canebière, Étoile Chain, Notre-Dame-de-la-Garde Basilica and St-Nicolas and St-Jean Forts.

Follow Rue St-Laurent.

Below, on the right, are the remains of the ancient theatre.
By the Place de Lenche, the presumed site of the agora, and Rue Henri-Tasso you reach the Quai du Port.

Town Hall (Hôtel de Ville) (ET H). – The town hall has preserved an interesting 17C façade. The king's coat of arms above the main entrance is the mould of a work by Pierre Puget exhibited in Longchamp Palace *(p 136)*.

Ⓥ **St-Ferréol** (ET). – Facing the old port, St-Ferréol or Church of the Augustinians raises its Renaissance façade, rebuilt in 1804. Inside will be found a Gothic nave and an 18C marble altar.

THE CANEBIÈRE (EFT) *time: 2 hours*

Marseilles' most famous street is lined with department stores, hotels, cafés and banks. Created during the expansion of the city in the 17C, the street's name comes from hempfields *(chènevières)* as hemp was once cultivated here.
Sailors from all the countries who had docked in this great Mediterranean port spoke of this street at all their ports of call; it symbolised this loud and vital city.

Place Général-de-Gaulle (ET 31). – On the Place Général-de-Gaulle is the Square Alexandre 1ᵉʳ where a monument to Pierre Puget stands; it is the meeting place of many of the local population. Across from it stands the stock exchange (Centre Bourse – inside of which is the Maritime Museum).

Ⓥ **Marseilles's Maritime Museum (Musée de la Marine de Marseille)** (ET M⁴). – Located on the stock exchange's ground floor, which also houses the chamber of commerce is this museum devoted to maritime history and to the history of the port of Marseilles, concentrating on the 17C to the present.
To illustrate its evolution several models of sailboats and steamships, paintings, watercolours, engravings and plans are exhibited.
Opening on the south side of the Canebière are the Rues Paradis and St-Ferréol, commercial arteries, either one of which takes you to the Cantini Museum.

★**Cantini Museum (Musée Cantini)** (FU M⁵). – The sculptor Jules Cantini donated
Ⓥ his collection and the 17C Hôtel de Montgrand to the city. The majority of the museum is occupied by the **Regional Foundation of Contemporary Art** which has assembled more than 400 works in different mediums *(exhibited in rotation)* representing the various tendencies: New Realism, New Figurative... etc.
Exhibited are sculpture by César, Ipoustéguy and Arman, collages by Michaux and Magnelli, paintings by Alechinsky, Masson etc, alternating with a newer generation of artists represented by Adami, Viallat, Jaccard etc. The Surrealist section, where the works of Picabia, Mirò, Arp and Antonin Artaud (a very rare drawing) can be seen, is dominated by the large *Monument to the Birds* (1927) by Max Ernst.
A **gallery of Marseilles and Moustiers faience**★★ composed of some 600 objects makes up the second half of the museum. Among the rare 17 and 18C pieces, note a small fountain by Leroy, a fine platter by Robert, a Veuve Perrin fish service, an ewer by Gaspard Robert, a Clerissy hunting dish, and the Olerys' tablet with a monkey motif.
As you go up the Canebière, you will pass by one of Marseilles's most animated streets, Rue de Rome.

St-Vincent-de-Paul (GST). – Neo-Gothic in style, the church was built on the site of a chapel of a reformed Augustinian monastery, thus its familiar name Church of the Reformed.
The area between the church and Boulevard Dugommier is the site of a Santons Fair held from the last Sunday in November to Epiphany.

NOTRE-DAME-DE-LA-GARDE (EV) *time: 2 hours*

Ⓥ **Notre-Dame-de-la-Garde Basilica (Basilique de N.-D.-de-la-Garde).** – *A ramp of 10-12% – 1 in 10 – 1 in 8 gradients – and a passage with a 15% 1 in 6 1/2 gradient; slippery surface in rainy weather. From Rue de Rome turn left into Rue de Dragon; then, left on Rue Breteuil, right on Boulevard Vauban and right again on Rue du Fort-du-Sanctuaire which comes out onto Le Plateau de la Croix (car parks).*
The basilica was built by Espérandieu *(qv)* in the mid-19C in the then fashionable Romano-Byzantine style. It stands on a limestone spike (162m – 532ft altitude) on the site of a 13C chapel also dedicated to Our Lady. Surmounting the belfry is a huge gilded statue of the Virgin.

The interior is faced with multi-coloured marble, mosaics and mural paintings by the Düsseldorf School. Numerous ex-votos cover the walls while in the crypt note the lovely Mater Dolorosa in marble carved by Carpeaux.

The **panorama★★★**, however, is the principal reason for the visitors' climb to the basilica: to the left rise the Pomègues and Ratonneau Islands, If Castle and in the distance Marseilleveyre Massif; opposite is the port overlooked by St-Jean Fort (14-17C) and Pharo Park in the foreground; further to the right is the city and in the background the Estaque Chain; in the distance is the Étoile Chain.

A popular pilgrimage to Notre-Dame takes place annually on 15 August.

★**St Victor's Basilica (Basilique St-Victor)** (DU). – The church is the last relic of the famous abbey known as the key to Marseilles' harbour, founded in the early 5C by St John Cassian, a monk from the Far East, in honour of St Victor, patron of sailors and millers, who suffered martyrdom in the 3C by being slowly ground between two millstones. The sanctuary, destroyed in a Saracen raid, was rebuilt in c1040 and subsequently remodelled and strongly fortified.

From the ouside it is truly a fortress. The porch which opens into Isarn Tower is roofed with heavy pointed vaulting which, built in 1140, are among the oldest in Provence. The interior presents two very distinct parts: the nave and aisles, with the 13C vaulting are a good example of the Primitive Gothic style, the chancel and transept are 14C. The high altar dates from 1966.

★★**Crypt.** – The most interesting part is made up of the 5C basilica, erected by St Cassian, which was submerged when the 11C church was built. Near it are the cave of St Victor and the entrance to the catacombs where, since the Middle Ages, St Lazarus and St Mary Magdalene *(see below)* are venerated.

In the neighbouring crypts a remarkable series of ancient, pagan and Christian sarcophagi can be seen.

In the central chapel, near the said St Cassian sarcophagus is a shrine (3C) discovered in 1965, which contained the remains of town martyrs on the tomb of which the abbey was built.

Every year on 2 February an enormous crowd, including the fishmongers gather at St Victor's for the Candlemas procession. The candles, which the faithful carry during the ceremony, are green in colour: the same colour as the vestment enveloping the much venerated statue of Our Lady of Confession.

Everywhere on that day small cakes in the form of a boat, called *navettes,* are sold; they commemorate the arrival of St Lazarus and the Stes Mary Magdalene and Martha *(qv)* on Provençal soil some 2 000 years ago.

Pharo Park (Parc du Pharo) (DU). – The park is situated on the promontory commanding the harbour entrance. From the terrace situated near Pharo Palace, the former residence of Empress Eugénie, wife of Napoleon III, there is a good **view★** of the Old Port (telescope).

★★**Corniche Président-J.-F.-Kennedy** (AZY). – *See town plan p 130.* This corniche road (more than 5km – 3 miles long) follows the coast for most of the way.

It goes by the **Memorial to the Dead in the Orient** (Monument aux Morts d'Orient – AY B) and offers lovely views of the offshore islands and coast dominated by the Marseilleveyre Massif *(qv).*

Right after, cross a bridge, below is the picturesque fishing village, **Vallon des Auffes** (AY), one of the most characteristic places in Marseilles.

The Promenade de la Plage, which is an extension of Corniche Président-J.-F.-Kennedy, skirts the immense Prado beach of 21ha – 52 acres. It consists presently of a resort park and three small protected beaches which are framed to the north by a pool for sailing. When all the work is over the area of park and beach will have doubled; four new protected beaches are planned.

At the roundabout where Avenue du Prado ends stands a statue of David (1951) (BZ T).

BORÉLY PARK (PARC BORÉLY) (BZ) *time: 1 1/2 hours*

The extensive park with its network of paths *(all automobile traffic prohibited)* is hemmed in to the west by the race course and to the east by the **botanical gardens** (a wide variety of species), located at the bottom of the English garden. To the south lies Château Borély.

Held annually in the park is the popular Provençal Boules Competition *(p 200).*

Château Borély (BZ Mᵉ). – This imposing edifice was called Borély in memory of the wealthy Marseilles merchants who had it built between 1767-78. It houses a fine 18C group of rooms furnished in the style of the period and an archaeological (Egyptian, Celtic, Greek, Roman) and lapidary collection which is to be transferred to the Old Charity Cultural Centre *(p 133).*

★**Museum of Mediterranean Archaeology** (Musée d'Archéologie méditerranéenne). – The ground floor houses the **collection of Egyptian antiquities★★** which includes such objects as amulets, wood statues, funerary furnishings, sarcophagi, mummies...

The 1st floor contains hundreds of Greek and Roman pieces of pottery covering all ages, Etruscan, Greek and Roman bronzes and fine pieces of ancient glass; collection of Oriental antiquities (Cyprus, Susa, etc.).

The 2nd floor covers the Feuillet de Borsat Gift which includes drawings from the 18C French School (Boucher, Fragonard, Ingres...), sanguines by Greuze, Hubert Robert and Watteau, as well as works by the Italian (Pannini, Tiepolo, Titian), Flemish (Bruegel) and Dutch (Moucheron, Willem Mieris) Schools.

Lapidary Museum. – Located in Château Borély's outbuildings. Several rooms, surrounding a small archaeological garden where diverse objects of the ancient city have been placed, contain items pertaining to the region.

One of these rooms displays remarkable Celtio-Ligurian sculpture discovered on the Roquepertuse site (in the *commune* of Velaux, Bouches-du-Rhône *département*): a portico from a sanctuary, decorated with skulls, two kneeling heroes wearing scapulars, a stone bird, a lintel adorned with stylised horses' heads and the admirable **group of two heads back to back**★ called Hermes from 3C BC. The two faces are different and earless; they were originally enhanced with colour.

The other rooms of the museum contain exhibitions of Greek sculpture (6C BC Ionic capital probably from Apollo's temple) and Roman objects (busts, votive altars, sarcophagi...).

LONGCHAMP QUARTER (QUARTIER LONGCHAMP) (GS) *time: 2 hours*

★★**Grobet-Labadié Museum** (Musée Grobet-Labadié) (GS **M⁷**). – This town house built
in 1873 for Alexandre Labadié, a Marseilles merchant was donated to Marseilles in 1919 by his daughter Marie-Louise, wife of Louis Grobet, a music lover and art collector. She considerably varied and enriched the collection with her own personal acquisitions.

The bourgeois interior has been kept with its fine Flemish and French (16-18C) tapestries, furniture, 18C faience, religious gold and silver plate, wrought iron work and old musical instruments.

Fine paintings hang on the walls: Flemish, German and Italian Primitives, French School covering the 17-19C.

★**Longchamp Palace** (Palais Longchamp) (GS). – This imposing building was constructed by the Nîmes architect Henri Espérandieu (he also built Notre-Dame-de-la-Garde Basilica, *p 134*) from 1862-9.

In its centre stands a well-disguised water tower animated by fountains; it is linked by colonnades to the Museum of Fine Arts (on the left) and the Museum of Natural History (on the right).

★**Museum of Fine Arts** (Musée des Beaux-Arts) (**M⁹**). – On the first level two large
galleries house **16 and 17C paintings:** the French School is represented by Vouet *(Virgin with a Rose),* Le Sueur, Rigaud, Largillière; the Italian School by Perugino, Cariani, Carracci, Guercino; the Flemish School by Velvet Bruegel, Jordaens and Rubens (Portrait – presumed to be of – Hélène Fourment), Teniers.

The Provençal School is represented especially by the works of Michel Serre and Jean Daret.

A room containing **African art** displays sculpture from French speaking African countries; paintings by Dufy and Gleizes.

On the ground floor a large room exhibits the works of **Pierre Puget** (1620-94) native of Marseilles, sculptor, painter, architect. In the centre are castings of monumental sculptures found either in the Louvre or in Genoa. On either side of the room are the **original works**★: drawings, paintings – of remarkable imagination *(Infant Jesus Sleeping),* statues *(The Faun)* and low reliefs *(The Plague at Milan, Louis XIV Riding).* In the stairwell are two murals by Puvis de Chavannes: *Marseilles as a Greek Colony* and as the *Gateway to the Levant.*

The second level contains several galleries devoted for the most part to **18-20 French painting:** to the left are Courbet *(Deer Taking Water),* Millet, Corot, Girodet, Gros, Gérard, Ingres and David; to the right the Provençal painters Guigou and Casile; sculpture by **Daumier** (the famous caricaturist born in Marseilles in 1808); Courbet, Verdilhon, Lombard, Camoin, Marquet, Ziem, Signac *(Entering the Port of Marseilles,* 1911) and Dufy.

Found on the mezzanine are fine paintings by Nattier, Verdussen, Watteau de Lille, Carle Van Loo, Françoise Duparc, Greuze, Joseph Vernet *(A Storm),* Mme Vigée-Lebrun *(Duchess of Orléans)* and sculpture by Chastel.

★**Museum of Natural History** (Muséum d'histoire naturelle) (**M⁹**). – Rich zoological,
geological and prehistorical collections are exhibited.

A gallery is devoted to the Provençal flora and fauna.

In the basement a Mediterranean and tropical **aquarium** displays fresh and saltwater fish from the five continents.

Zoo (Jardin zoologique) (CXY). – *Town plan p 131.* The zoo is located behind Longchamp Palace bordering the public gardens. It contains felines, wild, exotic and European animals.

★★THE PORT (AXY)

The modern port of Marseilles, constructed entirely by artificial means, was born of the new needs created by the introduction of ships of heavy tonnage and by the continual growth of the seaborne trade.

With a total traffic of 98 200 000 metric tons in 1986, it has taken a predominant position in this domain.

Origin and development. – The old port had become inadequate – ships were crowded 4 and 5 rows deep; in 1844 a law authorised the construction of a dock at La Joliette. This new dock had hardly been completed when a new decree provided for the creation of two further docks, Le Lazaret (later incorporated into Grande Joliette Dock) and Arenc.

The port was later enlarged to the north with the addition of the docks National, La Pinède, Président-Wilson, Léon Gourret and Mirabeau. When the troops of General de Montsabert liberated Marseilles on August 28, 1944, the port had just been almost completely destroyed by the German mines.

An immense effort was made immediately after the war which enabled the port to play an important role in the French economy.

Its reconstruction (refitting of the port, repair of quay equipment etc) was accompanied by a work of expansion and modernisation. The Mirabeau bordered by the Mourrepiane marshalling yard and the new La Pinède dock offer better facilities for containers. The traditional Marseilles installations (sprawled over 19km – 11 1/2 miles of docks offering more than 140 jobs and in places 15m – 49ft deep) have been remodelled.

Port activity. – Most of the facilities specialise in roll-on/roll-off operations (the ship's hold being accessible to trucks from all over Europe). Marseilles is one of the world's largest ports in this domain, especially for the shipping lines from the Mediterranean Basin and the Red Sea. The two terminals of Mourrepiane and La Pinède are used for coastal traffic, handled with containers, and commercial traffic with Africa.

Bulk foodstuffs retain an important position as Marseilles supplies Europe in fruit and vegetables (700 000 metric tons in 1986) and it holds as well an interest in sugar and grain.

A variety of industrial bulk is handled: alumina, clinkers (elements used in cement-making) etc.

Some 1 200 000 passengers entered the port in 1986 from the regular shipping lines of Corsica and North Africa (La Joliette Passenger Ship Terminal) and the cruise ships (North Passenger Ship Terminal).

Finally 55% of the naval repair in France is done in Marseilles thanks to ten dry docks and one floating. The number 10 Dock (465m × 85m – 1 526ft × 279ft) can handle the largest ships in the world.

⊙ TOUR

By the Traverse and Arenc Bridge you reach the outer breakwater (Digue du Large). Do not stay on the vehicle roadway but walk through either its upper or outer section. From the upper part, paved and lined with benches, there is a good view of the port installations, the ships, the roadstead and the offshore islands. The outer part of the breakwater is popular with amateur fishermen.

EXCURSIONS

★★ **If Castle (Château d'If).** – About 1 1/2 hours including boat trip and a tour of the castle; embarkation Quai des Belges.

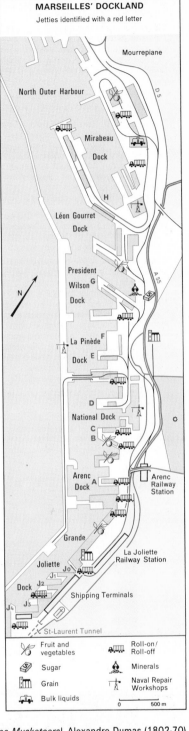

MARSEILLES' DOCKLAND

Jetties identified with a red letter

The popular French 19C author *(The Three Musketeers)*, Alexandre Dumas (1802-70) gave the castle literary fame by imprisoning two of his fictional heroes (from *The Count of Monte Cristo*) here: Count of Monte Cristo and Abbé Faria. Built rapidly from 1524-8, If Castle was an outpost destined to protect the port of Marseilles. In the late 16C the castle was encircled by a bastioned curtain wall.

No longer useful, the castle became a state prison where Huguenots, the Man in the Iron Mask, and various political prisoners were held; their cells can be visited. The **panorama**★★★ from the old chapel terrace is remarkable: note the roadstead, city and the Ratonneau and Pomègues Islands linked by the new port of Frioul.

Marseilleveyre Massif (Massif de Marseilleveyre). – 13km – 8 miles south. Leave Marseilles by Promenade de la Plage.

The **road**★★ skirts Prado Beach, crosses Pointe Rouge; after La Madrague-de-Montredon, it climbs into the Marseilleveyre Massif past Mount Rosé (alt 81m – 266ft) on the right; good views of Cape Croisette and Mairie Island.

Callelongue. – In a very lovely **spot** several houses stand at the end of the inlet which shelters a fleet of fishing boats and some yachts.

Old lookout post (Ancien poste de vigie). – *3/4 hour on foot; bear right into the path between two houses, continue to a retaining wall and then bear right again.* From the terraces of this old lookout post the **view★** embraces Pomègues Island and Estaque Chain to the northwest, Marie Island and the villages of Les Goudes and Callelongue to the west, Jarre and Riou Islands to the southeast and Cape Aigle to the east.

Other walks may be undertaken in Marseilleveyre Massif by following the signposted paths, however, a certain agility is required.

Sormiou and Sugiton Inlets (Calanques de Sormiou et de Sugiton). – *8km – 5 miles. Leave the city centre by ③ (on the town plan pp 130-131). Access: to Sormiou (1/2 hour on foot) from Beaumettes; to Sugiton (1 hour on foot) through the university centre "Domaine de Luminy".*
The walk from Marseilles to either inlet makes for a magnificent excursion for experienced walkers and climbers, who should beware of the summer heat and the lack of drinking water.
The Port-Miou, Port-Pin and En-Vau Inlets, situated further east, are described *p 103.*

Château-Gombert; Loubière Caves. – *11km-7 miles northeast. Take Avenue de St-Just (CX) and Avenue de Château-Gombert.*
Located northeast of Marseilles, Château-Gombert and the Loubière Caves are included in the city's built-up area.

Château-Gombert. – The plane tree shaded main square is overlooked on one side by a 17C church and opposite by the mansion which now houses a museum.
The **church** houses several works of art including, in particular, a *Resurrection of Lazarus* by Finsonius *(p 66)*, a 17C Flemish painter.
The interior of a Provençal house has been reconstituted in the local **Museum of Popular Arts and Traditions** (musée des Arts et Traditions populaires du Terroir marseillais) including a kitchen with its large chimney, Marseilles, Moustiers and Montpellier ceramics, pewter, glassware as well as a living room and bedroom both handsomely furnished; note the *radiassié,* a vast couch which used to be in the *bastide.* Recalling the local customs are traditional costumes of Marseilles and Arles women as well as the waggoner's, agricultural tools, and dress harnesses used in St Eligius' feast day processions.

Leave Château-Gombert in direction of Marseilles and bear right on Traverse de la Baume Loubière.

Loubière Caves (Grottes Loubière). – Discovered in 1829 these caves, offer a series of 5 galleries covering approximately 1 500m – 1 1/3 miles. They are decorated with finely coloured concretions: stalagtites, stalagmites, imposing columns, translucid draperies, delicate eccentrics...

MARTIGUES
Pop 42 039

Michelin map **84** folds 11 and 12 or **245** fold 43 or **246** folds 13 and 14 – Local map p 90 – Facilities

The Birds' Looking Glass, Martigues

Martigues took its name in 1581 after the union of the three villages of Jonquières, Ile and Ferrières established here since the Middle Ages.
Set on the banks of Berre Lagoon *(qv)* and linked to the sea by the Caronte Canal, Martigues, once a small fishing village, has been transformed and enlarged due to the expansion of the oil industry and its subsidiaries around Lavéra-Berre Lagoon. Painters (Corot, Ziem) and writers (Claude Maurras), were captivated by the luminosity and charm of this typical Provençal port; and due to this Martigues acquired a great renown in literary and artistic circles.

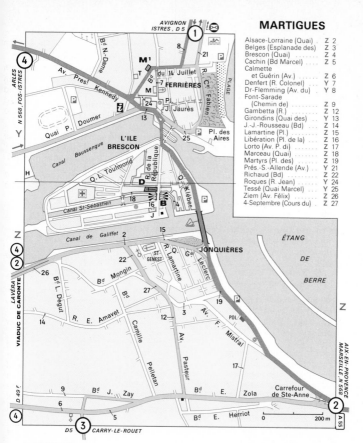

Alsace-Lorraine (Quai) .	Z	2
Belges (Esplanade des) .	Z	3
Brescon (Quai)	Z	4
Cachin (Bd Marcel)	Z	5
Calmette et Guérin (Av.)	Z	6
Denfert (R. Colonel) . . .	Y	7
Dr-Flemming (Av. du) . .	Y	8
Font-Sarade (Chemin de)	Z	9
Gambetta (R.)	Z	12
Girondins (Quai des) . . .	Y	13
J.-J.-Rousseau (Bd)	Z	14
Lamartine (Pl.)	Z	15
Libération (Pl. de la) . . .	Z	16
Lorto (Av. P. di)	Z	17
Marceau (Quai)	Z	18
Martyrs (Pl. des)	Z	19
Prés.-S.-Allende (Av.) . .	Y	21
Richaud (Bd)	Z	22
Roques (R. Jean)	Y	24
Tessé (Quai Marcel) . . .	Y	25
Ziem (Av. Félix)	Z	26
4-Septembre (Cours du) .	Z	27

SIGHTS

St-Sébastien Bridge (Pont St-Sébastien) (ZB). – The bridge on Brescon Island, is a vantage point from which to view★ the brightly coloured pleasure craft moored along St-Sébastien Canal and Quai Brescon. This has long been a favourite spot with painters and is known as the Birds' Looking Glass *(photograph opposite)*.

Ste-Madeleine-de-l'Ile (YZ D). – The 17C church beside the St-Sébastien Canal on Brescon Island, has a Corinthian style west front and pilasters, cornices and an imposing organ loft inside.

Ziem Museum (Musée Ziem) (Y M¹). – Grouped around the works of Félix Ziem (1821-1911) painter of landscapes and oriental scenes, who made an important donation to the city, are works by Provençal artists from the 19 (Guigou, Manguin, Monticelli, Hurard, Loubon) and 20C (Seyssaud).
Also exhibited in the museum are collections of local ethnology and archaeology. A collection of contemporary art completes the museum.

★Caronte Road Viaduct (Viaduc autoroutier de Caronte). – *By Avenue F.-Ziem* (Z 26). Since 1972 the Caronte Canal, which connects the lagoon with the sea, has been spanned by a spectacular 300m – 984ft long road bridge comprising a metal deck suspended 50m – 164ft above the water between inclined supports. It affords a good, bird's-eye view of the town.

EXCURSIONS

★Berre Lagoon. – *Round tour of 113km – 70 miles by ① on the town plan, the D 5. Description p 90.*

Notre-Dame-des-Marins Chapel (Chapelle N.-D.-des-Marins). – *3,5km – 2 1/4 miles. Leave Martigues by ④ on the town plan, the N 568; after 1,5km – 3/4 mile from the centre bear right at the main crossroads into the D 50 (towards the hospital); 1,2km – 1/2 mile further just before the top of the hill, turn right into a surfaced path to the chapel (car park).*
From the precincts of this chapel, the **panorama★** sweeps around Port-de-Bouc, Fos, Port-St-Louis, Lavéra complex, the Caronte railway and road bridges, Estaque Chain, Martigues, Berre Lagoon with the Arles Canal linking it to Fos-sur-Mer, Étoile and Vitrolles Mountain Chain, Mount Ste-Victoire and on clear days Mount Ventoux, Marseilles-Provence airport, the town of Berre and St-Mitre-des-Remparts.

★Fos Complex. – *9km – 5 1/2 miles by ④ on the town plan, the N 568.*

Port-de-Bouc. – Pop 20 106. A port protected by a fort built by Vauban (military architect) in 1664 on the south bank of the channel. The 12C tower, incorporated into these fortifications was transformed into a lighthouse. Confronted by the problems of industrial reconversion, the town shifted to maritime activities. A new fishing port and pleasure boat harbour (450 berths) was set up in 1985.

Follow the N 568.

★Fos Complex. – *Description p 116.*

★★ MARZAL Chasm (Aven de MARZAL)

Michelin map 🔟 fold 9 or 🔟 folds 2 and 15 or 🔟 fold 23 – Local map p 61

Buried under Gras Plateau, this chasm *(photograph p 19)* is remarkable for the great number and variety of limestone formations which range in their oxyde colouring from brown ochre to snow white.

The discovery. – The local word *marzal* identifies a wild grass. The word, *marzal*, was given in *c*1810 to the forester from St-Remèze, Dechame, after he had fined his wife who had picked some for her rabbits. A little later Marzal was murdered and thrown into a well, the said Trou de la Barthe, with his dog. The crime was discovered and the local people began calling the well, Marzal.

The chasm was not really discovered until 1892 when the speleologist E.-A. Martel (1859-1938) explored it for the first time, but its exact location was lost through incorrect signposting. It was, therefore, not until 1949 that it was rediscovered by the speleologist Pierre Ageron, after years of searching on Gras Plateau amidst the holm oaks.

Excavations near the chasm have uncovered, among the glacier layers, bones of horses, reindeer and bear.

⊙ **Museum of the Underground World (Musée du Monde Souterrain).** – It evokes the great names and great moments of French speleology: Martel's "Berthon" boat (1890) and ladder, a speleologist's equipment (1892); Robert de Joly's (inventor of material and equipment adapted for the underground world's demands) costume; Elisabeth and Norbert Casteret's *(qv)* helmet, electrical material and waterproof bag, Guy de Lavaur's diving equipment (1946).

⊙ **Chasm (Aven).** – *Inside temperature: 14 °C–57 °F.* A metal staircase (743 steps) leads to the natural opening used by Pierre Ageron in 1949. The vision before you is remarkable: great flows of coloured limestone in jellyfish-like shapes or huge Roman columns. The chasm, a natural well, opens into the Great Gallery or Tomb Gallery, nearby are bones of animals (bear, stag, bison) that fell into the cave.

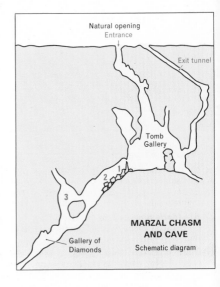

Cave (Grotte). – The Dog Gallery (1), the entrance of which is surmounted by a flow of white draperies, contains a large variety of concretions, eccentrics, brightly coloured organs, disc-like formations and shapes resembling bunches of grapes. Pine Cone Gallery (2) is interesting for the wealth of its colours. The Gallery of Columns (3), was the bed into which an underground river (since disappeared) cascaded. The Gallery of Diamonds (130m – 426ft below ground) ends the visit; it is a sparkling image of fairylike colours reflected in the glinting crystals which line the walls.

⊙ **Prehistoric Zoo (Zoo préhistorique).** – Along a shaded path (800m – 1/2 mile) reproductions of animals (life-size) from the Primary (Dimetrodon, Moschops) Secondary (Stegosarus, Tyrannosaurus) to the mammoth of the Quaternary Era are on view. The mammoth was contemporary to prehistoric man; various scenes of their day to day life have been reconstituted into life-like scenes. Note also the fossilized dinosaur eggs and a mammoth's tooth which was found in the North Sea.

★ MÉNERBES   Pop 1 027

Michelin map 🔟 fold 13 or 🔟 fold 30 or 🔟 fold 11 – Local map p 124

This old village occupies a picturesque site on a promontory of the Luberon's *(qv)* north face.

In 1573 the Calvinist's captured the stronghold by ruse and it took five years and a large ransom to dislodge them.

Place de l'Horloge. – The square is overlooked by the town hall's bell tower with its simple wrought iron bell cage *(p 31)*. In one corner of the square stands a noble Renaissance mansion with a round-arched doorway.

⊙ **Church (Église).** – The church stands at the end of the village and dates back to the 14C when it was a Priory dependent of St-Agricol of Avignon *(p 80)*. Behind the east end there is a fine **view★** of Coulon Valley, the villages of Gordes and Roussillon (with its ochre cliffs), Mount Ventoux, Vaucluse Plateau and the Luberon.

Citadel (Citadelle). – This 13C fortress (rebuilt in the 16 and 19C) has preserved part of its defence system with its corner towers and machicolations. Due to its strategic position it played an important part during the Wars of Religion.

MONTAGNETTE Hills (La MONTAGNETTE)

Michelin map 🛇 fold 11 or 🔳 folds 28 and 29 or 🔳 folds 25 and 26

Between the Durance River and Tarascon, the Montagnette is a range of hills, none of which tops 200m – 656ft, which parallels the Rhône as it flows southwest below Avignon. On a small scale it offers a typical Provençal landscape of rock escarpments, hillsides fragrant with wild flowers and aromatic herbs, quiet hollows sheltering olive, almond and apricot trees, pines, poplars and cypresses.

Barbentane. – *Description p 85.*

★**Beaucaire.** – *Description p 88.*

Boulbon. – Pop 1 042. An impressive fort marks the site of the town laid out like
ⓥ an amphitheatre against the Montagnette hillside. The local Romanesque **St-Marcellin Chapel** contains a number of statues, particularly the 14C recessed tomb with a recumbent figure and weepers.
On 1 June each year a picturesque Bottle Procession makes its way to the chapel for the blessing of the local wine *(p 199)*.

Graveson. – Pop 2 276. Standing amidst orchards, the church has a Romanesque oven-vaulted apse with a low, delicately carved blind arcade.

Bretoul Mill (Moulin de Bretoul). – Set in pine woods, south of Barbentane *(qv)*, this mill is the only well preserved windmill left of the many which at one time were scattered across the countryside.

St-Michel-de-Frigolet Abbey. – *Description p 165.*

★**Tarascon.** – *Description p 179.*

★ MONTMAJOUR Abbey

Michelin map 🛇 fold 10 or 🔳 fold 28 or 🔳 fold 26

On a hill overlooking Arles Plain lie the ruins of Montmajour Abbey, the buildings of which represent two different periods: medieval and 18C.

The struggle against the marshes. – The hill was, for a long time, surrounded by marshes. A Christian cemetery was established here and a group of hermits, who safeguarded the burial ground, were at the origin of the abbey, founded in the 10C under Benedictine rule. Inspite of the fact that the monk population was not large, the abbey possessed a number of priories. The main occupation of these people was the drying up of the marshland: between the Alpilles Chain and the Rhône, solid land was reclaimed little by little. To finance these projects a pardon was created in the 11C; at one time 150 000 pilgrims were counted.

Decadence. – In the 17C the abbey consisted of about 20 monks and "religious" laymen, officers of the crown, to whom the king granted a position in the community and especially part of the revenues. One could see, mingling in the processions with the monks in sackcloth, these young colourfully, dressed men strutting and flirting with the lovely women of Arles.
The congregation of reformed monks of St-Maur, in charge of restoring discipline sent new monks to the abbey in 1639; the former monks, expelled soldiers, pillaged the abbey.
In the 18C part of buildings collapsed, they were replaced by magnificent edifices. The last abbot, the Cardinal of Rohan, was implicated in the affair of the Queen's necklace; thus Louis XVI pronounced as punishment in 1786, the suppression of the abbey.

The misfortunes of a national property. – In 1791, Montmajour was sold as a national property. It was bought by a second-hand dealer for 62 000 *livres*, payable in twelve years. To help repay the debt she broke up the buildings: furniture, panelling, lead, timberwork and marble were loaded on carts and sold. In spite of that, the woman was late in her payments and in 1793 the sale was annulled. The abbey was allocated for 23 000 *livres* to an estate agent. He broke up the fine stonework and sold the old buildings to people who inhabited them. During the last century, the people of Arles, friends of old monuments, and the town itself recovered the buildings little by little: 6 000 Francs for the tower, 2 000 Francs for the church. In 1872 the restoration of the medieval buildings was started; the 18C buildings remained in ruins. The abbey is now state property.

★ABBEY
ⓥ *time: 3/4 hour*

★**Notre-Dame.** – The 12C building in the main part includes an upper church and a crypt or lower church.

Upper church. – The upper church was never completed and consists of a chancel, transept and a nave with two bays; the transept crossing was covered with pointed vaulting in the 13C.

★**Crypt.** – Due to the incline of the land, the crypt was in part built into the sloping rock and in part raised. Its plan was different from that of the upper church: on a cruciform plan with a central chapel and two chapels at either end of the arm of the transept. It is remarkable for the size of its vaulting and the fine dome which covers the chancel. Five apsidal chapels open onto the ambulatory.

★**Cloisters.** – The cloisters were built at the end of the 12C but three of the galleries were rebuilt at different periods: north gallery in the 19C, west gallery in the 18C, south gallery in the 14C. Only the eastern gallery has preserved its Romanesque characteristics. These galleries of three bays, nevertheless, contain some fascinating sculpture.

MONTMAJOUR Abbey★

The capitals carry a re-
markable historiated dec-
oration which has been
associated with that of
St-Trophime in Arles
(p 66). The base of the
columns is also carved
at the four corners. Un-
der the galleries are Gothic recessed tombs; in the
courtyard there is an
ancient well and laurel
bushes.

Monastic buildings. –
Included in these build-
ings, still standing, are
the chapterhouse with
rounded barrel vaulting,
the refectory with its
interesting pointed bar-
rel vaulting (access from
the exterior) and the dormitory, on the first floor
above the refectory.

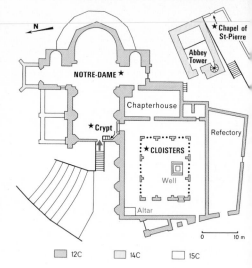

Abbey Tower. – This
fine keep (1369), the machicolations of which were rebuilt, was the abbey's main
defence.
From the platform (124 steps) a fine **panorama**★ embraces the Alpilles Chain, Crau
Plain, Arles, Cévennes, Beaucaire and Tarascon.

★**Chapel of St-Pierre.** – When the abbey was founded, this tiny church was built
half-carved out of the hillside. It includes a church with two naves (capitals carved
with geometric designs) and an hermitage, prolonging it, formed from natural caves.

★**Ste-Croix Chapel.** – This charming 12C building is located outside the abbey
precincts (200m – 218yds to the right towards Fontvieille). It is built in the form
of a Greek cross: a square surmounted by a dome with triangular pediments and
a bell tower surrounded by four apsidal chapels with oven vaulting. This was the
funerary chapel for the Montmajour cemetery.
Note the ancient tombs hewn out of the rock and stretched out over the rocky
platform.

NAGES Oppidum

Michelin map 🎱🎱 fold 8 or 🎱🎱🎱 fold 27 – 10km – 6 miles southeast of Nîmes

On Les Castels Hill, overlooking Vaunage Plain, the Nages-et-Solorgues **oppidum**, a
fortified township, is a fascinating archaeological site. A rocky path climbs up the
hill (signposted) to the site.
Nages was one of the five *oppida* of the Iron Age (800-50BC) that housed the
Vaunage population. The islands of living quarters, arranged on the slope's incline
separated by parallel streets 5m – 16 1/2ft wide, suggest an early urban plan and
give an insight into the characteristics of the Gauls' living arrangements.
You can very clearly discern the rows of small uniform houses with drystone walls,
sometimes quite high. They were all covered by roofs made of cobwork applied to
branches supported by beams which themselves were retained by posts.
To begin with these dwellings were on a one-room plan with a hearth at its centre;
in the 2C they were enlarged and subdivided but the comfort remained rudimentary.
The settlement was surrounded by fortifications (there were four successive ones
from 300-150BC) interspersed with round towers (one of them from the 3C was
11m – 36ft in diameter) and gates (a part of which has been successfully
excavated).
No public monument was uncovered except for a *fanum*, a small native temple
(70BC). Roman infiltration did not hinder the *oppidum's* development which was at
its greatest between 70 and 30BC, the period in which the specialists noticed the
beginning of economic specialisation (presence of a forge).
On the return trip down, at the village's entrance, take the first street to the left,
which leads to the Roman cistern, which still feeds several of the village's fountains.

Archaeological Museum (Musée archéologique). – Located in the town hall, on the
1st floor, the museum displays pottery and various items excavated from Les Castels
site. Different aspects of the successive inhabitants' daily life are evoked; food
orientated activities (agriculture, husbandry, hunting), crafts (metal work, pottery
making, weaving), arms, toilet requisites and funerary objects.

*The **Michelin Guide France** revises annually its selection of establishments offering*

– a good but moderately priced meal
– prices with service included or net prices
– a plain menu for a modest price
– free overnight parking

Elegant, sunny, hospitable and bustling, Nîmes lies at the foot of the *garrigues'* limestone hills. Influenced by its position as a great city of arts, Nimes is proud of its prestigeous Gallo-Roman past.

In addition each year the amphitheatre, Fountain Garden, and Temple of Diana serve as a stage for cultural events.

A city of old traditional industries (clothes, shoes), which transforms the local agricultural products as well (canning of fruit, wine production) and the administrative capital *préfecture* of Gard), Nîmes has tried in the past couple of years to develop its agricultural activities.

Among the city's gastronomic specialities note: *brandade de morue (p 41),* marinated olives, the *caladon,* an almond biscuit, and the Croquant Villaret.

Nîmes is also the centre of tauromachy. The *corridas,* with their set rules, which take place in the amphitheatre, and the race of the *cocarde (qv)* through the streets, have brought immense popularity and fame to the city.

The city of Nîmes suffered considerable damage following the extensive flooding in October 1988: some sites may be closed.

HISTORICAL NOTES

The chained crocodile. – Capital of Volcae Arecomici, Nemausus (Nîmes's ancient name originated from a sacred spring around which the town settled) was at the head of a vast territory of 24 settlements between the sea and the Cévennes and from the Rhône River to the Sète Mountains, when it accepted Roman domination. The date of Roman colonisation, its founder and the ethnic origin of its colonists is today a controversial subject. Two theories have been evoked: Augustus who settled here in 31BC with a Roman colony of veterans of the Egyptian campaign (the colonisation of which has been depicted by the famous coin which was stamped with the chained crocodile), or Caesar with a Latin colony in 44BC.

In any case of the two who founded Nîmes, Augustus was the one who heaped privileges on the town and allowed it to surround 200ha-494 acres with fortifications. It then proceeded to embellish itself, building splendid edifices: a forum with the Maison Carrée on its south side, an amphitheatre which could hold 24 000 people, a circus, baths and fountains fed by an imposing aqueduct, the Pont du Gard *(qv)* which yielded 20 000m³ – 7 063ft³ of water a day.

In the 2C the city benefited from the privileges granted to it by the Emperors Hadrian and Antoninus Pius (the in-laws of which originated from Nîmes) and continued to flourish and build (Plotinius's Basilica, arrangement of the Fountain quarter etc), reaching its zenith.

The surrounding countryside profited as well from all this attention; the land was surveyed and improved and large agricultural holdings, seeking to imitate the urban life *(p 32)* fed this brilliant metropolis.

The centuries of Roman occupation have left vivid memories: first names like Numa, Flavien, Adrien and Antoninus are still frequently employed. In the city's coat of arms appears the chained crocodile, the symbol of the conquest of Egypt and the Nile by its legionnaries, who subsequently became citizens of Nîmes.

Religious struggles. – The most significant period of Nîmes history together with that of the Roman occupation is the religious differences.

In the 5C the Visigoths, who ruled over the country (from Toulouse to the Rhône River), clashed with the Catholic population, when they tried to impose their beliefs: churches were closed and the Catholics were persecuted well into the 6C.

In the 13C the people of Nîmes sided with the Albigensians (a heretical Christian sect that believed in the separation of Good and Evil – Good was symbolised by God who ruled over a spiritual world of light and beauty; Evil was the material world ruled by the Devil). Simon de Montfort *(qv)* headed the terrible crusade against these heretics, the city preferred surrendering without resistance in 1213.

In the 14C a wave of intolerance fell upon the Jews, they were expelled from the city and their possessions confiscated.

In the 16C Nîmes became a Huguenot city. It was the Geneva of France: 3/4 of its population believed in the Reform.

On 29 September 1567 the Michelade tragedy occurred: 200 Catholics, most of whom were priests were massacred. There ensued a long sombre period of persecution and war which extended into the 17C and ended only at the Revolution, considered as a revenge of the Protestants on the Catholics.

Nîmes Academy. – The Nîmes Academy is more than 300 years old. In 1682 Louis XIV conferred upon the Academy the same privileges as the French Academy (in Paris). Concerned for the most part with historical and archaeological subjects, the Nîmes Academy also concentrates on the fields of literature, art and music.

Economic expansion. – Several times in Nîmes history, the city has shifted from prosperity to poverty. In the early 15C, the wars, road bandits, earthquakes and the plague had made of the flourishing ancient city of Nemausus but a small village under the Vivarais bailiwick. At the end of the 15C the town prospered: wood, leather, silk and glass, were manufactured. Louis XI (1461-83) ordered the founding of a textile manufacture. But it was mostly during the reign of François I (1515-47) that Nîmes developed; the textile industry prospered and progressed constantly (fabric *de Nîmes* – meaning from Nîmes – was contracted and the word used was *denim.*). In the 18C the textile mills (silk and serge) employed 10 000 people and 300 looms. The textile industry was handled by the Protestant middle class.

In the 19C the arrival of the railway favoured the industrial activities and the extension of the Gard vineyards.

20C Nîmes has stagnated, its industries have aged; the city has been supplanted by Montpellier in eastern Languedoc.

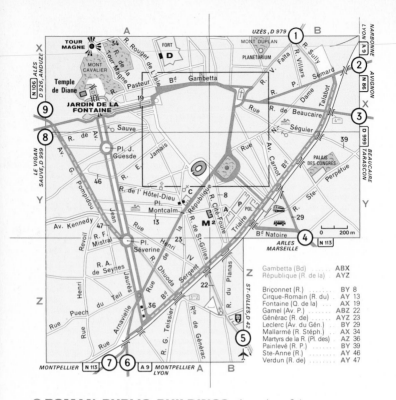

⊙ ROMAN PUBLIC BUILDINGS *time: about 3 hours*

***Amphitheatre (Arènes) (CV). – *See p 33.* This beautifully preserved amphitheatre
⊙ is twin to the one at Arles; most likely from the same period (late 1 – early 2C),
same layout, similar dimensions and capacity (133m × 101m – 436ft × 331ft;
capacity 24 000). Its differences are slight architectural ones such as the galleries
with barrel vaulting of Roman construction which are replaced by the Greek
trabeated form. The Nîmes amphitheatre because of its axial dimensions is ranked
9th out of the 20 important amphitheatres discovered in Gaul; however, it is the
best preserved of the Roman ones especially in its upper storey where remain, in
several places, sockets that held posts carrying a huge adjustable awning, the
velum, to shelter the spectators from the sun and rain. From the exterior, the
building presents two storeys each of 60 arcades (total height : 21m – 65 1/2ft)
crowned with an attic. The building material in hard limestone from Barutel did not
require detailed ornamentation: pilasters on the lower register and engaged Doric
columns above. Four axial doorways correspond to the four entrances. The main
northern gateway has kept its pediment adorned with bulls. Note in front of the
amphitheatre traces (tower and curtain wall) of the Augustinian fortifications.
Inside (climb to the topmost tiers to have a view of the whole) the *cavea* (all of the
tiers) was divided into 34 tiers of seats grouped into 4 independent *maenia* (a group
of 4 tiers below then 3 times 10 tiers rising to the top); the spectators were seated
according to their social station. An ingenious system of corridors, stairways,
galleries and *vomitaria* (sloping corridors) made it possible for all the spectators to
reach their seats quickly without crowding and without any mingling of the classes.
Under the arena itself a substructure (68 × 37m – 223 × 121ft) made of two vast
galleries served as backstage...

The Games. – The games included fighting of three kinds (between animals, between
gladiators and animals, and between gladiators), Olympic games and chariot races.
Performances were announced in advance by painted posters, giving the names of
the performers and details of the programmes in sensational terms. Long before
opening time the crowd, who loved to see bloodshed and prowess in the arena,
waited at the doors. As soon as these were opened they invaded the upper tiers
of seats. Distinguished spectators arrived on litters or in sedan-chairs.
To neutralise the smell of animals and stables incense-burners were set up in the
arena and slaves armed with scent sprays aimed clouds of perfume *(sparsiones)* at
the notables. An orchestra punctuated the games with gay music. Friends met in
the promenades during the intervals, and food and drink were sold in the galleries.
Carnivorous and exotic beasts: lions, tigers, panthers, elephants and rhinoceroses,
brought over in small numbers from the African provinces, were reserved for Rome
or for games in the provinces attended by the emperor; but more frequently bulls,
bears, wild boar and trained mastiffs were used. To relax the nerves of the
spectators after sensational contests, birds of prey were released against hares,
rabbits and pigeons, while dogs got bloody muzzles by attacking porcupines.
Performing animals were also on show.
Most gladiators were slaves or prisoners but among them, also, were free
Barbarians: Germans, Syrians or Berbers who had entered this dangerous profession
for sheer love of fighting. These combatants had barracks to themselves; they
formed teams carefully trained by impresarios who hired them out, for large fees,
to rich citizens, usually candidates for high office.

In principle, a duel between gladiators had always to end in the death of one of the opponents. A man who could fight no more would raise his finger to ask for quarter. If he had pleased the public, the President of the Games would turn up his thumb, and the man would be reprieved; if he turned down his thumb, the winner would cut the loser's throat.

Executions also took place in the amphitheatre: the condemned, not Roman citizens, were delivered to the beasts or the executioner: the first Christians were more than once the victims of this procedure. Furthermore, it is under the influence of Christianity that the gladiator combats were forbidden in 404.

The amphitheatre's role through the centuries. – Having lost their main purpose, the amphitheatre was transformed into a fortress by the Visigoths: arcades boarded up, towers added, a deep moat, was dug around the arena itself and perhaps backed up by a small rampart wall (ruins can be seen in the basement of the Law Courts). In the eastern part of the building, the castle of the Viscounts of Nîmes was later built (two walled arcades opened with small Romanesque windows were preserved). The watch was undertaken by a group of knights made up of a feudal aristocracy which aided the viscount. This cavalry of knights declined in the 12C and disappeared when the king established his rule in Nîmes in 1226.

The amphitheatre was, like the one at Arles *(p 65)*, overtaken by houses, streets and two chapels; a village was established and counted 700 inhabitants in the 18C. The demolition of these buildings began in 1809 and restoration began. The first *corrida* was performed in 1853.

★★★**Maison Carrée** (CU). – This
Ⓥ magnificent temple, known as the Square House, is the best preserved of the Roman temples still standing. It was built under Augustus's (late 1C BC) reign by an architect from the Narbonensis *(qv)* who was inspired by the Temple of Apollo in Rome. It stands a rectangle 26m – 49ft long, and 15m – 85ft wide and 17m – 55 1/2ft high; it rests on a podium which is reached by a stairway of 15 steps (the uneven number of steps was calculated so that by starting to mount the steps on the right

Maison Carrée in Nîmes

foot, one arrived on the podium on the same foot one started with).

Like all the Classical temples, the Maison Carrée's layout consisted of a *proanos* (vestibule) lined by a colonnade and a *cella* (the room which contained the statue of the divinity). Consecrated to the Imperial cult and dedicated to Augustus's grandsons, the temple faced the forum and was surrounded by a portico of finely carved columns.

The purity of the line and building construction, its harmonious proportions, and the elegance of its fluted columns denote Greek influence, which is also found in the temple's ornamentation: Corinthian columns, architrave divided by lines of pearls, a scrolled frieze, a modillioned cornice with rosettes, lion's heads... The entrance façade and the façade at the opposite end are both surmounted by a triangular pediment. The ten columns of the *proanos* stand alone with an ease rarely seen elsewhere whereas the other twenty columns are engaged in the *cella* wall. Under the podium, rooms were set up for the sanctuary's archives and the treasury.

Like the amphitheatre, the Maison Carrée's fortunes have varied: it has served as a public building (early Middle Ages), been a canon's house (*c*1015), consuls' house (until 1540), private house, stables, church belonging to the Augustinian order (in 1670). Sold as public property during the Revolution, it was acquired by the *département* which began restoration in 1816.

★**Museum of Antiquities** (Musée des Antiques). – Located in the *cella*, the museum exhibits interesting objects contemporary to the Maison Carrée. Note a bronze head of Apollo, a colossal statue of the same god, a white marble head of Venus from the Fountain's sanctuary, mosaics, a reassembled statue of Venus, a bust of Jupiter, the eagles frieze, the nymphs' frieze and cippi.

★★**Fountain Garden (Jardin de la Fontaine)** (AX). – The garden is the unexpected creation of an 18C army engineer, J.-P. Mareschal. Planted with tall densely foliated trees, pines and cedars, shading lawns, terraces and stone balustraded paths, and filled with flowers, the gardens extend from the famous Nemausus spring up the slopes of Mount Cavalier to the white octagonal form of Tower Magne *(p 146)*. Since the creation of the garden in the 18C, the spring water has been collected in a mirror-like pool surrounded by balustraded walks, before flowing through pools to the canal.

During Antiquity, this sacred quarter included the spring, a theatre, temple and baths. Recent excavations have uncovered some of the surrounding area; to the east on Rue Pasteur an opulent 2C *domus (p 34)*, to the west behind the Temple of Diana, a popular quarter (razed in the 2C most likely because it did not mix with Antoninus Pius's projects of architectural splendour), to the south at the crossroads of Boulevard Jaurès and Rue de Sauve, a sumptuous public building (2C), the function of which is still being sought. Discovered at the same time were lovely mosaics, fragments of mural paintings, a marble head of a man etc.

NÎMES

Temple of Diana (Temple de Diane) (AX). – This building which dates from the first half of the 2C is known as the Temple of Diana but its true function is unknown. It was most likely part of a vast architectural ensemble, still buried, made up of several different levels (traces of stairs).

Occupied by the Benedictine nuns in the Middle Ages, who converted it into a church without too many modifications, it was destroyed during the Wars of Religion.

There appears to be a large room (perhaps the *cella*) flanked with aisles and covered with barrel vaulting. Niches with pediments (alternatively triangular or rounded) are carved into the side walls and most likely contained statues.

★**Magne Tower** (Tour Magne) (AX). – Located at the top of Mount Cavalier, the city's highest point, the tower is the most remarkable vestige of the powerful fortifications built in 15BC. Its line of fortifications and some 30 towers have recently been identified these last couple of years.

Originally the tower was part of a pre-Roman rampart and was simply reinforced and raised during Augustus's reign. It is a three storey polygonal tower standing 34m – 112ft since Traucat's digging (in 1601 Traucat, the gardener, was convinced that under the tower was a hidden treasure left by the Romans; he was authorised by Henri IV to keep digging – 2/3 of the treasure going to the crown – the digging was stopped when it was discovered that the tower was falling). There is a good **view**★ (140 steps via an inside staircase to the platform) of Mount Ventoux, the Alpilles Chain, Nîmes, Vistre Plain and the *garrigues*.

From the Rue Stéphane-Mallarmé there is a fine view of the tower.

Castellum (AX D). – A unique ruin of its kind, this old Roman water tower was the Roman distribution tank from which water, from Uzès, was brought by the Pont du Gard aqueduct and deposited into a circular basin and then distributed in the town by means of 10 lead canal ducts (40cm – 15 1/2in in diameter). Above it stands the citadel built in 1687 to watch over Protestant Nîmes.

Augustus's Gate (Porte d'Auguste) (DU F). – This gate, a ruin of the Augustinian fortified wall on the Domitian Way, was flanked originally by two semi-circular towers enclosing an interior courtyard, an effective defensive procedure. It still has the two wide passages for chariots and the two more narrow passages for pedestrians. There is also a bronze copy of the statue of Augustus.

ADDITIONAL SIGHTS

★**Museum of Archaeology** (Musée d'Archéologie) (DU M¹). – Located in the former Jesuit College. In the ground floor gallery, numerous carvings displayed are pre-Roman: busts of Gaul warriors, steles and friezes. Upstairs the 1st gallery contains Gallo-Roman items used daily (toilet articles, head-dresses, kitchen utensils, tools), funerary steles, oil lamps; 2nd gallery contains glassware (flasks, funerary vases, bone and bronze objects); 3rd gallery exhibits pottery (Archaic Greek, black and red figure, Far Eastern influenced, Etruscan and Punic). The last room houses the Maison Carrée's **medal collection** rich in coins (Greek, Roman, Gallo-Roman and medieval). The **Jesuits Chapel** (1673-78) holds temporary exhibitions.

Natural History Museum (Muséum d'histoire naturelle). – Located in the former Jesuit College's first floor. The museum houses an ethnographic section (arms, head-dresses from Africa, Asia, Oceania and Madagascar) and local natural history.

★**Museum of Fine Arts (Musée des Beaux-Arts)** (ABY M²). – The museum is devoted
ⓥ to important contemporary and modern art exhibitions. There is also a large Roman
mosaic, discovered in Nîmes in 1882, representing the marriage of Admetus.
The upper floor contains works of art from the French, Italian, Flemish and Dutch
Schools (15-20C). Among the important paintings note the mystical *Marriage of
St Catherine* by Giambono (Venetian 15C), *St Luke Painting the Virgin Mary* by
Pieter Coecke, *Suzannah and the Old Men* by Jocopo Bassano.
Note as well the works by Renaud le Vieux (native of Nîmes), Subleyras, Boucher
and Natoire. French 19 and 20C are represented by paintings by Delaroche,
Sigalon, Jalabert, Chabaud, Valtat, Marinot.

Birthplace of Alphonse Daudet (Maison natale d'Alphonse Daudet) (CU E). – *20
Boulevard Gambetta.* Bourgeois town house, with columns flanking its entrance.

Pradier Fountain (Fontaine Pradier) (DV). – Built in 1848. The statue, which
symbolises Nîmes, had as a model Juliette Drouet, friend of Pradier and Victor Hugo.

Old Nîmes. – This preserved quarter lies around the cathedral and presents a group
of narrow alleyways upon which open picturesque covered passages.

ⓥ **Notre-Dame and St-Castor Cathedral** (CDU K). – Built in 1096 and often remodelled
over the centuries, the cathedral was almost entirely rebuilt in the 19C. The west
front, surmounted by a classical pediment has preserved a partly Romanesque frieze
where scenes of the Old Testament are depicted (Adam and Eve, Cain and Abel).
Inside in the third south chapel is a Christian sarcophagus.

★**Museum of Old Nîmes (Musée du Vieux Nîmes)** (CU M³). – Located on the ground floor
ⓥ of the former episcopal palace (17C) in the heart of Old Nîmes. This recently
rearranged museum presents a number of local exhibits in a beautifully restored old
fashioned interior. The summer antichamber contains lovely carved **cupboards** (said
of Suzanna, Jacob and Genesis), a painted cupboard from Uzès, pewter (from Nîmes
and Languedoc), a collection of pipes and lighters. The summer room contains
Directoire and Empire style furnishings, a marriage cupboard and old views of Nîmes.
The winter antichamber holds 18C furnishings, a 17C carved sideboard, a cupboard
said of Moses, a glass display case exhibiting writing material and paintings. The
winter room displays pottery and gold and silver plate from the region, Regency,
Louis XVI, and local (18C walnut marriage cupboard) furnishings and paintings,
pastels and astronomical tools.
In the wardrobe is a **Charles X style billiard table** with inlaid work (by the eldest
Bernassau son from Nîmes), billiard cue rests, several herbal-tea holders, Empire
living room, varied furnishings and portraits.
The great living room is decorated with Regency and Louis XV style furnishings
(note the child's bergère), the large console table with the stamp of the local
carpenter Gaboret (18C), faience (Moustiers and Alcora), Directoire furnishings and
portraits. The dining room displays faience from Uzès, St-Quentin-la-Poterie and
Vauvert.

Rue du Chapitre (CU 12). – *No 14* (L). The Hôtel de Regis presents an 18C façade
and a lovely 16C paved courtyard.

Rue de la Madeleine (CU 32). – *No 1* (N). The house offers a finely carved
Romanesque façade.

Rue de l'Aspic (CUV). – *No 8* (S). The porch is adorned with three paleochristian
sarcophagi imbedded in the wall and a cippus; lovely Renaissance stairway door.
No 14 (V) has a 17C double spiral grand staircase.

Rue de Bernis (CV 6). – *No 3* (Z). Fine 15C façade with mullioned windows. The
inside courtyard has a well, inspired from the antique style.

EXCURSIONS

Garrigues. – *11km – 7 miles by* ① *on the D 979 to join the itinerary described
on p 117.*

Round tour of 44km – 27 miles. – *About 2 1/2 hours. Leave Nîmes by Rue
Arnavielle* (AZ) *which becomes the D 40, the road to Sommières.*

Caveirac. – Pop 1 879. An imposing 17C horseshoe shaped château houses the town
hall. Two corner towers roofed with glazed tiles, mullioned windows, amusing
gargoyles and a fine staircase with a wrought iron balustrade enhance the edifice.
The porch is so big that it bestrides the road (D 103).

Continue along the D 40 and enter Calvisson from the right.

Calvisson. – Pop 1 793. A village amidst vines in the centre of Vaunage Plain.

*In the centre of town take the CD 107 in the direction of Fontanès; leave the
village and bear left on the signposted road indicating Roc de Gachonne.*

From the viewing table located at the top of the tower, there is a picturesque **view**
of the red tile roofed village, Vidourle Valley (southwest), St-Loup Peak (west) and
on the horizon the Mediterranean and the Pyrenees.

*Take the D 40 towards Nîmes and bear right on the D 137 to the Nages
Oppidum.*

Nages Oppidum. – *Description p 142.*

*Continue on the D 345 through Boissières, overlooked by a very restored
medieval castle, to the D 107, bear right on the N 113 then left on the D 139.*

ⓥ **Perrier Spring** (Source Perrier). – The spring forms an underground lake 15 ºC-50º F;
the abundant natural gas which escapes is captured and reinserted in the water
under pressure. The tour includes a visit to the bottle making, bottling, labelling...
The production now exceeds 800 million bottles.

Take the N 113 back to Nîmes.

NOTRE-DAME-DE-GRÂCE Sanctuary
(Sanctuaire de N.-D.-DE-GRÂCE)

Michelin map 81 fold 11 or 245 folds 15 and 16 or 246 fold 25 – 18km – 11 miles west of Avignon.

On a hillock at the edge of Rochefort Forest stands Notre-Dame-de-Grâce Sanctuary. Built on the site of a Benedictine priory founded in 798, ravaged in the 18C and restored in the 19C by the Marist Fathers, the sanctuary has sheltered, since 1964, an almshouse.

⊙ **TOUR** *time: 1/2 hour*

In the sparsely decorated chapel note the lovely wrought iron grille closing off the chancel; the altar in polychrome marble is surmounted by a statue of Our Lady of Grace.

On entering the chancel, on the south pillar, hangs an ex-voto (1666) offered by Anne of Austria for the birth of the future Louis XIV, in 1638, after 23 years of childless marriage. In a room off the chapel are exhibited more than 100 ex-voto (naive religious paintings) from the 17-20C. In the cloisters the echo chamber permitted hearing the confessions of lepers; two people stand in opposite corners facing the wall, when they speak quietly, they can hear each other distinctly.

Go around the reception office on the south side and take the Way of the Cross.

From the terrace a lovely **view★** can be had of the Lance Mountains, Mount Ventoux, Vaucluse Plateau, the Montagnette and Alpilles Mountain ranges and the Rhône Plain.

NYONS   Pop 6 293

Michelin map 81 fold 3 or 245 folds 4 and 17 or 246 fold 9 – Facilities

Situated within a protective ring of mountains *(see p 26 for the town's legend)* astride the Eygues River, where it emerges from a gorge into the Tricastin Plain, Nyons enjoys a pleasant climate where exotic flora blooms outside; this warm winter climate attracts people who are in retirement.

The olive groves surrounding Nyons (the olives and oil *(qv)* of which are one of the town's local enterprises) give the town a very Provençal look. The town has a truffle market and produces jam and fruit jellies.

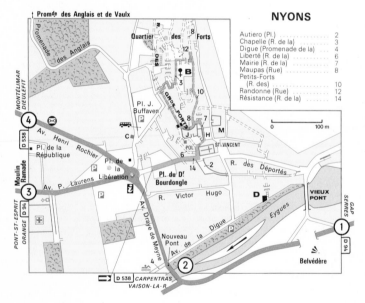

NYONS

Autiero (Pl.)	2
Chapelle (R. de la)	3
Digue (Promenade de la)	4
Liberté (R. de la)	6
Mairie (R. de la)	7
Maupas (Rue)	8
Petits-Forts (R. des)	10
Randonne (Rue)	12
Résistance (R. de la)	14

SIGHTS

Forts Quarter (Quartier des Forts). – This old quarter is built on a hill overlooking town.

Start from the arcaded **Place du Dr-Bourdongle.**

Take the Rue de la Résistance and Rue de la Mairie to Rue des Petits-Forts.

This is a narrow alley lined with low roofed houses (early 14C).

Randonne Tower (Tour Randonne) **(B)**. – The 13C tower houses the tiny chapel of Notre-Dame-de-Bon-Secours.

Bear left on Rue de la Chapelle.

★ **Rue des Grands Forts.** – This is a long covered gallery where the thick walls have been pierced with windows to allow the light to filter through.

Go under the tall vaulted gateway, the ruins of a feudal castle, and bear left into Rue Maupas, a stepped street which leads back to Rue de la Mairie.

★**Old Bridge (Vieux Pont)**. – The 13-14C humpbacked bridge, spanning the Eygues with a single 40m – 131ft arch, is one of the boldest in the Midi.

Oil Mills (Moulins à huile). – The oil mills are in operation full time between November and February.

Ⓥ **Ramade Oil Mill** (Moulin Ramade). – *Access via ③, Avenue Paul-Laurens and the fourth street on the left*. The first gallery contains millstones and presses which are used in the production of olive oil. The second gallery is used for refining and stocking. The Nyons olive, the Tanche variety, is processed here.

Ⓥ **Autrand Oil Mill** (Moulin Autrand) (**D**). – *Access via Avenue de la Digue*. Old 18C oil mills can be seen; oil is produced according to traditional methods.

Ⓥ **Oil and Wine Cooperative** (Coopérative oléicole et viticole). – *Place Olivier-de-Serres. Access via ③, Avenue Paul-Laurens*. In two adjacent rooms the production of virgin olive oil (70% of the production) obtained by only one mechanical pressing without further treatment. The remaining olives, the Tanche variety, or Nyons black olives, are used for canning.

Ⓥ **Olive Museum** (Musée de l'olivier). – *Avenue des Tilleuls. Access by ③, Avenue Paul-Laurens, then northwest of Place Olivier-de-Serres*. The museum includes a wide variety of utensils, presses, tools... used in the production of olives and olive oil; there is as well, a number of items, such as lamps, showing how oil can be used. Documents enhance the collection. Note as well the giant fossil weighing 148kg – 326lbs.

Viewpoint (Belvédère). – *Cross the Eygues over the Nouveau Pont, bear left on the D 94, leaving the Vieux Pont on the left; pass under the tunnel and turn right*. From the rocky spike (bench) the **view** embraces old Nyons overlooked by Angèle Mountain (alt 1 606m – 5 268ft), the deep, narrow Eygues Valley to the right contrasting with the wide basin, to the left, where the new town has spread.

EXCURSION

Promenade des Anglais et de Vaulx. – *Round tour of 8km – 5 miles. Leave Nyons Promenade des Anglais (northwest of town plan) and after 300m – 274yds turn right*.
The narrow, winding but nicely laid out road runs along the hillside through olive groves. It offers good views of Nyons, Eygues Valley and the Baronnies Massif.

> *On the descent to the D 538, leave the road on the right to Venterol and return to Nyons via the D 538.*

Use the Michelin Maps with your Michelin Guide.

★★ ORANGE   Pop 27 502

Michelin map 🎇 folds 11 and 12 or 🎇 fold 16 or 🎇 fold 24

Gateway to the Midi, the crossroads of two motorways, Orange is famous for its prestigeous Roman public buildings which include the triumphal arch and the Roman theatre. These monuments serve as the stage for the international music festival created in 1869 called **Chorégies** *(qv)*.
An important market centre for fruit and early produce, Orange also has industrial (canning, chemicals) and military (air base, Foreign Legion) obligations.

Roman Orange. – Ancient Arausio was a Celtic settlement, when in 105BC a terrible battle erupted between the Roman legions and against the army of the Cimbrians and Teutons. The Romans were defeated, risking, unfortunately, to compromise their recent conquest of Gaul. And yet they recovered quickly returning 3 years later under the command of the brilliant General Marius and won. The battle took place near Aix *(p 46)*. Established in 35BC, the Roman colony of Orange welcomed the veterans of the 2nd Gallica. The town had a well ordered urban plan, enhanced by public buildings and surrounded by fortifications which protected some 70ha – 173acres.
It was at the head of a vast territory, which the Roman land surveyors laid out with precision. Lots were attributed with priority to the veterans, the other more mediocre lots were rented out to the highest bidders and the remaining lots belonged to the collectivity. In this way the Roman state facilitated colonisation and the improvement of the soil at the natives expense. The cadastral plan several times revised, was posted publicly, several parts of it (in good condition) can be seen in the Municipal Museum *(p 152)*.
Until 412, the date the town was ransacked by the Visigoths, Orange prospered. Because it was a bishopric two synods took place here one in 441 and the other in 529.

Dutch Orange. – In the second half of the 12C, the town became the seat of a small principality in Comtat Venaissin *(qv)*. Through marriage and heredity Orange ended up belonging to a branch of the Baux family heir, also, to the German principality of Nassau. In the 16C the then Prince of Orange and Nassau, William the Silent transformed his fief into the United Provinces with himself as first stadtholder. At the same time, the town became Protestant and was victim to the ravages of the Wars of Religion, but it succeeded in preserving its autonomy.
Orange is justly proud of the fact that the preferred title of the glorious royal dynasty of Holland is Prince or Princess of Orange; and its name is identified to a state, cities, rivers, etc... in Australia, South Africa and USA.

ORANGE

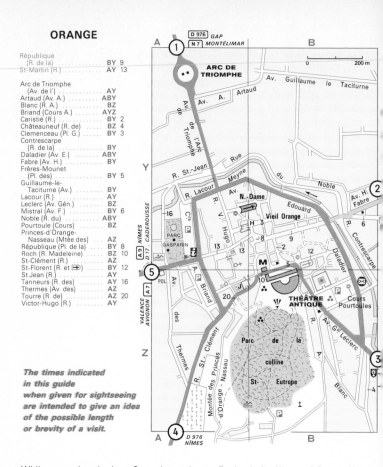

*The times indicated
in this guide
when given for sightseeing
are intended to give an idea
of the possible length
or brevity of a visit.*

While governing the Low Countries and even England, the House of Orange-Nassau
did not forget its tiny enclave in France.
In 1622 Maurice of Nassau surrounded the town with strong ramparts and built a
large castle.
Unfortunately, for economic reasons as well as lack of time, he took the stones
necessary for his fortifications from the Roman ruins which had not been destroyed
by the Barbarian invasions. Yet this time nothing was left standing except the
theatre, part of the ramparts and the triumphal arch which had been transformed
into a fortress.

French Orange. – During the war against Holland, Louis XIV wanted the Principality
of Orange.
It was the Count of Grignan, Lieutenant-General to the king in Provence and Mme
de Sévigné's *(qv)* son-in-law who captured the town. The ramparts were razed and
the castle demolished. In 1713 the *Treaty of Utrecht* ceded Orange to France. At
the Revolution, Orange was joined to the Drôme *département,* then Bouches-du-
Rhône and finally to Vaucluse.
The prosperous Roman town of Arausio became the main town of a canton.

ROMAN PUBLIC BUILDINGS *time: 1 hour*

★★★Roman Theatre (Théâtre Antique) (BZ). – The Roman theatre, has, justly so, been
⊘ the city's pride as it is the most well preserved not only in Provence but the Roman
empire as well.
Each summer, within these walls, the Chorégies takes place. This is a high quality
festival of music where notably great operas are performed.

Exterior. – Built during
Augustus's reign, the
theatre has the same
dimensions as the the-
atre in Arles *(p 65);* the
cavea (all of the tiers)
was built onto a natural
height which allowed
for a quicker and more
economical construc-
tion. The formidable
stage wall (103m –
338ft long and 36m-
118ft high), which
Louis XIV had qualified
as the finest wall of the
kingdom, is the the-
atre's outside façade.

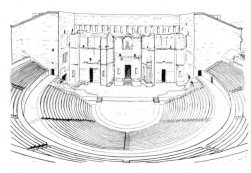

Roman Theatre in Orange

Its upper storey was made up of two rows of corbels which were pierced with holes to hold up the poles for the *velum (p 144)*, which shaded the spectators from the sun. Below 19 blind arcades corresponded with rooms inside, corridors and staircases. In front of it stood a portico 8m – 26ft wide, the foundations of which can be seen.

The present-day square before the theatre was most likely occupied by a garden encircled by a vast portico, the portico mentioned above was one of its side walls.

Interior. – The building is almost complete, however, the portico which crowned the top of the tiers, the roof sheltering the stage and of course its decoration are missing.

The semicircle, the *cavea,* contained 9-10 000 spectators seated according to their social station. It was divided into 3 sections of 37 tiers of seats and separated by walls.

Below, the orchestra was in the shape of a half circle, along it 3 low tiers of seats were where moveable seats were set up for the high ranking citizens.

On either side of the stage large rooms, one on top of the other (entrance is now from the lower room west side) were for receiving the public, and housed the backstage.

The stage floored with wood, under which the machinery was kept, measured 61m – 200ft long and 9m – 30ft of performing area; it overlooked the orchestra by about 1m10 – 3 1/2ft. It was held up by a low wall, *pulpitum.* Behind was the curtain slot (the curtain was dropped during the performances).

The stage wall was at the same level as the topmost tier, and presented an overly ornate decoration of marble facing, stucco, mosaics, several tiers of columns, and niches for statues including the imperial one of Augustus (3m55 – 11ft) which was brought back to its original location in 1951. The stage wall had three doors, each of which had a particular function. The centre one represented the palace door, while the two side doors were for the hosts. A roof protected the stage and was also acoustically useful.

From the top row one can hear someone speaking in the semicircle.

Performances. – The Roman theatre was used as a hall for political meetings, lectures and concerts. Competitions, lottery drawings and distribution of bread or money took place here. Conjurors, bear-leaders, tight-rope walkers, illusionists, sword-swallowers, jugglers, acrobats, mimes and marionettes could be seen, and there were already cock fights. When they became more elaborate – thus more costly – there was scenery and a number of walker-ons as in present day music halls. But the chief function of the theatre was the performance of comedies and tragedies. And yet neither the plays nor their authors are known; it is believed that Greek plays were frequently performed but it seems they did not attract much success from the Gallo-Roman audience. The more popular Roman comedies attracted large crowds especially when a lot of scenery, accessories, actors... were used.

There were also the performances inspired from mythology, in relation to the religious calendar.

In fact the theatrical performances became licentious and in the 5C they were abolished under the influence of Christianity.

The actors, grouped in a troop financed by wealthy citizens wore pasteboard masks. Each type of character: father, mother, daughter, young man, parasite, slave, tyrant etc... had a distinctive mask; as soon as the masked actor entered, one knew what role he or she played. The tragic actors, to appear even more awesome, wore sandals with a thick cork sole.

All sorts of means were used to obtain perfect acoustics. The mouths of the actors' masks were little megaphones; the large sloping roof over the stage threw the sound downwards, the upward curve of the seats received it smoothly, the colonnades broke up the echo and carefully graduated sounding-boards under the seats acted as loud-speakers. One detail will show how far these refinements were carried: the doors on the stage were hollow and made like violins inside. When an actor wished to amplify his voice he would stand against one of these sound-boxes. *For more on theatres, accompanied by an explanatory drawing see p 33.*

Theatre district. – Near the theatre, the excavations undergone by Jules Formigé have uncovered the substructures of a temple and a mysterious edifice which ended in a semicircle parallel to the theatre *(access by the theatre)*.

In the centre of this semicircle, raised on a platform, stood a large temple, probably built under Hadrian (2C) on the site of a sacred spring; the podium and some vestiges remain.

A double staircase climbed 28m – 92ft higher to a smaller second temple which with its annexes occupied what is now the site of the city's reservoir. Overlooking the whole, it seems that an immense group of three temples (60m – 197ft wide) stood on a rectangular platform extending east to west and supported on the north and west side by powerful buttresses. One can imagine the magnificent perspective realised.

★★**Triumphal Arch (Arc de Triomphe)** (AY). – The arch stands on the north side of the city on the old Via Agrippa which linked Lyons to Arles. It ranks third among the Roman constructions of this type due to its dimensions (22m – 72ft high, 21m – 69ft wide and 8m – 26ft deep; it is one of the best preserved, particularly the north face (the west has been restored).

Built *c*20BC and dedicated later to Tiberius, the arch commemorated the campaigns of the II Legion.

It has three openings flanked by columns and presents two unusual architectural features: a pediment above the central opening and two attic storeys. It was surmounted, at its construction with a bronze quadriga (a chariot drawn by four horses harnessed abreast) flanked by two trophies.

ORANGE ★★

Its exuberant decoration is linked to Roman Classicism and the plastic beauty of the Hellenistic style. To be admired are the scenes of battles and arms captured (1, 3, 6, 7) which recall the conquering of Gaul, naval accessories (2) pertaining to Augustus's victory over Actium, more than the fall of Marseilles under Caesar.

Triumphal Arch in Orange

North Face

1) Fighting between Gauls and legionaries. Prisoners.
2) Naval accessories: prows, beaks of galleys, anchors, robes, tridents.
3) Trophies: helmets, armour, javelins, military banners, flags.
4) Fruit, flowers, ancient ornamentation.
5) Coffered vaulting adorned with rosettes and various designs.

East Face

6) Trophies
7) Chained prisoners.

ADDITIONAL SIGHTS

St-Eutrope Hill (Colline St-Eutrope) (BZ). – *Drive up Montée des Princes-d'Orange-Nassau. Leave the car in the car park in front of the public gardens.*
The main avenue crosses the moat of the former castle of the Princes of Orange, the excavations (left of Square Reine-Juliana) have uncovered important ruins.
At the far north end of the park, near a statue to the Virgin, there is a viewing table offering a beautiful **view★** of the Roman theatre in the foreground, the city of Orange, the Marcoule nuclear power centre and the Rhône Plain hemmed in by mountains. On the left are ruins of the Roman capitol.

Municipal Museum (Musée de la ville) (BYZ M). – This museum presents in the courtyard and ground floor lapidary vestiges from the Roman monuments (no longer standing) and the Princes of Orange's castle. In one gallery are exhibited fragments (meticulously reconstituted) of the renowned Roman **land survey** of Orange *(p 149)*, unique in France. On these marble tablets, the historians have identified the well planned grid pattern (with its *cardo* and *decumanus*), the administrative subdivisions and topographical references (roads, mountains, rivers, swamps) and finally written information on the judicial and fiscal status of the land. The pieces found belong to three successive surveys: the first one dates from 77, the second from Trajan's reign (2C), the third is posterior. The historians have been able to position the second survey: south of Montélimar to north of Orange, bounded to the west by the Rhône River and extending to the east probably as far as Vaison and covering 836km² – 323sq miles.
Some of the land around Orange still clearly shows the influence of the Roman subdivisions.
The museum's other rooms are devoted to the history of Orange, local traditions, painting, and the making of printed fabrics in 18C Orange.

Former Cathedral of Notre-Dame (Ancienne cathédrale Notre-Dame) (AB Y). – This Romanesque building was very badly damaged during the Wars of Religion and the majority of it had to be rebuilt. Carvings of Ancient influence decorate the southern porch.

Old Orange. – The town centre's streets are very animated and pleasant to amble along. Start at the Roman theatre, take Rue Caristié and the streets around the town hall (17C belfry) and cathedral which end in lovely Provençal-like squares with their café terraces shaded by plane trees.

EXCURSIONS

J.-H. Fabre House (Harmas – maison – J.-H. Fabre). – *8km – 5 miles by ① on the N 7 and the D 576.* On entering **Sérignan-du-Comtat** stands the house of Jean-Henri Fabre, the famous entomologist (1823-1915) who lived here the last 36 years of his life. The visit includes the scientist's office, where display cases contain his own collections: insects, shells, fossils, minerals, and a gallery in which his watercolours (mushrooms of the region) are hung. A tour of the land around his house, which was his main field of observation, has become a botanical garden.

Caderousse. – *6km – 3 1/2 miles by ⑤ on the D 17.* Pop 2 007. This village is located on the banks of the Rhône and has often been subject to its flooding. On the town hall's façade left of the door, four plaques indicate the level reached by the rise of the floodwaters.
Since 1856 a dike protects the village from the floodwaters; ramparts encircle the whole village and only two doors open at the cardinal points.

St-Michel. – The church is in the Provençal Romanesque style. Inside, south of the chancel, St-Claude's Chapel in the Flamboyant style was added in the 16C; its vaulting is lovely.

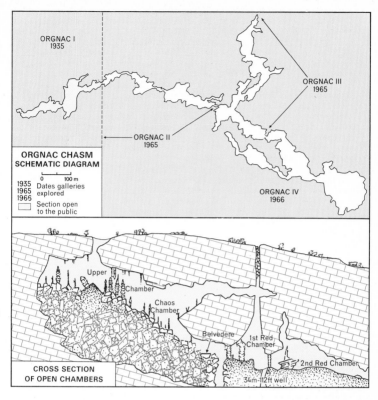

ORGNAC I
1935

ORGNAC III
1965

ORGNAC II
1965

**ORGNAC CHASM
SCHEMATIC DIAGRAM**

0   100 m

1935
1965   Dates galleries
1966   explored

Section open
to the public

ORGNAC IV
1966

Upper
Chamber

Chaos
Chamber

Belvedere

1st Red
Chamber

2nd Red Chamber

34m-112ft well

**CROSS SECTION
OF OPEN CHAMBERS**

The great hole in the ground was known of by the local people but ignored until October 1935 when the speleologist **Robert de Joly** (1887-1968) descended into it. In the garden a stela was built in memory of the engineer and speleologist, who explored this region, Cévennes (where he lived); he also played an important role in improving the equipment and techniques used in underground exploration *(p 140)*.

This cave is fascinating because of the natural development of underground streams, fed by infiltration and through fissures in the calcareous rock. The first concretions, which were at times 10m – 33ft in diameter were broken by a major earthquake at the end of the Tertiary Era. These columns, broken or turned upside down, served as a base to more recent stalagmites.

Climatic variations which occurred in the area during the Quaternary Era provoked irregularities in the building up of the concretions. Their growth, which could reach 5cm – 1 3/4in a century during the warm humid periods, was interrupted during the dry ice ages, when the water activity ceased. Thus when the thaw brought a rush of waters new channels were formed which explains the bayonet-shape and cantilever walls that these concretions formed.

New galleries were discovered and explored (Orgnac II, III, IV, and IV bis). The vast network of chambers will be closed to the public for sometime.

Stalagmites in Orgnac Chasm

Ⓥ **TOUR** *time: about 1 hour*

Interior temperature 13 ℃ – 55 ℉. 788 steps.

The Upper Chamber, in which there is a vast cone of rubble, is astonishing by its dimensions and perspectives. The dim light which comes from the cave's natural opening illuminates the chamber with a strange bluish light, 17 to 40m – 23 to 131ft high, 250m – 820ft long and 125m – 410ft wide, this chamber contains magnificent stalagmites. The largest are in the middle; a number of growths give them the shape of pine cones. Unable, due to the height of the vault, to join the stalagtites to form pillars, the stalagmites have thickened at the base, and become quite large; other more recent and thinner stalagmites have piled on top of them like a stack of plates. Along the walls of the chamber, note the delicate columns which came after the earthquake; some are very tall either in bayonet-shape or standing very straight. In the niche of a buffet-like concretion is an urn containing the heart of R. de Joly. In the Chaos Chamber, encumbered by concretions which have fallen in from the Upper Chamber, magnificent curtains of varied colours escape from a fissure in the vault.

On level with the belvedere of the first Red Chamber, the water filtering in, enriched with carbonate of lime through the calcareous layer, has encouraged the formation of a mass of concretions. Immense flows of ferruginous clay in a lovely dark red colour cover the walls and floor. Nearby is the well, the deepest in the cave at 34m – 112ft which leads into another chamber at 180m – 591ft deep. Another belvedere overlooks the second Red Chamber where the play of light enhances the beauty of the concretions.

ORGON   Pop 2 341

Michelin map 🔢 fold 12 or 🔢 fold 30 or 🔢 fold 12 – 7km – 4 miles south of Cavaillon – Local map 57

Orgon, crossed by the N 7, is in the Durance Plain. It overlooks the ridge which separates the Alpilles Chain to the west and Luberon Mountains to the east.

Napoleon's woes. – Escaping Avignon in April 1814, Napoleon, on his way to exile on Elbe Island, stopped at an inn in Orgon. A hostile crowd, allerted by the Royalist drummers gathered. The excited mob wanted to lynch him but he was saved by the mayor of Orgon and fled. He was able to reach the Auberge de La Calade near Aix.

Ⓥ **Church (Église).** – 14C. The choir and nave are slightly out of alignment; the chapels were added in the 17C. On the nave's north side hang fine 14C painted panels.

Notre-Dame-de-Beauregard Chapel (Chapelle N.-D.-de-Beauregard). – Crowning the hill overlooking the town to the south *(road subject to restrictions)*, the chapel's terrace presents a fine view of Durance Valley, Luberon Mountains, and Côtes Chain.

★ PAÏOLIVE Woods (Bois de PAÏOLIVE)

Michelin map 🔢 fold 8

This limestone area of Lower Vivarais stretches over about 16km² – 6sq miles southeast of Les Vans on either side of the Chassezac. The ground consists of a grey Jurassic limestone (Secondary Era *p 12*), which is both hard and permeable making it resistant to wind and weather erosion but susceptible to rain water, full of carbonic acid, which has enlarged the fissures into deep defiles and remoulded the rocks into strange forms. Elsewhere residual rock has turned to clay and permitted the growth of vegetation (especially the common oak).

TOUR

time: about 2 hours

The D 252 crosses the woods west to east.

About 200m – 219yds from the D 901 some 20m – 65 1/2ft off to the right coming from Les Vans stand the rocks known locally as the Bear (L'Ours) and the Lion (Le Lion).

★ **Clearing** (Clairière). – A clearing is accessible to cars near the D 252 in a left hand bend coming from Les Vans, not far from the kilometre-marker indicating "Casteljau 4km". It is established on a doline *(qv)* or sinkhole (picnic area).

★★ **Le Chassezac Corniche** (Corniche du Chassezac). – *3/4 hour on foot Rtn. Take the trail to the left, which is an extension of the D 252 coming from Les Vans and passes under a telephone wire (leave on the left another trail also passing underneath the telephone wire).*

After having walked several feet, Casteljau Manor-House, flanked by two corner towers of the same height, can be seen in the distance. Continue along the trail using the manor-house as a guide, the silhouette of which becomes more defined.

After a couple of hundred feet the trail branches slightly off to the left, heading still towards the manor-house. After less than 10 minutes walk you suddenly come upon the grandiose Chassezac Gorge winding past below, at the foot of the cave pitted cliffs. The corniche 80m – 262ft above the water follows to the left, across from the manor-house, to a belvedere located upstream.

Return by the way you came or for those who like to walk by the trails marked on the map p 154.

Mazet-Plage. – *A surfaced path off of the D 252 leads 300m – 328yds to a couple of houses along the river bank.* Walk along the Chassezac, going towards the left for about 500m – 1/3 mile along the shingly beach with its small willows across from the bizarre cave pitted cliffs *(1/4 hour on foot Rtn).*

Banne. – Pop 505. *6km – 3 1/2 miles from the crossroads of the D 901 and the D 252. Leave the car on the square; climb up the slope behind the Calvary.* The path leads to a platform overlooking the Jalès Depression. From the top, upon which lies the ruins of Banne's old citadel, there is a vast **panorama**★ extending from the Gard River to Lower Ardèche. Half-buried in the platform's southwest side a long vaulted gallery can be seen which served as Banne Castle's stables.

PERNES-LES-FONTAINES
Pop 6 961

Michelin map 81 folds 12 and 13 or 245 fold 17 or 246 fold 11

The town located on the border of Vaucluse Plateau was the former capital of Comtat Venaissin (968-1320) before Carpentras *(qv)*. It is the home town of Fléchier (1632-1710) one of the best orators of the late 17C; his funeral orations included one for Turenne and Marie-Thérèse of Austria, as well.

Like most of the towns on the Vaucluse Plateau, Pernes-les-Fontaines has canning factories. Fruit – cherries, strawberries, melons, grapes – is especially abundant in the region.

★**Notre-Dame Gate (Porte Notre-Dame).** – An old corbelled bridge, spanning the Nesque River preceeds this 16C gate. On one of the bridge's piles is a small 16C chapel (**B**). The bridge, chapel, gate and keep (**D**) make a charming picture. Known as the Clock Tower, the keep was formerly from the castle of the Count of Toulouse.

Notre-Dame-de-Nazareth. – The oldest parts of the church date from the late 11C. The south porch opens by a lovely door (in bad condition) inspired from antiquity. Inside, the pointed barrel vaulted nave is adorned with a cornice; Gothic chapels.

Cormoran Fountain (Fontaine du Cormoran) (E). – An 18C fountain.

Brancas (R. de)	2
Briand (Pl. Aristide)	3
Corti (Pl. et Square D.)	4
Gambetta (R.)	5
Giraud (Pl. L.)	6
Jaurès (Av. Jean)	7
Neuve (R.)	8
Notre-Dame (Pont)	10
Notre-Dame (R. Porte)	12
Raspail (R.)	13
République (R. de la)	15
Victor-Hugo (R.)	16

Town Hall (Hôtel de Ville) (H). – Old 17C hôtel.

Ferrande Tower (Tour Ferrande) (F). – Hemmed in by houses, this quadrangular crenellated tower overlooks a little square where Gigot Fountain plays. By a narrow staircase, climb to the 3rd floor which is adorned with fine 13C frescoes.

Covered Cross (Croix Couverte) (K). – Elegant 15C monument.

Villeneuve and St-Gilles Gates (Portes de Villeneuve et de St-Gilles). – Remains of the 14 and 16C curtain wall.

PEYROLLES-EN-PROVENCE
Pop 2 561

Michelin map 84 folds 3 and 4 or 245 fold 32 – Local map p 113

Located in the valley, Peyrolles spreads itself along the EDF Canal *(qv)* which drains part of the Durance River. All that is left of the medieval fortifications are a belfry crowned by a wrought iron bell cage *(qv)* and a round tower (in ruins) near the church.

St-Pierre (Église St-Pierre). – Inspite of being many times remodelled in the 15 and 17C, the church has kept a Romanesque pointed barrel vaulted nave.

Chapel of St-Sepulcre (Chapelle du St-Sépulcre). – The plan of this 11-12C chapel is a Greek cross: 4 oven vaulted apsidal chapels frame a square surmounted by a small bell gable.

Château. – This vast 17C château houses the town hall. The courtyard is opened by a large doorway.

155

Michelin map 80 fold 19 or 245 fold 15 or 246 fold 25

This aqueduct, one of the wonders of Ancient Times, is worth a journey. It is part of a system which brought spring water captured near Uzès *(qv)* to Nîmes; it was built *c*19BC and inspite of its 2 000 years is in very good condition.

Pont du Gard

Aqueduct (Aqueduc). – The Romans attached a great deal of importance to the quality of the water which they required for even the smallest town (imagine the water needed for the baths, public fountains and domestic use). The water was collected preferably on the north slope so that it did not heat in the reservoirs. The water channel was made entirely of stone, either vaulted or tiled and pierced with openings only for ventilation and maintenance. Some aqueducts were equipped with settling tanks. The form of the land was crossed with an exceptional engineering ability – the aqueduct followed its course via bridges, ditches, tunnels and siphons. The aqueduct of Nîmes some 50km – 31miles had an average incline of 34cm per km or 1:300 falling more steeply just before the valley to reduce the height of the bridge. Its daily flow was about 20 000m³ – 44 million gallons.

Whenever Nîmes was besieged, as often happened, the aqueduct was breached. From the 4C it ceased to be maintained, so that lime deposits built up, until finally by the 9C the course had become blocked and it had fallen into disuse. Land holders along the course, thereupon, began to remove the dressed stones for their own use.

In 1743, on to the aqueduct was added, downstream, a road bridge.

★★★ **Bridge (Pont).** – The aqueduct spans Gardon Valley. The golden coloured tone of the old stones harmonises beautifully with the surrounding countryside.

It is composed of colossal dressed blocks of masonry some weighing as much as 6 tons, which were laid without mortar, the courses being held together with iron clamps. The stone was lifted into position by block and tackle with goats as auxiliaries and a winch worked by a massive human treadmill.

In order to break the sense of monotony the three stages are recessed, the piers in line one above another. Statistical details are: height above the Gardon at low water: 49m – 160ft; lowest level: 6 arches, 142m long, piers 6m thick, arches 22m high (465ft, 20ft, 72ft); middle level: 11 arches, 242m long, piers 4m thick, arches 20m high (792ft, 13ft, 65ft); top level, the one carrying the canal: 35 arches, 275m long, piers 3m thick, arches 7m high (900ft, 10ft, 23ft). The bridge was restored under Napoleon III. The architect varied the span of the arches very slightly within each range; each arch was constructed independently to give flexibility in the event of subsidence. The stones obtruding from the face were scaffolding supports, and were left not only to facilitate maintenance work but to add interest to the surface, as do the ridges on the piers which held the semicircular wooden frames on which the arches were constructed.

TOUR

⊙ *Leave the car in the car park beside the D 981 downstream from the bridge (during the summer the bridge is one-way).*

Walk. – Time: 1 hour. On the south bank of the Gardon off the D 981 is a small road which passes underneath the aqueduct.

Continue on the road to the Château de St-Privat and the banks of the Gardon from where the view of the aqueduct is superb.

Return towards the aqueduct, 54 1/2yds before passing underneath it, bear right onto a winding path up through the undergrowth.

When you reach the third bend a path on the right leads to a **viewpoint** from where there is a good view of the aqueduct and the village of Castillon framed by one of the arches.

Continue up the winding path to the top level of the aqueduct (those who do not want to cross the bridge can take the path on the left, which passes under the last span of the bridge ending downstream from the bridge on the D 981.

Walk across the bridge, either in the canal trough (impeded in places by chalk deposits), a safe but dull path because it has no outlook, or, if you have a good head for heights, along the canal's stone roof from where, of course, there are views on all sides.

At the end descend the spiral staircase and turn right.

By the river. – Hire of canoe or kayak for the Pont du Gard (time: 1/2 or 1 hour) or the Gardon Gorges (time: 1/2 or 1 day – p 117). It is essential to be able to swim.

PONT-ST-ESPRIT   Pop 8 135

Michelin map 🔟 fold 10 or 🔢 fold 15 or 🔢 fold 23 – Local map p 61

The town owes its *raison d'être* and name to the bridge built 1265-1309 by the Bridge Brotherhood under the protection of the Holy Spirit (Saint Esprit); it subsequently became an important halting place on the Rhône.

PONT-ST-ESPRIT

Haut-Mazeau (R.)	8
Joliot-Curie (R.)	
Minimes (R. des)	
Mistral (Allées F.)	15
République (Pl. de la)	21
St-Jacques (R.)	25
Allègre-Chemin (Bd)	2
Bas-Mazeau (R.)	3
Bruguier-Roure (R. L.)	4
Couvent (R. du)	5
Doumergue (Av. G.)	6
Gaulle (Av. du Gén. de)	7
Hôtel-de-Ville (Pl. de l')	9
Jaurès (Allées J.)	10
Jemmapes (R.)	12
Paroisse (R. de la)	17
Plan (Pl. du)	18
St-Pierre (Pl.)	26
19 Mars 1962 (R. du)	28

*The main shopping streets
are printed
in a different colour
in the list of streets.*

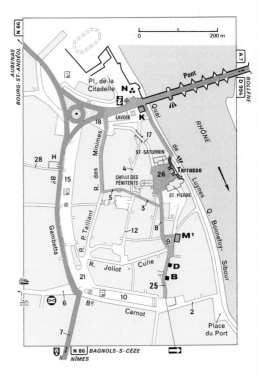

SIGHTS

Park the car at the end of Allées Jean-Jaurès.

Rue St-Jacques (25) is lined with old houses notably: 17C Hôtel de Roubin (no 10 – **B**), 12-16C Knights' Mansion (no 2 – **D**) with its lovely Romanesque window. On the Place de l'Hôtel-de-Ville stands the Paul Raymond Museum.

Ⓥ **Paul Raymond Museum (Musée Paul Raymond)** (**M¹**). – This museum, in the former town hall, contains collections pertaining to local prehistory and religious art (silver-gilt chalice and patera from the Languedoc area, 1650, and a canvas by the Provençal Primitive painter Raymond Boterie portraying the *Fall of the Angels*, 1510). Of particular interest is the pharmacy, from the former hospital with its splendid array of about 220 jars from the early 18C pottery workshops of Montpellier. Note also the fine selection of 17 medieval Hispano-Moorish pieces. In the basement is the town's former ice house (1780).

Take Rue Haut-Mazeau to reach Place St-Pierre.

Terrace (Terrasse). – It lies on the east side of Place St-Pierre bounded to the north by the 15C parish church, to the southwest by the baroque façade of the Penitents' Chapel (Chapelle des Pénitents) and to the southeast by the former 17C Church of St-Pierre (no longer in use) topped by a dome. From the terrace there is a good overall view of the bridge.
A monumental double flight of stairs leads to Quai de Luynes. Left, almost at the foot of the bridge, the Roy Mansion (**K**) is pierced by Renaissance windows.

Bridge (Pont). – The bridge, nearly 1 000m – 3 281ft long, is slightly curved upstream against the current; 19 of the 25 arches are old. It used to be defended at either end with bastions and two towers in the middle – this whole defensive system was destroyed.

To facilitate navigation – the passage through the bridge had, over the centuries, always been feared by sailors – the bridge's first two arches were replaced by one arch (it was subsequently destroyed during the Second World War and rebuilt in reinforced concrete.

From the bridge there is a fine view of the Rhône and the town. North of the bridge, where there is now a vast terrace, the citadel once stood; it was built in 1595 and fortified by Vauban in the 17C. From the centre of the terrace the view extends to the 15C Flamboyant doorway of the former Plan Collegiate Church (**N**).

To get a better look at the door's details (partly uncovered) take the stairs to the right of the tourist information centre.

Cross the intersection and then take old Rue des Minimes and left on Rue du Couvent; continue along Rues Bas-Mazeau, Haut-Mazeau and St-Jacques to the car.

*Travel with the **Michelin Regional Map Series** (1:200 000) they are revised regularly.*

★ PORT-CAMARGUE

Michelin map 👁👁 folds 8 and 18 – Local map p 96 – Facilities

Located west of the Camargue; near Espiguette Point, the resort of Port-Camargue is part of the *commune* of Le Grau-du-Roi *(qv)*. It represents the far most eastern resort created in the development of the Languedoc-Roussillon coast.

It is a good departure point for wanting to cruise along this coastline.

Port. – This project began in 1969 and was entirely man-made; it covers 150ha – 371 acres of which more than half is taken up by water. It provides mooring for more than 4 000 pleasure craft and includes transient docking facilities, winter dockage, a harbour master's office, shipyard, depots, and watersports facilities.

Resort. – The buildings never exceeding two storeys with smooth-stepped façades interspersed with gardens advance into the harbour on crooked finger-like promontories.

PORT-CAMARGUE

0 — 500 m

🎾 Tennis ⚓ Sailing Sch.
🏠 Harbour Master's Office
🐎 Riding School

MEDITERRANEAN

SEA

LE-GRAU-DU-ROI

North Beach

Promenade de la Plage

Y.C.M.
Outer Harbour

Short-term dockage

Winter dockage

Winter dockage

Hotels

Marina

INDUSTRIAL ZONE

Rte des

des

Marines

Channel

Carrefour 2000

Hotel

Pine Forest

Marines

Rte des

D 62ª LE GRAU-DU-ROI, Phare de l'Espiguette

Altier (R. de l') 2	La Superbe (Av.) 8
Centurion (Av. du) 3	Le Foudroyant (Av.) 9
Hermione (Av. de l') 6	Petite-Caroline (Av. de la) ... 10

Espiguette Lighthouse (Phare de l'Espiguette). – *6km – 3 1/2 miles south by a road off the intersection (carrefour) leading into Port-Camargue, opposite the direct road to Le Grau-du-Roi.*

This lighthouse which overlooks Espiguette Point (Pointe de l'Espiguette) stands amidst a typical Camargue *(qv)* landscape where on windswept dunes tamarisk, thistles, sea rockets and cakiles grow. From the beach the view embraces the Sète coastline.

★ LA ROQUE-SUR-CÈZE   Pop 133

Michelin map 👁👁 fold 9 or 👁👁👁 fold 15 or 👁👁👁 fold 24

The village appears grouped around its Romanesque chapel on a hilltop darkly plumed by cypresses. An old arched bridge with pointed cutwaters spans the Cèze River. Coming from the north on the D 980 the **site**★ is a delight.

★**Sautadet Waterfall (Cascade du Sautadet).** – This waterfall is unique by its deep cut into the river bed and by the complicated network of crevasses in which the Cèze runs.

Arriving at La Roque-sur-Cèze via the D 980 and the D 166, before crossing the bridge, take the path on the north bank.

Blocking the river's route, the limestone rock was attacked by the water, carving rifts, and pot holes into it. This unique amalgam of natural features (pot holes, small falls, pools...) is the Sautadet.

If you continue beyond the abandoned mill-race you will come to the deeper ravines plumbed by the Cèze River; from the southern end there is a lovely view.

Michelin map 🗺 fold 13 or 🗺 folds 18 and 31 or 🗺 fold 11 – Local map p 59
– Facilities

The village stands on an unusual **site★** on the highest of the hills between Coulon Valley and Vaucluse Plateau. These hills, composed of ochre rock of 16 or 17 different shades and reflected in the local houses, enhance the village and the surrounding countryside. *For the legend behind ochre see p 26.*

★**Village.** – Leave the car in the car park; walk along Rue des Bourgades and bear right on the narrow, picturesque, stepped and partly covered **Rue de l'Arcade** to the church and castrum on the cliff top.

Castrum. – Viewing table. From this platform the view extends northwards to Vaucluse Plateau and the white crest of Mount Ventoux, southwards to Coulon Valley and Grand Luberon.

ROUSSILLON

0   100 m

Abbé-Avon (Pl. de l')	2	Jeu-de-Paume (R. du)	7
Bistourle (Pl. de la)	3	Lauriers (R. des)	8
Burlière (Av. de la)	4	Mairie (Pl. de la)	9
Église (R. de l')	5	Mathieu (Pl. C.)	12
Fontaine (Rte de la)	6	Pasquier (Pl. du)	13

Go back down to Place de l'Abbé Avon and turn right on Rue du Jeu de Paume.

Continue to the village's opposite end, to the place called Porte Aurouse; from here there is a lovely view of the **Needles of Fairys' Valley** (Aiguilles du Val des Fées), vertical slices in the ochre cliff face.

Turn round; return to the car via a staircase on the right and Rue des Bourgades.

★★**Chaussée des Géants.** – *Time : 3/4 hour on foot Rtn. Start at the car park on the road towards Apt and turn left on the first surfaced path.*
From the first platform a lovely view of the village and its site opens out. Continue on the path, passing a cemetery on the left to the cliff's edge for a view onto the Chaussée des Géants (Giants' Way), a length of jagged rust red cliffs, relieved by a scattering of pines and evergreen oaks.

Chaussée des Géants in Roussillon

ST-BLAISE Archaeological Site

(Site Archéologique de ST-BLAISE)

Michelin map 84 fold 11 or 245 fold 43 or 246 fold 13

With the sea, Rhône River, Berre Lagoon as well as other small lagoons and the vast Crau Plain not far, the *oppidum* of St-Blaise (on the *commune* of St-Mitre-les-Remparts) is a historic site, the wealth of which depended on, during the Hellenic occupation, the working and commerce of salt. After being abandoned some 400 years, it was reoccupied between the 4-14C.

TOUR *time 3/4 hour*

> *Leave the car in the car park and climb a path on the left to the medieval wall surrounding the excavations.*

On the left stands the small Chapel of St-Blaise (12-13C) and adjacent to it a 17C hermitage.

Ancient St-Blaise. – The settlement of St-Blaise (its ancient name has not been identified, it could be Heraclea or Mastramellè), is presented like a fortified spur, the natural defences of which, huge vertical cliffs, are reinforced by ramparts from the Hellenistic period; these were built on the most accessible side which overlooks Lavalduc Valley.

The oldest traces of human existence date back to early 5 000BC. The group of small lagoons which link the east arm of the Rhône River to Berre Lagoon most likely contributed to the discovery of the site by Etruscan sailors in the 7C BC. They established a trading post and began a successful commerce: exchanging salt collected here for wine from Etruria. The settling of the Phocaeans at Marseilles *(p 128)* in *c*600BC developed serious competition between St-Blaise and Marseilles, nevertheless, as the discovery of Etruscan, Corinthian and Ionian pottery has proved, the settlement progressed.

In the second half of the 7C, the settlement formed a proto-urban town surrounded by a wall. Like Entremont *(qv)* a lower and upper town were established. The dwellings were built of stone with a square plan; one of them in the lower town still has its walls at a height of 0m90 – 35in.

A long period of transition (475-200BC) then took place, after a fire, marked by the departure of the Etruscans from the trading post and, Marseilles took over. It has been suggested that there was a possible period of withdrawal due to the absence of human dwellings.

From the late 3 to the mid 1C BC the settlement reached its apex: commerce picked up under the influence of Marseilles who held St-Blaise without, however, making it a colony.

Large projects of levelling of the terrain preceeded the establishment of an urban plan and a strong fortified wall. The lower town was built on a regular grid plan where the squaring off formed island-like units; the façades were all lined up, the streets rectilinear (sometimes with a sidewalk) and the small dwellings were made up of two, three or four rooms. The commercial and small-scale production related activities have left a great number of vestiges: cellars full of urns, metal-founder's workshop etc... St-Blaise, thus, played the role of store-house.

The very high **Hellenistic ramparts★** were raised under the direction of Greek craftsmen between 175 and 140BC; it is more than 1km – 1/2 mile long and cut by towers and bastions, equipped with three posterns and a gateway and crowned at the top with merlons. It was equipped with a system of water evacuation via channels. The wall had hardly been finished that the settlement underwent a violent siege (dozens of cannon-balls have been discovered) which the historians are seeking to date. According to a recent theory, St-Blaise, a salt trade center, having escaped the control of Marseilles a short time after the ramparts completion, may have been taken over by the Romans during their conquest from 125-123BC.

After this event, St-Blaise went through a period of total decline; after its brief re-occupation in mid-1C BC the site was totally abandoned for 4 centuries.

Besides the Hellenistic constructions, St-Blaise has also revealed the presence of a native sanctuary similar to the ones found at Roquepertuse, Entremont *(qv)* and Glanum *(qv)*; a building in the form of a portico with skulls, votive steles...

Paleochristian and medieval St-Blaise. – Before the rise of insecurity at the end of the Roman empire, the old settlement was once again inhabited. The Hellenistic fortifications were re-used: in the 5C the wall was surmounted by an ornamentation of irregular blocks of stone. Two churches were built: St-Vincent (the apse of which is near the ancient main gate) and St-Pierre (destroyed in the 9C). A necropolis (tombs carved into the living rock) extended to the south. The living quarters of this settlement were unfortunately difficult to identify among the other vestiges.

In 874, Ugium (the name of the settlement at that time) was destroyed by the Saracens. It recovered slowly, St-Pierre rebuilt in the 10C, then burned, was reconstructed again in the 11C (substructures have been found near the Chapel of St-Blaise). In 1231, at the plateau's northernmost point a new wall was built to protect the town of Castelveyre (its new name) with its new church Notre-Dame-et-St-Blaise around which the dwellings hovered.

In 1390 Raymond de Turenne's *(qv)* band of brigands pillaged the town. The site was never ever resettled; the last inhabitants settled at St-Mitre. At the end of the spur, a fine view of Lavalduc Lagoon and the Fos Complex *(qv)* opens out.

Museum (Musée).

Museum (Musée). – In the car park, in the former salt-makers customs office building, a small museum presents a small portion of the items unearthed during the excavation of the St-Blaise site *(the majority of excavated material can be found at the Hôtel de Sade p 169)*: pottery, Etruscan amphorae, Eastern Greek vases, vases made locally, Campanian pottery from the Ancient period; reconstruction of a cave tomb and dishes and utensils used at Ugium during the Middle Ages.

Michelin map 👓 fold 9 or 👓 fold 28 or 👓 fold 26 – Local map p 97 – Facilities

Gateway to Camargue *(qv)*, and of agricultural importance (fruit, Costières wines), St-Gilles's claim to fame is the old abbey church, the west front of which considerably influenced Romanesque sculpture in Provence *(p 35)* and in the Rhône Valley.

St Giles and the hind. – Legend has it that in the 8C St Giles, who lived in Greece, was touched by the grace of God and gave all his money to the poor. He set out from Greece aboard a raft which was borne by the sea to Provence. The hermit was befriended by a hind which he later saved from a huntsman, miraculously snatching the arrow in mid-flight, and so amazing the bowman that he, being of a rich and noble family, founded an abbey on the site in commemoration of the event. St Giles journeyed to Rome to obtain recognition for the new foundation and was presented, by the Pope with two doors for the abbey, which he promptly launched on the Tiber and which, after being carried out to sea, landed on the Provençal shore at the same time and place as the saint on his return.

The influence of St Giles (11-12C). – On the site of St Giles's tomb, a sanctuary was raised which became the object of a fervent cult and a place of pilgrimage, even more frequented because of its location on one of the four major roads to Santiago de Compostela *(see Michelin Green Guide to Spain)*. Popes and the Counts of Toulouse protected and enriched the Benedictine monastery which since 1066 had been affiliated to the Cluny order.
In 1096 the powerful **Count Raymond IV** received Pope Urban II, who consecrated the altar of the new abbey church; the count vowed never to return to his land so as to devote himself entirely to the conquest of the Holy Land, which he did, founding the county of Tripoli, where he died.
In the 12C the monastery reached its peak: the town surrounding it had 9 parishes and was extraordinarily prosperous. It benefited from the Crusades: in its port a large amount of Far Eastern goods passed through; the crusading pilgrims embarked from here and the people of St-Gilles had trading posts with privileges in the Latin States of Jerusalem.
The St-Gilles Fair held in September was in full expansion; it was one of the great trading centres between the Mediterranean and northern countries. This prosperity diminished in the 13C due to the competition of the royal port of Aigues-Mortes *(qv)*.

Excommunication. – Before the progress of the Albigensian heresy *(qv)*, Count of Toulouse, Raymond VI was called before Pope Innocent III and ordered to fight against his heretical subjects. It was at St-Gilles, the extreme limit of the county, that the Papal Legate was received; the next day, 15 January 1208, he was assasinated. The Pope immediately excommunicated Raymond VI and preached the Crusades. The count submitted and did penance in St-Gilles on 12 June 1209. However, he soon revolted, again, fighting a losing battle against **Simon de Montfort**, and was killed at Muret in 1213.

ST-GILLES
time: 3/4 hour

In order to understand the abbey's greatness in the end of the 11C and during the 12C, try to imagine the chancel of the former abbey church extending beyond the present chancel; on the church's south side the cloisters, the courtyard of which was surrounded by the chapterhouse, refectory, kitchens and basement storeroom, while other monastic buildings stretched as far as the present Rue de la République and Rue Victor-Hugo.
In the 12C, therefore, stood, on the site of an old sanctuary which had housed the tomb of St Giles, a vast abbey church;

ST-GILLES

Brèche (R. de la)	2
Canal (Quai du)	3
Cimetière (Montée du)	4
Griffeuille (Av. François)	6
Hôtel-de-Ville (R. de l')	7
Jaurès (Pl. Jean)	8
Porte-des-Maréchaux (R.)	9
République (Pl. de la)	12
République (R. de la)	13
Soleil (R. du)	14
Zola (R. Émile)	15
11-Nov.-1918 (Av. du)	16

but due to lack of funds the church had still not been completed the following century. Its plan, influenced by its Burgundian counterparts *(see Michelin Green Guide to Burgundy)*, presented three naves seperated by cruciform pillars an extended transept and an ambulatory with radiating chapels; underneath the nave was the large crypt.
Secularised and established as a collegiate church in 1538, it suffered irrevocable destruction in 1562 during the Wars of Religion. The Huguenots threw the monks into the crypt's well and set the monastery on fire: the church's vaulting collapsed; in 1622 the great belfry was destroyed. In the 17C the church was shortened by half and its vaulting was lowered so that in the future there would be less upkeep. Thus what is left of a magnificent medieval building are the fine west face, remains of the chancel and the crypt.

★★Façade. – Considered one of the finest examples of Romanesque sculpture of the south of France, the façade dates from the mid-12C.

Its architectural ordonnance which evokes a Roman triumphal arch is made up of three doorways with pilasters and porticoes. The upper part was demolished when the building was lowered in the 17C; much of the sculpture was mutilated during the Wars of Religion and especially the Revolution; several columns and capitals were restored in the 19C. The work was carved at one time, according to an initial project which was modified during its carving by several different schools of sculpture. The story told is that of Salvation through the different stages in the life of Christ. The carvers were inspired by the Antique style, notably from the paleochristian sarcophagi, as is shown, by their use of high relief and the representations of volumes (anatomical proportions) and forms (pleated clothing).

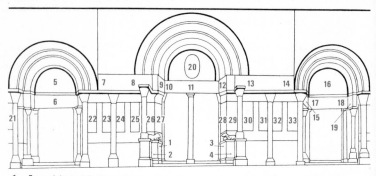

1 – From right to left: Cain offers a grain of wheat to the Lord. Abel sacrifices a lamb.
2 – Murder of Abel by Cain.
3 – A centaur shoots a stag with a bow and arrow.
4 – Balaam and his ass.
5 – Adoration of the Magi.

The great frieze reads left to right and recounts all the events of Holy Week from Palm Sunday to the morning of Pascal Resurrection and the discovery of the empty tomb by the Holy Women.

6 – Christ's entry into Jerusalem (note the realism of the staggering procession).
7 – Judas returning the thirty pieces of silver.
8 – Christ driving out the merchants from the temple.
9 – Christ announcing the prophecy of Peter's denial.
10 – Washing of the feet.
11 – The Last Supper.
12 – The kiss of Judas.
13 – Flagellation.
14 – The carrying of the Cross.

15 – Mary Magdalene prostate before Jesus.
16 – The Crucifixion (note the realistic anatomy of death by suffocation of the crucified who leans on the steps of the cross to catch his breath).
17 – The Holy Women buying spices.
18 – The Holy Women at the Sepulchre of Christ.
19 – Christ appearing before his disciples.
20 – Christ in Majesty surrounded by the symbols of the four Evangelists *(p 66)*.

The art historians identify five stylistic groups with the name of only one master known, that of Brunus.

– Brunus: Matthew (**22**), Bartholomew (**23**), John the Evangelist (**26**), James the Greater (**28**), Paul (**29**); characteristics: antique style, heavy, plain.

– Master "of St Thomas": Thomas (**24**), James the Less (**25**), Peter (**27**), low reliefs of the centre door (**1-2-3-4**); this carver would have worked in the west of France; characteristics: linear quality and animated with a typically Romanesque treatment.

– Soft Master: apostles (**30-31**), left splay of the centre door (**9-10**), tympanum (**5**) and lintel (**6**) of the north door; characteristics: supple drapery modelling the folds around the arms and legs.

– Hard Master: apostles (**32-33**), south door (**15-16-17-18-19**); characteristics long envelopping drapery with voluminous and hard folds sometimes represented in a spiral form, contrasts accentuated by light and shade.

– Master of "St Michael": entablatures on either side of the centre door (**7-8** and **13-14**), St Michael slaying the dragon (**21**); characteristic: very expressive style.

Former Chancel (Ancien chœur) (B). – Outside of the actual church, it corresponds to the part which was devastated in the 17C and razed during the Revolution. The base of the pillars and the walls indicate precisely the former chancel's layout with its ambulatory and radiating chapels. On either side of the ambulatory, two small bell towers were served by spiral staircases, the one on the left remains: Screw of St Giles *(p 167)*.

★Crypt (Crypte). – This low church (50m – 164ft long, 25m – 82ft wide) was the scene of one of the West's most important pilgrimages. It lasted three days and some 50 000 people marched past the venerated tomb of St Giles. It was once covered with groined vaulting, which remains in several bays to the right of the entrance. Pointed vaulting from the mid-12C is what remains in the crypt; this vaulting is among the oldest accounted for in France. The decoration of certain arches adorned with a plain band contrast with some of the others elegantly ornamented with ribbons and ovolo moulding in the bay preceeding the tomb (11C); there is a lovely keystone of Christ Blessing and Smiling. An antique-like influence can be detected, this same influence is seen in the pillars' fluting.

Note the staircase and ramp the monks used to reach the upper church. Sarcophagi, antique altars and Romanesque capitals are also worth admiring.

★ **Screw of St Giles** (Vis' de St-Gilles). – This spiral staircase served the abbey
Ⓥ church's north bell tower. Completed in 1142 it has always been admired by the
Brotherhood of Stonemasons who during their habitual tour of France stopped to
study it (they left graffiti), made in reduced size, it has been the object of numerous
stonemasons' masterpieces. Climb to the top (50 steps) to appreciate the rare
quality of the cutting and joining of the stone.

The steps rest on the central core and the cylindrical walls. The perfection of the
interlocking stone composes a spiral vault of nine voussoirs. The art of the
stonemason appears in the double concavity and convexity of each voussoir.

ADDITIONAL SIGHTS

Ⓥ **Monks Storeroom** (Cellier des Moines) (D). – The storeroom presents three 11C
bays on pointed arches.

Ⓥ **Romanesque House** (Maison Romane) (E). – This house is the birthplace of Guy
Foulque, elected pope in 1265 under the name of Clement IV.

It houses, on the ground floor, a small lapidary museum containing the ruins of the
former abbey church: tympanum, capitals, keystone, 12C low reliefs where the
apostles can be identified, 3C sarcophagi in white marble. The 1st floor is devoted
to local fauna (ornithology).

On the 2nd floor, which has preserved its chimney with a conical canopy (12C),
there is a view of the town's red tiled roofs.

A room, known as the Old St Giles's room, presents tools and objects relating to
the old trades: the shepherd, coopery, life in the fields, the vineyards, olive groves
and domestic life.

Aristide Dumont Pumping Station (Station de Pompage Aristide Dumont). – *5km –
3 miles northeast on the D 38 to the place called Pichegu.*
This pumping station is one of Europe's most important: it is the heart of the
hydraulic system for the Lower Rhône and Languedoc regions.

The station is located at the intersection of two canals; one of which is the main
irrigation canal which starts 12km-7 1/2 miles from there in the Rhône, north of
Arles to reach the Montpellier region and the Costières Canal which goes north. The
station raises the water to a level by which it can flow by gravity through the
Languedoc Plain in order to irrigate it.

ST-JULIEN   Pop 825

Michelin map 🆃🆃 west of fold 5 or 🆃🆃🆃 fold 33 – 14km – 8 1/2 miles south of
Gréoux-les-Bains

The village overlooks the Provence Plateau carpeted with a thin layer of shrubbery.
Here and there a small village or town becomes the centre of an area of cultivated
land where cereals, vineyards and olive groves grow. Above the village (alt 579m
– 1 900ft), a terrace offers a **view★** over Upper Provence: Durance Valley, Valensole
Plateau, Alps of Provence, and Ste-Baume and Ste-Victoire Mountains.

Church (Église). – 11C. This is the typical kind of church found in Upper Provence.
It contains a 17C high altar in gilt wood and a rood beam (well conserved). The
chancel is lit by a square bell tower which forms a lantern.

Ramparts (Remparts). – Continue northwest into the street, which is an extension
of the road you arrived on, to a fortified gateway. From here another lovely **view**
of the surrounding countryside opens out. The ruins of the 13C ramparts are all that
is left to show that this was once a stronghold.

ST-MARCEL Caves (Grottes de ST-MARCEL)

Michelin map 🆃🆃 fold 9 or 🆃🆃🆃 fold 15 or 🆃🆃🆃 fold 23 – Local map p 61

Overlooking the Ardèche Gorges, these caves offer huge corridors decorated with
voluminous stalagmites and crystallisations.

Ⓥ **Tour**. – After a 1/2 hour walk you will reach a vast gallery remarkable by the
regularity of its vaulting; then proceed to the upper gallery. A platform made of
enormous *gours (qv)* – vast basins, sometimes in the form of holy water basins made
by the calcite-filled water – lead to a third level of galleries with lovely concretions;
sparkling vaulting, eccentrics, cave flowers. The visit ends in the enormous Dining
Hall (Salle du Repas) the roof of which is in the form of an inverted ship's hull. The
speleologists have uncovered more than 20km – 12 miles of cave network.

★★ ST-MAXIMIN-LA-STE-BAUME   Pop 5 552

Michelin map 🆃🆃 folds 4 and 5 or 🆃🆃🆃 fold 33

St-Maximin, lies at the centre of a small basin, once the bottom of a lake; not far
from the source of the Argens in a region of flat depressions; the village is flanked
to the north by wooded hills and vineyards and to the south by the mountainous
foundations of Ste-Baume Massif *(qv)*.

Former new town the grid pattern of which presents irregularities, St-Maximin,
enlivened by small shaded squares and fountains, groups its houses around the
admirable basilica.

The church stands on the spot, where according to legend Mary Magdalene *(p 171)*
and later St Maximinus were buried.

When St Maximinus died, the village, of Gallo-Roman origin, took his name and acquired fame during the 13C when the tombs of the two saints were discovered. (Mary Magdalene, after having lived many years of penitence in the Ste-Baume Cave – p 173 is said to have been buried in the crypt of St Maximinus). The sarcophagus contained the relics of the saint which were hidden in 716 for fear of the Saracens who were devastating the region, and uncovered in 1279 by Charles of Anjou, brother to St Louis. The spot was indicated by the saint herself in a dream. In 1295 Pope Bonifacio VIII recognised the relics and on the site of the crypt Charles of Anjou had built a basilica and monastery.

The monastery was a vast U-shaped three storey building built on to the basilica. He installed the Dominican friars who were in charge of guarding the relics and supervise what soon became a major pilgrimage. During the Revolution the Dominicans were expelled but by great good fortune the basilica and monastery housed **Lucien Bonaparte,** Napoleon's youngest brother, then officer in charge of military store. He turned the cathedral into a food depot and saved the organ from harm by having the *Marseillaise* played regularly upon it. The young officer, with an intelligence second only to Napoleon's, became a well-known figure in the town, as he developed into a rousing speaker and was elected president of the local Jacobin club.

In 1858 the Royal Convent of St Maximinus became a School of Theology, reoccupied by the Père Lacordaire.

In 1957 the Dominicans left the convent; it was bought in 1966 by an association of public and private benefactors and today houses a **cultural centre** (Centre culturel de Rencontre: le Collège d'Échanges Contemporains) which organises a number of programmes, especially in the summer.

★★**Basilica.** – Time: *3/4 hour.* The basilica's construction, on the foundations of a 6C Merovingian church, began in 1295 by command of Charles II, Prince of Salerno future king of Sicily and Count of Provence. Work continued until 1316 (chancel followed by five bays of the nave); halted for more than a century, work began again in 1404 when the crypt of the old church was reduced to ground level to allow for the construction of the new basilica floor. From 1508-32 work proceeded and the building took on its present state.

Exterior. – Devoid of transepts and ambulatory, the basilica has a squat appearance reinforced by the absence of a belfry, its incomplete west front, and the massive buttresses reaching the nave walls high up. It is nonetheless the most important example of the Gothic style in Provence combining the influences of the north, especially of Bourges, with the local architectural traditions.

Interior. – The building comprises a nave, chancel and two aisles of remarkable height.

The two storey 29m – 95ft high nave has pointed vaulting; its keystones picture the arms of the Counts of Provence and Kings of France; the very large chancel is closed off by a pentagonal apse. The aisles, which were only 18m – 92ft high to allow for a clerestory, end with quadrangular apsidal chapels. The side chapels were raised less than the aisles so as to allow the light to filter through.

1) The organ, which has a double case and still has the pipes saved by Lucien Bonaparte, was made by the lay Dominican, Isnard of Tarascon and ranks with the one in Poitiers Cathedral, as one of the finest 18C instruments in France.

2) Fine gilded wood statue of John the Baptist.

3) 15C altarpiece of the Four Saints: Lawrence, Anthony, Sebastian and Thomas Aquinas.

4) Reliquary containing the sumptuous cope of St Louis of Anjou, Bishop of Toulouse (1274-97); 30 silk embroidered medallions of different colours illustrating the lives of Christ and the Virgin encircled by four winged cherubim *(electric switch on the pillar).*

5) Rosary altar adorned with 18C gilded wood statue of the Virgin; 16C altar front carved with four low reliefs recounting the life of Mary Magdalene.

6) 17C choir screen carved in wood with wrought iron inlets emblasoned with the arms of France.

7) Choir stall panelling enclosing 94 stalls, decorated with 22 medallions of men and women saints of the Dominican Order, carved in the 17C by the lay brother, Vincent Funel.

8) 17C stucco decoration by J. Lombard before which stand, to the right, a terracotta of Mary Magdalene's communion, to the left, a marble of the saint's ecstasy and, at the centre, the altar surmounted by a glory.

9) Pulpit carved in 1756 by the Dominican, Louis Gaudet, with representations on the sounding board, in great size, of the ecstasy of Mary Magdalene, and on the staircase, panels of her life. The rail is cut from a single piece of wood and is a masterpiece in itself.

10) 15C Provençal School predella (lower part of of the altarpiece) illustrating the beheading of John the Baptist, St Martha taming the Tarasque *(qv)* on Tarascon Bridge and Christ appearing to Mary Magdalene.

11) 16C painted wood **retable★** by Ronzen of the Crucifixion, surrounded by 18 medallions.

Crypt (Crypte). – The crypt was the funeral vault of a late 4 – early 5C Roman villa. It contains 4 sarcophagi of the 4C: Saint Mary Magdalene, Saints Marcella and Susan, Saints Maximinus and Cedonius. At the back there is a 19C reliquary containing a cranium long venerated as that of Mary Magdalene's. Four marble and stone tablets depict carved figures of the Virgin, Abraham and Daniel (c500).

★Former Royal Monastery (Ancien Couvent Royal). – Started in the 13C at the same time as the basilica, against which it has been built to the north; it was completed in the 15C. The **cloisters★** with a

Sarcophagus of St Cedonius (detail)
in the Basilica of St Maximinus

great purity of line include 32 bays. At their entrance note the 1C milestone. Its garden contains an abundance of foliage: boxwood, yew, lime and cedars. It serves as the stage set for the St-Maximinus Musical Evenings (Soirées musicales de St-Maximin) in the summer.

The conventual buildings include a former chapel, with fine vaulting in the form of a depressed arch, the former refectory of five bays (on the north wall note the lectern) and the **chapterhouse**, with its lovely pointed vault above slender columns ending in foliated capitals and held by very low corbels; it is entered through a door flanked by two windows. The large 17C guest house now houses the town hall.

Old Quarter. – South of the church opens a covered passageway which joins Rue Colbert; lined with 14C arcades, it indicates the location of the old Jewish ghetto. On the street's other side is the house lived in by Lucien Bonaparte from 1793-4 and the old hospital.

Retrace your steps, and you will reach a small square dominated by the Clock Tower (Tour de l'Horloge) and its bell cage.

On the right as you walk to Rue de Gaulle, there is a fine 16C house with a corbelled turret.

ST-MICHEL-DE-FRIGOLET Abbey

Michelin map **81** fold 11 or **245** fold 29 or **246** fold 25 – 18km – 11 miles south of Avignon

The abbey is nestled in a hollow, fragrant with rosemary, lavender and thyme and sheltered by cypresses, pines and olives.

Ten centuries of pilgrimages. – The abbey was founded in the 10C by monks from Montmajour (qv), who came to this idyllic spot to recover from the feavers they contracted while draining the marshes around their mother house. They dedicated the chapel to Our Lady of Goodly Remedy (Notre-Dame-du-Bon-Remède), which became the object of a pilgrimage which continues even to this day.

Religious of different orders inhabited the conventual buildings before all was confiscated at the Revolution and later converted into a boarding school attended by Frédéric Mistral (qv) from 1839-41. The school shut down in 1841 and the abbey was abandoned. In 1858 the abbey was bought and Premonstrants were installed. The owner, a certain R.P. Edmond, had the idea in the mid-19C to surround the abbey with a neo-medieval curtain wall complete with towers, crenellations and machicolations. Vast pilgrim guest houses as well as a farm, workshops and a lavishly ornate church were added.

Expulsions. – In 1880 religious persecution chased the monks out and the abbey underwent a real siege at that time. The religious community was once again dispersed in 1903, the result of the Law of Congregations: the Premonstrants fled to Belgium. During World War I the abbey was converted into a concentration camp; later the Premonstrants returned to their abbey.

ABBEY time: 3/4 hour

The beauty and simplicity of the religious ceremonies are one of the abbey's charms.

Abbey church (Église Abbatiale) and Notre-Dame-du-Bon-Remède. – Built in the 19C by R.P. Edmond, the abbey church possesses lavish decoration. The 11C **Chapel of N.-D.-du-Bon-Remède,** which was the abbey's precursor, serves as the apse of the church's north nave; it contains lovely gilt **panelling★** a gift of Anne of Austria, who had come in pilgrimage to ask for a son after many years of childless marriage; her son, Louis XIV, was born in 1638.

The panelling has framed 14 canvases attributed to the school of Nicolas Mignard. In the hall, added in the 19C, onto which opens the refectory, note the handsome modern *santon* figures in olive wood.

Cloisters (Cloître). – Early 12C. In the north gallery a number of Roman ruins have been collected: friezes, capitals, masks.

Chapterhouse (Salle Capitulaire). – 17C. The monks who resisted were arrested here in 1880.

Museum (Musée). – The museum contains Provençal furniture, a fine collection of 18-19C pharmacy jars and the chapel's Renaissance doorway.

St-Michel. – This very plain 12C church is the monastery's former church. It has a fine stone roof topped by an openwork crest. The façade was redone in the 19C. The interior was heightened 1m 1/2 – 4ft thus modifying the building's equilibrium.

★ ST-RÉMY-DE-PROVENCE   Pop 8 439

Michelin map 🎔 fold 1 or 🎔 fold 29 or 🎔 fold 26 – Local map p 56 – Facilities

Gateway to the Alpilles Chain *(qv)*, St Rémy symbolises beautifully what Provence is, whether it be through its decor of plane tree-shaded boulevards, fountains splashing in the squares, charming old town alleyways or the atmosphere which reigns especially on market day and traditional fairs.
The village, founded after the destruction of Glanum *(p 167)*, developed under the protection of the Abbey of St-Remi of Reims, from whence it got its name.
A town of gardeners due to this region, which is a great fruit and market gardening centre; it has been, for a long time, specialising in the production and trade of flower and vegetable seeds. However, its main source of income is tourism enhanced by its thyme and rosemary laden streets and by the presence of moving Roman ruins.
Birthplace of Nostradamus, St-Rémy has been dazzled by the genius of Van Gogh and by the inspiration of the Provençal poets from Roumanille to Marie Mauron *(p 25)*.
South of town, the Chapel of N.-D.-de-Pitié houses part of the works given to France by the painter Mario Prassinos (1916-85).

★★ROMAN MONUMENTS (LES ANTIQUES) *time: 1 1/2 hours*

Leave St-Rémy by ③ on the town plan (p 168).

The Roman Monuments lie on a plateau below the Alpilles's last foothills, 1km – 1/2 mile south of St-Rémy. In this pleasant spot, from where the view extends over the Comtat Plain, Durance Valley and Mount Ventoux, stood the prosperous city of Glanum. It was abandoned after Barbarian invasions in the end of the 3C; two magnificent monuments – the mausoleum and commemorative arch – remain.

★★Mausoleum (Mausolée).

– This monument is 18m – 60ft high and is one of the most outstanding in the Roman world and the best preserved; it lacks but the pine cone finial crowning its dome. For a long time it was believed to have been built as a sepulchre for a noble from Glanum and his spouse, however, the excavations conducted by Henri Rolland have established that it was not a tomb but a cenotaph, that is to say a monument built in memory of the deceased.
Low reliefs representing battle and hunting

Roman Monuments in St-Rémy-de-Provence

scenes adorn the four walls of the square podium. The first storey, pierced by four arches evoking a commemorative arch, shows on the frieze (depicting naval scenes), of the northern architrave an inscription which says "Sextius, Lucius Marcus sons of Gaius of the Julii family, to their parents". This most likely implies a posthumous dedication in honour of Emperor Augustus's grandsons, Gaius and Lucius nicknamed the Princes of Youth. The second storey is made up of a rotunda with a Corinthian colonnade which encloses the statues of the two figures.
The archaeologists date the mausoleum to *c*30BC and attribute it to a Rhône Valley workshop under the direction of Italian master craftsmen.

★Commemorative Arch (Arc Municipal). – Perhaps contemporary to the mausoleum, that is to say the first years of Augustus's reign; this arch is the oldest Roman arch of the Narbonensis region. It indicated, on the great way of the Alps, the entrance to Glanum. Its perfect proportions (12.50m – 40ft long, 5.50m – 17ft wide and 8.60m – 27ft high) and the exceptional quality of its carved decoration show Greek influence, quite evident at Glanum.
The sole arcade is carved with a lovely festoon of fruit and leaves; inside, it is adorned with a finely carved hexagonal coffered ceiling. To be seen on either side

of the opening are allegorical symbols of victory and on the sides groups of two prisoners, men and women, at the foot of the booty. The despondency shown on the figures is well rendered.

Art historians feel that the unique form of this arch, mutilated very soon after construction, has inspired some of the 12C Romanesque doorways such as St-Trophime at Arles *(p 66)*. The tiled roof was put on in the 18C.

★**Glanum Excavations.** – The excavations, unearthed since 1921, are located at the
Ⓥ Alpilles Chain's main gap, which dominates them. The site consists of a group of complex structures caused by the existence of several different periods of occupation grouped by the archaeologists into three phases.

The origin of the site is a sacred spring venerated by Celtic-Ligurian people known as the Glanics. This native settlement rapidly came into contact with the merchants of Massalia due to its location at the crossroads of two important roads.

Glanon (or Glanum I) developed under Hellenistic influence which can be seen in the construction, particularly in the technique of bonding (large carved blocks of stone perfectly set without mortar) in the 3 and 2C BC. This Hellenistic community included public buildings (temple, agora, assembly hall, perhaps a theatre), houses with a peristyle and a fortified quarter to the south (sanctuary).

The second phase (Glanum II) began with the Roman conquest during the late 2C *(p 22)* and by the occupation of the country by Marius's army which stopped the Teutonic army. The town most likely suffered when the Teutons passed through; the new buildings were then made by the bonding of irregular stones.

The last phase (Glanum III) follows the conquest of Marseilles by Caesar in 49BC *(p 128)*. Romanisation intensified and under Augustus the town was rebuilt.

In the centre, the old buildings were razed, their debris levelled and filled to make room for a vast horizontal esplanade on which were erected the great public buildings: forum basilica, temples, baths... The private dwellings, which had not disappeared were adapted and transformed, others were built. The walls were in regular ashlar work stuck with mortar.

In *c*270, Glanum was prey to the Germanic tribes and it was abandoned. The canals, no longer maintained, clogged up, and the alluvium descending from the Alpilles, slowly covered the site. The excavations unearthed with caution an enormous quantity of ruins, the interpretation of which, still today, has a number of theories: the vestiges discovered are exhibited at the Hôtel de Sade *(p 169)*.

Antes's House. – This lovely house of the Greek type, built according to the 2C BC taste, was laid out around a peristyled central courtyard and cistern. The entrance bay *(antes)* of one of the rooms has preserved its two pilasters. The ruins of a staircase and the low columns lead to believe that the house had one storey. It was modified during the Gallo-Roman period.

Fountain basin. – Elegant 2C BC fountain.

Atys's House. – Beside Antes's House, this house was divided, in its primitive period, into two parts (peristyled court to the north and pool to the south) joined by a large door. Consequently, a sanctuary to Cybele was set up in the area where the peristyle stood; note the votive altar dedicated to the goddess's ears.

Baths. – These baths date back to the time of Julius Caesar. Its plan is easily recognised and followed the classical route *(p 34)*: a *gymnasium* (**1**), *frigidarium* (**2**), *tepidarium* (**3**), *caldarium* (**4**), *palestra,* set up for physical exercise and athletic games, once lined with porticoes, cold swimming pool perhaps, finally, with running water. The lovely mosaics (**5, 6**) came from a house razed when the baths were constructed.

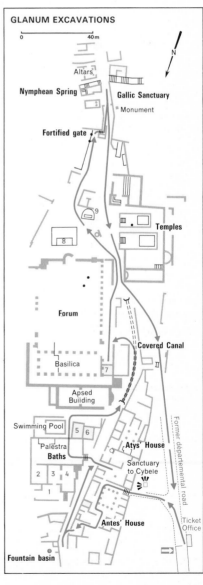

GLANUM EXCAVATIONS

0 ——————— 40m

N

Altars

Nymphean Spring

Gallic Sanctuary

Monument

Fortified gate

Temples

9

8

Forum

Covered Canal

Basilica

Apsed Building

Swimming Pool

5 6

Palestra

Baths

Atys' House

Sanctuary to Cybele

2 3 4

1

Antes' House

Ticket Office

Former départemental road

Fountain basin

Covered canal. – This remarkable work, probably a drain, was so constructed that the stone covering also served as Glanum's main street pavement. It skirts an apsed building near which a great number of altars dedicated for the most part to Silvanus, the god with the mallet, were found.

Forum. – The forum was built on the ruins of Pre-Roman buildings which the archaeologists are seeking to identify. It was closed to the north by the basilica (a multi-purpose building mostly for commercial and administrative purposes) of which 24 foundation pillars remain and under which Sulla's House was discovered. In the house were uncovered mosaics (7), most likely the oldest ones accounted for in Gaul. South of the basilica lay the forum square lined on each side by a covered gallery and closed to the south by a great decorated apsidal-ended wall. Discovered underneath the forum were a house and the Greek **agora** which was surrounded by colonnades (fragments) magnificently decorated with figure-hewn capitals (exhibited at the Hôtel de Sade).

Temples. – Southwest of the forum (on the right as you go south) stood two twin temples surrounded by a *peribolus,* the southern part of which covered an assembly hall (the Greek bouleuterion) with its tiered seats. These Roman public buildings, the oldest of this kind in Gaul, date back to 30BC and like the mausoleum *(p 166)* were posthumously dedicated to Gaius and Lucius. Important vestiges of their lavish decoration (blocks of cornice, roof decorations, etc) as well as exquisite sculpture (particularly the portraits of Octavian and Julia which will be found in the Hôtel de Sade) have been excavated.

Facing the temples, in front of the forum, was a triangular square on which stood a paved platform (8) and a monumental fountain (9). Further east was the theatre district.

Fortified gate. – This remarkable Hellenistic vestige used, like at St-Blaise *(qv)*, the Massaliote technique of large well-matched rectangular blocks of stone with merlons and gargoyles. The ramparts defended the sanctuary, they included a postern with a zig-zag passageway and a carriage gate.

Nymphean spring. – The source round which Glanum developed is marked by a pool with masonry walls of large, Greek style stones. It was restored by Agrippa in 20BC who built right next to it a temple dedicated to Valetudo, goddess of health (ruins of three fluted columns). A staircase leads up to the swimming pool still fed with water from the spring. On the south side, a sanctuary to Hercules was established; a statue of the demi-god and several votive altars have been discovered.

Gallic sanctuary. – Set up in terraces, orientated towards the rising sun, this sanctuary, dates from the 6C BC. In this area were uncovered kneeling warriors and stelae with carved skulls identical to those found in the great Salian towns.

⊘ **Former Monastery of St-Paul-de-Mausole (Ancien monastère de St-Paul-de-Mausole).** – Located near the Roman monuments, to which its name is linked, this monastery of Augustinian and then Franciscain canons was transformed into a convalescent home in the mid-18C. It preserves the memory of Van Gogh *(qv)* who voluntarily interned himself from 3 May 1889 to 6 May 1890. He had, at his disposal, a workroom on the ground floor and a bedroom on the 1st floor. He continued to paint: his life at the hospital, nature *(Cypress Trees, The Sower)*, self-portraits and copied the great masters including Rembrandt, Millet, Delacroix, Gustave Doré *(The Prisoners' Watch)* and the extraordinary *Starry Night*.

The small church dates from the end of the 12C (18C façade) and has a fine square bell tower adorned with Lombard arcades. Beside it the **cloisters★** present a fine Romanesque decor: the capitals of the small columns are carved with varied motifs (foliage, animals, masks etc) in a style similar to that of Montmajour and St-Trophime in Arles.

THE TOWN OF ST-RÉMY-DE-PROVENCE *time: 1 hour*

Start at Place de la République

Place de la République. – Beside the ring road, this square is on the site of the medieval ramparts and is the heart of the town, animated by its café terraces and the bustle on its market days.

St-Martin presents an imposing 19C classical façade which had to be rebuilt in the 1820s after collapsing; it has preserved its 14C bell tower. Inside there is a fine organ case.

Take Avenue de la Résistance, then right immediately onto the small Rue Hoche.

Rue Hoche is lined by the ruins of the 14C fortifications; standing in bad condition is the **birthplace of Nostradamus (D)**.

ST-RÉMY-DE-PROVENCE

0   200 m

LES ANTIQUES
ST-PAUL-DE-MAUSOLE

Turn around by taking Rue du 8-Mai 1945 which goes into Place Jules-Pélissier.
On this square stands the town hall which was formerly a 17C monastery.

Take Rue Roux and then Rue Carnot.

At no 5 Rue Carnot, the Roux House, Gounod *(qv)* gave his first audition of *Mireille* in 1863. A couple of yards further on Place Favier (Le Planet or the former herbal market place) is lined with fine 15 and 16C *hôtels,* converted into museums.

Hôtel de Sade (B). – This 15-16C townhouse contains an important **archaeological collection★** (part of which is open to the public) where remarkable finds from the Glanum excavations can be seen.
Ground floor: Gallic funerary stelae in the form of obelisks, votive altars, sarcophagi, columns, acroterions and cornice fragments from the temples of Gaius and Lucius. In the back of the courtyard are remains of 4C baths, and a 5C baptistry, evidence showing the origins of St-Rémy having succeeded the founding of Glanum.
First floor: capitals, very fine acroterion from the temple dedicated to the goddess Valetudo (represented with a torque or necklace), miscellaneous ex-votos, votive altars, statue of a captured Gaul, statue of Hercules from Hercules's sanctuary, lovely low relief with the effigy of Hermes and Fortuna.
Second floor displays objects evoking daily life at Glanum from the Greeks to the Gallo-Roman occupation: tools, bronze and wood objects, funerary urns, pottery, oil lamps (among them note the rare candelabrum with two rows, one above the other, of lamps), jewellery (note the magnificent ring made of rock crystal adorned with the finely carved head of a woman). Prehistoric collection (flints, bones).

Pierre de Brun Alpilles Chain Museum (**Musée des Alpilles Pierre-de-Brun**) (**M**). – The museum is located in the vast 16C Mistral de Mondragon Mansion built round a fine courtyard with a round turreted staircase and overlooked by loggias. The exhibits concern popular arts and traditions.
Documents concerning Nostradamus as well as minerals from the Alpilles Chain are also displayed.

★★ STE-BAUME Massif

Michelin map ▨▨ fold 14 or ▨▨▨ folds 45 and 46

Ste-Baume is the name of a forest and of a cave – *baoumo* is Provençal for cave. The cave, where Mary Magdalene retired, which subsequently gave its name to this massif, is now a well-known place of pilgrimage. The forest is magnificent and unique for several reasons. The massif forms at its summit a long crest, one of the peaks of which, St Pilon (alt 994m – 3 261ft), offers a splendid panorama.

GEOGRAPHICAL NOTES

The massif. – Covering the most surface and the highest of the Provençal mountain ranges, Ste-Baume Massif reaches an altitude of 1 147m – 3 763ft at the Ste-Baume Signal Station. It answers to the general east-west orientation of the mountain system of Pyrenean origin which predominates in Provence *(details on land formation p 12).* The assymmetrical relief, frequent in this region is very accentuated, like at Ste-Victoire, but in the opposite sense.
The arid and barren southern face climbs in a gentle slope from Cuges Basin up to the 12km – 7 1/2 mile crest; the northern face, a steep vertical slope approximately 300m – 984ft high shelters the famous cave; below lies the state forest beside the Plan d'Aups's permeable plateau, similar to the Causses.
This massif, typically Provençal by its poor soil and brilliantly white rocky ridge is northern in aspect because of its forest cover.
Mountaineers can climb from the Bertagne Peak to the eastern extremity of the chain, peaks of more than 100m – 328ft (some rise 250m – 820ft).

★★ **The forest.** – Sprawled over 100ha – 247 acres and varying in altitude from 680 to 1 000m – 2 231 to 3 281ft, the position this forest holds among French forests is exceptional. Of glaciary origin, this forest was most likely a sacred wood at the time of the Gauls and this tradition has come down over the centuries. From time immemorial and even today, Ste-Baume cannot be cut down; the continuation of each species is carefully watched.
Its other unique aspect is its forest cover: giant beech, enormous lime trees intermingling with maples. Their high vaulting of light foliage close over the thick, dark undergrowth of yew, spindle, ivy and holly. It is astonishing to see deep in Provence a forest cover typical of the forests of Ile-de-France, which can be explained by the fact that the shadow given by the steep cliff, which on the southern side overlooks the wooded area, retains a cold and humid region genuinely northern in climate. As soon as this ridge ends Mediterranean foliage reappears.

HISTORY AND LEGEND...

Mary Magdalene. – Mary Magdalene, a princess of royal blood, born the same year as Jesus Christ led a dissolute life until the day she heard Christ preaching. The repentant Mary Magdalene subsequently became a follower of Christ.
For 13 years after the Crucifixion, Mary Magdalene lived with Jesus's mother until, according to an oral Provençal legend, together with Lazarus and his sister, Martha, St Maximinus and other saintly people, she was set adrift in a boat which came ashore at Stes-Marie-de-la-Mer *(qv).* Mary Magdalene preached the Evangile with St Maximinus, Aix's first bishop. Finally in order to atone her past faults, she retired to the cave at Ste-Baume.

The saint spent 33 years in the solitude of her cave praying and contemplating. Anticipating death she descended into the plain and sought out St Maximinus who gave her last communion and later buried her. At the place where, according to tradition, her last communion took place, on the right of the road coming down from Ste-Baume, some hundred yards before the entrance to St-Maximin Abbey, Petit Pilon Monument stands.

The pilgrimage. – The cave has been venerated since the beginning and in the 5C the monks of St Cassien settled here and in St-Maximin Abbey. Its fame attracted a number of pilgrims, among them the illustrious.

Then in the 11C, it was said that the relics of Mary Magdalene were stolen and taken to Vézelay which became one of the main pilgrim centres of Christianity *(see Michelin Green Guide to Burgundy)*. But in 1279 Charles of Anjou discovered the saint's remains at St-Maximin Abbey and the Provençal pilgrimage replaced the one at Vézelay. A number of French kings (including St Louis), several popes (especially those from Avignon), thousands of lords, millions of the faithful flocked to Ste-Baume. One of Good King René's first public appearances was to go to the cave, accompanied by his nephew Louis XI.

Tradition has it that each engaged couple built on the path up to the cave a pile of rocks; the number of rocks in the pile meant the number of children desired in the future household. Beside the proud rock piles stood unassuming menhirs.

As of 1295 the Dominicans had the protection of the cave. Their guest house situated right close to the cave was burned down during the Revolution. Traces of its site are still visible on the rock side.

In 1859 Père Lacordaire brought the Dominicans back to the cave and to St-Maximin Abbey. The guest house was rebuilt according to his directions below the plateau. It functions under the spiritual direction of the Dominicains but for a lay director, who is there to supervise all the technical services.

For the feast day of Mary Magdalene 21-22 July as well as at Easter and Christmas nocturnal masses are held in the cave.

ROUND TOUR FROM GÉMENOS

69km – 43 miles – about 3 hours, not including the ascent of St-Pilon

Gémenos. – Pop 4 548. Facilities. The small town, where the 17C château now serves as the town hall, stands where the small green St-Pons Valley opens into the larger Huveaune.

> *Drive 3km – 2 miles up the D 2 along St-Pons Valley.*

★**St-Pons Park** (Parc de St-Pons). – *Park the car before the bridge and walk along the path beside the stream.* An old watermill fed by St-Pons stream, a Vauclusian spring, and the extensive ruins of a 13C Cistercian abbey, abandoned in the 15C, are set in a wooded park of beech, hornbeam, ash and maple, uncommon trees for so southerly a latitude. In the spring there are Judas trees in flower.

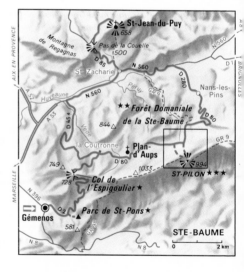

The road climbs the steep bare southern slope cut into a deep circus.

★**Espigoulier Pass** (Col de l'Espigoulier). – Alt 728m – 2 390ft. The views from the pass extend over the Ste-Baume Massif itself, Aubagne Plain, St-Cyr Chain, Marseilles and Étoile Chain.

The descent down the north face offers further views of the Étoile and of Mount Ste-Victoire beyond Fuveau Basin.

> *At La Couronne turn right into the D 80.*

Plan-d'Aups. – The small health resort is distinguished by a correspondingly small Romanesque church.

Guest house (Hôtellerie). – The guest house 675m – 2 215ft up on the plateau in the lee of the forest, was rebuilt in 1863; and continues to house pilgrims. It became a cultural and spiritual centre in its own right in 1968; in 1972 a chapel was created in the elegant vaulted hall, the original pilgrim shelter.

To the left of the guest house is the austere cemetery.

Access to the cave. – *1 hour on foot Rtn. There are two alternative starts to the route: the first is along a path left of the guest house and through the Canapé, a group of moss-covered rocks; the second, which is easier, is from the D 80-D 95 or the Oak Tree crossroads (Carrefour des Chênes), along the "Kings' Way" (Chemin des Rois). After a pleasant walk through the lovely Ste-Baume forest cover, the two paths meet at the Oratory crossroads (Carrefour de l'Oratoire), where a wide path on the right leads to a flight of steps cut into the rock face; halfway up there is a door decorated with a shield with fleur-de-lis and a bronze Calvary in a niche to the left.*

Terrace (Terrasse). – The stairway (150 steps) ends at a terrace on which a stone Cross and bronze *Pietà* (it has been set up as the 13th Station of the Cross) stand. The terrace itself commands a **view★** of Mount Ste-Victoire, Mount Aurélien, which prolongs it to the right and in the foreground, Plan d'Aups, the guest house and dense woodland.

Cave (Grotte). – The semicircular cave lies north of the terrace at an altitude of 946m – 3 105ft. Inside, to the right of the high altar, is a shrine with relics of Mary Magdalena brought from St-Maximin-la-Ste-Baume Abbey *(qv);* behind the altar, 3m – 10ft up the wall, is an irregular cavity, the only dry place in the cave, known as the Place of Penance, which contains a recumbent statue of the saint.

★★★ **St-Pilon.** – *2 hours on foot Rtn starting at the Oratory crossroads (Carrefour de l'Oratoire). Pass in front of the oratory and follow the right hand path (red and white GR 9 signs) which climbs to the abandoned Parisians' Chapel (Chapelle des Parisiens) and continues by a zigzag route and a turn to the right to the St-Pilon Pass (Col du St-Pilon). A column, since replaced by the small chapel, formerly marked the summit – hence the name. According to legend, angels bore Mary Magdalena to this spot seven times a day so that she might listen to the music of paradise.*

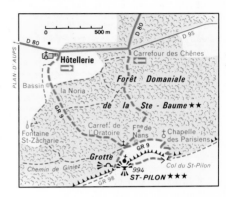

From St-Pilon (alt 994m – 3 261ft) a magnificent **panorama★★★** (viewing table) can be had: to the north the guest house, in the foreground Mount Ventoux in the distance, the Luberon, Mount Olympe and nearer Mount Aurélien; to the southeast Maures Massif, southwest onto Ste-Baume Massif and La Ciotat Bay; northwest on to Alpilles Chain and Mount Ste-Victoire.

Return to the car and make for Nans-les-Pins along the D 80.

The road as it descends through the woods affords views of Mount Regagnas.

In Nans-les-Pins turn left into the D 280 which crosses a pinewood before meeting the N 560 where you turn left to travel the Upper Huveaune Valley to St-Zacharie.

St-Jean-du-Puy Oratory (Oratoire de St-Jean-du-Puy). – *9km – 6 miles from St-Zacharie, plus 1/4 hour on foot Rtn.* Turn right into the D 85 from which, as it climbs by means of hairpin bends, there are views of St-Zacharie Basin and, in the distance the Ste-Baume Massif. Shortly after the Pas-de-la-Couelle, a narrow track on the right leads up a short slope to a military radar post. Park the car and continue on foot to the oratory. From the site there is a good **view★** of Mount Ste-Victoire and the St-Maximin Plain to the north, the Maures and Ste-Baume Massifs to the southeast, Mount Regagnas in the foreground and the Étoile Chain and Aix countryside to the west.

Continue along the N 560 to Le Pujol where you turn left into the D 45ᴬ.

The road first ascends the Valley of the Vede, a stream at the foot of terraced hillsides, before turning aside to overlook the bare, rock walled gorges.

At La Coutronne, turn right for Gémenos along the road taken in the opposite direction at the outset.

★ STES-MARIES-DE-LA-MER   Pop 2 045

Michelin map 🗺 fold 19 or 🗺 fold 41 or 🗺 fold 27 – Local map 97 – Facilities

Between the Mediterranean and the Launes and Impérial Lagoons, in the heart of the Camargue, Stes-Maries-de-la-Mer can be distinguished by its fortified church.

The saintly ship. – According to the Provençal legend, in *c*40, in the boat, abandoned to the waves by the Jews of Jerusalem, which, without the aid of sail or oar, fetched up safely on the shore where Stes-Maries is now situated, were Mary, the mother of James, Mary Magdalene, Martha and her brother Lazarus, St-Maximinus, Mary Salome, the mother of James Major and John, and Cedonius, the man born blind. Sarah, the two Marys' black servant, left behind on the shore, wept aloud until Mary Salome threw her mantle on the water so that Sarah could walk over it to join the others. The legend continues that after erecting a simple oratory to the Virgin on the shore, the disciples separated; Martha went to Tarascon *(qv)*, Mary Magdalene to Ste-Baume *(qv)*, Lazarus to Marseilles *(qv)*, Maximinus and Cedonius to Aix *(qv)*. The two Marys and Sarah remained in Camargue and were buried in the oratory.

19 centuries of pilgrimage. – The saints' tomb rapidly became the object of a cult attracting pilgrims from afar while gipsies and other nomads developed a particular veneration for Sarah.

By the mid-9C the oratory (believed to date from the 6C) had been replaced by a fortified church which, in 869, was being incorporated in the town ramparts under the personal supervision of the Archbishop of Arles, when suddenly the Saracens made a lightning raid and carried off the archbishop.

In the short time it took to collect the ransom of 150 livres of silver, 159 mantles, 150 swords and 150 slaves, the prelate died; unperturbed, the Saracens returned with the corpse, set apart on a throne, and departed with the ransom before the Arlesians discovered their losses.

In the 11C the monks of Montmajour established a priory and in the 12C rebuilt the church which was at the same time incorporated into the fortifications. In the end of the 14C the church's war-like appearance was inforced by the addition of machicolations.

During the Barbarian invasions the saints' remains were buried under the chancel. In 1448, King René *(qv)* ordered the exhumation of the saints whose relics were then enshrined with great ceremony and have remained the object of a deep and widespread veneration ever since.

Stes-Maries-de-la-Mer's feast days. – Two vast celebratory pilgrimages are still held here each year for the Virgin Mary's two half-sisters on 24 and 25 May, the **Gipsy Celebration**★★, for Mary, the mother of James and the Sunday in October closest to 22 October for Mary Salome.

On the afternoon of the first day, the shrines are brought down from the upper chapel to the chancel. The next day the saints' statues preceeded by the women of Arles in costume, surrounded by Camargue *gardians* on horseback are marched in procession through the streets, to the beach and into the sea. Finally, after vespers, the shrines are returned to their chapel on high.

The arrival of gypsies who come here from the world over add to the picturesque charm of these festivities. They take over the church's crypt where their patron saint, Sarah, lies. They, too, the first day march the richly dressed statue of Sarah through the streets to the sea. They elect their queen here every 3 or 4 years.

26 May, is Baroncelli-Javon *(see Baroncelli Museum p 173)* Memorial Day; the day is one of much celebration and local colour. Camargue *gardians* with the women of Arles in traditional costume take part in such events as the local dance, the *farandole,* the roundup *(ferrade),* horse racing and bull running.

SIGHTS

★**Church (Église)** (B). – From the exterior the massive crenellated walls of this fortified church are decorated with Lombard arcades at the east end. The keep-like structure of the upper chapel, surrounded at the base by a watchpath and surrounded by a crenellated terrace, is dominated by a bell gable (restored in the early 20C).

On the south side note the two fine lions devouring their prey which are believed to have supported a porch.

Interior. – *Enter through the small door on Place de l'Église.* The Romanesque nave (lengthened by two bays in the 15C) is very dark. The chancel raised when the crypt was constructed presents blind arcading held up by 8 marble columns with splendid carved capitals, two of which are historiated one illustrating the incarnation, the other illustrating the Sacrifice of Isaac and the other six are decorated with leaf-work masks and busts of men. South of the nave, protected by a wrought-iron railing is a well of fresh water for use in time of siege.

In the third bay on the north side, above the altar is the boat of the Saint Marys' which is carried in procession by the gypsies in May and the parishoners in October.

South of this altar note the Saints' Pillow a worn block of marble incorporated in a column and discovered during the excavations of 1448 when the saints' relics were discovered.

In the 4th north bay is a pagan altar.

Crypt. – Built under the sanctuary. The altar has been built with part of a sarcophagus; it holds the reliquary containing the presumed relics of St Sarah. Right of the altar stands the statue of Sarah and ex-votos offered by the gipsies.

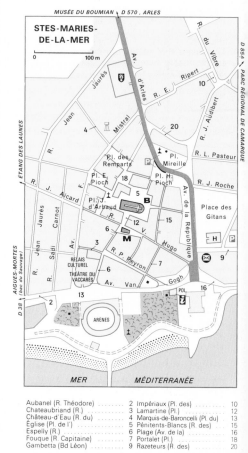

MUSÉE DU BOUMIAN ▷ D 570 , ARLES

STES-MARIES-DE-LA-MER

0   100 m

MER   MÉDITERRANÉE

Aubanel (R. Théodore)	2	Impériaux (Pl. des)	10
Chateaubriand (R.)	3	Lamartine (Pl.)	12
Château-d'Eau (R. du)	4	Marquis-de-Baroncelli (Pl. du)	13
Église (Pl. de l')	5	Pénitents-Blancs (R. des)	15
Espelly (R.)	6	Plage (Av. de la)	16
Fouque (R. Capitaine)	7	Portalet (Pl.)	18
Gambetta (Bd Léon)	9	Razeteurs (R. des)	20

⊘ **Upper Chapel** (Chapelle haute). – The chapel is richly panelled in bright green and gold in the Louis XV style. It houses the reliquary shrine of the two Marys, which is exposed on the nave's clerestory sill; except during pilgrimages.
Mistral *(qv)* set the final scene of his romance *Mireio* in the chapel where his heroine, Mireille, came to pray for help.
There is a statue of *Mireille* by A. Mercié standing in the main square.

⊘ **Watchpath** (Chemin de ronde). – 53 steps. Climb to the paved watchpath which circles the church roof, commanding a **view** of the sea, the town, and the vast Camargue Plain.

⊘ **Baroncelli Museum (Musée Baroncelli) (M).** – Located in the former town hall, the museum exhibits documents relating to Camargue which were amassed by Marquis Folco de Baroncelli-Javon (1869-1943). The marquis was a true *manadier (p 97)* who brought Camargue and its customs back to life. Display cases showing fauna as well as paintings, furniture and tools used by the *gardians* evoke Camargue life.
A narrow spiral staircase (44 steps) leads to a terrace with a **view** of the church and town, Vaccarès Lagoon, Petit Rhône and Camargue.

★★ Mount STE-VICTOIRE

Michelin map 🅱🅰 folds 3 and 4 or 🅰🅰🅴 fold 32

East of Aix-en-Provence lies Mount Ste-Victoire, a limestone range which reaches an altitude of 1 011m – 3 297ft at Mouches Peak. Orientated west to east, this range presents on its south side a sheer drop down to the Arc Basin while on its north side it slopes gently in a series of limestone plateaux towards Durance Plain. A striking contrast exists between the bright red clay of the foot of the mountains and the white limestone of the high mountain ridges especially between Le Tholonet and Puyloubier.
The mountain, immortalised by Cézanne *(qv)* in his paintings was the site of the battle in which Marius's legions overcame the Teutons as they were about to start an advance on Rome *(qv)*.

ROUND TOUR STARTING FROM AIX-EN-PROVENCE

74km – 46 miles – allow 1 full day not including the tour of Aix – local map below

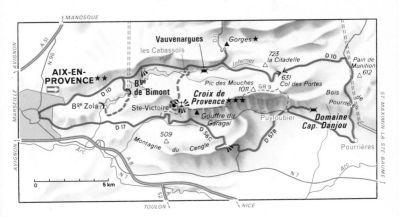

★★**Aix-en-Provence.** – *Tour: 4 hours. Description p 46.*

Leave Aix-en-Provence by the D 10 going east; turn right towards the Bimont Dam.

Bimont Dam (Barrage de Bimont). – The vaulted dam across the Infernet River, is the principal undertaking in the Verdon Canal *(p 111)* extension. It stands in a beautiful, wooded site at the foot of Mount Ste-Victoire; downstream, superb gorges descend *(1 hour on foot Rtn)* to the Zola Dam (built by François Zola, father of the famous author, Émile Zola) the second undertaking in the scheme which supplies water to local towns and villages and irrigation to some 60 local *communes*.

Return to the D 10 and turn right.

The road offers fine views of the dam.

★★★**Cross of Provence.** – *3 1/2 hours on foot Rtn. Park the car to the right of the road at Les Cabassols Farm and walk along the Venturiers path, a muletrack which rises rapidly through a pinewood before easing off into a winding path (easier walking).* The road offers fine views of the reservoir up the hillside. The first staging post is at 900m – 2 950ft, the Notre-Dame de Ste-Victoire Priory, built in 1656 and occupied until 1879. It comprises a chapel, a conventual building and parts of cloisters; a terrace laid in a breach in the wall gives a **view** of Arc Basin and Étoile Chain.
Bear left of the cloisters to make the short climb to the 945m – 3 100ft high summit marked by 17m – 56ft Cross (croix) upon an 11m – 36ft base.
The **panorama**★★★ of Provençal mountains includes: Ste-Baume Massif and Étoile Chain to the south, then turning towards the right the Vitrolles, Crau Plain, Durance Valley, Luberon, Provençal Alps and more to the east Mouches Peak.
To the east on the crest is **Garagaï Chasm** (Gouffre du Garagaï) 150m – 492ft deep, a source of legends and superstitions.

Ⓥ **Château de Vauvenargues.** – The 17C château stands on a rock spur overlooking Infernet Valley. Pablo Picasso who lived here at the end of his life (1881-1973) is buried in the park in front of the château.

> *Beyond Vauvenargues turn left into the D 11 towards Jouques continuing for about 1km – 1/2 mile.*

The road follows lovely steep **gorges★**.

> *Return to the D 10.*

The road goes up the wooded Infernet Gorges, overlooked on the left by the 723m – 2 370ft high Citadelle, and reaches Portes Pass (Col des Portes). During the descent, the Alpine foothills can be distinguished on the horizon.

Take the D 23 to the right which skirts Mount Ste-Victoire on its eastern side and crosses Pourrières Woods; to your left is the Pain de Munition (alt 612m – 2 005ft).

> *In Pourrières turn right to Puyloubier.*

The region is a grape growing area.

Ⓥ **Captain Danjou Pensioners' Hospital** (Domaine Capitaine Danjou). – In Puyloubier, a path to the right leads to Château le Genéral now the Foreign Legion's *(p 87)* Pensioners' Hospital. The tour visits the workshops (pottery, bookbinding, ironworks) and a small museum.

> *Return to Puyloubier and take the D 57ᴮ and then turn right into the D 56ᶜ.*

Good views continue of Mount Ste-Victoire, also of Trets Basin and Ste-Baume Massif before the road climbs the slopes of Mount Cengle. The D 17, on the left, winds between the imposing mass of Mount Ste-Victoire and the Cengle Plateau to reach Aix.

★ SALON-DE-PROVENCE   Pop 35 845

Michelin map 🔢 fold 2 or 🔢 fold 30 or 🔢 fold 12 – Facilities

The town is at the heart of France's olive growing country, which was established here in the 15C and developed by Colbert. Today mineral oils hold an important position in the town's commerce.

A large agricultural market centre, Salon is also the seat of the officers training school for the French Air Force, which was established in 1936. The town is in two parts: the old city climbing up the hill to the castle *(see below)* and the new quarter which lies at its feet, divided by a broad belt of tree-shaded avenues.

The **Salon Jazz Festival** (Festival de Jazz) has gained a solid reputation and is the origin of much of the town's events in the summer *(p 200)*.

On 11 June 1909 the area from Salon to Aix was badly shaken by a severe earth tremor destroying the villages of Vernègues and Rognes and causing ruins in Salon, Lambesc and St-Cannat; some 60 people died.

Adam de Craponne. – Salon's native son, the civil engineer Adam de Craponne, (1527-76) made the region fertile through the construction of the irrigation canal bearing his name which carries water from the Durance along the original river course through the Lamanon Gap to Berre Lagoon and the sea *(p 111)*.

Michel Nostradamus. – Nostradamus chose Salon as his home. Born in St-Rémy *(qv)* in 1503, he studied medicine in Montpellier and traveled during twelve years in Europe and the Far East to try and improve the remedies which he kept secret; and he also studied esoterism.

The success he obtained with his remedy for the plague epidemics of Aix and Lyons roused the jealousy of his colleagues. When the epidemics ceased, he retired to Salon (1547) and took up astrology. His book of predictions entitled *Centuries,* written in the form of verse quatrains, was fantastically successful and attracted the attention of Catherine de' Medici. She came to him and had him read Charles IX's horoscope and showered him profusely with gifts. Nostradamus then attempted meteorology and his Almanach was also successful. He died in Salon in 1566. His son César wrote a remarkable work entitled *Stories and Chronicles of Provence.*

TOWN CENTRE *time: 1 1/2 hours*

> *Follow on foot the itinerary indicated on the town plan (p 175).*

Ⓥ **Empéri Castle (Château de l'Empéri)** (BYZ). – Built on top of Puech Rock, the massive castle dominates the old town. Once the residence of the archbishops of Arles, lords of Salon, the castle was begun in the 10C, rebuilt in the 12 and 13C and remodelled in the 16C; it was transformed into barracks in the 19C and suffered during the 1909 earthquake. A vaulted passage leads to the court of honour decorated with a Renaissance gallery.

The 12C Chapel of Ste-Catherine, the main reception room with its finely carved chimney and some 20 rooms house the Empéri Museum.

★★ **Empéri Museum** (Musée de l'Empéri). – This museum presents the collections of Raoul and Jean Brunon acquired in 1967 by the Paris Army Museum *(see Michelin Green Guide to Paris)*. It covers the history of the French army from the time of Louis XIV to 1918. The fine rooms enhance the pleasant exhibit of 10 000 items (uniforms, flags, decorations, cutting and thrusting weapons and firearms, cannons, paintings, drawings, engravings, figures on foot or on horseback) illustrate the military past with special reference to the Napoleonic years.

Town Hall (Hôtel de Ville) (BY H). – Elegant 17C mansion with two corner turrets and a carved balcony.

On the Place de l'Hôtel de Ville stands the statue of Adam de Craponne (fountain).

All town plans are north orientated.

St-Michel (BY). – This 13C church possesses two bell towers one which is a fine 5-bay arcaded one and the other which was added in the 15C. Note the portal's (12C) carved tympanum where, in the centre, St Michael surrounded by two snakes stands above the Paschal lamb in a stylised floral decoration.
In the chancel there is an imposing gold gilt wooden altar (17C); and in the third south chapel the statue of the Virgin (17C).

Bourg-Neuf Gate (Porte Bourg-Neuf) (BY F). – The gate is what is left standing of the old 13C ramparts.

Nostradamus's House (Maison de Nostradamus) (BY M¹). – In the heart of old Salon stands the house in which the famous sage lived the last 19 years of his life. It houses a small museum which contains items (family tree, reconstituted office, 17C editions of *Centuries* and *Oracles,* and the works of his son César) pertaining to Nostradamus.

Clock Gate (Porte de l'Horloge) (BY K). – 17C ruins of the old ramparts.

Mossy Fountain (Fontaine moussue) (BY R). – On the Place Crousillat stands this charming 18C fountain.

St-Laurent Collegiate Church (Collégiale St-Laurent) (BY). – Of the 14 and 15C this church is a good example of southern French Gothic.
Inside, the first chapel north of the chancel contains a monolithic 15C polychrome Descent From the Cross; the 3rd north chapel has a 16C alabaster Virgin and Nostradamus's tomb; in the 5th chapel is a 15C low relief in marble.

EXCURSION

Round tour of 51km – 31 1/2 miles. – *About 3 hours. Leave Salon-de-Provence eastwards, the road to Pélisanne (D 17). Bear left on the road to Val de Cuech and immediately left again Rue du Pavillon (signposted road).*

Salon and Crau Museum (Musée de Salon et de la Crau). – The museum in a huge 19C mansion, known as the Pavilion is mainly concerned with displays of regional fauna. Provençal furnishings and paintings by local artists of the Salon region complete the exhibit.
One room is concerned with popular beliefs; two other rooms, (now being arranged) will evoke the Crau Plain and the making of Marseilles soap.

Continue along the D 17; in Pélissanne turn left into the D 22ᴬ.

★**La Barben Castle.** – *Description p 85.*

Continue along the D 22ᴬ and turn left into the D 572.

The road follows the fertile Touloubre Valley and passes beneath the Marseilles Canal *(p 111)* before offering a lovely view of Trévaresse Range before you.

St-Cannat. – Pop 2 384. The town was the birthplace of Admiral Suffren (1729-88), who was in constant and usually successful action against the Royal Navy throughout a career which spanned the Seven Years' War and the American War of Independence. The house in which Suffren was born is now the town hall (small **museum**). In the church a fine Ancient reliquary chest, decorated with small figures carved in high relief, serves now as the stoup.

Lambesc. – 5 353. The small town now by-passed by the N 7, has a large 18C church which incorporates a 14C bell tower of an earlier sanctuary. The spire collapsed in the 1909 earthquake.
On a 16C gate is a belfry with a Jack.

Continue along the N 7, in Cazan turn left into the D 22.

Château-Bas. – *Description p 104.*

Continue along the D 22 and turn right into the D 22ᶜ.

As the road rises a very fine view extends to include, besides the Luberon and Durance Valley, the Côtes Range and Aix countryside.

Vernègues. – Pop 377. The post-1909 village was built on the plateau after the earthquake had destroyed the original perched settlement.

Vieux-Vernègues. – The uphill road circles the village (ruins are not open to the public) and goes on to the small tower from where there is a vast **panorama★** (viewing table) of a large area of Provence; the Alpilles Chain stands out in the west.

Return to Vernègues, bear right on the D 22ᴮ and left on the D 68.

The road goes into the small Cuech Valley with its lovely gorges.

At the entrance to Pélisanne turn right into the D 17.

★★ SÉNANQUE Abbey

Michelin map 🕮 fold 13 or 🕮 fold 17 or 🕮 fold 11

Nestled in the hollow of a small canyon of the Senancole, which opens onto the Vaucluse Plateau, appears in a desolate **site★**, the harmonious ensemble of buildings of Sénanque Abbey (lovely view coming from Gordes on the D 177). As you arrive, facing the abbey church's east end, set, in the summer, in a sea of lavender and bathed in sunlight, one senses perfectly the tranquil atmosphere which it exudes.

Foundation and development. – The foundation, in 1148, of Sénanque by a group of monks who had come from Mazan Abbey (Upper Vivarais) fits into the great Cistercian expansion of the 12C.

This monastic movement, directed and inspired by St Bernard of Clairvaux, preached an ascetic ideal and prescribed extremely rigorous conditions in the application of the early Benedictine rule in his monasteries: isolation, poverty and simplicity must lead the monk to purity and beatitude.

The way of life of the Cistercians was thus very demanding, very difficult even: divine service, prayer and pious reading alternated with manual labour to fill very long days where time of rest did not exceed seven hours; meals taken in silence were frugal and the monks all slept in a common dormitory without any comfort. Cistercian austerity influenced the architectural and artistic conceptions of the Order. St Bernard decreed that buildings be exceedingly plain and stripped of all ornamentation that could divert the attention of those who prayed: no coloured stained glass windows, statues, paintings, or carved tympana and proud bell towers. This lack of ornamentation can be found in the other two Provençal abbeys, daughter-houses of Sénanque: Thoronet Abbey *(see Michelin Green Guide to French Riviera)* and Silvacane Abbey *(qv)*. They have come down to us almost as they were at the height of the Cistercian movement.

Sénanque prospered very rapidly to the point that, as early as 1152, the community had enough members that it founded another abbey in Vivarais. It profited from numerous gifts starting with the land of the Simiane family and the land of the lords of Venasque, too. The monastery rapidly set up, sometimes quite far, outlying farms (known as *granges*) worked by lay brothers recruited from the peasant population who performed the duties essential to the running of a farm.

Sénanque's peak occurred in the early 13C, but as elsewhere, success and prosperity caused corruption. As with the Cluny Order in the past, the Cistercian Order accumulated wealth incompatible with its vow of poverty: disorder followed.

Decadence and renaissance. – In the 14C Sénanque entered a decadent period. Recruitment and fervour diminished while lack of discipline increased. And yet, thanks to the energetic rule of an abbot during the end of the 15C, the situation improved and until the mid-16C, the monastery strove to respect the ideals of its founders.

Unfortunately in 1544, Sénanque is victim of the Vaud revolt *(qv)*: monks were hanged by the heretics and several buildings were razed. This was the final blow, the abbey was unable to recover.

In the end of the 17C, inspite of the diserving efforts of the abbots, the community counted but two monks. In spite of this the south wing of the monastery was rebuilt in the early 18C.

Sénanque Abbey

Sold as state property in 1791, Sénanque fell miraculously into the hands of an intelligent owner who not only preserved it from destruction but also consolidated it. Bought by an ecclesiastic in 1854, it found, soon after, its monastic vocation; new buildings were added flanking the older ones and 72 monks were installed. The anticlerical beliefs of the Third Republic brought about their eviction twice. In 1927 a dozen monks returned and remained some 40 odd years.

Ⓥ Today the abbey's preservation continues, it houses a **cultural centre** (Centre Culturel de Rencontre) which organises artistic and cultural events.

TOUR

time: about 1 hour

This is a fine example of Cistercian architecture. The early monastery is almost complete with the exception of the lay-brothers wing, which was rebuilt in the 18C. The medieval parts are built in local ashlar-stone. The abbey church has kept its original roof of limestone slabs *(lauzes)* surmounted by a small square bell tower; contrary to what was customary it was not built orientated to the east, but to the north as the builders had to compensate for the rigours of the local terrain.

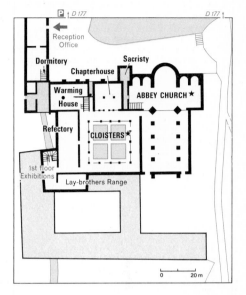

> The tour starts on the 1st floor of the dormitory, northwest of the cloisters.

Ⓥ **Dormitory (Dortoir).** – This vast pointed barrel vaulted room with transverse arches, lit by a twelve lobed oculus and narrow windows, is paved in brick. This is where the monks slept fully dressed on a simple straw pallet. They were roused in the middle of the night for the first service (nocturns) which took place at 2am, soon followed by a second matins at dawn. The dormitory now houses an exhibition on the abbey's construction. On the 1st floor there is also an interesting exhibition with as its theme: The Sahara of the Nomads, the Deserts of Man.

★ **Abbey Church (Église).** – Begun in 1160 with the sanctuary and transept, the
Ⓥ church was completed in the early 13C with the nave. The purity of line and great and severe beauty, emphasised by the absence of all decoration, create a place of worship worthy of meditation.
Stand in the back of the nave to admire the harmony of the proportions and volumes. The façade did not have the customary central door, one entered through two small doors opening onto the aisles; this indicated that the church was not made to receive flocks of worshipers in this secluded spot. The five-bayed nave is roofed with pointed barrel vaulting without transverse arches, the aisles are in rampant pointed barrel vaulting, and are joined with the nave's arches with great arcades with double recessed orders. The transept crossing is crowned by a large dome on elaborate squinches (small arches, curved stone slab, fluted pilasters which recall the style of churches from Velay and Vivarais.). The sanctuary ends with a semicircular apse pierced by three windows, symbolising the Trinity, and flanked by four apsidal chapels, which, on the outside have been incorporated into the rectangular mass. The four side altars and high altar are the original ones. In the right arm of the transept, the wall of which is opened by a window with ten rays, is the tomb of a Venasque lord, one of the abbey's benefactors in the early 13C. Nave, transept and aisles are covered with flat stones resting on the vault itself. Note the lack of all ornamentation which left the monk alone to confront God the Father.
Off the north façade is the sacristy.

★ **Cloisters (Cloître).** – Late 12C. The cloisters' galleries are covered with rounded
Ⓥ barrel vaulting with transverse arches held up by carved brackets. Under great relieving arches are two groups of small twinned columns alternating with square pillars. Decoration appears on the capitals (leaf-work, flowers, rope and palm-leaf moulding and interlacing) and yet it remains discreet.
The cloisters open onto the different rooms of the conventual buildings each of which has their specific function.

★ **Conventual buildings (Bâtiments conventuels).** – An extension of the abbey church's
Ⓥ left arm of the transept are: chapterhouse, warming house, dormitory *(see above)* upstairs and west and south are the refectory and lay-brothers range.

Chapterhouse (Salle capitulaire). – The room is roofed with six pointed vaults held up at the centre on two pillars flanked by four small engaged columns. Under the abbot's leadership the monastic community met here to read and comment on the Scriptures, receive the novices' vow, to keep vigil over the dead and to make important decisions. The monks sat in tiers.

Warming house (Chauffoir). – Access via a narrow passage (parlour or day room), the warming house is roofed with groined vaulting which is held up by a massive central pillar perched on a pedestal. One of the two original chimneys remains in a corner. The heat was essential to the transcribers who were bent over their manuscripts all day.

Refectory (Réfectoire). – Parallel to the cloisters west gallery. Somewhat destroyed during, the 16C *(p 176)*, it was then rebuilt and recently restored to its original appearance.

An exhibition of the Cistercian Order can be seen.

⊙ **Lay-brothers Range** (Bâtiment des convers). – South of the cloisters, this building, remodelled in the 18C, lodged the lay-brothers (who carried out duties too distracting for the monk and lived seperately from the monks) meeting them only during certain services or when working in the fields.

The ground floor and 1st floor house exhibitions.

★★ SILVACANE Abbey

Michelin map **84** folds 2 and 3 or **245** fold 31 or **246** fold 12 – Local map p 113

Set in a pastoral landscape on the Durance's south bank, Silvacane Abbey, with its pink tiled roofs and small mutilated square bell tower, offers a beautiful example of plain Cistercian beauty.

From its founding to the present. – In the 11C the monks from St-Victor of Marseilles established themselves on this infested land surrounded by reeds.

The monastery became affiliated with Cîteaux and in 1147 received a donation from two benefactors: Guillaume de la Roque and Raymond de Baux while a group of Cistercians from Morimond Abbey (an abbey which has since disappeared, located on the boundary of Champagne and Lorraine) settled here.

Protected by Provence's great lords, the abbey prospered; it accomplished large land improvement projects in the region and in turn founded Valsainte Abbey near Apt. In 1289 a violent confrontation occurred between it and the powerful Montmajour Abbey of the Benedictine Order; monks pursued each other and some even became hostages. The affair ended in a trial and Silvacane was returned to its rightful owners, the Cistercians. But even more serious were the pillaging of the abbey in 1358 by the Lord of Aubignan and the great freezes of 1364 which destroyed the olive and wine crops. This set off a period of decline which ended in 1443 by the annexation of the abbey to the chapter of St-Sauveur Cathedral in Aix. It became the village of Roque-d'Anthéron's *(qv)* parish church in the early 16C, and suffered during the Wars of Religion. When the Revolution broke out the buildings were already abandoned; sold as state property, it was converted into a farm. Bought by the state in 1949, the buildings are slowly being restored.

TOUR *time: about 1 hour*

⊙ **Church** (Église). – Built between 1175-1230 on a slope, it presents different levels which are noticeable when viewing the west façade. This façade is pierced by openings: a central door (on the tympanum the canons of St-Sauveur placed their coat of arms), two side doors topped with small off-centred windows, three windows and an oculus adorned with mouldings on the upper floor. The three-bayed nave ends by a flat east end. Each arm of the transept has two orientated chapels.

The vaulting is surprisingly varied: pointed barrel with transverse arches in the nave, rampant barrel in the aisles except the third north bay which is half-barrel, transverse barrel vaulting for the arms of the transept, pointed vaulting for the transept crossing and apsidal chapels.

The chancel is illuminated by three round arched windows surmounted by an oculus; the south aisle is also lit by an opening at each bay. Note how the architect had to take into account the very steep slope of the land by placing at different levels the south aisle, nave, north aisle and cloisters. Like at Sénanque all decoration was forbidden; the building with its simplicity evokes the rigid Cistercian rule.

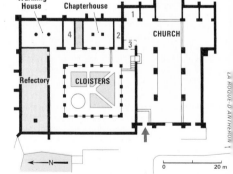

In the north chapel of the north arm of the transept (1) are the fragments of the tomb of Bertrand de Baux, grandson of the founder, who began the church's construction.

⊙ **Cloisters** (Cloître). – Located at a lower level (1m60 – 4 1/2ft) than the church, the cloisters date from the second half of the 13C. Nevertheless, the gallery vaulting is still Romanesque with rounded barrel vaulting on transverse arches except three corners which have pointed vaulting. Powerful rounded arches open on the yard; they were originally adorned with paired bays.

ⓥ **Conventual buildings (Bâtiments conventuels).** – Except for the refectory they were all built between 1210-30.
The **sacristy** (2) is a long narrow room next to the **library** (3) located under the north arm of the transept. The **chapterhouse** recalls the one at Sénanque *(qv)*: six pointed vaults falling on two different central pillars: one flanked by four small columns the other with fluted rope moulding. After the **parlour** (4), which was used as a passage to the exterior, is the **warming house** also with pointed vaulting, it has kept its chimney. Above is the **dormitory.**
ⓥ The large and magnificent **refectory** was rebuilt between 1420-5. The capitals are more decorated than in the other rooms; high windows and a large rose window profusely illuminate the room; the pulpit remains.
The lay-brothers range has completely disappeared. Excavations have uncovered, outside, the ruins of the gatehouse and the abbey's precinct wall.

SUZE-LA-ROUSSE   Pop 1 396
Michelin map 🗺 fold 2 or 🗺 fold 16 or 🗺 fold 23 – Facilities

Suze-la-Rousse, picturesquely terraced on the south bank of the Lez, was, during the Middle Ages, the most important town of Tricastin.
The hill is dominated by its imposing feudal castle. One of its lords, wounded during the siege of Montélimar in 1587, was hoisted on to his mare, also wounded, and before returning home, kindly said to her: "come on my grey, let us go die at Suze". The former town hall presents a lovely 15 and 16C façade.

ⓥ **Castle (Château).** – Crossing a plantation of truffle oaks (some 30ha – 74 acres) the alley leads to the castle's only entrance.
It dates, for the most part from the 14C and its towers are a good example of military architecture of this period. It was remodelled inside during the Renaissance. The court of honour offers fine Renaissance façades.
The ground floor houses the staff and service quarters, the stables and 12C kitchen. The apartments are reached by a monumental grand staircase. Note the Four Seasons Room and the armoury with its painted ceiling and great chimney flanked by two frescoes (restored) representing the siege of Montélimar.
In one of the corner towers there is an octagonal room. A fine view of Mount Ventoux, Lance Mountain and the Dauphiné Prealps can be had.

★ TARASCON   Pop 11 024
Michelin map 🗺 fold 10 or 🗺 fold 28 or 🗺 fold 26

A tradition going back some 2 000 years has made Tarascon, the city of Tarasque. Last century Alphonse Daudet *(qv)* brought fame to the town through his character Tartarin (a fat bearded figure invented by Daudet in 1872). And yet it has its own claim to fame through its magnificent castle, the walls of which drop straight down to the swift Rhône River.
The city is on the boundary of a rich region of market gardening and has thus become an important fruit and vegetable dispatching centre.

The Tarasque. – Massalia's trading post, Tarascon was established on an island in the Rhône. The Romans took it over after the defeat of the Massaliotes. The present castle stands on the site of the Roman camp built by the legionaries.
According to a Provençal legend, an amphibious monster periodically climbed out of the Rhône into the town where it devoured children and cattle and killed anyone attempting to cross the river. To save the town, St Martha *(qv)* came from Stes-Maries-de-la-Mer and quelled the beast with the sign of the cross; the beast subsequently became docile and was thereupon captured by the townspeople.
In celebration of the miracle, Good King René *(qv)* who often resided in the castle, organised stupendous festivities in 1474. The legend is recalled in an annual fête and procession. A huge model of the Tarasque with clamping jaws and swinging tail is paraded through the streets, with a snap of its tail, the monster knocks down those he can reach.

Tarasque

★★ **CASTLE** (Château) (Y) *time: 1 hour*

ⓥ Due to its location on the banks of the Rhône, its massive appearance, which contrasts with its inside architecture, and the exceptional quality of its preservation, this building is one of the finest medieval castles in France. In the 13C, the castle, facing the royal city of Beaucaire, defended Provence's western boundary. Captured by Raymond de Turenne *(qv)* in 1399, it was restituted, soon after, to its legal owners, the Anjou family; Louis II, father of René *(qv)* decided to have it entirely rebuilt.

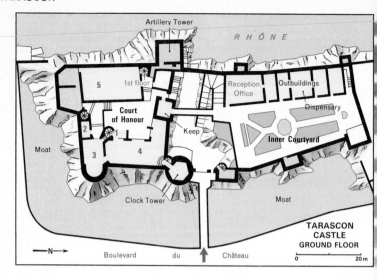

Construction began with the fortified walls and towers built between 1400-6 and continued under Louis III between 1430-5 with the inside courtyard and the east and southeast wings; the master craftsman was the Provençal architect Jean Robert. From 1447-9, King René completed the building, which was his favourite residence, contributing all his taste and refinement to the interior decoration.

Here he organised splendid festivities (notably the famous tournament, Pas de la Bergère which went on for 3 days in June 1449), wrote the *Tournaments Treatise*, composed music, received prominent guests, like the future Louis XI and Charles of Orléans, the famous troubadour.

More or less abandoned, Tarascon Castle became a famous prison in the 17C. It remained a prison until 1926. Since restored it has rid itself of its numerous accretions and its moats were cleared giving the castle the appearance it had 500 years ago. It is made up of two independent buildings: the seignorial living quarters on the south side flanked by round towers on the town's side and square towers on the Rhône side offering a compact mass of walls rising up 48m – 157ft (towers and curtain wall were of the same height, which facilitated artillery movement on the terraces built for that purpose) and the inner courtyard on the north side, defended by shorter rectangular towers.

Interior. – A wide moat, crossed by a bridge (once a drawbridge) isolates the two groups of buildings. Enter the seignorial living quarters through the keep's zigzag passageway to the court of honour around which are the apartments with their lovely finely carved façades adorned with mullioned windows. A graceful polygonal staircase turret (1) serves the different floors; near it a niche shelters the busts of King René and Jeanne de Laval *(qv)*, his second wife.

Still on the south side of the court of honour, climb up some steps to the Flamboyant screen of the chantry (2), then opening onto the corner tower is the lower chapel (3) and above it the upper chapel.

To the east and north lie the L-shaped main living quarters which partly overlook the town and include the private apartments, which rise above a lovely gallery (4), with pointed barrel vaulting, and communicate with the Clock Tower (which had a military function). To the west stands the Artillery Tower.

The tour of the west wing, which rises above the river, is a visit through the state rooms: the ground floor – dining hall (two chimneys) (5); 1st floor – reception hall (two vast rooms with painted wood ceilings). Then continue to the king's bedroom (in the southwest tower) with a chimney and heating platter; on the 2nd floor are the Audience Chamber and Counsel Room, which were vaulted to support the terraces.

Admire, while touring these rooms, several fine 17C Flemish tapestries the subject of which is: *"Scipio Africanus's Gesture"*.

Return to the south wing to see the Chaplain's Room (sacristy, host oven, corner for the treasury) and the royal chapel, which has kept the king's and queen's oratories and from where they could hear the chantry voices.

Terrace (Terrasse). – The terrace offers an all encompasing **panorama**★★ of Beaucaire, Tarascon, the Rhône, Vallabrègues Undertaking, the Montagnette, Alpilles Chain, Fontvieille, Montmajour Abbey, Arles and St-Gilles Plain.

It was through the crenellations of this platform that Robespierre's local partisans were thrown into the river in 1794. These terraces were dominated by a fort, crowning the keep; its base remains.

Go back down by the Clock Tower, the ground floor of which houses the Galley Room, named such in memory of the graffiti and boat drawings made by the past prisoners.

Outbuildings. – Annexe of the castle which it joins but independant of it, this section includes the inner courtyard, as such, and the service buildings where under René a large staff of personnel worked.

Recently remodelled, these buildings house the Hospital of St-Nicolas's **dispensary:** in a finely panelled 18C room 200 apothecary jars (ceramics from St-Jean-du Desert and Montpellier).

TARASCON

*The main car parks
are indicated
on the town plans.*

ADDITIONAL SIGHTS

★**Ste-Marthe** (Y). – Founded in *c*10C, the church was rebuilt in the 12C when the saint's body was found, then rebuilt for the most part in the 14C and remodelled the following centuries.

The church was restored after having been partly destroyed in 1944. The south door is a fine example of the Romanesque style; unfortunately, its lovely carved decoration has partially disappeared.

Inside among the numerous paintings hanging in the side chapels note: St Thomas Aquinas and St Catherine of Siena by Pierre Parrocel (3rd south chapel) and the works of Vien and Nicolas Mignard retracing St Martha's life. Found in the north aisle are a fine 15C triptych (last bay's chapel); St Francis of Assisi by Carle Van Loo, a reliquary bust and a marble recumbent figure from a 17C mausoleum (Ste-Marthe's Chapel, 2nd bay).

In the staircase going down to the crypt is the tomb of Jean de Cossa (former seneshal of Provence) a fine Renaissance style work attributed to the school of Francesco Laurana.

The crypt itself contains the sarcophagus (3-4C) of St Martha, ornamented with carvings.

Town Hall (Hôtel de Ville) (Y H). – This 17C building presents an elegantly carved façade enhanced by a stone balcony.

In the nearby Rue des Halles are picturesque arcaded houses (15C).

Tartarin's House (Maison de Tartarin) (Y B). – Arranged in hommage to the most famous of Tarascon citizens, the fictitious Tartarin *(p 179)*, this house consists of three rooms decorated in the 1870s style. On the ground floor are the office and living room, above is the bedroom. Costumed models, furniture and documents help relive the atmosphere of Daudet's *(qv)* novel: *The New Don Quixote or the Wonderful Adventures of Tarascon.*

Behind the house is a tropical garden.

Le THOR   Pop 5 025

Michelin map **81** fold 12 or **245** fold 17 or **246** fold 11

Once the capital of the white dessert grape, Chasselas, Le Thor has diversified its agricultural activities to include market gardening and trees and shrub growing. The bridge over the Sorgue, the church and its precinct create a picturesque scene. Remaining from the Middle Ages are the ruins of the ramparts and the belfry.

★**Church** (Église). – *Time: 1/4 hour.* Completed in the early 13C, the church as a whole is Romanesque in style yet its single nave is covered with Gothic vaulting which counts among the most ancient in Provence. The exterior is imposing with its massive buttresses supporting the tall tower, its apse adorned with Lombard arcades and its heavy unfinished central bell tower. The doors were directly inspired from Ancient art, particularly the south door.

The interior is austere presenting a single nave and a fine dome on squinches. Note the keystone at the entrance to the four-sided apse: Lamb of God encircled by five eagles.

Thouzon Cave (Grotte de Thouzon). – *3km – 2 miles to the north; the trail to the cave branches off the D 16.*

The cave opens at the foot of the hill crowned by the ruins of Thouzon Castle and a monastery (small Romanesque chapel quite closeby). It was discovered in 1902 by chance after a blast on the site of a former quarry. The tourist walks 230m – 755ft along the old underground river bed, which carved this gallery, to a not very deep chasm.

On the cave roof, which rises to 22m – 72ft, are fistuliform stalactites of rare quality. In addition the cave presents oddly-shaped, beautifully coloured concretions.

La TOUR-D'AIGUES

Pop 2 479

Michelin map 🔲 fold 3 or 🔲🔲 fold 32 – 6 km – 3 1/2 miles northeast of Pertuis

Nestled at the foot of the Luberon, Aigues Country, open onto Aix-en-Provence, appears to be a favoured region: its smiling countryside made up of fertile and well exposed land where vineyards, orchards (cherries) and market produce grow, contrasts with the wild barrenness of its neighbouring mountains.
Founded in the 10 or 11C, the town owes its name to a tower (*tour* in French) which preceeded the keep of the present castle.

Château. – Rebuilt between 1555-75, on the foundations of a medieval castle in the Renaissance style by an Italian architect (Ercole Nigra), the château occupies, on a vast terrace overlooking the Lèze, 1 400m² – 15 070sq ft. Burned in 1782 and again in 1792 when it was ruined, it is now being progressively restored by Vaucluse *département*.
The monumental **entrance gate** stands like a triumphal arch with an abundance of decoration: Corinthian columns and pilasters, a frieze of the attributes of war and an entablature surmounted by a triangular pediment. On either side rise two imposing square pavilions with three storeys of windows (the pavilion on the left has preserved its tall chimney).
In the centre of the bailey is the massive keep; in a corner the chapel.

◯ **Museum of the History of Aigues Country and Ceramics Museum** (Musée de l'Histoire du Pays d'Aigues et musée des faïences). – *Enter by the tourist information centre (a branch office of the Luberon Regional Nature Park – qv)* These two museums have been set up in several of the chateau's cellars. The first cellar presents a modern display concentrating on audio-visual methods: a history of Provençal man's evolution from his origins to the present. Slides, illuminated maps, miscellaneous objects and models depict the evolution of local rural life.
The second cellar presents a collection of ceramics, illustrating the production of a ceramics factory, which has since disappeared from the château.
The tour of the cellars and underground passages complete the visit.

Church (Église). – This unusual building possesses a Romanesque nave with an apse which is now the façade, while the transept and chancel were added in the 17C.

★ UZÈS

Pop 7 826

Michelin map 🔲🔲 fold 19 or 🔲🔲 fold 14 or 🔲🔲 fold 25 – Facilities

Set in the severe yet charming *garrigues (qv)* countryside, Uzès established itself at the tip of a limestone plateau, overlooking Alzon Valley.
A ducal seat, bishopric and consular seat, Uzès has preserved its lay-out as a medieval stronghold, which in the 17 and 18C embellished itself due to its economic prosperity acquired through its fabrication of linen, serge and silk. The town, flowing over its former fortifications, now replaced by boulevards, has developed on the plateau.

The duchy of Uzès. – The old House of Uzès goes back to Charlemagne through its women. In 1486 the last heir of the lords of Uzès, married the Count de Crussol, governor of Dauphiné ; one of their descendants, Antoine de Crussol received from Charles IX, in 1565, the title of Duke of Uzès. After the execution, in 1632, of the Duke of Montmorency in Toulouse, the Duke of Uzès became the first duke and peer of the kingdom.
As early as 1547 there appeared in Uzès a powerful Protestant church. From then on there began a long period of religious wars which resulted in the submission and exile of Huguenots under Louis XIII and Louis XIV. In the meantime a strong rivalry divided, until recently, the Uzès religious population of Catholics and Protestants.

Poet in exile. – Uzès is important in the history of French literature because it is here that **Jean Racine** (1639-99) stayed in 1661 when he was 22 years old.
After having been educated in the severe discipline of Port-Royal and the Jansenist College of Harcourt in Paris, Racine emancipated himself. His family, who watched with horror their son thinking of a career in the theatre sent him to his uncle, vicar general of Uzès. To pull him away from his worldly associations, his uncle promised him a benefice once he had entered into the orders. Racine spent a bit more than a year at his uncle's. In his letters, full of humour, he spoke little of theology but of the countryside, the food, the local dialect (which he did not understand) and his first poems.
A trial arose concerning his benefice, he did not understand a thing and lost: this pettifoggery is said to have been the origin of his only comedy *Plaideurs* (*The Litigants,* a 3 act play written in 1668). The young poet did not pursue the religious vocation so desired by his family and returned to Paris to become France's greatest classical dramatist.

Jean Racine (School of Mignard)

The Gide family. – Uzès is also the birthplace of the Gides. Paul Gide (1832-80) an eminent lawyer and Charles Gide (1847-1932) the famous economist, were both born in Uzès and were respectively the father and uncle of the author André Gide (1869-1951) who was awarded the Nobel Prize for Literature in 1947. Gide spent his holidays with his grandmother in Uzès and recounts his sojourns in *If It Die... (Si le grain ne meurt).*

SIGHTS

Start at Avenue de la Libération and turn right onto Boulevard des Alliés.

ⓥ **St-Étienne** (A). – This 18C church presents a curved west face decorated with flame ornaments. On its north side, it is flanked by a 13C square tower.

On the Place de l'Église stands the house (A **D**) Charles Gide *(see above)* was born in.

Rue St-Étienne (A **25**). – *No 1.* An imposing Louis XIII style faceted door. Further on to the left in a blind alley, fine Renaissance façade.

Place aux Herbes (A **15**). – The square is surrounded by covered arcades, *couverts,* and shaded with plane trees. Among the old houses note the 17C **Hôtel d'Aigaliers** (A **E**) set back on the west side.

> *At the end of the square turn right into an alleyway.*

It leads to the unusual and narrow **Rue Pélisserie** (A **18**).

> *Advance into Rue Entre-les-Tours.*

Place aux Herbes in Uzès

Clock Tower (Tour de l'Horloge) (A). – Dating from the 12C this tower was the bishop's tower; its confronted the duke's tower and king's tower at a time when these three powers shared Uzès.

Hôtel Dampmartin (A **K**). – *1 Rue Jacques-d'Uzès.* This mansion presents a Renaissance façade flanked by a round tower; a carved frieze surrounds the 1st floor window. Enter into the Renaissance courtyard (staircase).

> *Cross Place Dampmartin.*

Hôtel de Joubert et d'Avéjan (A **L**). – *12 Rue de la République.* Fine Henri II style façade (restored).

> *Return to Rue Jacques-d'Uzès and turn left.*

★**Ducal Palace** (Duché) (A). – From the outside, the palace appears as a feudal mass
ⓥ with buildings of various periods exemplifying the rise of the Uzès family.

Courtyard. – To be noted from left to right are: Viscounty Tower (14C) with its octagonal turret, commemorating the lords of Uzès's elevation to a viscounty in 1328 ; Bermonde Tower, a square 11C keep, named after the lord who had it built, the top of it, damaged during the Revolution was rebuilt in the 19C.

To the right, at a right angle, lies the Renaissance **façade**★ erected by the first duke in c1550 to plans by Philibert Delorme (c1510 – c1570). It is one of the first examples of the superimposition of the classical orders – Doric, Ionic and Corinthian. At the façade's far end stands a Gothic chapel (restored in the 19C).

Bermonde Tower (Tour Bermonde). – 148 steps. Access by an elegant Renaissance staircase, with coffered and faceted vaulting.

From the tower's terrace there is an interesting **view**★ onto the old roofs of Uzès baked by the sun and the *garrigues* countryside.

Apartments. – In the grand Louis XV drawing room ornamented with stucco decoration there is a Trianon console in gilt leaf with a lovely Delft vase, Louis XV and XVI style furniture and costumes dating from the period of Charles X.

The dining room furniture dates from the Renaissance and Louis XIII period. On leaving, the 12C watch tower (Tour de Vigie) is on the left.

Town Hall (Hôtel de ville) (AB H). – A finely laid-out 18C courtyard.

⊘ **Crypt** (Crypte) (AB N). – Note the baptistry and the two low reliefs: one of the low relief's figures has been given glass eyes; in the 4C early Christian sanctuary the niches were intended to hold cult objects.

Continue along Rue Boucairie.

At the corner of Rue Rafin stands the **old mint** (hôtel des Monnaies) (B); a sign reminds us that the bishops of Uzès were permitted to strike their own coins during the Middle Ages.

Hôtel du Baron de Castille (B R). – The late 18C front of this mansion is preceded by a colonnade – a particular predilection of the baron's, it would seem, since his other residence, Château de Castille *(qv)* is similarly adorned.

Former Episcopal Palace (Ancien palais épiscopal) (B S). – This sumptuous palace, built at the end of the 17C, houses in its right wing the public library and museum.

⊘ **Local museum** (Musée Municipal). – The museum's collections include *garrigues* flora *(qv)*, fossils, shells, prehistory, archaeology (1st gallery) ; old documents, popular arts and traditions, African art, furniture (2nd gallery) ; pottery from St-Quentin, porcelain (3rd gallery) ; paintings, lithographs, Daumier caricatures (4th gallery), and souvenirs of the Gide family (5th gallery).

St-Théodorit Cathedral (B V). – The 17C cathedral behind a 19C remodelled west front contains a fine Louis XIV style **organ**★. It has preserved many of its 18C pipes; in the past, during Lent, painted shutters were closed over the instrument (they can still be seen). Note also the triforium gallery with wrought iron rails above the tall arcades, and in the chancel, on the left, the handsome 17C lectern.

⊘ ★**Fenestrelle Tower** (Tour Fenestrelle) (B). – The tower which abuts the cathedral's south wall is 12C and is the only relic of the former Romanesque cathedral destroyed during the Wars of Religion, This kind of round bell tower is unique in France: it rises 42m – 138ft above a square base with six stories which recede one above the other. The variety of the openings adds elegance and avoids monotony.

Promenade Jean-Racine (B). – This avenue, which runs into Promenade des Marronniers, overlooks the ducal park, the *garrigues,* and Alzon Valley where the Eure River has its source by the Romans and diverted along the Pont du Gard aqueduct *(qv)* to provide water for Nîmes. To the left stands **Racine Pavilion** (B X), an old tower, once part of the fortifications, restored in the late 18C.

Le Portalet House (Maison du Portalet) (B). – *19 Le Portalet.* A lovely Renaissance house, the façade of which is partly hidden by a wall closing off the courtyard.

Turn right into Rue Paul-Foussat.

At no 3 there is the lovely Renaissance door of the mansion (A Z) where Grimoard du Roure lived before becoming Pope Urban V *(p 73).*

EXCURSION

⊘ **Castelnau Castle** (Château de Castelnau). – *19km – 11 1/2 miles via the D 982 and the D 186. Leave Uzès by ③ on the town plan. Car park.*
This fortified castle stands on a rocky spur. Castelnau was transformed into barracks and the top of its towers and its crenelations razed after a dramatic event which occurred in August 1704, when the leader of the Camisards (a guerilla type organisation of local people revolting against the king) was caught and killed here. It was restored in the 19C.

In the form of a quadrilateral flanked by 4 towers – 2 round and 2 square – the castle is made up of different architectural elements covering the 11-12C, 17 and 19C. Access to the keep allows you to walk along part of the watchpath.

From the terrace there is a lovely view of Uzès, Mount Ventoux, Mount Bouquet, Lozère Mountains and Gardon River.

Inside on the 1st floor the visit includes the drawing room, gallery and bedroom furnished with interesting 17, 18 and 19C furniture. The ground floor contains the dining room and kitchen.

The inside courtyard lined with a gallery, preserves several Gallo-Roman stelae built into the wall; note the 25m – 82 ft deep well.

Note, on leaving, a small chapel adorned with 16C gilt wood paintings. Amble through the park shaded with trees.

Michelin map 🟫 fold 2 or 🟥 fold 17 or 🟥 fold 9 – Local maps pp 110 and 191
– Facilities

Built along the banks of the Ouvèze River, in the middle of a corrie of wooded hills, Vaison-la-Romaine, a small Provençal town full of charm will enchant those who love old stones... Rarely has a town offered such a complete and picturesque ensemble: vast fields of ancient ruins, Romanesque cathedral and cloisters, old quarter dominated by its castle...
An animated tourist centre during the music festivals *(pp 199-200)*, Vaison also thrives as an agricultural centre where wine, fruit and mountain products (honey, lavender, truffles etc...) give rise to prosperous trading.

VAISON-LA-ROMAINE

Fabre (Cours H.)	Y 13
Grande-Rue	Y 18
Montfort (Pl. de)	Y 25
République (R.)	Y 32
Abbé-Sautel (Pl.)	Y 2
Aubanel (Pl.)	Z 3
Burrhus (R.)	Y 4
Cathédrale (Square de la)	Y 5
Cevert (Av. François)	Y
Château (R. du)	Z 7
Choralies (Av. des)	Y 8
Église (R. de l')	Z 9
Évêché (R. de l')	Z 12
Ferry (Av. Jules)	Y
Foch (Quai Maréchal)	Z 14
Fours (R. des)	Z
Gaulle (Av. Gén. de)	Y
Gontard (Quai P.)	Z 17
Haute-Ville (Montée de la)	Z 20
Horloge (R. de l')	Z 21
Jaurès (R. Jean)	Y 22
Mistral (R. Frédéric)	Y 24
Noël (R. B.)	Y 27
Pasteur (Q.)	Y
Poids (Pl. du)	Z 29
Poids (R. du)	Z 30
St-Quenin (Av.)	Y 34
Verdun (Q. de)	Z
Victor-Hugo (Av.)	Y 35
Vieux-Marché (Pl. du)	Z 38
11-Novembre (Pl. du)	Y 40

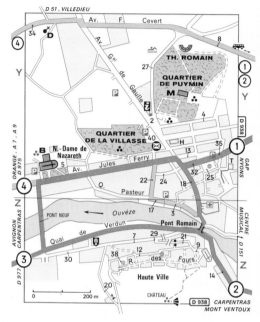

HISTORICAL NOTES

The city of the Vocontii. – Southern capital of the Vocontii, a Celtic tribe, Vaison (Vasio Vocontiorum) became part of Roman Provence; it was conquered in the end of the 2C BC *(p 22)* and covered all southeastern Gaul. Very early it received the status of federated city (and not colony) which allowed a great deal of autonomy. Allied with Caesar during the Gallic Wars (58-1BC), the Vocontii lived side by side with the Romans; and among them illustrious men appeared: the historian Trogue-Pompée and Nero's tutor Burrhus.
Cited as one of the Narbonensis's *(qv)* most prosperous cities under Roman rule, Vaison covered some 70ha-173 acres and had a population of approximately 10 000. Contrary to the colonial examples of Arles, Nîmes, Orange... the city did not expand with a Romanised urban plan, as was customary, because a pre-existing rural plan prevented the surveyors from tracing a regular grid plan and placing living quarters and public buildings in their rightful place. The result was a very loose urban plan.
Immense dwellings were built right in the centre of the city, replacing the earlier edifices. It was only in the last third of IC AD, under the Flaviens that it was decided to make straight streets, which forced the properties to: readjust the houses to realign their façades and modify their axis, while porticoes and colonnades were erected. The large public buildings, except for the theatre and baths, were not discovered.
The archaeologists have established that the luxurious *domi (p 31)* were much larger than those in Pompeii. They were built over a period of time, 250 years, and yet Vaison was not restricted to just this kind of dwelling, excavations have unearthed small palaces, modest dwellings, huts and tiny shops.

Over the centuries. – Partially destroyed in the late 3C, Vaison rose again during the 4C with a reduced urban plan. The seat of a bishopric, it ranked highly in the 5 and 6C inspite of Barbarian occupation, and two synods took place here in 442 and 529.
The following centuries were marked by a net decline and by the desertion of the lower town to the profit of the old town on the river's south bank where the Count of Toulouse built a castle. The medieval upper town was protected; it was abandoned in the 18 and 19C and the modern town fortified the Gallo-Roman city. Excavations began in the 1840s, Mérimée (the Minister of Culture at that time) came to the site. And yet the major part of the work was accomplished from 1907-55 by Canon Sautel, to whom we owe the discovery and uncovering of two quarters and the theatre. His work is actually being pursued by a highly qualified team of archaeologists.
At the same time, the upper town is under restoration, due to private donations, and is taking on a new appearance with its atmosphere of days past...

★★ROMAN RUINS (RUINES ROMAINES) (Y) *time: about 2 hours*

The ancient ruins are spread over 13ha – 32 acres. The centre of the Gallo-Roman city (forum and precincts) is covered by the modern town and, therefore, only the peripheral quarters, rich with information on life at Vaison in 1C AD, especially its private life, have been uncovered.

The excavations progress on the one hand towards the cathedral in the La Villasse Quarter and on the other hand around Puymin Hill where a shopping district and a sumptuous *domus*, the Peacock villa *(see below)*, with its mosaics were recently unearthed.

On the northern boundary of the ancient town, the excavated baths (some 20 rooms) have revealed that they were used until the late 3C and subsequently destroyed.

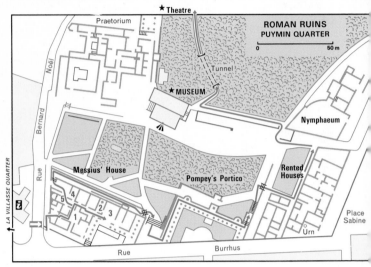

PUYMIN QUARTER

Messius's House. – This *domus,* a large urban dwelling belonging to a wealthy Vaison family (partly buried under the modern road network) exemplifies a very elaborate interior which constituted a sumptuous and comfortable life style. Upon entering, via the Roman street, a vestibule then a corridor lead to the *atrium* (1) around which the different rooms have been laid out including the *tablinum* (study and library reserved for the head of the family). The *atrium* had in its centre, under the open section, a square basin *(impluvium)* which caught the rainwater.

Note the room (2) where Venus's head (in the museum; *photograph p 20)* was found, the main reception hall or *oecus* (3), the peristyle and its basin. The annexes include the kitchen (4) with its twin hearths and the private bath (5) with its three rooms: *caldarium, tepidarium, frigidarium.*

Pompey's Portico. – This elegant public promenade, a sort of public garden, 52m – 171ft square, consisted of 4 galleries with *exedra,* covered originally with a lean-to-roof and, surrounded a garden and pool, in the centre of which stood a square aedicule. *For the definition of terms used see pp 30-31.*

The nicely excavated north gallery presents 3 exedra into which were placed the casts of the statues of Sabine, Diadumenos (Roman copy of the statue by Polyclitus which is exhibited at the British Museum) and Hadrian.

The west gallery is also almost entirely excavated, while the other two galleries are lodged among the modern buildings.

Rented Houses. – This residential complex consists of a block of dwellings (to rent) several storeys high for citizens of modest means. Note the large urn (dolium) for provisions.

Nymphaeum. – The various buildings of a cistern set around a spring, which was collected into an elongated basin, called nymphaeum.

Further on to the east were excavated the shopping district and **Peacock villa.**
From the nymphaeum take the Roman tunnel, which the inhabitants on this side of the hill used for convenience, to the theatre.

★Roman Theatre. – The theatre was built in the 1C, repaired in the 3C and dismantled in the 5C. Its dimensions (95m – 312ft diameter, 25m – 82ft high) reveal that it was slightly smaller than the one in Orange (103m – 338ft, 36m – 118ft); it had a seating capacity of 6 000 people (Orange held 9 – 10 000 spectators). Also like the theatre in Orange, it was built against the hillside, but its tiers were rebuilt by Jules Formigé (1879-1960; Inspector-General of Historical Monuments). The entire stage was hewn out of the rock and the pits containing the machinery and curtain have been well preserved. Discovered amidst the ruins are the fine statues exhibited in the museum. Another feature, unique among the Roman theatres in Provence, is the partial existence of a top gallery portico.

Return to the west side of the Puymin Quarter.

Here lies a group of buildings called the *praetorium,* and yet it is in fact an immense *domus* with frescoes and latrines.

★**Museum** (M). – Opened in 1974, this fascinating and pleasant museum presents the finds excavated at Vaison. Different aspects of Gallo-Roman civilisation are evoked thematically: religion (altars, funerary inscriptions, dedications), living quarters, pottery, glassware, arms, tools, ornaments, toiletries and Imperial coins. The statues are remarkable. They are all in white marble; in chronological order: Claude (dating from 43) whose head is adorned by a heavy oak crown, armoured Domitian, naked Hadrian (dating from 121) who evokes a majestic feeling in the Hellenistic manner, Sabine, his wife, represented more conventionally as a great lady in state dress. The acephali statues are those of municipal figures whose heads were interchangeable.

Two other pieces are worthy of interest: the 2C marble head of Venus crowned with laurel leaves *(photograph p 20)* and a 3C silver bust of a patrician.

Empress Sabine

LA VILLASSE QUARTER

Main street and baths. – On entering the site of the excavations, walk on the paved main street, under which runs a drain which goes down towards the Ouvèze and the modern buildings.

On the west side of the street, it is doubled by a way lined with colonnades, which was reserved for pedestrians only; shops, located in the main houses' dependencies, lined it.

On the east side of the street lie the baths – for a long time thought to be a basilica – which are surrounded by deep drains. The great room 12.5m – 40ft wide has a pilastered arcade.

House of the patrician of the silver bust. – Across from the baths in the shop street is the entrance (1) to the vast *domus,* in which was discovered the silver bust *(see museum above)* of its opulent owner.

Sprawled over about 3 000m² – 32 292sq ft the *domus* is complete: paved vestibule, *atrium* (2), *fablinum* (3) and a first peristyle with garden and pool and then a second larger peristyle also enhanced with garden and pool.

On this house's south side stands another house where mosaics (4) were found as well as frescoes around an atrium.

North of the second larger peristyle is the private bath (5) preceeded by a courtyard. Nearby lies a large hanging garden which enhanced the wealthy property.

For the definition of these words and more see pp 30-31. An explanation of the Roman house with a drawing appears on p 34.

Dolphin House. – In its early stages *c*40BC, this house occupied the northeastern section of a large enclosure in a non-urban setting. The main residence was enclosed by a peristyle while an outbuilding housed the first private baths known of in Gaul.

North of the large peristyle, a couple of steps lead down into another peristyle (6) with its pool. To the right covering 50m² – 538sq ft lies the private baths (7) flanked by latrines. Cross the state dining room or *triclinium* (8) and several other rooms before reaching the *atrium* (9).

To the south stands another peristyle, a pleasant garden enhanced by a large pool, with 3 exedra and decorated with white marble verneer as well as fountains and formal gardens.

Colonnade Street. – Not completely excavated, this street borders the Dolphin House along 43m – 141ft.

It was not a paved street; its surface, like many other street surfaces, was made of gravel.

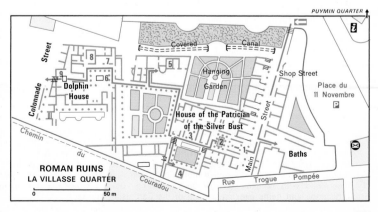

ROMAN RUINS
LA VILLASSE QUARTER

ADDITIONAL SIGHTS

Ⓥ **Old Notre-Dame-de-Nazareth Cathedral** (Ancienne cathédrale N-D-de-Nazareth) (Y). – This fine cathedral, in the Provençal Romanesque style *(p 35)* succeeds several buildings, the vestiges of which remain. The east end's foundations lie on the parts taken from a Roman temple; below, the ruins of an apse, with small bonding, date from the late 4C. Succeeding this first Paleochristian church was a 6 or 7C Merovingian church as is proven by the apse and the base of a fluted column uncovered in 1951 in the first bay of the north aisle. One can imagine, with some caution, this building's appearance: a triple nave with a timber roof supported by 12 columns. Rebuilt in the 11C (belonging to this period are a part of the outside walls and the south bay preceeding the apse), the church was raised in the mid – 12C and completed in the early 13C: the nave and aisles date from this period. The outside decoration presents cornices and foliated friezes imitating Antique decoration. The apsidal chapels are of unequal size and the square bell tower is off-centred.

Inside, the nave includes two bays with pointed barrel vaulting and one bay topped by a dome on squinches decorated with the symbols of the Evangelists. The central apse (6C) is adorned with an arcade held up by re-employed Antique columns. It has preserved its original lay-out: the bishop's throne preceeded by three stone steps, which were used as benches by the faithful. The sarcophagus of St-Quenin, bishop of his native Vaison, and the **high altar★** in white marble supported on four small columns, also most likely from the 6C. In the apsidal chapel, north of the chancel, there is another marble altar dating from the 6C. The only more recent additions to the church are the 14C recessed tombs and the 15C main window.

★ **Cloisters** (Cloître) (Y **B**). – Built in the 11C and remodelled in the 12C, the cloisters
Ⓥ were very restored in the 19C.
A small museum of Christian art has been set up in the cloisters. It displays a miscellaneous group of stone fragments: primitive altar, sarcophagus, 15C two faced cross, tombstones, fragments of Carolingean fretwork, funerary inscriptions etc.
From the cloister-garth the long Latin inscription which runs under the cathedral's nave cornice can be seen; its meaning has created much controversy among the specialists.

★ **St-Quenin's Chapel** (Chapelle de St-Quenin) (Y **D**). – The unusual triangular apse and its remarkable decoration have produced a number of theories from the archaeologists. Some see it as a temple of Diana others as a Merovingean chapel. It is now believed to be a Romanesque building constructed in the 12C with older elements. The nave was redone in the 17C. Re-employed Paleochristian and Merovingean decoration above and to the left of the door.

Roman Bridge (Pont Romain) (Z). – The bridge has but one arch, 17m – 56ft wide. Besides the parapet, redone in the 19C, the bridge is as it was 2 000 years ago.

Upper Town (Z). – Start from Place du Poids and walk through the maze of alleyways and small squares of the upper town, which dates from the 13 and 14C and then abandoned. The houses constructed of warm-coloured stone and roofed with colourful old Roman tiles have been successfully restored creating a typical Provençal village of yesteryear.
Go through the 14C fortified gateway, dominated by the belfry tower and its 18C wrought iron bell cage *(qv)*. Take the time to amble through the charmingly picturesque streets (Rue de l'Église, Rue de l'Évêché, Rue des Fours) and squares (Place du Vieux-Marché) decorated with lovely fountains.
The church, which was the cathedral until the Revolution, dates from the 15C and was remodelled in the 17 and 18C (façade).

Reach the castle by a steep path.

Built in the late 12C the castle was transformed in the 15C following the progress in military architecture of the time; it is now abandoned. The castle overlooks the upper town commanding a **view** (at the foot of the castle) of Ouvèze Valley, Les Baronnies and Mount Ventoux.

VALBONNE Charterhouse (Chartreuse de VALBONNE)

Michelin map 80 fold 9 or 245 fold 15 or 246 fold 23

The Valbonne Charterhouse is buried under glazed tile roofs in the centre of a thick forest. Founded in 1203, rebuilt in the 17 and 18C, the charterhouse is presently occupied by a medical establishment.
In the middle of a long building, flanked by two Provençal-style turrets, is the main gate. A 17C door leads to the central courtyard, in the corner of which (on the right) is a door with rustication dating from the reign of Henri II, which leads to small cloisters.
Facing the entrance door stands the baroque church.

Ⓥ **TOUR** *time: 1/2 hour*

The **interior decoration★** is sumptuous: in the middle of the stucco decorated chancel is the baroque high altar surmounted by a small baldachin with small twisted columns. The white stone rose pattern vaulting is of rare workmanship.
Via a passage opening onto the church's south side enter into the immense glassed in cloisters, offering a perspective more than 100m – 328ft long and which were
Ⓥ once lined with monks' cells. A **monk's cell** has been recreated and contains furnishings and items evoking the life of the Carthusian monks.

VALLON-PONT-D'ARC
Pop 1 907

Michelin map 🗺 fold 9 or 🗺 fold 1 or 🗺 fold 23 – Local map p 61 – Facilities

Vallon is the recommended starting point for the descent of the Ardèche Gorges *(qv)* by boat.
Southeast of the locality, on the hillside, stand the ruins of old Vallon, a feudal village.

⊘ **Town hall's tapestries (Tapisseries de la mairie).** – The town hall is located in an old Louis XIII style mansion.
In a ground floor gallery hang 7 Aubusson tapestries remarkable for their bright colours. Six of them depict episodes of the deliverence of Jeruselam; the seventh tapestry, the ancient art of grafting a tree.

⊘ **Tour of a silkworm farm (Visite d'une magnanerie).** – *3km – 2 miles towards Ruoms on the D 579.* In the village of **Les Mazes** one of the last Vivarois silkworm farms still functioning can be seen.

> *Access on a road branching off to the left coming from Vallon.*

From the covered terrace, *couradou (qv),* visit the cocoonery, a vast room containing silkworms on trays made of reeds. The tour shows the evolution of the silkworm from a tiny worm, the size of a pin's head, to a cocoon envelopped in silken threads. These cocoons are sent to the Alès Institute of Silkworm Breeding.

VALRÉAS
Pop 8 796

Michelin map 🗺 fold 2 or 🗺 folds 3 and 4 or 🗺 fold 9 – Facilities

Lying in the fertile Coronne Valley, Valréas is an important centre for agriculture and light industry (printers, factories of metal furniture, pasteboard articles...).

The popes' enclave. – The papacy located in Avignon *(qv)* wanted Valréas, a neighbour to the Comtat Venaissin *(qv).*
In 1317, John XXII bought Valréas from the Dauphin Jean II, Visan in 1318, Richerenches *(qv)* in 1320 and Grillon in 1451; and yet a strip of land still separated the two pontifical states.
Worried about the expansion of the papal lands in this region, the King Charles VII, forbade further sales of land to the popes, thus creating this papal enclave. In 1791, after a referendum, France annexed the territory.
Still today, Valréas once an enclave, is a *canton* of Vaucluse *département* entirely surrounded by Drôme *département.*

Little St John. – This is a charming tradition which has survived 500 years. Every year, the night of 23 June, a small boy (3-5 years) is crowned Little St John.
Symbolising the relics of St-Martin, the city's patron saint, Little St John parades through torch lit streets on a litter blessing people along the way. A procession of 300 costumed figures follow him in a colourful and animated atmosphere.
For 1 year Valréas is placed under his protection.

SIGHTS

The town lies within plain tree-shaded boulevards planted on the site of former ramparts of which only the Tivoli Tower (**B**) remains.

⊘ **Town Hall (Hôtel de Ville) (H).** – This former 18C mansion belonged to the Marquis de Simiane, who married Pauline de Grignan, grand-daughter of Mme de Sévigné *(qv).* The oldest part of the mansion dates back to the 15C; a majestic façade overlooks Place Aristide-Briand.
The 1st floor contains the **council room** which presents a painted ceiling and friezes.
The library with its 17C wood panelling from the former hospital contains papal bulls and Mss.
The 2nd floor room with its fine timber work ceiling contains works by the Austrian painter Scharf (1876-1943) who retired to Valréas.

VALRÉAS

All symbols on the town plans are explained in the key p 42.

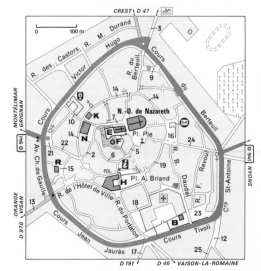

Notre-Dame-de-Nazareth. – This 11 and 12C Provençal Romanesque church was remodelled in the 14 and 15C (transept crossing and side chapels). It is most interesting for its south door of four recessed orders resting on small columns. Inside is a 16C organ.

White Penitents Chapel (Chapelle des Penitents Blancs) (E). – On Place Pie a lovely wrought iron gate announces the way to the 17C chapel. Enter the section reserved to the faithful. The chancel is adorned with carved stalls and a lovely flowered coffered ceiling.
The garden is overlooked by Château Ripert or Clock Tower (F); from the terrace there is a lovely view of old Valréas and the hills of the Tricastin.

Old houses. – At 36 Grande-Rue is the Hôtel d'Aultane (K), the door of which is topped by a coat of arms; corner of Rue de l'Échelle is Hôtel d'Inguimbert (N) adorned with modillions and mullioned windows; on Place Gutenberg stands Delphinal Castle (R) with machicolations.

EXCURSION

Round tour of 40km – 25 miles. – *About 2 hours. Leave Valréas west on the D 941.*

★**Grignan.** – *Description p 119.*

Take the D 541 and turn left into the D 71.

Chamaret. – Pop 349. A clock tower, converted from a fine belfry, relic of the massive castle perched high on a rock, dominates the landscape with an all encompassing view of Tricastin.

Continue along the D 71.

The road is bordered by fields of lavender separated by truffle oaks and cypresses.

Montségur-sur-Lauzon. – Pop 925. The modern village stands at a crossroads.

In front of the town hall, take the street on the left, turn right and then take the uphill path to the hillock on which lies the old village.

A network of streets through the old town leads to the old half-troglodyte church (restored).
From the watchpath, a fine **panoramic view** of the Tricastin countryside, Baronnies and Mount Ventoux can be had.

Take the D 71^B going east.

There are good views of Lance Mountain and the Nyons countryside.

Richerenches. – Pop 590. This former commandery was founded in the 12C by the Knights Templars. It was a place of work and worship; they raised horses and sheep and subsisted on the sale of wool and wheat. The town is now an important truffle market *(p 15)*. Built on a rectangular plan, it still retains its fortified wall flanked by four round corner towers; go through the belfry, a rectangular machicolated tower with a heavy nailed door.
Left of the church lie important temple ruins.

The D 20, southeast, crosses Visan and continues on to Notre-Dame-des-Vignes.

Notre-Dame-des-Vignes Chapel (Chapelle N.-D.-des Vignes). – This 13C chapel is decorated in the nave with 15C panelling, in the chancel is a 13C polychrome wood statue of the Virgin, the object of a popular pilgrimage on 8 September.

Via Visan and the D 976 return to Valréas.

VENASQUE   Pop 656

Michelin map 🄱🄱 fold 13 or 🄰🄰🄵 fold 17 or 🄰🄰🄶 fold 11

Venasque built on a foothill of Vaucluse Plateau dominates Carpentras Plain. The village was, before Carpentras, the Comtat's bishopric and gave its name to the Comtat Venaissin *(qv)*.

★**Baptistry (Baptistère).** – Entrance right of the presbytery. The baptistry dating most likely from the 6C or the Merovingian period and remodelled in the 11C, is one of France's oldest religious buildings. The Greek cross plan, with groined vaulting over the centre square, has arms of unequal length ending in apsidal chapels, each oven vaulted and decorated with blind arcading on slender marble columns with Antique or, in the case of the east apsidal, Merovingian capitals. The hollow in the floor was for the font.

Notre-Dame. – The church, which is 12 and 13C with considerable 15-18C alterations, contains, in the chancel, a 17C carved altarpiece and a tabernacle door of the Resurrected Christ appearing to the disciples of Emmaus. In 2nd north chapel is a 15C Avignon School Crucifixion.

EXCURSION

Venasque Woods; Murs Pass (Forêt de Venasque; Col de Murs). – *10km – 6miles east on the D 4 towards Apt.*
This winding yet picturesque road through Venasque Woods goes up the **gorges★**, often dry but quite pleasant. After climbing some 400m – 1 312ft the road reaches Murs Pass (alt 627m – 2 057ft).
Beyond the pass the first bends on the way down to Murs reveal extended views of Apt Basin and Roussillon.

Michelin map 81 folds 3, 4, 13 and 14 or 245 folds 17 and 18 or 246 fold 10

Mount Ventoux is the most dominant feature of Provence's Rhone Valley. It proudly commands the Rhône Valley to the west, Vaucluse Plateau to the south and the small Baronnies Range to the north.

The climb to Mount Ventoux is one of the loveliest excursions of Provence; the panorama obtained from the peak is immense. With only a height of 1 909m – 6 263ft, Mount Ventoux cannot rival the Alps or Pyrenees for altitude; and yet its location in front of the Alps, far from any rival peak, the bold way in which it stands above Carpentras Plain and Vaucluse Plateau, all these elements combined give it an astonishing majesty.

Weather. – There is nearly always a wind on Mount Ventoux, as its name suggests (*vent* means wind) particularly when the *mistral* is blowing. The temperature at the top is on average 11°C – 20°F lower than at the foot; rainfall is twice as heavy and filters through the fissured limestone of Vaucluse Plateau. In winter the temperature may drop at the observatory to -27°C (-17°F) the mountain is usually snow-capped above 1 300m – 4 265ft to 400m – 4 593ft from December to April, and the slopes at Mount Serein on the north side and Chalet-Reynard on the south provide good skiing.

Vegetation. – The lower slopes are covered with the trees and plants typical of Provence; while at the summit polar species such as Spitzbergen saxifrage and Icelandic poppy flourish. The flowers are at their best the first fortnight in July. The forests which once covered the mountainside were felled from the 16C on to supply the naval shipyards in Toulon; replanting has been going on since 1860. Aleppo pine, holm and downy oaks, cedar, beech, pitch pine, fir and larch form a forest cover which at about 1 600m – 5 249ft is replaced by a vast field of white shingle.

During the autumn a climb to the top through the multicoloured landscape is enchanting.

The conquest of the summit. – From 1902-73 the road between Bédoin and the summit was used for motor car hill trials; the pre 1914-18 record established by Boillot in a Peugeot was 17' 38" (73kph – 45mph); in 1952 Manzon in a Simca-Gordini was 13' 17"7/10 (averaging 97.480kph – 60mph); in 1973 Mieusset in a March was 9' 03' 6/10 (averaging 142.278kph – 90mph). The summit is sometimes included in the Tour de France cycle race.

The description below concerns the ascent of Mount Ventoux's north face; the ascent is also possible on the eastern face starting from Sault (see Michelin Green Guide to Alpes du Sud, in French only).

**ASCENT BY THE NORTH FACE

Round tour starting from Vaison-la-Romaine
63km – 39miles – allow 1 day – local map below

Ⓥ The itinerary uses the D 974, a road made in 1933 for tourists ascending Mount Ventoux.

Although the incline is the same type as the one on the south side, it is less trying during the hot summer months because of the breeze. During a storm, the road can be hindered by fallen earth for the last 3km – 2 miles but does not stop traffic. These conditions simply require more attention on behalf of the driver.

So as not to strain the engine we suggest you go up this way, and take the Bédoin road down.

** **Vaison-la-Romaine.** – *Description p 185.*

Leave Vaison-la-Romaine by ② on the town plan, the D 938.

The road goes up the smiling Groseau Valley overlooked on the west by the Dentelles de Montmirail *(qv)*.

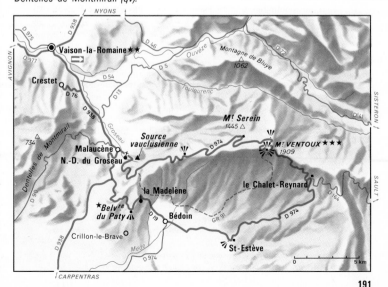

Crestet. – *2.5km – 1 1/2 miles on the D 76. Description p 110.*
Malaucène. – *Description p 110.*

Leave Malaucène east on the D 974.

ⓥ **Notre-Dame-du-Groseau Chapel** (Chapelle N.-D.-du-Groseau). – This chapel is all that is left of a Benedictine abbey which depended on St-Victor's of Marseilles. The square building is the 12C abbey church's former chancel, the nave of which has since disappeared.
Inside, a fine octagonal dome rests on squinches decorated with the symbols of the four Evangelists.
The Antique, classical style decor shows the influence of the Rhone Valley School.
In the early 14C, Clement V, first of the dynasty of French popes at Avignon, liked to stay in this charming spot.

La Groseau Vauclusian Spring (Source vauclusienne du Groseau). – The spring forms a pool of clear water as it emerges from several fissures, at the foot of a more than 100m – 328ft steep slope, beneath trees to the left of the road. The Romans had built an aqueduct to carry the water to Vaison-la-Romaine.

The road continues up the northern slope revealing a good view of Vaucluse Plateau, climbing up the steepest and most ravined face of the mountain; it crosses pastures and pinewoods near the Mount Serein refuge.
The belvedere beyond the Ramayettes hut offers a fine **view★** of the Ouvèze and Groseau Valleys, the Baronnies Massif and Plate Summit.

Mount Serein. – Winter sports resort: chalets are charmingly set in the snow fields; and it is well equipped with ski lifts.
The panorama becomes wider and includes the Dentelles de Montmirail and the heights along the Rhône's west bank. Two more long hairpin bends bring you to the top.

★★★ **Mount Ventoux Summit.** – The 1 909m – 6 263ft summit is spiked with scientific equipment: an air force radar station and a television mast.
In summer the summit may be shrouded in cloud or midday mist, it is advisable to set out early or remain at the top until sunset.
In winter the atmosphere tends to be clearer but the last stage of the ascent has to be made on skis.
The view from the car park extends over the Alps and particularly the Vercors Range (viewing table).
But it is from the platform on the south side that an almost circular **panorama★★★** (viewing table) can be had: it swings from the Pelvoux Massif to the Cévennes by way of the Luberon, Ste-Victoire, Estaque Hills, Marseilles, Berre Lagoon, Alpilles Chain and Rhone Valley.
On very clear days the Canigou is visible way over to the southwest in the Pyrenees.
At night the Provençal plain is transformed into a dark carpet studded with clusters of glittering lights. The sight extends to the Berre Lagoon and coast where the lighthouses regularly probe the darkness.

The corniche road, which winds down the south face through white shingle to woods, is the oldest road built (in *c*1885) to serve the observatory. In 22km – 13 1/2miles of hairpin bends to Bédoin (alt 310m – 1 017ft), it descends 1 600m – 5 249ft.

Le Chalet-Reynard. – Excellent local slopes have made Le Chalet-Reynard a popular resort for skiers from Avignon, Carpentras and other nearby towns.

The road goes through the forest; pine trees are followed by beeches, oaks and a lovely cedar grove. Provençal vegetation begins to appear: vines, peach and cherry orchards and a few small olive groves. The view extends across the Comtadin Plain; beyond Vaucluse Plateau appears the Luberon.

St-Estève. – From the famous sharp bend, now straightened, which the car racers had to take when climbing the summit, there is a good **view★** on the right of the Dentelles de Montmirail, Comtat Plain, and left onto Vaucluse Plateau.

Bédoin. – Pop 1 842. Perched on a hill this village has picturesque small streets, which lead to the classical Jesuit style church, which contains several elegant altars.

Take the D 19.

ⓥ **La Madelène Chapel** (Chapelle de la Madelène). – Below the road stands this priory. The modest 11C chapel is pure Provençal Romanesque in style with three small apsidal chapels covered with stone slabs and a disproportionately massive square bell tower with twin bays above the chancel.

★ **Le Paty Belvedere** (Belvédère du Paty). – From this belvedere, a panoramic **view★** can be had below of the picturesque stepped village of Crillon-le-Brave and the ochre clay quarries; to the right emerges the Alpilles Chain, facing it the Comtat Venaissin, bounded by Vaucluse Plateau to the left and Mount Ventoux.

Via the D 19, which crosses a wooded area, and the D .938 return to Vaison-la-Romaine.

★ VILLENEUVE-LÈS-AVIGNON

Pop 9 535

Michelin map 🔳 folds 11 and 12 or 🔳 fold 16 or 🔳 fold 25 – Facilities – Plan of Avignon's built-up area in the Michelin Red Guide France

A tour of Villeneuve-lès-Avignon is the natural complement to a visit to Avignon. This town, the "City of the Cardinals" offers, onto the City of the Popes a view, which makes up one of the most famous in the Rhône Valley. It is in late afternoon, under the setting sun that Avignon appears in all its splendour.

Historical notes. – After the Albigensian Crusade, the King of France, Philip III, the Bold, acquired in 1271 the county of Toulouse which extended to the banks of the Rhône. On the opposite shore was Provence and the Holy Roman Empire.
The river belonged to the crown which raised the thorny question of rights: whenever the river flooded parts of Avignon, the French king claimed them as his territory and demanded taxes from the inundated citizens.
At the end of the 13C, Philip the Fair, founded in the plain a new town (in French: *ville neuve)* which rapidly became populated. Grasping the great military importance of the spot, he built, at St-Bénézet's entrance, a powerful fortification.
The cardinals arriving at the papal court in the 14C and finding no suitable accommodation in Avignon, began to build magnificent residences *(livrées)* across the river in Villeneuve, until at one time there were 15.
The prosperity, which the cardinal's patronage of churches and monastic houses brought to the town, remained long after the papal court had returned to Rome. The kings, John the Good and Charles V, had built St-André Fort in order to watch over the neighbouring papal kingdom. In the 17 and 18C fine *hôtels* lined the Grande-Rue. In the monasteries, which became veritable museums, an active and brilliant life flourished until the Revolution swept away the aristocratic and ecclesiastical regimes.

★VAL DE BÉNÉDICTION CHARTERHOUSE
(CHARTREUSE DU VAL DE BÉNÉDICTION)
Time: 1 hour

ⓥ In 1352 the papal conclave met in Avignon and elected the General of the Carthusian Order as pope, but he refused the throne out of humility. To commemorate this gesture Innocent VI, who became pope instead, founded a charterhouse on his *livrée* in Val de Bénédiction. The house, enlarged by the pope's nephews after his death, became the most important one in France.
The Carthusian Order was founded in 1084 by St Bruno. It consisted of Fathers, who used the title Dom, and Brothers, who lived a communal life like monks in other orders. The Fathers, however, lived singly in cells spending their time in prayer, study and manual work. Three times a day the monks met in chapel to sing the offices; they took their meals alone except on Sundays when brief periods of conversation were allowed.
ⓥ The charterhouse is now a **cultural centre** (Centre International de Recherche, de Création et d'Animation – C.I.R.C.A.)

 Enter at 60 Rue de la République by the great door.

A plaque on the right of the door marks the highest flood level reached by the Rhône on 1 May 1856.

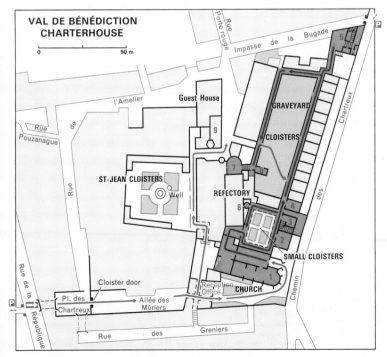

Cloisters' door. – It separates Place des Chartreux from Allée des Muriers. The proportions and ornamentation of the 17C door can be admired from inside: fluted consoles supporting balconies, lions' heads, fir cones decorating the pediment...

Pass through the reception and skirt the church's south side.

Church. – Go through the nave, the apse opens out with a view on to St-André Fort *(see below)*. On the north side, the apse of the other nave and a bay contains the tomb of Innocent VI (**1**): the white marble recumbent figure lies on a high plinth of Pernes stone decorated with arcading; the Flamboyant Gothic canopy has been restored. The two chapels that follow, dedicated to St Michael and St Bruno are open only during exhibitions.

Small Cloisters. – The east gallery opens into the chapterhouse (**2**) and the Sacristans yard (**3**) with its well and picturesque staircase.

Graveyard Cloisters. – The great cloisters, 80m – 262ft × 20m – 66ft, with their warm Provençal colouring, are lined with cells for the Fathers, each cell consisting of a small open court and two rooms, one of which communicates with the cloisters by a hatch. The first cell (**4**) can be visited.

At the northeast end of the cloisters a corridor leads to the *bugade* (**5**), the depressed groin vaulted wash-room, which has preserved its well and chimney for drying clothes. Opening off the west gallery is a small chapel of the dead (**6**) off of which is another chapel (**7**) which was part of Innocent VI's *livrée*; it is decorated with lovely frescoes attributed to Matteo Giovanetti (14C), one of the decorators of the Palace of the Popes *(p 74)*. They illustrate scenes from the life of John the Baptist and the life of Christ. Particularly fine are the Presentation in the Temple and the Entombment.

Cross the Graveyard Cloisters to the lavabo skirting the north side of the Small Cloisters.

The lavabo (**8**) is a small circular building beneath a beautiful 18C dome.

⊙ **Refectory** (Réfectoire). – The former Tinel (18C) is now a concert hall.

Pass by the church and reception office to reach the St-Jean Cloisters.

St-Jean Cloisters (Cloître St-Jean). – The cloisters' galleries have disappeared; however, several of the Fathers' cells remain.

In the centre stands the monumental St-Jean's Fountain (18C) which has kept its well and lovely old basin.

On leaving the cloisters, skirt the crenellated east end of the Tinel; note the bakery (**9**) with its hexagonal tower.

On the northeastern side, the **guest house**, remodelled in the 18C presents a lovely façade on the north side.

ADDITIONAL SIGHTS

★**St-André Fort (Fort St-**
⊙ **André).** – In the Middle Ages, St-André Hill, called Mount Andaon was still an island with an hermitage and later a monastery on it.

The tributary of the Rhône which circled it on the landward side, dried up and was taken by the local people.

The fort, built in the second half of the 14C by John the Good and Charles V, includes: a magnificent **fortified gate★**, flanked by twin towers (**B**) – this is one of the finest examples of medieval fortifications to be seen – and a fortified wall which included a Benedictine Abbey, the 12C Roman-
⊙ esque **Notre-Dame-de-Bel-vézet Chapel** (**D**) and the village of St-André, of which remain but a few walls.

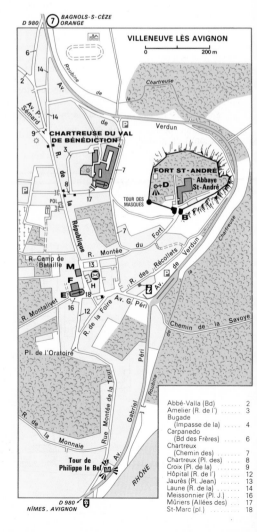

VILLENEUVE LÈS AVIGNON
0   200 m

CHARTREUSE DU VAL DE BÉNÉDICTION

FORT ST-ANDRÉ
Abbaye St-André

TOUR DES MASQUES

Access to the west tower of the fortified gate allows the tourist to discover the chamber from which the portcullises were controlled and an 18C bakery.
The terrace (85 steps) commands a very beautiful **view★★** of Mount Ventoux, Rhône River, Avignon and the Palace of the Popes, Comtadin Plain, the Luberon, Alpilles Chain, and Philip the Bold's Tower.

St-André Abbey (Abbaye St-André). – From the Benedictine Abbey founded in the 10C on the ancient pilgrim's way to St Casarie (6C – patron saint of Villeneuve) and partly destroyed during the Revolution, there remains the entrance gate, left wing and terraces, held up by massive vaulting. Walk through the pleasant formal Italian style gardens; from the upper terrace a lovely **view★** of Avignon, Rhône Valley and Mount Ventoux opens out.

Church (Église) (E). – This former collegiate church was founded in 1333.
The tower which ends the building on the east side was built as a separate belfry, the ground floor of which straddled the public footpath. The monks obtained permission to redirect the path. They blocked off the belfry arcade, converted it into a chancel and linked it to the existing church by adding an extra bay to the nave. Inside a number of works of art can be found: starting from the back of the church note the tomb of Cardinal Arnaud de Via, rebuilt with its original 14C recumbent figure (2nd north chapel), a copy of the famous *Pietà* kept in the Louvre since 1904 (3rd south chapel), *St Bruno* by Nicolas Mignard and a *Calvary* by Reynaud Levieux (above the chancel's entrance).
The 18C high altar is adorned with a low relief of *Christ Laid in the Tomb* from the charterhouse; right of the high altar an old abbot's chair (18C) from St-André Monastery. Note, as well, the nave's finely carved corbels (partly destroyed).

Cloisters (Cloître) (F). – They date from the late 14C.

Rue de la République. – The street is lined with a number of *livrées* (nos 1, 3, 45 and 53). One of these palaces (recently restored), which belonged to Cardinal Pierre de Luxembourg, a cardinal who died in the odour of sanctity at the early age of 19 (in 1387), houses the local museum.

Pierre de Luxembourg Museum (Musée municipal Pierre-de-Luxembourg) (M). – It presents four floors of magnificent works of art. On the ground floor is the 14C polychrome ivory **Virgin★★**, which takes the form of the elephant's tusk from which it was carved, it is one of the finest works of its kind.
Also worth admiring are the two-faced Virgin in marble from the School of Nuremberg (15C), the death mask of Jeanne de Laval, second wife of King René, by Laurana, Innocent VI's chasuble, and the 18C veil of the Holy Sacrament, adorned with small pearls. On the 1st floor admire the museum's most beautiful work of art: **Coronation of the Virgin★★** painted in 1453 by Enguerrand Quarton, from Laon, this artist painted in Aix, then Avignon (from 1447). Fascinated by landscapes and Provençal light, he used bright colours which emphasised the scene's greatness. The Virgin with her large cloak dominates this composition which encompasses heaven and earth through the subjects painted; the Holy Spirit is symbolised by a dove, the open wings of which unite God the Father and His Son. Paintings by Nicolas Mignard (*Jesus in the Temple*, 1649), Philippe de Champaigne (*Crucifixion* c1644) are also worth noticing.
On the 2nd and 3rd floors, works of Nicolas Mignard, Philippe de Champaigne *(Visitation)* Simon de Châlons, Parrocel *(St Anthony and Infant Jesus)*, Reynaud Levieux are exhibited. Miscellaneous items (17C door, 17C cupboard) from the charterhouse and pewter from the guest house can also be seen.

Philip the Bold's Tower (Tour de Philippe le Bel). – Built on a rock, near the Rhône, this was the key structure in the defence work at St-Bénézet Bridge's west end, on royal land. When it was first built (1293-1307) it was the present 1 storey high building. The second floor and watch turret were added in the 14C. From the upper terrace (176 steps) a very lovely **view★★** can be had of Villeneuve and St-André Fort, Mount Ventoux, Rhône River, Avignon, St-Bénézet Bridge, Palace of the Popes, Montagnette and Alpilles Chain.

VITROLLES   Pop 22 739
Michelin map 🟦 fold 2 or 🟦🟦 folds 31 and 44 or 🟦🟦 fold P – Local map p 90

Located east of Berre Lagoon overlooking the A7 motorway, which links Lyons to Marseilles, Vitrolles is an industrial zone (240ha – 593 acres) of light industry: metal construction, chemical products and foodstuffs. Near the industrial zone is a large long and short haul lorry depot. These activities have created, around the old town, a vast residential zone of warm ochre coloured houses.
The town is also known for the unusual runiform rock which dominates it.

Walk to the rock. – *1/4 hour on foot Rtn. After having taken the path around the rock, leave the car in front of the cemetery's main gate, climb 75 steps.* The path goes up to the top of the rock, where on its southernmost tip is a Saracen's Tower (11C), and on the opposite side a chapel dedicated to Notre-Dame-de-Vie, the aviators' guardian.

★**Panorama.** – This immense panorama embraces to the southwest onto the Lagoons of Berre and Bolmon, Estaque Chain separated from St-Mitre Heights by the Caronte Depression and the port and oil installations of Lavéra. On the banks of the lagoons can be seen the mouth of Arles Canal, Fos-sur-Mer, La Mède and its refinery, Marignane and the airport, Berre and its factories. To the southeast Étoile Chain and Pilon du Roi can be seen; further to the east the impressive Mount Ste-Victoire stands out.

Practical Information

The French Government Tourist Offices at 178 Piccadilly, London WIV OAL, ☎ (01) 49.76.22 and 610 and 628 Fifth Avenue, New York, ☎ (212) 757-1125 will provide information and literature.

How to get there. – You can go directly by scheduled national airlines, by commercial and package tour flights, possibly with a rail or coach link-up or you can go by cross-Channel ferry or hovercraft and on by car or train.
Enquire at any good travel agent and remember if you are going during the holiday season or at Christmas, Easter or Whitsun, to book well in advance.

CUSTOMS AND OTHER FORMALITIES

Visa for U.S. citizens. – An **entry visa** is required for all U.S. citizens visiting France in accordance with a French security measure.
Apply at the French Consulate (visa issued same day; delay if submitted by mail).

Papers and other documents. – A valid national **passport** (or in the case of the British, a Visitor's Passport) is all that is required.
For the car a valid **driving licence, international driving permit, car registration papers** (log-book) and a **nationality plate** of the approved size are required. Insurance cover is compulsory and although the Green Card is no longer a legal requirement for France, it is the most effective form of proof of insurance cover and is internationally recognised by the police.
There are no customs formalities for holidaymakers importing their caravans into France for a stay of less than 6 months. No customs document is necessary for pleasure boats or outboard motors for a stay of less than 6 months but you should have the registration certificate on board.

Motoring regulations. – The minimum driving age is 18 years old. Certain motoring organisations run accident insurance and breakdown service schemes for their members. Enquire before leaving. A **red warning triangle** or hazard warning lights are obligatory in case of a breakdown. It is compulsory for the front passengers to wear **seat belts.** Children under ten should be on the back seat.
The **speed limits,** although liable to modification, are: motorways 130kph – 80mph (110kph – 68mph when raining); national trunk roads 110kph – 68mph; other roads 90kph – 56mph (80kph – 50mph when raining) and in towns 60kph – 37mph. The regulation on speeding and drinking and driving are strictly interpreted – usually by an on the spot fine and/or confiscation of the vehicle. **Cede priority** to vehicles joining from the right. There are tolls on the motorways.

Medical treatment. – For EEC countries it is necessary to have Form E III which testifies to your entitlement to medical benefits from the Department of Health and Social Security. With this you can obtain medical treatment in an emergency and after the necessary steps, a refund of part of the costs of treatment from the local Social Security offices (Caisse Primaire d'Assurance Maladie). It is, however, still advisable to take out comprehensive insurance cover.
Nationals of non-EEC countries should make enquiries before leaving.

Currency. – There are no restrictions on what you can take into France in the way of currency. To facilitate export of foreign notes in excess of the given allocation, visitors are advised to complete a currency declaration form on arrival.
Your passport is necessary as identification when cashing cheques in banks. Commission charges vary with hotels charging more highly than banks when "obliging" non-residents on holidays or at weekends.

DULY ARRIVED

Consulates: British – 24 avenue du Prado, 13006 Marseille; ☎ 91.53.43.32.
American – 12 boulevard Paul Peytral, 13006 Marseille; ☎ 91.54.92.00 or 91.54.92.01

Embassy: British – 35 rue du Faubourg-St-Honoré, 75008 Paris; ☎ 42.66.91.42.
American – 2 avenue Gabriel, 75008 Paris; ☎ 42.96.12.02.

Tourist Information Centres or *Syndicats d'Initiative* 🛈 are to be found in most large towns and many tourist resorts. They can supply large scale town plans, timetables and information on entertainment facilities, sports and sightseeing.

Poste Restante. – Name, Poste Restante, Poste Centrale, *département's* postal code number, followed by the town's name, France. The Michelin Red Guide France gives local postal code numbers.
Postage via air mail to: UK letter 2.20F; postcard 2.20F
US aerogramme 4.20F; letter (20 g) 6F; postcard 3.40F.

Where to stay. – In the Michelin Red Guide France you will find a selection of hotels at various prices in all areas. It will also list local restaurants again with prices. If camping or caravanning consult the Michelin Guide Camping Caravaning France.

Electric Current. – The electric current is 220 volts. European circular two pin plugs are the rule – remember an electrical adaptor.

Public holidays in France. – National museums and art galleries are closed on Tuesdays. The following are days when museums and other monuments may be closed or may vary their hours of admission:

New Year's Day	Ascension Day	The Assumption (15 August)
Easter Sunday and Monday	Whit Sunday and Monday	All Saints' Day (1 November)
May Day (1 May)	France's National Day (14 July)	Armistice Day (11 November)
Fête de la Libération (8 May)		Christmas Day

In addition to the usual school holidays at Christmas, Easter and in the summer, there are week long breaks in February and late October-early November.

SPORTS AND OUTDOOR ACTIVITIES

Rambling. – The long-distance footpaths Topo Guides are edited by the: Fédération française de la Randonnée pédestre – Comité national des sentiers de Grande Randonnées. To buy them enquire at the information centre, 64 Rue de Gergovie, 75014 Paris, ☎ 45.45.31.02.
They give detailed maps of the paths and offer valuable information to the rambler. For local short-distance footpaths enquire in the tourist information centres. To explore thoroughly the Colorado Provençal, Luberon, Mount Ventoux and Dentelles de Montmirail use the pamphlets: *Circuits de Découverte* by F. and C. Morenas (Saignon, Auberge de Jeunesse).

Riding holidays. – The National Association for Riding Holidays (Association Nationale pour le Tourisme Equestre – A.N.T.E. – 15 rue de Bruxelles, 75009, Paris, ☎ 42.81.42.82 edits a pamphlet with addresses of all regional and *département* associations:
– ATEP (Bouches-du-Rhône, Vaucluse), 28 place Roger Salengro, 84300 Cavaillon; ☎ 90.78.04.49.
– ATECREL (Gard), 14 rue des Logis, Loupian, 34140, Mèze; ☎ 67.43.82.50. The Rental Association of Camargue horses (Association des Loueurs de Chevaux de Camargue) organises through the *manades*, marshes, or beaches: 55-60F 1 hour, 100-110F 2 hours, 140F 1/2 day, 200-220F 1 day; ☎ 90.97.86.27.

Boat tours. – To visit If Castle or the inlets of Sormiou, Sugiton, En-Vau, Port-Pin and Port-Miou see times and charges pp 201-214 where their access appears under their name. Apply to the tourist information centre for other boat tours.
Compagnie Naviginter offers daily cruises early July to mid-September between Le Grau-du-Roi and Aigues-Mortes (time: 1 1/2 hours) aboard the *Cigalou,* embarkation Le Grau-du-Roi quay across from Avenue de la Gare; for information and reservations: ☎ 66.53.06.09 or 66.53.01.01.
The same company organises cruises on the Rhône (Lyons – Valence – Avignon – Arles and in the opposite direction); can pick the boat up mid-way; information and reservations: Naviginter, 3 rue de l'Arbre-Sec, 69001 Lyon ☎ 78.27.78.02.
Tour of Petit Rhône. – See p 210.

Water sports. – For information apply to the particular sport's national or *département* federation.

Sailing. – Fédération Française de Voile, 55 avenue Kléber, 75084, Paris Cedex 16; ☎ 45.53.68.00.

Canoe and kayak. – Fédération Française de Canoë-Kayak, 17 route de Vienne, 69007, Lyon; ☎ 78.61.32.74. For Ardèche Gorges see times and charges for admission p 202.

Skin diving. – Fédération Française d'Études et de Sports Sous-Marins (24 quai de Rive-Neuve 13007 Marseille; ☎ 91.33.99.31) has about 1000 member clubs and publishes an annual on underwater activities in France.
Regional commitees of this federation: FFESSM:
– Comité Régional de Provence, 38 avenue des Roches, 13007 Marseille; ☎ 91.52.55.20.
– Comité Régional Languedoc-Roussillon, 29 rue de Bouleaux, 31200 Toulouse; ☎ 61.47.43.63.

Fishing. – Amateur deep-sea fishing does not require a permit.
Freshwater fishing: obey national and local laws; become a member (for the year in progress) of an affiliated fishing association in the *département* of your choice, pay the annual fishing tax, or buy a day card.
The map (with information) called Fishing in France (Pêche en France) can be obtained at the Conseil Supérieur de la Pêche, 10 rue Péclet, 75015 Paris, ☎ 48.42.10.00; map in the process of being re-edited.

Hunting. – For information enquire at St-Hubert Club de ·France, 10 rue de Lisbonne, 75008 Paris, ☎ 45.22.38.90 or locally.

Mountaineering. – For information enquire at Club Alpin Français, 12 rue Fort Notre-Dame, 13007 Marseille, ☎ 91.54.36.94.

Speleology. – For information enquire at Section Spéléologie du Club Alpin Français de Provence *(For address and phone number see above "Mountaineering").*

Archaeological excavations. – Apply to the local *département* agency of the Directions des Antiquités Préhistoriques et Historiques:
– Ardèche, Drôme: 23 rue Roger Radisson, 69322, Lyon Cedex ☎ 78.25.79.16 or 78.25.87.62.
– Bouches-du-Rhône, Var, Vaucluse: 21-23 boulevard du Roy René, 13617 Aix-en-Provence; ☎ 42.27.98.40.
– Gard: 5 bis rue de la Salle Évêque, 34000 Montpellier; ☎ 67.52.85.85.
Also the magazine *Archeologia* publishes every spring the list of sites needing volunteers.

Cycling holidays. – Tourist information centres have a list of places to rent bicycles. Some railway stations propose 3 types of bicycles: Aix-en-Provence, Avignon, Le Grau-du-Roi, L'Isle-sur-la-Sorgue, Fontaine-de-Vaucluse. Fee of rental degressive according to duration. Fédération Française de Cyclotourisme, 8 rue Jean-Marie Jégo, 75013 Paris; ☎ 45.80.30.21.
Ligue Provence de la FFCT (Bouches-du-Rhône, Vaucluse); M. Jacques Maillet, 15 lotissement de la Trévaresse, 13540 Puyricard; ☎ 42.92.13.41.
The Comité départemental du Tourisme du Gard (3 place des Arènes, 30000 Nîmes) offers a free pamphlet *cyclotourisme*.

Skiing. – Down-hill or cross country skiing is possible at the resort of Mount Serein (Mount Ventoux's second highest peak alt 1 445m – 4 741ft). Information at Beaumont-du-Ventoux town hall (Mairie, Beaumont-du-Ventoux 84350); ☎ 90.65.21.13 or at the welcome office ☎ 90.63.49.44.

Arts and crafts. – There are craftsmen – blacksmiths, weavers, *santon* makers, potters – which open their workshops to tourists and would-be craftsmen in summer; for information apply to the tourist information centres.

Tour of wine cooperatives. – Tours possible in all the wine growing areas along the east and west banks of the Rhône River (Aix, Cassis, Beaumes-de-Venise...).

SOME USEFUL ADDRESSES

Accommodation. – See p 8.

For **ramblers and trekkers** consult the guide: Gîtes et Refuges en France by A. and S. Mouraret, Éditions CRÉER, 63340 Nonette, ☎ 73.96.14.07.

Rural accommodation. – Enquire at the Maison des Gîtes de France, 35 rue Godot-de-Mauroy, 75009 Paris; ☎ 47.42.25.43 which will then give you their local headquarters' address.

Tourist information centres. – Listed below are the local, regional, *département...* tourist information centres:

– **Comité Régional du Tourisme Provence – Alpes – Côte d'Azur (Bouches-du-Rhône, Var, Vaucluse).** – 22A rue Louis Maurel, 13006 Marseille, ☎ 91.37.91.22.

– **Loisirs Accueil Bouches-du-Rhône** (offers accommodations, holidays and discount activities guaranteeing rapid reservations). – Domaine du Vergon, 13770 Mallemort, ☎ 90.59.18.05.

– **Comités départementaux du Tourisme:**
– Ardèche: 8 cours Palais, 07000 Privas; ☎ 75.64.04.66.
– Bouches-du-Rhône: 6 rue Jeune Anacharsis, 13001 Marseille; ☎ 91.54.92.66.
– Drôme: 1 avenue de Romans, 26000 Valence; ☎ 75.43.27.12.
– Gard: 3 place des Arènes, 30000 Nîmes; ☎ 66.21.02.51.
– Var: 1 boulevard Foch, 83300 Draguignan; ☎ 94.68.58.33.

– **Chambre départementale de Tourisme de Vaucluse.** – La Balance, place Campana, 84008 Avignon Cedex; ☎ 90.86.43.42.

Tourism for the Handicapped

Some of the sights described in this guide are accessible to handicapped people. They are listed in the publication *Touristes quand même! Promenades en France pour les voyageurs handicapés* produced by the Comité National Français de Liaison pour la Réadaptation des Handicapés (38 boulevard Raspail, 75007 Paris). This booklet covers nearly 90 towns in France and provides a wealth of practical information for people who suffer from reduced mobility or visual impairment or are hard of hearing.
The **Michelin Red Guide France** and the Michelin **Camping Caravaning France** indicate rooms and facilities suitable for physically handicapped people.

BOOKS TO READ

A Guide to Provence by M. Jacobs *(Viking Penguin)*

Food Lover's Guide to France by P. Wells *(Eyre and Spottiswoode)*

South of France by A. Lyall *(Collins)*

Two Towns in Provence by M.F.K. Fisher *(Chatto & Windus)*

Riviera was Ours by P. Howarth *(Century)*

A Little Tour in France by H. James *(Sidgwick & Jackson)*

Provence by F.M. Ford *(Ecco)*

The Camargue by C. Dix (Victor Gollancz)

Discovering the Camargue by M. Krippner (Hutchinson)

Camargue by K. Weber and L. Hoffmann (Kümmerly & Frey)

*The current **Michelin Guide Camping Caravaning France***
indicates the facilities and recreational amenities offered
by each individual site.
Shops, bars, laundries, games room, tennis courts,
miniature golf, children's play area, paddling pool,
swimming pool...

PRINCIPAL FESTIVALS *(1)*

2 February
Marseilles .... Candlemas procession

Sunday before Mardi Gras
Graveson .... Carnival procession of floats *(corso)*

Good Friday to Easter Monday
Arles .... Easter Festival *(feria)*. Spanish style (to the death) bull fights

Easter weekend
Barjac .... Antiques Fair

Easter Monday
Le Beaucet 🗺 fold 13 ...... Pilgrimage to the sanctuary of St Gentius

Late April
Villeneuve-lès-Avignon .... Feast of St Mark (patron saint of winegrowers): procession of beribboned vine stock

Late April-early May
Arles .... Gardians *(qv)* Festival

Mid-May
Le Beaucet 🗺 fold 13 ...... Pilgrimage to the sanctuary of St Gentius

Sunday and Monday after 15 May
Monteux .... Feast of St Gentius *(p 101)*

Ascension weekend
Roussillon .... Festival of ochre and colours

24 and 25 May
Stes-Maries-de-la-Mer .... Gipsy Pilgrimage *(p 172)*

Whitsun
Apt .... Horse show; music festival
Nîmes .... Whitsun Festival; bullfights and contests

June to September
Nîmes .... Bullfighting contests

1 June
Boulbon .... Bottle procession; canticles in praise of St Marcellinus and blessing of the wine

First or 2nd Sunday in June
Courthézon 🗺 fold 12 ...... Vine stock festival; sermon in Provençal.

23 June
Valréas .... Feast day of Little St John *(p 189)*

Sunday following 24 June
Allauch .... Provençal Festival of St John the Baptist; blessing of the animals

Mid-June to mid-September
Fontaine-de-Vaucluse .... *Son et Lumière* on the fountain's site

Last weekend in June
Tarascon .... Tarasque Festival; folk procession with Daudet's character Tartarin; bullfights *(p 179)*.

Late June to late July
Arles .... Arles Festival (dance, music, opera, theatre)

July
Fontaine-de-Vaucluse
L'Isle-sur-la-Sorgue,
Lagnes (🗺 fold 13) **Saumane** (🗺 fold 13), **Le Thor** Sorgue Festival (music, theatre, dance)

July-August
Villeneuve-lès-Avignon ...... International Summer Meetings at the charterhouse

1st Saturday in July
Martigues .... Venetian Water Festival; nocturnal procession of decorated boats

1st Sunday in July
Châteaurenard .... St Eligius's cart decorated and drawn by 40 horses in Saracen harness; bullfights

1st Monday in July
Arles .... Provençal style bullfight: *course à la cocarde d'or*

Early July to early August
Aix-en-Provence .... International Music Festival *(p 63)*
Vaison-la-Romaine .... Vaison Festival (music, theatre, dance)

Early July to late August
Cassis, St-Martin-de-Crau (🗺 fold 10),
Salon de Provence .... Mediterranean Festival

July to September
Arles .... Bullfights: Spanish style (to the death) and Provençal style *(courses à la cocarde)*

---

(1) For places not described in the guide the number and fold of the relevant Michelin map are given.

First fortnight in July
Marseilles .... Château-Gombert's International Folklore Festival

2nd weekend in July
Nyons .... Olive and folklore festival

2nd week in July
Arles .... International Photography Meeting *(p 64)*

1 week mid-July
Marseilles .... Borély Evenings: opera and theatre

Mid-July
Carpentras .... Festival of Our Lady of Good Health; nocturnal procession of floats *(corso)*

St Maximin-la-Ste-Baume . St Maximinus's musical evenings

Mid-July to early August
Orange .... Chorégies: operas, orchestral concerts *(p 149)*

2nd fortnight in July
Martigues, Port-de-Bouc,
St-Mitre .... Popular Festival: theatre, dance, music, exhibitions

Uzès .... Musical evenings

Mid-July to mid-August
Avignon .... Dramatic Arts Festival *(p 72)*

Carpentras .... International Festival "Offenbach and his Epoch"

Mid-July to mid-September
St-Rémy-de-Provence .... "Organa" Festival: organ recitals

3rd week in July
Nîmes .... International Jazz Festival in the amphitheatre

Salon-de-Provence .... Jazz and Music (South American, African, Rock, Salsa...) Festival *(p 174)*

21 and 22 July
Ste-Baume .... Mary Magdalene Festival *(p 170)*

Last week in July and first fortnight in August
Aigues-Mortes .... Dramatic Arts Festival

Last Sunday in July
Graveson .... St Eligius's Festival

Late July-early August
Marseilles .... *Boules (qv)* contest in Borély Park

Late July to late August
Valréas .... Evenings of the Popes Enclave (dramatic arts)

August
La Roque d'Anthéron .... International Piano Festival

1st Saturday and Monday in August
Valréas .... Lavender Festival; nocturnal procession of floats *(corso)*

1st Sunday in August
Châteaurenard .... Magdalene Festival; flowered carts

1st fortnight in August every 3 years (next time: 1989)
Vaison-la-Romaine .... International Choral Festival

Week of 15 August
Barjac .... Antiques Fair

3rd week in August
Séguret .... Provençal Festival and Winegrowers Festival

Tuesday following the 4th Sunday in August
Monteux .... St John's Fireworks *(p 101)*

Late August
Aigues-Mortes .... St Louis's Festival

Every Sunday in September
Le Beaucet 🗺 fold 13........ Pilgrimage to the sanctuary of St Gentius

Two weeks in September
Arles .... Rice Festival

Last weekend in September
Nîmes .... Wine harvest Festival

Sunday closest to 22 October
Stes-Maries-de-la-Mer .... Procession to the beach and blessing of the sea *(p 172)*

Last Sunday in November to Epiphany
Marseilles .... Santons Fair *(p 134)*

Early December to early January
Arles .... International santon-makers show

24 December
Allauch, Les Baux-de-
Provence, Fontvieille,
St-Michel-de-Frigolet,
Ste-Baume, Séguret .... Christmas Eve mass

Times and charges for admission

As times and charges for admission are liable to alteration, the information below is given for guidance only.

The information applies to individual adults. However, special conditions regarding times and charges for parties are common and arrangements should be made in advance. In some cases admission is free on certain days, eg Wednesdays, Sundays or public holidays.

Churches do not admit visitors during services and are usually closed from noon to 2pm. Tourists should refrain from visits when services are being held. Admission times are indicated if the interior is of special interest. Visitors to chapels are accompanied by the person who keeps the keys. A donation is welcome.

Lecture tours are given regularly during the tourist season in Aix-en-Provence, Arles, Avignon, Beaucaire, Carpentras, Marseilles, Nîmes, Nyons, Orange, St-Gilles, Uzès, Vaison-la-Romaine and Villeneuve-lès-Avignon. Apply to the tourist information centre.

When guided tours are indicated, the departure time of the last tour of the morning or afternoon will be up to an hour before the actual closing time. Most tours are conducted by French speaking guides but in some cases the term "guided tours" may cover groups visiting with recorded commentaries. Some of the larger and more frequented sights may offer guided tours in other languages. Enquire at the ticket office or book stall. Other aids for the foreign tourist are notes, pamphlets or audio-guides.

When parking your car in unattended car parks or isolated sites please make sure to leave no valuables in your car.

Enquire at the tourist information centre for local religious holidays, market days etc.

Every sight for which there are times and charges is indicated by the symbol ⊘ in the margin in the main part of the guide.

AIGUES-MORTES

Constance Tower and Ramparts. – Welcome office: bottom of the tower. Open daily early July to mid-September; the rest of the year mornings and afternoons; closed 1 January, 1 May, 1 and 11 November and 25 December; 15F; tickets are no longer sold 1/2 hour before closing time posted. For guided tours ☎ 66.53.61.55.

Notre-Dame-des-Sablons. – Open mornings and afternoons.

Chapels of White Penitents and Grey Penitents. – Guided tours July and August apply at the tourist information centre ☎ 66.53.73.00.

Midi Salt Marshes. – Guided tours July and August organised by Aigues-Mortes tourist information centre (☎ 66.53.73.00). Wednesday and Friday afternoons and by Le Grau-du-Roi tourist information centre (☎ 66.51.67.70) Tuesday and Thursday afternoons.

AIX-EN-PROVENCE

Natural History Museum. – Open mornings and afternoons; closed Sundays and holidays September to May; 4F; ☎ 42.26.23.67.

Saint-John Perse Collection. – Open mornings and afternoons; closed Saturdays, Sundays, holidays and most of April; ☎ 42.23.41.81 extension 525; audio-guides during exhibitions.

Museum of Old Aix. – Open mornings and afternoons; closed Mondays, October and holidays; 10F; ☎ 42.21.43.55.

Hôtel de Châteaurenard. – Open daily; closed Saturdays, Sundays and holidays.

Tapestry Museum. – Open mornings and afternoons; closed Tuesdays, late December to late January and 11 November; 8F (13F during exhibitions) ☎ 42.21.05.78.

St-Sauveur Cathedral. – Open mornings and afternoons; closed Tuesdays and Sundays. To see the Triptych of the Burning Bush and the door panels apply to the sacristan except during church services.

Paul Arbaud Bibliographical and Archaeological Museum. – Open afternoons; closed Sundays, holidays and October; 10F.

Times and charges

St-Jean-de-Malte. – Open mornings and afternoons (late afternoon Sundays); closed Wednesday mornings.

Granet Museum. – Open mornings and afternoons; closed Tuesdays (except July and August), most holidays and late December to late January; 11F (15F during exhibitions) ☎ 42.38.14.70.

Ste-Marie-Madeleine. – Open mornings and afternoons; closed Sundays and weekday afternoons July and August.

Vendôme Pavilion. – Open mornings and afternoons; closed Tuesdays and holidays; 7F; ☎ 42.21.05.78.

Vasarely Foundation. – Open mornings and afternoons; closed Tuesdays, 1 January, 1 May, and 25 December; 18F; ☎ 42.20.01.09.

Cézanne's Studio. – Guided tours (time: 1/2 hour) mornings and afternoons; closed Tuesdays and holidays; ☎ 42.21.06.53.

Entremont Plâteau Excavations. – Open mornings and afternoons; closed Tuesdays and holidays.

ALLAUCH

Museum of Old Allauch. – Open only Tuesday and Saturday afternoons and Sunday mornings and afternoons; 4F.

ANSOUIS

Castle. – Guided tours (time: 3/4 hour) afternoons only; closed Tuesdays, 1 January, 1 May and 25 December; 15F; ☎ 90.79.20.99.

Extraordinary Museum. – Guided tours (time: 1/2 hour) afternoons only; closed Tuesdays; 12F; ☎ 90.79.20.88.

APT

Old St Anne's Cathedral. – Guided tours early July to late September at 11am and 5pm; the rest of the year open mornings and afternoons; closed Mondays and Sunday afternoons.

Treasury. – Guided tours (time: 15 min) early July to early September mornings and afternoons; closed Mondays, Sundays and holidays.

Archaeological Museum. – Open mornings and afternoons; closed Tuesdays, Sundays and holidays; 3.40F; ☎ 90.74.00.34.

ARDÈCHE Gorges

According to the season and the water level allow 6-9 hours to descend. There are several difficult stretches due to rapids, which should be attempted only by those with experience; it is essential to know how to swim.
In addition it is recommended that you buy the waterproof map of the descent of the Ardèche Gorges (Plan de descente des Gorges de l'Ardèche; it can be found in the local shops) edited by the Association for the protection of the Ardèche Gorges.
Picnic spots have been set up along the bank but camping is only authorised on the Gaud and Gournier sites (5F per person per night).

Descent by boat. – The Ardèche Boat Association (Association des Bateliers de l'Ardèche) organises trips in 4 to 6 man boats piloted by two experienced boatmen. Departure 8am, return around 6pm. Information and reservations at the Vallon-Pont-d'Arc tourist information centre; ☎ 75.88.04.01.
M. J.-L. Tourre (at the farm in the Tiourre Valley, beyond Pont-d'Arc, route des Gorges, 07150 Vallon-Pont-d'Arc; ☎ 75.88.02.95) organises early March to late November trips in 4-man boats to Sauze; the return is by taxi from Sauze to the farm; 200F per person (return trip included).

Descent by canoe. – Apply to Locacano-Sports, Salavas, 07150 Vallon-Pont-d'Arc; ☎ 75.88.04.36; they hire out canoes or kayaks for the day or more April to September. Return trip guaranteed.

ARLES

Public buildings and museums (Amphitheatre, Roman Theatre, St-Trophime Cloisters, Museum of Pagan Art, Museum of Christian Art, Réattu Museum, Constantine's Palace, The Alyscamps). – Open daily early May to late September; the rest of the year mornings and afternoons; closed 1 January, 1 May and 25 December. In winter to visit Constantine's Palace apply to Réattu Museum's ticket office. 10F for each public building and/or museum; all inclusive ticket (including Museon Arlaten) 33F; ☎ 90.96.29.35.

St-Trophime's Doorway. – Under restoration.

Museon Arlaten. – Open mornings and afternoons; closed Mondays early October to late June, 1 May and 25 December; 8F; ☎ 90.96.08.23.

Van Gogh Cultural Centre. – Scheduled opening date of the media centre: late 1989.

AUBAGNE

Santon workshops. – Exhibit mid-July to early September.

Panoramic Christmas crib. – Exhibit early December to early February.

Small World of Marcel Pagnol. – Exhibit mid-February to mid-November.

Museum of the French Foreign Legion. – Open early June to late September mornings and afternoons; the rest of the year mornings and afternoons Wednesdays, Saturdays and Sundays; closed Mondays all year round and Tuesdays, Thursdays and Fridays out of season; ☎ 42.03.03.20.

AURIOLLES

Mas de la Vignasse. – Guided tours (time: 1 1/2 hours) early May to late September mornings and afternoons; 20F; ☎ 75.39.65.07.

AVIGNON

Palace of the Popes. – Tour accompanied (time: 3/4 hour) or unaccompanied daily early July to late September; Easter holidays to late June accompanied or unaccompanied mornings and afternoons; the rest of the year only accompanied tour mornings and afternoons; closed 1 January, 1 May and 25 December; 19F; ☎ 90.86.03.32.
Closed to the public: Treasury below the Jesus Room, library on the 4th floor of Angels' Tower, the Wardrobe Tower, Benedict XII's study on the 1st floor of the Study Tower and St-Michel's Oratory above the Stag Room.
To visit Benedict XII's Chapel occupied by the Archives Départementales apply in advance to the curator Palace of the Popes ☎ 90.86.16.18.

Petit Palais. – Open mornings and afternoons; closed Tuesdays and holidays; 13F; ☎ 90.46.44.58.

St-Bénézet Bridge and Chapel of St-Nicolas. – Open mornings and afternoons; closed January and February and Tuesdays except early June to late August.

St-Agricol. – Closed for restoration.

Le Roure Palace. – Guided tours of the apartments Tuesday mornings and afternoons; ☎ 90.82.57.51.

Calvet Museum. – Open mornings and afternoons; closed Tuesdays, 1 May, 14 July, 1 November and 25 December; 14F; ☎ 90.86.33.84.

Requien Museum. – Access to the library and study area mornings and afternoons; closed Sundays, Mondays and holidays; ☎ 90.82.43.51.

Lapidary Museum. – Same openings times and admission fee as Calvet Museum *(see above).*

Grey Penitents Chapel. – Closed Sunday and holiday afternoons and all day Tuesdays.

House of King René. – Closed: under restoration.

St-Didier. – Open late afternoons Monday to Saturdays and Sunday mornings.

St-Pierre. – Open Sunday mornings only.

Théodore Aubanel Museum. – Open mornings; closed Sundays, holidays and August.

Black Penitents' Chapel. – Closed: under restoration.

Louis Vouland Museum. – Open early July to late September mornings and afternoons; the rest of the year afternoons only; closed Mondays, Saturdays, Sundays and holidays; ☎ 90.86.03.79.

St-Symphorien. – Guided tours during the week early mornings and late afternoons; Sundays mornings and late afternoons; ☎ 90.82.10.56.

BAGNOLS-SUR-CÈZE

Modern Art Museum. – Open mornings and afternoons; closed Tuesdays, 1 and 2 January, 1 May, 25 and 26 December and February; 5,50F, combined ticket with Archaeology Museum; 8F; ☎ 66.89.60.02.

Archaeology Museum. – Open only Thursdays, Fridays and Saturdays mornings and afternoons; closed 1 and 2 January, 1 May, 25 and 26 December and February; 5,50; combined ticket with Museum of Modern Art: 8F; ☎ 66.89.74.00.

La BARBEN

Castle. – Open mornings and afternoons; closed Tuesdays and 25 December; 20F; ☎ 90.55.19.12.

Vivarium. – Open mornings and afternoons; closed 25 December; 20F; ☎ 90.55.19.12.

Zoo. – Open Mondays to Saturdays mornings and afternoons; Sundays all day; closed 25 December; 30F; ☎ 90.55.19.12.

BARBENTANE

Château. – Guided tours (time: 1/2 hour) mornings and afternoons; mornings and afternoons Sundays only from All Saint's Day to Easter; closed Wednesdays except in July, August and September, 1 January and 25 December; 18F; ☎ 90.95.51.07.

House of the Knights'. – Not open to the public.

Le BARROUX

Château. – Guided tours July and August mornings and afternoons; 15F.

Terrace. – Open all year round.

Les BAUX-DE-PROVENCE

Car park. – Unlimited parking: 7F.

Former Town Hall, Museum of Contemporary Art, Hôtel de Manville. – Open Easter to late October mornings and afternoons; all inclusive ticket (including Lapidary Museum and Deserted Village) 12F.

Lapidary Museum. – Open all day Easter to late October; all inclusive ticket (sights mentioned above and Deserted Village) 12F.

Picture Palace. – Open all day; closed Tuesdays in October and November and mid-November to late March; 28F; ☎ 90.54.38.65.

BEAUCAIRE

Power Station. – May be visited during the week after applying, at least two weeks in advance to: Compagnie Nationale du Rhône, 2 rue André, 69316 Lyon Cedex 04; ☎ 72.00.69.69 or 28 boulevard Raspail, 75007 Paris, ☎ 45.48.76.26.

Castle. – Open mornings and afternoons; closed Tuesdays; 10F.

Vignasse Museum. – Open afternoons; closed Mondays, Tuesdays and holidays; 5F; ☎ 66.59.47.61.

Notre-Dame-des-Pommiers. – Closed afternoons and holidays.

BOLLÈNE

Museum. – Open early April to late September mornings and afternoons; closed Mondays and Tuesdays; ☎ 90.30.14.43.

St-Martin Collegiate Church. – Apply to the tourist information centre; ☎ 90.30.14.43.

BONNIEUX

Old Church. – Apply to M. Bernard Gils, rue Pasteur.

New Church. – Apply to M. Bernard Gils, rue Pasteur.

Bakery Museum. – Open during spring holidays and early June to late September mornings and afternoons; closed Tuesdays, Mondays to Saturdays early October to late May, January and February and 25 December; 5F; ☎ 90.75.90.28.

BONPAS Charterhouse

Courtyards, Romanesque chapel and formal gardens open all day all year round; 5F.

BOULBON

St-Marcellin Chapel. – Apply to M. Betton, 10 rue de l'Enclos; ☎ 90.91.13.79.

BOUMIAN Museum

Open early April to late October mornings and afternoons; February, March and November Sundays and holidays mornings and afternoons; closed January and December; 15F; ☎ 90.97.87.42.

BUOUX Fort

Open all year round; 7F.

CADARACHE Centre on Nuclear Studies

Group tours on written application 3 weeks in advance to: Bureau des Relations Publiques du Centre d'Études Nucléaires de Cadarache, B.P. n° 1, 13115 St-Paul-lez-Durance.

CADEROUSSE

St-Michel. – The church's interior can be viewed through the glassed in entrance; for a guided tour apply to Mlle Léone Roche, 1 place de l'Église.

CAMARGUE

Regional Nature Park. – Information concerning the park's events and facilities can be obtained at the Centre d'Information et d'Animation de Ginès (see under Ginès) or in the local tourist information centres ☎ 90.96.29.35 in Arles; ☎ 90.47.82.55 in Stes-Maries-de-la-Mer; ☎ 42.86.82.11 in Salin-de-Giraud.

Nature Reserve. – For information concerning tours apply to the Centre d'Information de la Capelière (open Mondays to Fridays mornings and afternoons) located on the D 36ᴮ, east of Vaccarès Lagoon, 13200 Arles; ☎ 90.97.00.97.

Seawall. – A pedestrian walkway (20km – 12 miles) has been set up on the seawall and along the coast; no motor vehicles allowed.

CAPTAIN DANJOU Pensioners' Hospital

Guided tours of the workshops mornings and afternoons; closed Saturdays, Sundays and holidays; museum open mornings and afternoons; closed Mondays; ☎ 42.29.24.01.

CARPENTRAS

Old St-Siffrein Cathedral. – Open mornings and afternoons.

Treasury. – Open mornings and afternoons; closed Tuesdays, Sunday mornings and holidays; ☎ 90.63.04.92.

Law Courts. – Guided tours during the week; apply to the tourist information centre; ☎ 90.63.00.78.

Museums. – Guided tours mornings and afternoons; closed Tuesdays and holidays; 2F; ☎ 90.63.04.92.

Hospital. – Open mornings Mondays, Wednesdays and Thursdays; 5.50F; ☎ 90.63.00.78.

Synagogue. – Guided tours (time: 3/4 hour) mornings and afternoons; closed Saturdays, Sundays and Jewish holidays.

CASSIS

Local Museum. – Open afternoons; closed Mondays, Tuesdays, Thursdays and certain holidays; ☎ 42.01.88.66.

Les Baux Castle. – Not open to the public.

Inlets. – See under the inlet's proper name.

CASTELNAU Castle

Guided tours (time: 1 hour) daily in season; the rest of the year Sundays only; 17F; ☎ 66.83.21.04.

CASTILLE, Château de

Not open to the public.

CAVAILLON

St-Jacques Chapel. – Open mornings and afternoons; closed Tuesdays; ☎ 90.71.32.01.

Old Notre-Dame-et-St-Véran Cathedral. – Open mornings and afternoons; closed Sunday and Monday mornings; ☎ 90.71.32.01.

Synagogue. – Open mornings and afternoons; closed Saturdays, 1 January, 1 May, 25 December; 4F.

Museum. – Open mornings and afternoons; closed Tuesdays, 1 January, 1 May, 25 December; 4F.

CHÂTEAU-BAS

Roman Temple. – Open Sundays; to visit during the week; ☎ 90.59.13.16.

St-Césaire Chapel. – Same opening times as the Roman Temple *(see above)*.

CHÂTEAU-GOMBERT

Church. – Open Sunday mornings only.

Museum of Popular Arts and Traditions. – Open Monday, Wednesday (except during school holidays), Saturday and Sunday afternoons; guided tours Wednesdays at 3pm; 10F; ☎ 91.68.14.38.

CHÂTEAUNEUF-DU-PAPE

Winegrowers Museum. – Open mornings and afternoons; ☎ 90.83.70.07.

CHÂTEAURENARD

Feudal Castle (Griffon Tower). – Guided tours (time: 3/4 hour) mornings and afternoons; closed Tuesday, Thursday and Saturday mornings early June to late September, Tuesday and Friday afternoons and Saturday mornings early October to late May, 1 January, 25 December; 3F; ☎ 90.94.07.27.

La CIOTAT

Notre-Dame-de-l'Assomption. – Open mornings and afternoons; closed Saturday afternoons; ☎ 42.71.43.82.

Local Museum. – Open afternoons; closed Sunday afternoons and holidays early June to late September, and Tuesdays, Thursdays and Sundays the rest of the year; 5F; ☎ 42.71.40.99.

Mugel Gardens. – Open all year round; the belvederes are closed noon to 2pm. The Centre on Marine Life (Blue Workshop): ☎ 42.08.07.67

Verte Island. – Apply to the boat owners at embarkation; 16F Rtn per person in season.

COCALIÈRE Cave

Guided tours (time: 1 1/4 hours) early April to early November mornings and afternoons; 26F; ☎ 66.24.01.57.

CRESTET

Castle. – Under restoration.

CUCURON

Church. – Open afternoons.

Luberon Museum. – Closed for remodelling.

d - e

DAUDET'S Mill

Tour. – Mornings and afternoons; closed weekdays in January; 5F; ☎ 90.97.60.78.

EN-VAU Inlet

Boat tour (time: 3/4 hour Rtn) from Cassis, Quai St-Pierre; the excursion includes a tour of Port-Miou and Port-Pin Inlets; 25F.

f

FONTAINE-DE-VAUCLUSE

Car park. – 7F.

Underground World of Norbert Casteret. – Guided tours (time: 1/2 hour) mornings and afternoons; closed Mondays and Tuesdays except June, July and August, early November to late January; 15F; ☎ 90.20.34.13.

Museum. – Open mornings and afternoons. Weekends only early March to mid-April and mid-October to late December; closed Tuesdays mid-April to mid-October, January and February; 5F.

St-Véran. – Open daily Easter to late October.

FORESTIÈRE Chasm

Guided tours (time: 1 hour) early June to late August; April, May and September mornings and afternoons; 22F; ☎ 75.38.63.08.

FOS-SUR-MER

Tour of the harbour. – For guided tours apply to the public relations office: Service des Relations Publiques du Port Autonome, 23 place de la Joliette, 13002, Marseille; ☎ 91.91.90.66.

Fos Community Information Centre. – Tour and films shown mornings and afternoons; closed Wednesdays, Saturdays, Sundays and holidays; ☎ 42.05.03.10.

g

GINÈS

Camargue Information Centre. – Open mornings and afternoons; closed Fridays early October to late February and 1 January, 1 May and 25 December; ☎ 90.97.86.32.

GORDES

Château. – Open mornings and afternoons; closed Tuesdays in July and August, 1 January, 1 May and 25 December; 10F; ☎ 90.72.02.89.

Les Bories Village. – Open all day; 15F; ☎ 90.72.03.48.

Stained Glass Museum. – Open early February to late November mornings and afternoons; the rest of the year Sundays and holidays only mornings and afternoons; 14F combined ticket with the Museum of Oil Mills *(see below)*; ☎ 90.72.22.11.

Museum of Oil Mills. – Same times and charges as Stained Glass Museum (same telephone number as well).

GRIGNAN

Château. – Guided tours (time: 1 1/4 hours for lecture tour, 35 min for audio-visual tour) mornings and afternoons; closed all day Tuesdays and Wednesday mornings November to March and 1 January and 25 December; lecture tour: 16F, recorded commentary: 22F, tour of the gardens: 5F. *Son et Lumière* mid-July to mid-September; ☎ 75.46.51.56.

St-Sauveur. – In summer organ recitals are held.

IF Castle

Boat tour (time: 1 1/2 hours including tour of the castle); embarkation Quai des Belges in Marseilles's Old Port (Vieux Port); departures every hour in summer variable in winter; 30F; ☎ 91.55.50.09.

L'ISLE-SUR-LA-SORGUE

Church. – Open mornings and afternoons; closed late Sunday afternoons.

Hospital. – Guided tours early June to late September; no tours Sundays and holidays; apply to the caretaker, main door.

ISTRES

Museum. – Closed: under restoration; ☎ 42.55.04.97.

LABASTIDE-DE-VIRAC

Castle. – Guided tours (time: 1 hour) Easter to mid-October morning and afternoons; 15F; ☎ 75.38.61.13.

LOUBIÈRE Caves

Guided tours (time: 1/2 hour) afternoons; closed Tuesdays and 25 December; 15F; ☎ 91.68.15.02.

LOURMARIN

Château. – Guided tours (time: 3/4 hour) mornings and afternoons; closed Tuesdays early December to late February; 15F; ☎ 90.68.15.23.

LUBERON Regional Nature Park

Information Centres. – Maison des Pays du Luberon, 1 place Jean-Jaurès, 84400 Apt, ☎ 90.74.08.55. Pamphlets, temporary exhibits, geological and palaeontological regional centre (open mornings and afternoons, closed Sunday).
Château at La Tours d'Aigues, 84240 La Tour-d'Aigues, ☎ 90.77.50.33 or 90.77.48.80; for the opening times of the Museum of the History of Aigues Country and Ceramics Museum see p 213.

MADELEINE Cave

Guided tours (time: 1 hour) daily July and August; early April to late June and September mornings and afternoons; October Sundays only; 21F; ☎ 75.04.22.20.

La MADELÈNE Chapel

Apply to the tourist information centre in Bédoin; ☎ 90.65.63.95 Easter to September or town hall on weekdays; ☎ 90.65.60.08.

MAILLANE

Mas du Juge. – Not open to the public.

Museon Mistral. – Guided tours (time: 1/2 hour) mornings and afternoons; closed Mondays and most public holidays; 4F; ☎ 90.95.74.06.

MARCOULE

Exhibition. – The galleries are open July and August mornings and afternoons; April to June September and October afternoons except Tuesdays and Thursdays; school holidays – except summer – afternoons; the rest of the year Wednesday, Saturday and Sunday afternoons.

MARIGNANE

Town Hall. – The façade overlooking the inside courtyard is under restoration; open – apply for permission – during office hours; ☎ 42.88.13.41.

MARSEILLES

Historical Museum of Marseilles. – Open daily; closed Sundays, Mondays, 1 January, 1 May, 11 November and 25 December; 3F; ☎ 91.90.42.22.

Museum of Old Marseilles. – Open mornings and afternoons; closed Tuesdays, Wednesday mornings, public holidays and 26 December; 3F; ☎ 91.55.10.19.

Roman Docks Museum. – Open noon to late afternoons; closed Tuesdays, Wednesday mornings and public holidays; 5F.

Old Charity Cultural Centre. – Open noon to late afternoons and Thursday nights, as well. Transfer of the Borély Collections (Museum of Mediterranean Archaeology and Lapidary Museum); ☎ 91.73.21.60.

La Major Cathedral. – Open mornings and afternoons; closed Mondays; ☎ 91.90.53.57.

Old La Major Cathedral. – Guided tours (time: 1 hour) mornings and afternoons; closed Mondays; apply to M. Christian Lamothe, 1 avenue Robert-Schuman; ☎ 91.90.53.57.

St-Ferréol. – Closed noon to 3pm, Saturdays and Sundays and July to early October.

Marseilles's Maritime Museum. – Open mornings and afternoons; closed Tuesdays, public holidays and the feast day of the Sacred Heart; ☎ 91.91.91.51.

Cantini Museum. – Open noon to late afternoon; closed certain public holidays; 3F; ☎ 91.54.77.75; transfer of ceramics collection to Château Borély.

Notre-Dame-de-la-Garde Basilica. – Open with or without guided tour (apply to ☎ 91.37.42.82).

St-Victor's Basilica. – Open mornings and afternoons; 5F; ☎ 91.33.25.86.

Botanical Gardens. – Open daily; closed Tuesdays and Sundays; fee for 19C greenhouse: 7F; for guided tours apply to ☎ 91.55.25.51.

Château Borély. – Open mornings and afternoons; closed Tuesday and Wednesday mornings; 10F (12F during temporary exhibits). After the transfer of the chateau's collections to the Old Charity Hospise, a museum of decorative arts will be set up in the château. For information apply Monday, Tuesday and Thursday mornings; ☎ 91.73.21.60 or to the tourist information centre, 4 La Canebière ☎ 91.54.91.11.

Grobet-Labadié Museum. – Open mornings and afternoons, guided tour (time: 1 hour) on request; closed Tuesdays, Wednesday mornings and holidays; 3F; lecture-theme tours Wednesday and Sunday afternoons; ☎ 91.62.21.82.

Museum of Fine Arts. – Open mornings and afternoons; closed Tuesdays, Wednesday mornings and some public holidays; 3F; ☎ 91.62.21.17.

Museum of Natural History. – Open mornings and afternoons; closed Tuesdays and Wednesday mornings; 3F; ☎ 91.62.30.78.

Zoo. – Open daily; 5F.

Tour of the harbour. – Sundays and public holidays only; access to the Outer Breakwater (Digue du Large) is permitted, pedestrians only, 7am to 9pm (6pm early October to late March) by Gate no 2 (Arenc).
Weekdays guided tours of the harbour are organised; apply minimum 1 week before to: Direction du Port Autonome, Service des Relations Publiques, 23 place de la Joliette, 13002 Marseille, ☎ 91.91.90.66.

MARTIGUES

Ste-Madeleine-de-l'Ile. – Under restoration, however, church is open; ☎ 42.42.10.65.

Ziem Museum. – Open afternoons; closed Mondays, Tuesdays, 1 January, 1 May, 14 July, 1 November and 25 December; 5F; ☎ 42.80.66.06.

MARZAL Chasm

Museum of the Underground World: chasm and cave. – Guided tours (time: 1 hour) early May to late August mornings and afternoons; April, September and October afternoons, mornings as well Sundays and public holidays; March and November Sunday and public holiday afternoons; closed early December to late February; 26F; ☎ 75.04.12.45.

Prehistoric Zoo. – Open early May to late August mornings and afternoons; April, September and October afternoons only; March and November Sunday and public holiday afternoons only; closed early December to late February; 20F; ☎ 75.04.12.45.

MAZAN

Local Museum. – Open July and August afternoons; June and September Sunday afternoons only; ☎ 90.69.71.69.

MÉJANES

Pony trekking: 50F per hour; tour in miniature train: 10F.

MÉNERBES

Church. – Apply to town hall secretary Tuesdays to Saturdays mornings and afternoons; ☎ 90.72.22.05.

MONTFAVET

Church. – Group tours only; apply at the presbytery.

MONTMAJOUR Abbey

Open mornings and afternoons; St-Pierre Chapel open only with guided tour; closed Tuesdays, 1 January, 1 May, 1 and 11 November, 25 December and Sunday and public holiday afternoons early October to late March; 16F; ☎ 90.54.64.17.

Ste-Croix Chapel. – Not open to the public.

NAGES

Oppidum and Archaeological Museum. – For non-guided or guided (time: 2 hours) tours apply in writing in advance to Mme Py-Tendille, rue Basse, 30980 Langlade: 200F (for guided tour of *oppidum* and museum). Apply to town hall secretary; ☎ 66.35.05.26.

NÎMES

Roman Public Buildings. – Amphitheatre, Maison Carrée and Magne Tower open all day mid-June to mid-September, the rest of the year mornings and afternoons; closed 1 January, 1 May, 1 and 11 November, 24, 25 and 31 December; amphitheatre closed the day of a performance or *corrida*; 23F inclusive ticket for all Roman public buildings and museums, 12F for only one (except amphitheatre); museums closed Sunday mornings. Guided tours (in English) by bus daily July and August, closed Sundays and holidays; mid to late June and mid to late September Tuesdays, Thursdays and Saturdays; departure 9am place des Arènes (duration of tour: 3 1/2 hours); 40F, children 7 and under free; for information enquire at the tourist information centre; ☎ 66.67.29.11.

Museum of Archaeology. – Open daily mid-July to mid-September; the rest of the year mornings and afternoons; closed Sunday mornings; Tuesdays out of season, 1 January, 1 May, 1 and 11 November, 24 and 25 December. Combined ticket for the museums: 15F; ☎ 66.67.25.57.

Natural History Museum. – Same opening times and admission as Museum of Archaeology (see above); ☎ 66.67.39.14.

Museum of Fine Arts. – Same times and charges as the Museum of Archaeology (see above); ☎ 66.67.38.21.

Notre-Dame and St-Castor Cathedral. – Open mornings and afternoons.

Museum of Old Nîmes. – Same opening times and admission as Archaeological Museum. An expected transfer of the contents of the former episcopal palace to the museum is scheduled; ☎ 66.36.00.64.

NOTRE-DAME-DE-GRÂCE Sanctuary

Chapel and conventual buildings. – Apply under the porch to the right; ☎ 90.31.72.01.

NOTRE-DAME-DE-LUMIÈRES Sanctuary

Open mornings and afternoons.

NOTRE-DAME-DES-VIGNES Chapel

Guided tours early April to late November afternoons daily, closed Tuesdays; the rest of the year Saturday, Sunday and holiday afternoons only; ring the bell at the care-takers.

NOTRE-DAME-DU-GROSEAU Chapel

Apply at the presbytery in Malaucène; ☎ 90.65.20.19.

NOVES

Church. – Open mornings and afternoons.

NYONS

Ramade Oil Mill. – Open mornings and afternoons; apply in advance ☎ 75.26.08.18; closed Sundays and holidays.

Autrand Oil Mill. – Open mornings and afternoons; closed Sundays and 2nd fortnight in October; ☎ 75.26.02.52.

Oil and Wine Cooperative. – Open all day in summer; the rest of the year mornings and afternoons.

Olive Museum. – Open Easter to late September Saturday afternoons, July and August Thursday, Friday and Saturday afternoons; 5F; ☎ 75.26.12.12.

OK CORRAL Amusement Park

Open all day (merry-go-rounds are closed during lunchtime): March – 1 to 8 March and Sundays; in April and May – Wednesdays, Saturdays, Sundays, holidays and school holidays (all regions included); early July to late August – all day; September – Wednesdays, Saturdays and Sundays; October – Sundays and school holidays; 50F adults, 40F children up to 10 years old; ☎ 42.73.80.05 or 42.73.82.75.

ORANGE

Roman Theatre. – Open early April to early October Mondays to Saturdays all day, mornings and afternoons Sundays and holidays; the rest of the year Mondays to Sundays mornings and afternoons; closed 1 January, 1 May and 25 December; 10F combined ticket with Municipal Museum; guided tours during spring school holidays and early June to mid-September; for information apply to the tourist information centre ☎ 90.34.70.88.

Municipal Museum. – Open mornings and afternoons; closed 1 January, 1 May and 25 December; 10F combined ticket with Roman Theatre.

ORGNAC Chasm

Open mornings and afternoons; closed mid-November to late February; 26F; ☎ 75.38.62.51.

ORGON

Church. – Open only during services.

p - r

PERNES-LES-FONTAINES

Ferrande Tower. – Guided tours Thursday mornings July and August; apply to the tourist information centre; 5F; ☎ 90.61.31.04.

PERRIER Spring

Guided tours (time: 50 min) mornings and afternoons; closed Saturdays, Sundays, holidays and during week of Christmas holidays; ☎ 66.87.62.00.

PETIT RHÔNE Boat Trip

Boat tours (time: 1 1/4 hours) late March to early November; 4 tours per day July and August; 1 to 2 per day the rest of the year; 44F; for information and reservations apply to Captain E. Aupy, Bateau Tiki III, 13460 Stes-Maries-de-la-Mer; ☎ 90.97.81.68.

PEYROLLES-EN-PROVENCE

St-Pierre. – Apply to the presbytery, 15 rue de l'Église.

Chapel of St-Sépulcre. – Apply to the town hall.

PIOLINE, Château de la

Guided tours (time: 3/4 hour) apply in advance in writing to M. J.-L. Vian, Château de la Pioline, 13290 Les Milles; minimum 20 people.
Tour also possible in July during the festival at Aix-en-Provence with the Regional Historic Houses Tour; 85F; ☎ 42.26.02.93.

PONT DE GAU

Bird Sanctuary. – Open early March to mid-November; 16F; ☎ 90.47.82.62.

PONT DE ROUSTY, Mas du

Museum of the Camargue. – Open early April to late September; the rest of the year mornings and afternoons; closed Tuesdays early October to late March, 1 January, 1 May and 25 December; 12F; ☎ 90.97.10.82.

PONT DU GARD

Car park. – 7.50F for 24 hours.

PONT-ST-ESPRIT

Paul Raymond Museum. – Open mornings and afternoons; closed February, Tuesdays early June to late September, Mondays, Tuesdays, Fridays and Saturdays the rest of the year, 1 and 2 January, Easter, 1 May, 1 and 11 November and 25 December; 5F; ☎ 66.39.09.98.

PORT-MIOU Inlet

Boat tour (time: 3/4 hour Rtn) departing from Quai St-Pierre in Cassis; tour includes Port-Pin and En-Vau Inlets; 25F.

PORT-PIN Inlet

Same opening times and admission as boat tour of Port-Miou Inlet.

ROGNES

Church. – Apply in advance to M. Bonnaud, 10 avenue de la Libération, 13840 Rognes.

ST-BLAISE Archaeological Site

Excavations. – Open July to late September mornings and afternoons; the rest of the year Mondays, Wednesdays and Fridays afternoons only, Thursdays, Saturdays and Sundays mornings and afternoons; closed Tuesdays, 1 May, 1 and 11 November and 25 December; 5F.

Museum. – Temporarily closed.

ST-CHAMAS

Church. – Closed Sunday afternoons.

ST-CHRISTOPHE Reservoir

To visit the hydraulic installations first apply to the Société des Eaux de Marseille, Service Adduction, 25 rue Édouard-Delanglade, 13254 Marseille Cedex 6; then with your authorisation apply to the caretaker who lives in the administrative buildings along the D 543 and the reservoir.

ST-GABRIEL Chapel

To visit apply to St-Gabriel camping site: ☎ 90.91.19.83.

ST-GILLES

Crypt. – Open mornings and afternoons; closed January and February, Sundays except from early July to late September, 1 January, 1 and 11 November and 25 December; 8F combined ticket with Screw of St Giles; ☎ 66.87.33.75.

Screw of St Giles. – Same opening times and admission fee as the crypt.

Monks Storeroom. – Accessible only during lecture tours; ☎ 66.87.33.75.

Romanesque House. – Open early March to late December mornings and afternoons Mondays, Wednesdays and Fridays; ☎ 66.87.40.42.

ST-JEAN-DE-GARGUIER

Chapel. – Open Saturday and Sunday afternoons.

ST-LAURENT-DES-ARBRES

Church. – Closed Sundays. For a guided tour apply to Mme Vian, near the town hall; ☎ 66.79.44.73.

ST-MARCEL Caves

At the present time not open to the public; for information apply to St-Marcel-d'Ardèche's town hall; ☎ 75.04.66.11.

ST-MAXIMIN-LA-STE-BAUME

Cultural Centre. – For information ☎ 94.78.01.93.

Basilica. – Open mornings and afternoons; the organ is under restoration.

Former Royal Monastery. – Open early April to late October mornings and afternoons; closed 1 May; 7F; ☎ 94.78.01.93.

ST-MICHEL-DE-FRIGOLET Abbey

Daily tour of the church unaccompanied but accompanied for the cloisters; apply to the shop near the entrance on the right after the arch.
Weekdays: mass 11am, vespers 8.10pm; Sundays mass 10.30am. Special feast and holiday masses: Holy Week, Easter Monday (folklore festival), Sunday after 15 May (Notre-Dame-de-Bon-Remède feast day), last Sunday in June (the sick people's feast day), last Sunday in September (St-Michael's feast day with procession), Christmas night midnight mass with shepherds offering the lamb; ☎ 90.95.70.07.

ST-PANTALÉON

Church. – Closed; under restoration.

ST-PONS Park

Open daily; closed Mondays.

ST-RÉMY-DE-PROVENCE

Glanum Site. – Open mornings and afternoons; closed 1 January, 1 and 11 November and 25 December; 22F early April to late September; 10F the rest of the year.

Former Monastery of St-Paul-de-Mausole. – Church and cloisters open daily.

Hôtel de Sade. – Guided tours (time: 1 hour) early April to late September mornings and afternoons; March and October Saturdays, Sundays and holidays mornings and afternoons; closed Tuesdays in season and early November to late February; 8F; ☎ 90.92.08.10.

Pierre de Brun Alpilles Chain Museum. – Open early April to late October mornings and afternoons; March and November mornings and afternoons Saturdays and Sundays only; closed Tuesdays in season and early December to late February; 8F; ☎ 90.92.05.22.

ST-ROMAN Abbey

Open early July to mid-October; the rest of the year afternoons only Saturdays, Sundays, holidays and school holidays; closed Thursdays in season; 5F.

ST-SIXTE Chapel

Apply to Eygalières presbytery.

STES-MARIES-DE-LA-MER

Church. – Open early May to mid-September mornings and afternoons; the rest of the year all day. Time switch of the chancel (1F), nave (1F), vault (1F).

Upper Chapel. – Closed for restoration.

Watchpath. – Open early April to mid-November mornings and afternoons; closed Thursdays early April to mid-May and early October to mid-November; 9F.

Baroncelli Museum. – Open mornings and afternoons; closed Tuesdays early October to late May; 7F.

SALON-DE-PROVENCE

Empéri Castle. – Open mornings and afternoons; closed Tuesdays, 1 January, 1 May and 25 December; 6F; ☎ 90.56.22.36.

Nostradamus's House. – Open July and August mornings and afternoons; May and June Wednesday, Saturday and Sunday afternoons; the rest of the year apply to Salon and Crau Museum *(see below)*; closed Tuesdays in season; 5F.

Salon and Crau Museum. – Open mornings and afternoons; closed Tuesdays and Saturday, Sunday and holiday mornings and 1 January, 1 May and 25 December; 3F; ☎ 90.56.28.37.

SÉNANQUE Abbey

Cultural Centre. – For information ☎ 90.72.02.05.

Dormitory abbey church cloisters and conventual buildings (excluding Lay-brothers Range). – Open July and August daily; the rest of the year mornings and afternoons; closed Mondays to Fridays in January; 20F; guided tours in July and August on request; ☎ 90.72.02.05.

Lay-brothers Range. – Closed to the public.

SÉRIGNAN

J.-H. Fabre House. – Guided tours (time: 1 hour) mornings and afternoons; closed Tuesdays, October, 1 January, Easter, 1 May, 1 November and 25 December; 9F; ☎ 90.70.00.44.

SILVACANE Abbey

Church, cloisters, conventual buildings (excluding dormitory and refectory). – Open mornings and afternoons; closed Tuesdays, 1 January, 1 May, 1 and 11 November and 25 December; 16F April to September, 9F October to March; guided tours (time: 3/4 hour) on request; ☎ 42.50.41.69.

Dormitory. – Closed to the public.

Refectory. – Temporarily closed.

SORMIOU Inlet

Boat tour (time: 4 hours) July and August afternoons departing from Quai des Belges, Marseilles. The tour includes a tour of the following inlets: Sugiton, En-Vau, Port-Pin, Port-Miou; 70F; ☎ 91.55.50.09.

SUGITON Inlet

Same opening times and charges for boat tour as Sormiou Inlet *(see above)*.

SUZE-LA-ROUSSE

Castle. – Guided tours afternoons; closed Tuesdays, 1 January, 25 December and November; 8.50F.

TARASCON

Castle. – Guided tours (time: 3/4 hour) daily early June to late September; the rest of the year mornings and afternoons; closed Tuesdays, 1 January, 1 May, 14 July, 1 November and 25 December; 16F in season, 9F out of season; ☎ 90.91.03.52.

Tartarin's House. – Open mornings and afternoons; guided tours (time: 3/4 hour); closed holidays; 7F; ☎ 90.91.05.08.

TEILLAN, Château de

Guided tours (time: 1 hour) of the inside mid-June to mid-September afternoons; guided tours on request Easter to mid-June and mid-September to 1 November; closed Mondays unless it is a holiday and Tuesdays if Monday is a holiday; 15F; ☎ 66.88.02.38.

LE THOR

Church. – Open mornings and afternoons; closed Monday afternoons.

Thouzon Cave. – Guided tours (time: 35 min) early April to late October mornings and afternoons; 18F; ☎ 90.33.93.65.

LA TOUR D'AIGUES

Museum of the History of Aigues Country and Ceramics Museum. – Open mornings and afternoons; closed Mondays mid-September to mid-June, 1 January and 25 December; 12F; ☎ 90.77.50.33 or 90.77.48.80.

UZÈS

St-Étienne. – Open only during lecture tours; ☎ 66.22.68.88.

Ducal Palace. – Guided tours (time: 3/4 hour) mornings and afternoons; 20F; ☎ 66.22.18.96.

Crypt. – Guided tours (time: 20 min) mid-June to late October mornings and afternoons; closed Mondays; 5F; 6F Sundays and holidays; ☎ 66.22.68.88.

Local Museum. – Open mid-June to mid-September afternoons; closed Mondays; 3.50F; ☎ 66.22.68.88.

Fenestrelle Tower. – Not open to the public.

VAISON-LA-ROMAINE

Roman Ruins. – Open mornings and afternoons; combined ticket for all the monuments (including museum, cloisters, etc...); 17F available at each entrance; ☎ 90.36.02.11.

Peacock Villa. – Closed to the public.

Old Notre-Dame Cathedral. – Lecture tours in summer; apply to the tourist information centre; ☎ 90.36.02.11.

Cloisters. – Open mornings and afternoons; closed 1 January and 25 December; 4.80F; lecture tours at Easter and in summer apply to the tourist information centre *(see above)*.

VALBONNE Charterhouse

Open mid-March to mid-November mornings and afternoons; closed Sunday mornings and holiday mornings; 10F; ☎ 66.82.79.32 extension 30.

Monk's Cell. – Can be seen only during guided tours for groups.

VALLON PONT D'ARC

Town Hall's Tapestries. – Guided tours (time: 1/4 hour) mornings and afternoons; closed Sundays and holidays; 3F; ☎ 75.88.02.06.

Silkworm Farm. – Open mid-May to late September mornings and afternoons; closed Sundays; 17F; ☎ 75.88.01.27.

VALRÉAS

Town Hall. – Guided tours (time: 20 min) afternoons; closed Sundays and holidays; 5F during the temporary exhibitions in July and August; ☎ 90.35.00.45.

Notre-Dame-de-Nazareth. – Open mornings and afternoons.

White Penitents Chapel. – Guided tours weekday afternoons in July, August and September.

Times and charges

VAUVENARGUES

Château. – Not open to the public.

VENASQUE

Baptistry. – Open mornings and afternoons.

Notre-Dame. – Open mornings and afternoons.

VENTOUX, Mount

Access. – For information on driving conditions (mountain roads may be blocked between November and May) telephone Mount Serein 90.36.03.20 or Carpentras 90.67.20.88; see Skiing p 198. Note also that the D 974 is closed to traffic 15 November to 15 April between Chatel-Reynard and Mount Serein.

VILLENEUVE-LÈS-AVIGNON

Val de Bénédiction Charterhouse. – Open daily in July; the rest of the year mornings and afternoons; closed 1 January, 1 May, 1 and 11 November and 25 December; 16F; for guided tours: ☎ 90.25.05.46 or lecture tours: ☎ 90.25.61.33.

Cultural Centre. – For information on the centre and the international Summer Meeting ☎ 90.25.05.46.

Refectory. – Not open to the public.

St-André Fort. – From mid-May to late October ☎ 90.88.18.71 mornings and afternoons.

Notre-Dame-de-Belvézet Chapel. – Not open to the public.

St-André Abbey. – Gardens and terraces open mornings and afternoons; 5F; ☎ 90.88.18.71.

Church. – Open mornings and afternoons; closed Tuesdays, February, 1 and 2 January, 1 May, 25 and 26 December.

Pierre de Luxembourg Museum. – Open mornings and afternoons; closed Tuesdays, February and 1 May; 10F; ☎ 90.25.42.03 (town hall) or 90.25.61.33 (tourist information centre).

Philip the Bold's Tower. – Same opening times as Pierre de Luxembourg Museum *(see above)*; 5.60F.

The gardian's wayside cross

Index

217

otes